RARITAN
· *Reading* ·

RARITAN
· *Reading* ·

Edited by

RICHARD POIRIER

RUTGERS UNIVERSITY PRESS

NEW BRUNSWICK · LONDON

Library of Congress Cataloging-in-Publication Data

Raritan reading / edited by Richard Poirier.
    p.   cm.
    ISBN 0-8135-1504-1 (cloth)   ISBN 0-8135-1505-X (pbk.)
    1. Arts, Modern.   2. Literature, Modern—History and criticism.
    NX449.5.R37   1990
    700—dc20   89-36068
                                                          CIP

British Cataloging-in-Publication information available

We would like to thank the following individuals and publishers for permission to reprint material in this book:

Clifford Geertz, *Works and Lives: The Anthropologist as Author.* Copyright © 1988 by Stanford University Press. Used by permission.

Vicki Hearne, *Adam's Task: Calling Animals by Name.* Copyright © 1986 by Vicki Hearne. By permission of Alfred A. Knopf, Inc.

Richard Poirier, *The Renewal of Literature.* Copyright © 1987 by Richard Poirier. By permission of Random House, Inc.

Edward W. Said, *The World, the Text, and the Critic.* Copyright © 1983 by Edward S. Said. By permission of Harvard University Press.

Eve Kosofsky Sedgwick, *Between Men.* Copyright © 1985 by Columbia University Press. Used by permission.

Sara Suleri, *Meatless Days.* Copyright © 1989 by the University of Chicago Press. Used by permission.

With gratitude to
Edward J. Bloustein and Kenneth W. Wheeler

Contents

———

Preface

SINCE ITS FIRST ISSUE in 1981, *Raritan* and its contributors
have received a number of awards for articles that have appeared in its
pages, but none of these is more gratifying than the continuing loyalty of
its readers. Apparently they find something distinctive about the magazine even though it has proclaimed no particular mission for itself. Indeed, in preparing this brief introduction I have come to realize that as it
nears its tenth year *Raritan* still eludes, as its editors have always hoped it
would, any capsule definition. That is surely a virtue at a time when a
blind faith in categories and in their manipulation is one of the unfortunate marks of American intellectual life. Controversy seems to be carried
on in many other journals less by persons than by the labels to which they
have committed themselves, by a process that makes one term viable because of its power to generate and sustain its opposite. If the likely end of
the Cold War is even now depriving apologists on both sides of the rhetoric that has for so long served their purposes, a similar fate probably awaits
the rhetoric of those literary intellectuals who shuttle endlessly between
dichotomies like modernism/postmodernism, structuralism/poststructur-
alism, historicism/new historicism, logocentric/deconstructive. It is as if
these and similar pairings describe some evolutionary development,
when in fact they refer only to oppositions inextricably comingled throughout the millennia of cultural expression.

Of course no quarterly review which intends to engage itself with
contemporary issues can ignore the terms in which they are currently articulated. These terms have to be used if only to show that in reality they
are not very useful, particularly in a journal that gives considerable space
to a still misapprehended American intellectual tradition, passing from
Emerson and William James to the present, which has, even while pointing the way beyond them, long since taken on the burdens belatedly and
inadequately summarized by these terms. *Raritan* is intellectually skeptical without being rejectionist or exclusive; it is diverse and eclectic, working on the assumption that there is no synoptic subject or mode of analysis
more interesting than the person who proposes to care about them.

Raritan is therefore difficult to encapsulate even in a collection as lengthy as this one. I suppose it could be called a literary magazine, and yet that title seems rather narrow, not only because we publish relatively few poems and stories, none of which are included here, but because, more significantly, most members of the editorial board and most of its contributors do not share a widely held assumption of their colleagues on other magazines. I mean the assumption that literary appreciation or a capacity for literary interpretation or for literary production necessarily qualifies anyone to make political or cultural judgments superior to those made by people in other lines of work. The claims to such privilege that get regularly expressed within departments of literature and in the pages of literary journals are one of the comic aspects of the current scene, where people who can read the novels of Thomas Pynchon but who have trouble reading a map or the economic reports in the newspaper nonetheless feel empowered to arrange the geopolitical universe into THEM and US. Without sanctifying literature or philosophy or any other enterprise involving language, our contributors look for the spirit that has always been at work within such enterprises, which is why so many different kinds of interests are represented in the twenty-two pieces collected here out of the more than three hundred published in our first thirty-two issues.

I am perhaps making *Raritan* sound like a journal of theory even though it cannot properly be called one. Theory—which is implicit when not explicit and altogether inescapable in any use of the mind, itself only a theory—is not to be confused with the systematization of it in methods and vocabularies. Against these, anyone might have strong practical (and theoretical) objections. No one is likely to send an essay to *Raritan*, and none is printed here, which could more easily appear in any number of the important theoretical journals that now exist. While quite a few of our editors can be called theorists, and many of the articles we publish are necessarily involved in theoretical debate, the theoretical jargons which so often express intellectual submission even in articles that most vociferously attack institutions and systems are largely absent from *Raritan*. For us theory occurs as it occurs, and if Thomas Edwards or I, or Suzanne Hyman, in the editing of a piece, find its language too technical or too special, we simply ask if the sentences in question might not be given a more personal cast or phrased so as to prove less forbidding to, say, a recent college graduate who now works in an investment or law firm. It is hardly an abridgment of the freedom of any writer to ask that an argument be phrased so that it may solicit readers who would otherwise feel rejected by it.

It is difficult for any magazine nowadays to set a style for itself that assumes an educated readership fed up both with professionalist privatizations of language and with journalistic gloss. The difficulties are increased by the fact that since the sixties, in the United States as in most other countries, intellectual dissent has for the most part moved entirely inside the academy. Understandably it has there fallen prey to conformities no less binding than those it likes to attack, and to a shared discourse that is perceived by many of those also within the academy to be full of buzz words and tiresome cant. Universities and colleges, while maintaining the civilities traditional to them, have had to be equally hospitable to oppositional stances which are often, sometimes for good reason, quite harsh; the most painstaking scholars teach side by side with freewheeling radical opponents of some of the taxonomies of scholarship; and recondite theorists share office space with belletristic popularizers who, in the monthlies and metropolitan weeklies, cater to audiences which, under the guise of favoring the old verities, are at heart bitterly opposed to the pursuit of unaccustomed and uncomfortable truths.

To be in and of the academy is to be at the very heart of these various tugs, pulls, and contradictions. That is where *Raritan* is fortunate enough to find itself. Everyone on its board of editors is associated with a university here or in England, and its very existence depends on the generous support it receives from Rutgers, The State University of New Jersey, which allows us an editorial freedom that could not be expected from a private donor or a commercial publisher. *Raritan* is a journal in which contributors are encouraged to be individualistic, even eccentric, in their interests, to be autobiographical rather than institutional in their writing, to avoid as far as possible the snare of stylistic complicities. We aspire to a common sense which requires only so much dependence on the common sense now in place, that reader and writer might move together at least some distance beyond it, toward a shared sense of new possibilities.

Richard Poirier
New Brunswick, N.J.
June 1989

Pedagogy and Pederasty

LEO BERSANI

C AN WE write about sex without giving it up? Is the repudiation of sexuality inherent in the project of tracing its history?

I am prompted to ask these questions as a result of making what I take to be the necessary distinction between the history of sexuality in Western culture as Foucault describes it and the fate of sexuality within that historical description. In Volume 1 of *The History of Sexuality*, Foucault argues—with great originality and brilliance—that sexuality is the name given not to some hidden or profound human reality, but rather to a *dispositif historique* (an historical construct or apparatus) organized according to certain strategies of knowledge and power. Sexuality, far from belonging to our repressed or inhibited "nature," is an area of discourse historically produced in order to be expressed, talked about, one might even say "liberated." In the past few hundred years, according to this argument, sexuality has shown itself to be an ideally flexible or manipulatable economy of the body's pleasures. From the point of view of a controlling network of power and knowledge, the more we talk about sex, the better: to liberate sexuality may mean nothing more than to enlarge the confessional field in which the human may be interpreted, disciplined, and normalized.

These apparent paradoxes—and Foucault's obvious relish in producing them—were all quite thrilling, especially since Foucault concluded the first volume of his history with the passing but obviously crucial suggestion that our resistance to the powerful *dispositif de sexualité* in our culture should take the form, not of an appeal to an uninhibited, unrepressed sexuality, but rather of a new arrangement, a new, perhaps other-than-sexual economy of the body's pleasures. In Volumes 2 and 3, however, an apparently new ethic appears on the Foucauldian scene: an ethic, and, as we shall see, an esthetics of sexual asceticism. This can perhaps best be approached by way of Foucault's quite personal, and quite remarkable confession, at the beginning of Volume 2, of the type of pleasure which the historian gets from writing history. Foucault now confesses

1

his motive for writing these books: he defines it as a "type of curiosity" which allows one to "effect a kind of self-removal from oneself [se dé-prendre de soi-même]." The history of sexuality is to be thought of as what Foucault calls a "philosophical exercise." These volumes will per-haps answer the question of whether or not "the work of thinking one's own history can free thought from what it silently thinks and permit it to think differently or in other modes [lui permettre de penser autrement]." At the same time, however, the very passage which prefaces an announced attempt at a massive cultural self-disappropriation praises the function of the philosophical essay in our culture (with the hint that it may today unfortunately no longer serve that ennobling function) as "an ascesis, an exercise of or on the self through thought [une ascèse, un exercice de soi dans la pensée]." The pleasure of writing history is that of being onto-logically dispossessed.

The presence of this self-dispossessing motive can be felt especially in what I consider to be the intellectual and the ethical high point of Vol-umes 2 and 3: Foucault's discussion of *l'amour des garçons* in classical Greece. It is part of Foucault's always great originality that he is not inter-ested in locating the differences between then and now in questions of acceptance and rejection: in Greek culture, sex between males is officially all right; in Christian culture it is officially not all right. What interests Foucault is something quite different: how and why the Greeks prob-lematized homosexuality while not only accepting it but even, in a certain sense, glorifying it. The Greeks, it could be said, made no hermeneutical fuss about love-making between two men; such activity did not give rise, as it has in modern times, to analyses of different structures of desire in heterosexual and in homosexual love. Foucault emphasizes that the Greek suspicion of homosexuality is, first of all, part of a more general suspicion of intemperate appetites—whether those appetites be for men, women, or food. In this view, sex is a threat without being an evil; what is at stake is that self-domination or self-mastery which, as Foucault reminds us over and over again, is for the Greeks the supreme sign and achievement of the moral life. Furthermore, this individual morality is also a political philosophy. Foucault writes very well about what he calls the isomorph-ism between sexual and social relations: to be unable to govern oneself is to be unable to govern others. The exercise of political authority is insep-arable from the exercise of authority over the self.

L'amour des garçons, it could be said, exacerbates these ethical and political tensions and imperatives. In an extremely curious way, Foucault's analysis leads us to conclude that the Greeks were casual about (and even gave great value to) a relation which in fact they found nearly unthinkable. The general ethical polarity of self-domination and a helpless indulgence of appetites results in a structuring of sexual behavior in terms of activity and passivity, with a correlative rejection of the so-called passive role in sex. What the Athenians find hard to accept, Foucault writes, is the authority of a leader who as an adolescent was an "object of pleasure" for other men; there is a legal and moral incompatibility between sexual passivity and civic authority. The only "honorable" sexual behavior "consists in being active, in dominating, in penetrating, and in thereby exercising one's superiority." If, as Foucault suggests, the Greek ethic of temperance is grounded in the isomorphic privileging of self-domination and the domination of others, then the preferred, if by no means exclusive form of homosexual love in classical Greece—between a "guiding," sexually dominating, if also potentially rejected, adult male and an adolescent boy—becomes exactly the type of homosexuality which cannot take place. The preference for that particular type of relation within a wholly male-oriented, ejaculatory model is sexuality in which, at each step in the relation, one partner is, as it were, on top and the other on the bottom, means that homosexuality can be ethically articulated only by being erased.

Foucault analyzes the two principal strategies of this erasure. First, the relation is considered from the boy's point of view: how can his honor be preserved? And the answer is that he will be worthy of becoming a free adult Greek male citizen only if, while accepting the desires of the pursuant man, he manages not to share any sensations with him—that is, to experience any sexual pleasure. A kind of sublimation of sexuality is apparently possible within the sexual act itself: it is by mastering the pleasure of passivity in a situation in which he is defined *as* passivity that the boy lays the foundation for the spiritualizing transformation of sex into the socially acceptable relation of *philia*, or friendship. Foucault is, I think, particularly intrigued by the second solution, which consists in displacing the act of honorable renunciation of sex from the boy to the man. Instead of problematizing the honor of the boy as an object of pleasure, at this stage of reflection—and the principal texts here are *The Symposium* and *The Phaedrus*—the analysis is shifted to the lover, and, more specifically, to what it is he loves. Having eliminated the boy's pleasure from his sexual relation with a man, the problematizing analysis now dissolves the very terms of the analysis by eliminating the boy himself as an object of love.

What the man discovers is that he loves truth instead of (or rather, through) boys, a revelation which, by no means incidentally, has the enormous strategic benefit of making *him* the object of the *boy's* pursuit. The adult lover has been transformed from the suppliant pursuer to the master of truth. Boys anxious to see truth will turn to him, will love truth through him; he will be an object of love without, however, having to take a passive role. And he will remain dominant by resisting the now pursuant boy lover: the beloved master must guide the boy's love away from his person to the truth which is the real (if not fully conscious) object of the boy's desires. The pursuit of truth depends on a sexual asceticism by which the master of truth controls his student lovers. Thus a perhaps sexually undesirable teacher makes himself infinitely desirable by refusing to satisfy the desires of desirable boys. (One thinks of course of an unappetizing Socrates resisting an irresistible Alcibiades.) This complicated philosophical maneuver must, I think, be seen as a brilliant strategic achievement: the elimination of sex has transformed a relation of problematic desires into a pure exercise of power.

Exactly how does Volume 2 present that achievement? I should say at once that Foucault does not hesitate to call the Socratic ideal of love in *The Banquet* "another type of domination." But he is, I think, also seduced by a structure of domination which, while obviously different from what Volume 1 had analyzed as the contemporary model of sexuality normalized through confession, can hardly be thought of as a less restrictive economy of the body's pleasure. It is of course true that the Socratic philosophy of sexual asceticism is presented as simply one moment in the history of sexuality. But it is also true, first of all, that the Greek model profits from the tirelessly reiterated contrast between it and such later developments as the codification of sexual behavior in terms of good and evil, pure and corrupt, healthy and sick, and especially the hermeneutics of desire in our modern confessional civilization. The latter belong, precisely, to that power-knowledge network the very analysis of which in Volume 1 is to be thought of as an initial act of resistance to it. In the light of that analysis alone, the analytic procedure of comparison in Volume 2 and 3, of relentlessly reiterated contrasts (between pagan and Christian, ancient and modern), while they do not suggest that the Greek model can or even should be "resurrected," is inevitably a tendentious and even polemical strategy. (Foucault clearly wanted to protect himself from any suggestion that he thought a return to the Greeks possible or desirable.)

Even more: what could after all be read, in the Greek texts studied by Foucault, as a brutally calculated renunciation of sex for the sake of power is softened and glamorized by Foucault's continuous reference to such calculations as a way of "stylizing" an individual existence. I don't mean that the stylizing of the ethical is irrelevant to conceptions of the moral life in antiquity; what I am concerned with is the *nature* of Foucault's interest in certain scholarly investigations initiated, as he recognized, by others—that is, in how such investigations enter *his work*. In Volumes 2 and 3, astonishingly vague, and new, references to "style" and to the "esthetic" seem designed to impart a kind of superior imaginative refinement to what could equally be thought of as an exceptionally parsimonious economy of the self designed to center the self and to subjugate the other. The fact that this economy is not codified as law and has to be developed by an individual who must, through rhetorical talents, persuade others to love him for his renunciations, seems, for Foucault, to justify referring to this ancient "art of existence" as a "stylistics." But, without any definition or sustained analysis of what might be called the ontological boundaries of either the ethical or the esthetic, to live according to *une stylistique* seems perilously close to merely "living with style."

There is a striking analogy between the Greek ethic of sexual asceticism and what I referred to earlier as Foucault's confession of the pleasure of writing history—an analogy which suggests that the study of antiquity allowed Foucault to paganize and thereby to render somewhat less problematic a perhaps ambivalent interest in Christian self-mortification. Volumes 2 and 3 are permeated by a relatively superficial estheticizing of the familiar Christian value of ascetic self-denial: the historian writes in order to lose himself, the philosopher teaches truth by sacrificing his desire for his students. More precisely, the Greek model provides Foucault with the ideal of an asceticism which owes nothing to a prohibitive code. It appears to reconcile self-denial with self-affirmation, and the need for the reconciliation thus emerges as a primary pressure, a kind of obsessive thematics in Foucault's work. Finally, the most extraordinary ambitions of power are realized in both Socratic chastity and Foucauldian history writing: the historian presumably frees himself from the episteme which Foucault had previously led us to think could only be resided from within, and, in the case of the philosopher-teacher, the deceptively de-eroticized study of truth legitimates the teacher's claim to mastery and involves an extraordinary simplification of that play of desire and resistance in teaching which—happily, we might wish to add—helps to demystify and debunk any claim for teaching as the transmission of "truth."

I make these rather harsh remarks because nothing could be more at odds with both Foucault's own erotically playful style as a teacher and the intellectual promises of his earlier work, than the implicit estheticized idealization of power in his last two books. What happens in Volumes 2 and 3 of *The History of Sexuality* can perhaps best be understood in terms of the relation between writing and power. The move to antiquity, and the notion of history writing as an "ascesis," as the possibility of shedding the cultural conditions of possibility of one's own thought, are both aspects of a new kind of surrender to the very episteme which they presumably elude. The notion of history as an object of study, the view of the historian as distinct from his material, and finally, the image of the philosopher as someone capable of thinking himself out of his own thought: far from being premises which may allow us to move out of—or even to see critically, and therefore to begin to resist—the field within which our culture diagrams our thinking, are themselves among the fundamental assumptions of Western humanistic culture.

Nothing is more ominous than the unanimous reverence with which Volumes 2 and 3 have been received in France, or the hagiographical industry already at work on—really against—Foucault's life and writing. For they correspond to Foucault's own willingness to be tempted by the illusion—nurtured in our culture since, precisely, classical Greece—that philosophy and history are free, nonconditioned exercises of the mind rather than particular versions of self-replicative urgencies in philosophers and historians. This is precisely the sort of illusion which we might expect Foucault to be most suspicious of: it is a strategic encouragement of a belief in the power of the individual mind designed, one might say, to disguise the mind's conformity to its culture and to forestall its potential for resistance to that culture.

The writer's resistance to his culture can lie—as Foucault had abundantly shown in his earlier work—not in the factitious power of a mind mythically exercised into a kind of self-divestiture, but rather in the excessive passivity of his surrender to the coercive seductions of what he "silently thinks." In Foucault's case, this had taken the form—especially in *Les Mots et les choses*, *Surveiller et punir* and *La Volonté de savoir*—of extravagant and succulent replicative syntheses of his (of our) culture's networks of power and knowledge. He had demonstrated the corrosive power of what was after all his implausibly intelligible rethinking or diagramming of the ways in which we can't help but think. The recklessly synthesizing order of his prose had been anything but an "ascesis" or a self-dispossession. Foucault's talking about our compulsion to talk about sex in Volume 1 of *The History of Sexuality*, for example, had been at once an act of risky conformity to the cultural imperative he was also denouncing, and a pedagogical demonstration of how a particular *pouvoir-savoir* apparatus can produce discursive performances which subvert its own coercive intentionality. The ambiguous energetics of the power-knowledge network can work to defeat the immobilizing orders of power and of knowledge. But in the ascetic esthetics of Volumes 2 and 3 of the *History*, it is as if Foucault were striving to detach language from the excitement of its performance, or at least to control that excitement through the myth of dispassionate historical scholarship as an exercise in epistemic conversion. It is, in short, as if he were seeking a new, desexualized austerity in the very act of writing, to elude the exuberant despair of being had, of being penetrated, and possessed, by a language at once inescapably intimate and inescapably alien.

Criticism, Canon-Formation, and Prophecy: The Sorrows of Facticity

HAROLD BLOOM

I BEGIN WITH my search for a word, which I can't quite find, because the dictionaries don't have it, or else list it equivocally. What I need is a word that will describe our being so far inside a tradition, or inside a way of representing, or inside even a particular author, that only enormous effort can make us aware of how reluctant we are to know our incarceration. I need to say, here at the start, that I am not talking about a linguistic problematic, or any other development of Nietzsche's much misused trope of our being pent up in the prison house of language. There is a textual aspect to my subject, obviously, but the containment I address is considerably larger than textuality, unless you conceive textuality so diffusely that all human action is textual. Manifestly, that trivializes human action, and increasingly I distrust any critical mode that so reduces us. But my subject does have to do with something inescapable that reduces us constantly, and which I believe criticism must combat. There is a kind of brute contingency that compels us to misread figurative language as being literal; yet to call it "contingency" comes a little short of it. I could speak of "brute factuality" or even of "brute facticity," but I am aware that those words (or nonwords) are slow to enter the dictionaries. *Factuality* would mean just the state or quality of being fact or factual, as in "I question the factuality of their account." But *facticity*, if it becomes an acceptable English word, is better for my purposes. *Facticity* would mean the state of being a fact, as an inescapable and unalterable fact. To be caught in facticity is to be caught in the inescapable and unalterable. The stances or positions of freedom are not available, and the text or event reads us more fully and vividly than we can hope ever to read it.

Anyone who comes late into a story or a family or an institution is likely to have a sense that her or his status is forever uncertain. I do not identify this sense with what I call facticity, because uncertainty is something near to interpretive freedom, or can be converted into it. But belatedness has a peculiar relationship to facticity, and can be mistaken for it. Belatedness is a conscious anxiety, and results from a pervasive ambivalence. Facticity is a state or quality, not a mode of consciousness, and so pragmatically excludes any sense of ambivalence. And yet belatedness and facticity alike do follow from the assumption that everything has a meaning, or rather that there is sense in everything. If there is sense in everything, then all temporality is reduced to pastness, and invention becomes impossible. Dr. Johnson, the best literary critic in our language, insisted that the essence of poetry was invention. Belatedness threatens poetry, and yet can spur it; facticity, allowed a full sway over us, destroys poetry, by making trope irrelevant.

An easy but dangerous misunderstanding of what I am calling facticity is simply to see it as the negation of all irony. I think the negating force of facticity is larger, in that it also destroys every possibility of representation by synecdoche. As an instance I give Freud, the largest recent facticity that contains us. Freud depends upon the synecdoche that represents health by neurosis, which is to say that in his favorite trope, psychic health is completeness, and neurosis is a fragment, a broken symbol of health. Yet Freud is now so much himself a synecdoche for the facticity of our psychic containment that we must read his favorite synecdoche as a literalism. Indeed, facticity urges us to literalize all of Freud, so that we walk about now assuming that we are uneasy triads of id, ego, and super-ego, and mingled drives of Eros and Thanatos. It takes an effort to remember that the Freudian agencies and drives are tropes, and not actual entities or real instances of human life. This is the tribute we pay to Freud, and I mean "tribute" in more than one sense. We pay tribute to Freud involuntarily, as we do to all the powerful mythologies and idealisms that together constitute our historicized dungeon of facticity. Wittgenstein complained that Freud was a powerful mythologist. The complaint is useful, but even Wittgenstein was too enclosed by Schopenhauer's facticity to complain about that precedent mythology, of which Freud himself was never quite free. Philosophers, psychoanalysts, and those still involved with religion are all strikingly vulnerable to blindness about facticity, and to this grouping I would add literary critics who are enclosed by the facticity of Hegel and his tradition, down through Heidegger to Derrida. It is a charming irony that the conscious demystifiers of and by language are themselves unknowingly mystified by the larger entrapments of a containing facticity. Negation also has become a facticity, a literalizing of Hegel's prime trope, and this remystification is now the most squalid truth one can utter about contemporary advanced criticism.

What are the critical uses of a concept of facticity? Our culture in all of its most frozen aspects has been created by its literalization of anterior tropes. Indeed, our concept of culture itself is such a literalization. But I need to make clear that I hope not to be caught in the enclosure of merely literalizing the anterior trope of facticity that plays itself out in the early Heidegger. Heidegger's *Faktizität* is the modern equivalent of the *kenoma*, the emptiness into which we have been and are being thrown, according to the Gnosis of Valentinus. I follow Hans Jonas in so connecting Valentinus and Heidegger, and since I am a kind of belated Valentinian, I am all the more anxious to disengage my sense of facticity from Heidegger's. In the Heideggerian "hermeneutics of facticity," our understanding of the world and of ourselves is limited by our tradition and by our factual circumstance in history. Instead of the narcissistic ego of Freud, or the transcendental ego of Husserl, we have the factually existing ego, a thrown-clear fragment of Being. My own sense of facticity is a blend of the Freudian narcissistic and partly unconscious ego with a Gnostic or Kabbalistic *pneuma*, or spark, which has been thrown all right, but not clear or into a possible clearing.

When a reader is limited by facticity, the limitation goes beyond the facts of tradition and of history. Foucault has tried to engage "notions of chance, discontinuity, and materiality" at the origins of historical ideas, but his mode of engagement is unknowingly tropological, as Hayden White shows. Heidegger is not much interested in the brute contingency of all origins as such, since he privileges Greece and Germany; thus the absolute arbitrariness of the engendering of every tradition whatsoever would not suggest itself to him as a facticity. I tend to cite the erotic analogue in regard to facticity, because almost all of us have immediate knowledge of the contrast between the chance start of our love affairs and the inescapable vicissitudes that ensue from initial haphazardness. The facticity of erotic suffering is shockingly disproportionate to the apparent blunder of erotic venturing, a disproportion that is a clue to many quieter versions of cultural facticity. But I need an example, and for that I turn to the one inevitable work in Western literary culture, the Bible, which is neither Greek nor German. What happens to us when we attempt to read the first great story of a mingled belatedness and earliness, the story of Adam, Eve, and the serpent in Eden?

The strongest writer in the Hebrew language, fully the rival of Homer and Dante, of Shakespeare and Milton, we know fittingly by the

Kafkaesque name of the letter J, standing for the Jahvist. Fittingly, because J in one of his aspects is more Kafkaesque than Kafka, as in another he is more Tolstoyan than Tolstoy. J is a bewildering writer, uncanny beyond any other, and boundlessly difficult because wildly original, with an originality that perhaps three thousand years of commentary and revisionism have failed to subdue or even assimilate. This is originality in the strictest sense, for J is *our* original, as, say, *Gilgamesh* is not, precisely because J *was*. J was and is, and J has authority over us, whether we are Gentile or Jew, normative or heretic, concerned or indifferent. This is the authority of brute contingency, of our being imprisoned by what we might call J's facticity. J's stories are not merely just as familiar as Homer's. They are stories that were more than stories for most of our ancestors, and even if they are only stories for many or perhaps most of us, they are stories with a different aura than Homer's. Wrestling Jacob moves us more intimately than Odysseus confronting the Cyclops, and Yahweh walking down the road to Sodom is a touch more disturbing than Zeus swooping down as a swan. But why?

What I have called facticity or brute factuality is a truth about interpretation that we repress rather than neglect. These days we evade it also, by troping upon it, as the Franco-Heideggerians and their American *epheboi* trope, substituting the fashionable prison house of language for the dank dungeon of historical contingency. Reflecting upon the difficulties of reading J can help remind us *why* rather than just *how* we tend to misread tropes as literalisms. J was an astonishing ironist, and yet nearly every mode of interpretation has read him as being anything but ironic. I am going to offer a belated (and brief) reading of J's story of Eve and the serpent, a reading that will take into account some of the earlier interpretations, normative and Gnostic. But mostly I will attempt to take J's own irony into account, which means that I will try to escape the confinements of facticity, while acknowledging that it is quite impossible to do so. Still, I will try, while remembering that the irony of one age or language is not likely to be irony of another, no matter what our current linguistifiers tell us to the contrary.

So I commence with J's irony, or rather his ironies. His minor modes of irony have something in common with Dante's or Milton's, but only because those poets are so much imprisoned by the contingency of his being the Word of God for them. J is even more massively self-confident a writer than Dante or Milton, fierce and primal in his approach to human personality, and totally daring in his apprehension of divine realities. It is when human personality and divine reality collide that J is almost invariably ironic, in a mode that Kafka catches best among all the descendants of J. This irony is neither classical nor Romantic, Greek nor European. If irony is saying one thing while meaning another, or provoking an expectation that will not be fulfilled, then J is no ironist. But if irony ensues from the juxtaposition or clash of incommensurate levels of powerful realities, then J sets standards of irony that have not been met since. Consider Genesis 6: 1–4. The sons of the Elohim look upon the daughters of men, find them beautiful, and take them. Yahweh says: "Man is only flesh, and shall not be guarded by my spirit forever, so let him have just one hundred and twenty years." Why doesn't Yahweh say something about the sons of the Elohim, who certainly are showing that they are pretty fleshly also? The elliptical J makes no comment, except to observe that it was *then,* as well as later, that the Nephilim or Titans appeared on earth, presumably as the children of Elohistic mismatches. And he adds, rather drily, perhaps even wryly: "Those were the ancient heroes, men with a name." Here is the late E. A. Speiser's quite normative weak misreading:

> It is evident, moreover, from the tenor of the Hebrew account that its author was highly critical of the subject matter. It makes little difference whether J took the contents at face value or, as is more likely (cf. vs. 5), viewed the whole as the product of man's morbid imagination. The mere popularity of the story would have been sufficient to fill him with horror at the depravity that it reflected. A world that could entertain such notions deserved to be wiped out.

Well, J's fifth verse does say that Yahweh saw man's wickedness and evil schemes on earth, but *that* hardly seems a reference to the lustful antics of the sons of the Elohim. There is certainly sorrow in Yahweh's heart, but what J expresses is a kind of ironic apprehension and perhaps even appreciation. Men with a name—before the rather different ways in which Abram became Abraham, and Jacob became Israel, and Moses became the messenger of Yahweh—tended to spring from illicit marriages between earth and heaven. There is no horror and no morbidity in J's tone, but rather a high and sublime irony, which Speiser is too hemmed in by facticity to be able to hear.

But my example is the serpent in Eden, and not to hear J's irony in Eden is to be deaf to literature. First there is Yahweh's characteristic gesture, granting all yet ironically withdrawing that part of the grant which is incommensurate with the recipient. This is the problematic gift made to Adam, and more equivocal still is the irony of Yahweh originally making the serpent more fully conscious than the man and the woman, yet not conscious enough to know with certainty either their limits or his own. As befits a God whose name is presence (I will be when and where I will be), only Yahweh knows the limit of limits, the dialectics of infinite human aspiration and finite human limitations. And the irony of the serpent, much exploited by certain varieties of Gnosticism, is that he is both human-all-too-human and more than human, even if not of the Elohim. Any accurate reading of Genesis 3 begins with the realization that Adam's wife (unnamed until under the curse of Yahweh) is wholly unsurprised by the talking, standing, clever serpent, whether in its proper person or in its message. J clearly neither says nor implies that the serpent is bad or ill-motivated, but only rather shrewd or crafty, an attribute which in the Hebrew is connected by a pun to *nakedness*. Nor does J's serpent lie; a half-truth is quite enough to engender our disaster. The woman eats in order to gain wisdom; she gains instead the knowledge of death, and ultimately death itself, but only after Yahweh takes action against her and her husband. But that, as I think J implies, after all *is* a kind of wisdom, though it comes first as the previously nonexistent consciousness of sexuality—not, of course, as sexuality itself. The new consciousness arrives through its sign of nakedness, and so the serpent teaches that which it truly is: consciousness, or a sense of nakedness, or a certain subtle mode of quest, craftiness. J's God Yahweh marks the consciousness as one limit, a limit that he presumably never intended us to touch. We are expelled by God Yahweh lest we transgress further limits, and we achieve that sense of time without boundaries that Abraham, Isaac, Jacob, and their descendants are to achieve only through an agonistic blessing, and then only within very clear individual limits.

I turn now to some early interpretations of J's serpent drama, and I will state my conclusion before I start. Both the normative and the Gnostic interpretations are strong misreadings of J. I can scarcely decide which distorts or revises J more, and because both the normative and the Gnostic interpretations have enforced and maintained their own contingencies, I think we must call them equally strong misreadings. This is not to say that one cannot choose between them; I do not hesitate in finding the Gnostic misprision far more satisfying, morally, aesthetically, and indeed spiritually, than the Jewish and Christian normative misprisions. The normative interpretive is perhaps too familiar for commentary, or rather the strongest commentary is available in *Paradise Lost*. What is central in that commentary is the identity of the serpent with Satan, which of course has not the slightest relation to J's story. Early Jewish legend invented the serpent's sexual envy of Adam, expressed most forcefully by the fine touch of the serpent pushing Eve against the tree, while urging independence of God upon her. This emblematic movement is reinforced by the detail of the serpent shaking the tree violently, bringing down its fruit. The interpretative strength of these physical details is that they do return to the implications of J's pun upon the serpent's slyness and human nakedness.

Gnostic interpretations antithetically began with the opposite principle, and so with a pragmatic exaltation of the serpent. Perhaps reacting to tropes of seduction, involving Eve and the serpent, in St. Paul and later Christian texts, the Gnostics emphasize the serpent's role in the liberation of human consciousness. The most sublimely outrageous of Gnostic texts in this regard is the book Baruch by Justin, where the serpent is identified with the tree of the knowledge of Good and Evil, and a child of the Demiurge called Elohim and of the maternal figure called Eden, Eve being her later representative. Before Justin's rather tormented and grotesque story is over, the serpent has sexually violated *both* Adam and Eve, but in the interest of purging from both their souls all traces of the unfaithful Demiurge Elohim. The priapic function of the serpent is thus to purify consciousness by a kind of sexual scourging. As an interpretation of J, this is fantastic but exuberant. But as interpretations of J, all the normative accounts, Jewish and Christian, are fully as fantastic and very far, alas, from being exuberant. Rhetorically, the normative misreadings tend to literalize J's ironies, whereas the Gnostic misreadings hyperbolize those ironies. Our inability to this day to read J as being primarily an ironist, of his own very strange and difficult kind, is a dark tribute to his permanent originality.

Our inability adequately to read J extends to almost all of the Bible. But I intend eventually to write a full-scale study of facticity as the blocking agent that thwarts revisionism, and in such a study the Bible necessarily would take a central place. Here I am concerned with the function of criticism as an agonist wrestling with facticity, and I want to emphasize particularly two aspects of that function: canon-formation and prophecy, aspects that overlap but do not coincide. The greatest critics, such as Johnson, Coleridge, Hazlitt, Ruskin, Emerson, and Pater, perfect and extend the canon, while simultaneously prophesying changes in the use and understanding of the canon, changes which are not far in the unapparent, but rather extend the full awareness of what truly is the contemporary. Coleridge and Hazlitt had violently different affective reactions to Wordsworth and his poetry, but they shared absolutely the prophetic and canonical sense that Wordsworth was indeed in the process of inventing modern poetry. Emerson, despite all his later, genteel reservations, saw and said instantly and precisely just what Whitman was doing in the first edition of *Leaves of Grass*. If Wallace Stevens has displaced Eliot and Pound, to some large degree, or if John Ashbery is in the process of displacing Robert Lowell and John Berryman, such displacements are movements proper to criticism, which must protect and yet correct the canon while prophesying accurately the kinds of discernment appropriate to the time, time as it is breaking over and through us.

I hear and read continually the complaint that criticism is now too much concerned with itself, and too little devoted to the clarification of work more primary than itself. I am moved to the countercomplaint that criticism is still too little concerned with itself, because it manifests too much anxiety over method. The quest of contemporary criticism is for method, and the quest is vain. *There is no method other than yourself.* All those who seek for a method that is not themselves will find not a method, but someone else, whom they will ape and involuntarily mock. Poetry and fiction share with criticism the mystery that poststructuralist speculation seeks to deny: the spark we call personality or the idiosyncratic, which in metaphysics and theology once was called presence. Finally we read one critic rather than another for the same reasons we have to read one poet or novelist rather than another. He or she imposes upon us because there is something there that we cannot forget, in a very intimate way. I have a kind of preternatural memory for what I read, yet I remember Wallace Stevens or Nathanael West or G. Wilson Knight very differently than I remember Robert Frost or Thomas Pynchon or Lionel Trilling. This difference, unforgettable, I ascribe to the more successful revisionist struggle against facticity in Stevens, West, and Wilson Knight, a struggle against and yet *within* facticity. But to describe just *how* any revisionist struggles against facticity from within, I need to resort to the authentic precursors of so dialectical an agon. These precursors were the line of Hebrew prophets, from Elijah to the Jesus of the Gospels, which returns me to J, the Jahvist, as the textual founder both of this facticity and the prophets who emerged from it. There is a difficulty, always, in relating prophecy to facticity in J's tradition, a difficulty that is most saddening when we contemplate any idealization of that tradition. I cite here a great idealizer, Martin Buber, who impresses me now as a much more problematic figure than he seemed in my youth.

> The prophetic faith involves the faith in the *factual* character of human experience, as existence that factually meets transcendence. Prophecy has in its way declared that the unique being, man, is created to be a center of surprise in creation. Because and so long as man exists, factual change of direction can take place toward salvation as well as toward disaster, starting from the world in each hour, no matter how late.

I would say that what Buber omits here is indeed brute factuality, the facticity of the prophetic faith as *literary* experience. Man may be created to be a center of surprise in creation, but the writing prophet cannot hope to be a center of surprise in literary creation. Elijah *is* a center of surprise, but Isaiah and even Jeremiah are hemmed in by facticity. Originality is again the stairway of surprise when Elijah enters the Biblical text, because only the accents of breakthrough could allow the sudden violation of facticity that Elijah represents and accomplishes. The rhetorical cost is an abruptness that Biblical scholarship has been unable to assimilate.

> Now Elijah the Tishbite, of Tishbe in Gilead, said to Ahab: "As the Lord the God of Israel lives, before whom I stand, there shall be neither dew nor rain these years, except by my word."

This is not the uncanny tone of J, which acknowledges no possible antagonist, but rather a rhetoric of authority which presupposes enemies, though they be only the priests of the empty god Baal, who does not live. The chronicler of Elijah is like J only insofar as J contains him. J's irony, as exemplified, say, in the story of Eve and the serpent, is beyond the range of Elijah's narrator, who knows only the simple and savage irony of the unequal match between Yahweh and Baal. This decline in irony becomes sharper in the writing prophets, until irony becomes wholly reduced to a terrifying pathos with Jeremiah's sense of humiliation and abandonment.

I am suggesting that the prophets, while they rely upon their as-serted belief that they are returning to the God of Abraham, Jacob, and Moses, nevertheless are caught up in the facticity constituted for them by J's text. Or to employ the Gnostic trope that Heidegger associates with *his* concept of facticity, the prophets' relation to J's text is one of having been thrown. The uncanny Yahweh of J is literalized by the prophets, though less literalized than he was to be by later normative interpreters down to our own time. When we reach the popular vision of an old white-bearded sage up in the clouds, satirized by Blake as Urizen, we have at once the final product of J's facticity and the weakest possible misreading of J.

The popular mind is so given to enclosure by facticity as to be wholly innocent of any urge toward battling facticity. More of a concern for criti-cism is the urge to idealize literature that too frequently results in the idealization of facticity. Most literary exaltations of tradition, let alone *the* tradition, are concealed acts of worship directed toward literary facticity. I could cite here again the Eliot of "Tradition and the Individual Tal-ent,"where facticity masks as an atemporal "simultaneous order" of great works, but I am compelled to look at those who have affected me more intimately, at two of my own heroic precursors, M. H. Abrams and North-rop Frye. What appears in Abrams as the "Romantic heterocosm" and in Frye as the "verbal universe" are two more subtly veiled and idealized versions of facticity. Since Abrams and Frye are legitimate spokesmen for historical High Romanticism, it saddens me to say that they expose Col-eridge and Blake as grand weavers of facticity, dangerous idealizers of harsh and unpleasant literary realities.

Literature is a discursive as well as a linguistic mode, and no dis-course, alas, is autonomous. It is true that strong poems love and hate other strong poems, as it were, far more than they react to other modes of discourse. In the battle against facticity, against the confining strength of prior poetry, a poem has no weapons except the stances and positions of freedom, and for a poem these must be tropes. This limitation compels the subject matter of belated poetry, now dismissed by deconstruction as the rejected referential aspect of an achieved text, to take on a curious coloration, one that I have not been able to explain to nearly anyone's sat-isfaction or understanding. When I've said that a person, place, thing, or event, to get into a poem, has to be treated as though it already were a poem, I have been judged to be declaring the autonomy of poetry. Yet I thought I was expressing a limitation of poetry, rather than celebrating one of its powers. The self may not be what Nietzsche once called it, a rendezvous of persons, but even the strongest poem indeed *is* a rendezvous of poems. This means that even the most organized and written-through poem is necessarily fragmentary. Facticity reduces not only originality and autonomy, but also unity and self-sufficiency, the heterocosmic qualities that the spiritualizers and idealizers of literature are likeliest to discover, early and late.

Since I chose the facticity of J as my instance of that literary concept, I feel obliged to illustrate the idealizing refusal of facticity by a critic of the Bible, and Northrop Frye is now very much to hand. Frye's book *The Great Code: The Bible and Literature* culminates his lifelong work upon his favorite literary form, the anatomy, and so Frye implicitly treats the Bible as a vast anatomy. Nothing could be more imaginatively liberating, but alas, nothing is got for nothing, and that liberation is achieved at the expense of the Hebrew Bible, which indeed is consumed in Frye's great Blakean Code of Art, a fiery furnace worthy of the authors of *The Four Zoas* and *Fearful Symmetry*. Even the uncanny originality of J is melted down in the visionary flames of Toronto. Frye rightly insists that "There is no way of distinguishing the voice of God from the voice of the Deuteronomic redactor," but he does not explain away our ability to distinguish the voice of J from the voices of all of his redactors. Presumably Frye's answer would be this:

> It is futile also to try to distinguish what is "original" in the Bible, the authentic voices of its great prophetic and poetic geniuses, from the later accretions and corruptions sometimes alleged to surround them. The editors are too much for us; they have pulverized the Bible until almost all sense of individuality has been stamped out of it. . . . We are so possessed by the modern notion that all the qualities we admire in literature come from the individuality of an author that it is hard to realize that this relentless smashing of individuality could produce greater vividness and originality rather than less. But so it seems to be.

Frye's position here is consistent with his critical theory, and utterly at variance with my reading of the Hebrew Bible. Frye is curiously free of J's facticity, but this freedom is purchased by bondage to another facticity, the typological traditions of the Christian religion, which imprisoned even William Blake. Frye's Bible, as he says, "is the Christian Bible, with its polemically named 'Old' and 'New' Testaments." I myself would prefer to name these, not unpolemically, as the "Original" and "Belated" Testaments, since I join my ancestors in declining to see the earlier Testament as somehow being "fulfilled" in the later. But I do not see this so much as a quarrel between religions; rather, it is a struggle between critical theories. Frye is interested in the totality of literature, but I am interested primarily in the work of individual poets, those strong enough to force their way against facticity into a canon that is complete without them, and must be compelled somehow to need them. Frye has formulated what he calls a "myth of concern," which excludes any negation from the understanding of literature. Linguistic and rhetorical modes of negation, modern versions of the Hegelian negative, interest me rather less than Frye does, but negation as a psychic defense against belatedness, whether in Shelley or in Freud, is necessary to explain the agonistic element in poetry, which Frye's idealism denies in the face of endless evidence. Ambivalence, to Frye, is only an episode that poetic desire surmounts, but the desire of any individual poet is to surpass the precursors who created *him* through the Scene of Instruction. Frye's St. Paul is a refinement upon the prophets; the Paul I read is a strong misreader, an ephebe struck down on the road to Damascus by the light of the Necessity of Misreading, which became the muse of his own originality. There are no types and no archetypes; there is facticity and there is revisionism, and they battle either to a standstill or to facticity's yielding up of a new name to the revisionist.

Let me contrast Frye and Bloom on a single text, J's account of the wrestling match between Jacob and a nameless one among the Elohim, in Genesis 32:26. I've written about this episode twice before, in *The Breaking of the Vessels* and in the introduction to a volume of Martin Buber's essays on the Bible, and so I want to be brief about it here. Indeed, I want to imitate Frye's pithiness as best I can, since whatever my ambivalence, I worship that great critic's stance and style. Here is the last sentence of the seventh chapter of Frye's *The Great Code:* "The inference for the reader seems to be that the angel of time that man clings to until daybreak is both an enemy and an ally, a power that both enlightens and cripples, and disappears only when all that can be experienced has been experienced." I would say instead: "The angel of death that man clings to until daybreak is an enemy, a power that cripples, and disappears only when an impending death has been averted and a new name for man's persistence as an agonist has been won." Frye's reading has the virtue of balance, which I would call in this context a triumph for the Bible's facticity over Frye, or more simply, Frye has balance but J doesn't. Frye omits the angel's terror of daybreak, and the real viciousness of the nightlong struggle. The being who cries out desperately, "Let me go, for it is daybreak!" is no ally, and precisely what Jacob has refused to experience is literal death. Is it harsh for me to say that the idealizing or typological reading here, even when performed by a master, is by no means wholly adequate to the force of J's text?

Frye's ultimate idealization, always, is his moving faith that "imaginative literature" is *not* an "anxiety-structure." He concludes *The Great Code* by saying that man builds anxiety-structures around his religious and social institutions. What Frye cannot or will not see is that artistic institutions (including canons, and academies, and traditions) are necessarily anxiety-structures also. The Bible, like any real literary canon, is *an achieved anxiety,* and not a program to release us from anxiety. For what can a canon, or an academy, or a tradition be unless it has some residual authority over us? Such authority is now only rhetorical, but the Bible's rhetoric of authority, whether in J or in the prophets, is far more individual and personal than Frye, on principle, can allow it to be. How did Jeremiah, a prophet whom it would be kind to call "defeatist," ever manage to impose himself upon the canon? An acute individualizing of voice is almost certainly the only realistic answer. Jeremiah's sufferings became exemplary only because they are memorable, because they dramatize, with striking harshness, the endless dilemma of Jeremiah's people: caught throughout history, as they are today, between rival empires; always threatened, as they are today, by a much more numerous surrounding and hostile people. Frye says, quite wonderfully, and I think accurately, that "The prophet may be right or wrong, reasonable or unreasonable: the thing he does not do is hedge." Prophecy, in the Hebraic sense, indeed is oratory without qualification. The *nevi* speaks his *davar* or word, which is also Yahweh's. What is oldest and farthest back in the *nevi* is brought forward and presented straight out as an act. It is for this that the *nevi* was born—consecrated, as Jeremiah says he was, from the womb until death. But who will listen to an impersonal and generalized voice? Frye, I think, misses something of the meaning of *davar* when Jeremiah or Amos or Isaiah proclaims "Thus Yahweh speaks." The paradoxical evidence for the voice's authority, for the word being sent from Yahweh, is that the figuration be wholly personal and magnificently individual. A writing prophet is received only because of his rhetorical power, and this power of troping always must make its anxious way against the facticity of Moses, which means against the facticity of J.

I am arguing now not only against Frye, but against Buber, indeed against all Biblical criticism that I know, whether normative or scholarly-historical. But the prophetic figurations are to a considerable degree a kind of deceptive rhetoric. Contrast Isaiah's call, in chapter 6 of his book, to the call of Moses, upon whose authority supposedly it is founded. Moses attempts to evade the call, but Isaiah volunteers, saying: "Here am I; send me." Moses asks Yahweh to name Himself, that he, Moses, may declare Who sent him when he descends into Egypt to speak to his fellow Jews. Isaiah does not even know what he is being called upon to do or to say. The legacy of J declares itself only in the frightening irony of Yahweh's injunctions to Isaiah:

> Go, and tell this people:
> Hear ye indeed, but understand not;
> And see ye indeed, but perceive not.
> Make the heart of this people fat,
> And make their ears heavy,
> And shut their eyes;
> Lest they, seeing with their eyes,
> And hearing with their ears,
> And understanding with their heart,
> Return, and be healed.

Isaiah's irony, like J's, involves the clash of incommensurate orders of reality, the clash of Yahweh and his people—always a clash, rhetorically speaking, despite the promise of every covenant. But Isaiah's irony swerves away from J's into an irony less uncanny to us. J is never bitter; indeed, like Homer, J is sublimely beyond bitterness. Isaiah, strong poet though he be, falls into bitterness *in order to get started.* His bitterness is the cost of his call, or as we would say, the sign of his originality. It *individualizes* Isaiah, by making him memorable at the very start of his prophetic mission. J's Moses is genuinely bewildered that he, a man anything but eloquent, should have been chosen. Isaiah is a knowing latecomer, and he tropes his own conscious eloquence through the image of the glowing stone with which one of the seraphim touches his, the prophet's, mouth. That glowing stone upon the lips is as much Isaiah's mark for his own originality as the transparent eyeball was Emerson's, or the Holy Spirit brooding over the vast abyss to make it pregnant was Milton's. J as narrator of the tales of Jacob or of the Exodus feels no need for self-dramatization, though I hear his personal sign in the extraordinary tribute he pays Wrestling Jacob: "The sun rose upon him as he passed Penuel, limping on his hip." But Isaiah, like all of the writing prophets, and like the Milton of the invocations, cannot get started without dramatizing himself.

As critics we can only confirm the self-canonizations of the truly strong prophets and poets. What we cannot do is invent their canonization for them. Nothing, of course, is more pathetic in literature than the bathos of the false prophets and the weak poets. Pindar and Milton celebrate themselves, and we are happy to concur, but how embarrassed we are by the canonical gestures of those who cannot write their way out of a paper bag, let alone out of the facticity of giants. In a secular age, or more simply in a literary culture, why ought criticism to address itself to the almost undisplaced religious concept of prophecy, as well as to the clearly displaced notion of canon-formation? After all, no one thanks you for a canonical enterprise, and the academy certainly has no use for prophets. Were it not better done, as others use the discipline, to allow canonization to proceed as an implicit process, and to wait for consensus on all issues as to the nature and function of poetry and criticism? Professor Moldy Fig and Dame Gentility hold the field as they always have held it, and why should they not?

I would begin an answer mildly enough, by observing that poetry is not a criticism of life, but the criticism of poetry is or ought to be. It is very late in the West, and the academies increasingly serve as our sun-dials. In the evening land, you can see some things more clearly than before, or more clearly than elsewhere, and by our falling light poetry is seen for what it has become, a criticism of earlier poetry, an evasion of overwhelming facticities. A criticism that thinks itself through, in our situation, will prophesy unto us merely by being as and where it is. Our Elijah or Supreme Critic was Freud, who preferred to see himself as Moses, but the preference was misleading. Freud, like J, was an uncanny writer who created a new and enormous facticity for all of us, whether or not we are aware of it. We literalize Freud's tropes every day of our lives, and we have no way of freeing ourselves either of the tropes or of our literalizations. It is Freud who wrote the poems of our temporality, as opposed, say, to the poems of our climate.

I want to take as a closing text a few observations made by Freud in his last book, the unfinished but definitive work called, with a false modesty, *An Outline of Psychoanalysis*. Just before Freud breaks off his manuscript, he describes the relationship between the *I* and the *Over-I* or *Above-I*—the ego and the superego, as translation has taught us to call them:

> A portion of the external world has, at least partially, been given up as an object and instead, by means of identification, taken into the ego—that is, has become an integral part of the internal world. This new mental agency continues to carry on the functions which have hitherto been performed by the corresponding people in the external world: it observes the ego, gives it orders, corrects it and threatens it with punishments, exactly like the parents whose place it has taken. . . . The superego is in fact the heir to the Oedipus complex and only arises after that complex has been disposed of. For that reason its excessive severity does not follow a real prototype but corresponds to the strength which is used in fending off the temptation of the Oedipus complex.

Freud is moving overtly toward a scene of recognition in which he himself can identify the id with the organic past and the superego with the cultural past. This would be, I think, the Freudian explanation of what I have described as a literary state of facticity, and such an explanation apparently would be at variance with my own theory of facticity, which assigns to precursor figures something more of the role of the id than of the superego. But Freud is too subtle not to have anticipated this, as he anticipates all legitimate criticism. He goes on to doubt his own generalizations, and observes:

> Some of the cultural acquisitions have undoubtedly left a deposit behind in the id; much of what is contributed by the superego will awaken an echo in the id. . . .

Even as superego and id begin to blend together a little *in this specific context*, Freud manifests a realization of how he is affected by the facticity that Goethe's *Faust* constituted for him. He quotes a famous aphorism from Part I: "What you have inherited from your fathers,/Strive to make it your own." And to illustrate this Goethean paradox, Freud ends this unended and unendable last book with a remarkable declaration:

> Thus the superego takes up a kind of intermediate position between the id and the external world; it unites in itself the influences of the present and of the past. In the emergence of the superego we have before us, as it were, an example of the way in which the present is changed into the past. . . .

Why Freud breaks off just there we cannot know, but as our master he has taught us how to surmise in something of his spirit. The superego, being above the *I* (and above the *it* also), is, like the Freudian trope of the drive, a frontier concept, neither internal nor external, neither psychic nor societal, neither subjective nor objective. Freud wants us to believe that the superego represents all our abandoned object affections, as well as the revenge that the abandoned take upon us. Literary facticity, as I seek to describe it, assimilates the superego to the id and makes of the most powerful texts—the Bible, Shakespeare, Freud—a kind of drive within us as well as a partly internalized spirit of revenge. When the present is altogether changed into the past in the agon of reading, then facticity has triumphed over the reader's Sublime, which is to say, it has voided the function of criticism. So powerful is Freud's own facticity for us that it prevents us from seeing the extent to which his reductive authority has augmented our inability to be strong critics.

I would surmise, though, that Freud's belated invention of the super-ego marks the crisis in his own repressed sense of being hemmed in by cultural facticity—by the combined force of Hebraic and classical culture, of Moses or the Jahvist and of Homer, but also of Shakespeare and Goethe, and of those great precursor speculators, Schopenhauer and Nietzsche. Freud's own countertransference or cultural guilt, provoked by his own enormous usurpation of authority, results in what could be called the revenge of Yahweh or of the Jahvist, which is the belated, painful birth of the superego, or the spirit of revenge. As the strongest modern exemplification of the reader's Sublime, or the agon against facticity, Freud paradoxically fostered what has become the inevitable trope for facticity. Having been thrown, we are subject to the harshness of the superego, which religious rebels once enjoyed calling the Demiurge.

Criticism cannot teach us to be Freud, or even how to avoid imprisonment by Freud. The function of criticism at the present time, as I conceive it, cannot be to liberate us from the brute factuality of our dependent relation to culture, whether that culture be Biblical or Freudian. But criticism alone can teach us to stop literalizing our cultural dilemmas. Education, when it is most authentic, centers upon the precise project of showing the student just what degree of freedom is possible for her or him in relation to the presentness of the cultural past. The most critical of educations never will be capable of totally convincing us that the figurations of the past *are* figurations and not literal entities. Yahweh and the superego will go on haunting us, whether or not we are persuaded that they are ironies or synecdoches or whatever. The strong critic does not arrive to exorcise the colors of our involuntary imaginings, but she or he does stand at the threshold of culture's haunted mansion to admonish us to enter, not even as the most alert among spectators, but as agonists armed with the past's own weapons, the only weapons that will defend us honorably against the force of the past.

Edward Thomas and Modernism
DAVID BROMWICH

In any discussion of modern poetry Edward Thomas is apt to be praised in a subordinate clause; if the speaker has mastered the tone of patronage appropriate to a survey, the clause may well be: "though an interesting secondary figure, Thomas. . . . " *Interesting* in this case admits the integrity of a style which though never consciously modernist still does not feel archaic, sixty years later. In America Thomas is of course mentioned now and then in connection with Frost; but his poems are not read; few scholars of poetry could give the titles of five of them. In England, where both the poems and "writings on the English countryside" are more familiar, Thomas is seen as expressing unassimilable tendencies. Critics in search of his tradition have placed him with Clare and Crabbe for the poetry, and with Richard Jefferies and W. H. Hudson for the prose; Thomas is accordingly cherished as a writer of insular concerns, who worked in a genre now all the more appealing for being almost extinct. Different as the results are, Thomas has been poorly served by his reputation in both countries. The truth is that one cannot read widely in his work, including the criticism, reviews, and sketches of daily life, without growing convinced of his importance in the early history of modernism. He not only pointed the way for others, he himself exemplified the value of pursuing it. A great part of the change of mood, with the testing of a new eloquence, which is commonly associated with Yeats, Eliot, and Pound, he helped to create. His manner was calmer than theirs but not less decisive.

Edna Longley's anthology of Thomas's prose, *A Language Not to Be Betrayed*, reprints many of the articles he wrote after 1902 for the *Daily Chronicle*, where he took Lionel Johnson's place as regular reviewer. Here he soon established the continuity between Johnson and himself by an unstinting admiration for Hardy's poems: "The moan of his verse rouses an echo that is as brave as a trumpet." Here too, he considered volumes by Frost, Pound, de la Mare and the lesser Georgians, as they first appeared. These reviews, with their incidental statements of creed, are not otherwise available in permanent form, so that in one respect the anthology is a meticulous work of restoration. But the editor's feeling for what is essential in Thomas, in a discussion of Keat's odes, or of prose writers like Borrow and Cobbett with whom he felt an affinity, comprehends all his more substantial writings as well; and with twenty years' labor in prose so finely represented, it will no longer be plausible to regard Thomas as a man whose moment arrived quite suddenly with the war and passed as suddenly. Indeed, Edna Longley's selections after 1913 suggest that for Thomas the war was simply a large public event in which he could not help being interested, because it happened while he was alive. More grandly than that he never saw it. He wrote frank descriptions of the patriotic mood, of which he was critical, as a native may be critical; and when he came to write the poem that begins, "This is no case of petty right and wrong," he justified his decision to enlist by the sentiment of a place and not a generation: it was a confession of his attachment to home in the largest sense. Soldiers mattered to Thomas, hardly in a personal way, as part of the humanity he counted as his audience, and therefore part of his subject beyond war. He cared, not so much for writers who contributed to a public record, as for those who were or might become individual voices, and in the end he aimed to be known as such a voice. I will be quoting disproportionately from Thomas's criticism because it seems to me the least understood area of his achievement; but for readers who know his poetry, a tone it shares with the criticism may be worth keeping in mind from the start. In both, a certain reticence guards the stronger sentiments, and at the same time announces them more firmly than any imaginable emphasis. The result is a kind of writing in which sincerity becomes a well-defined term of praise.

The advance signalled by the criticism of T. E. Hulme, and of Eliot and Pound when they wrote as his disciples, might be reduced to a single perception. These critics saw that the language of the third and fourth generations of Romantic poets had been refined beyond the service of a living speech: by the twentieth century, it had become a machine for poemmaking. Much of their polemic was anticipated in Ruskin's criticism of the pathetic fallacy, and yet the new school had the wit to make theirs a battle not merely of practices but of personalities. Swinburne was only one, though perhaps the typical, object of routine derision, and it may seem in retrospect that the profuse monotony of his eloquence fostered bad habits of dismissal in those who had tired of it. Still, Hulme, Eliot, and Pound were admired by their contemporaries for the simple daring of having sought to dislodge a great reputation of the 1880s and 1890s, a name sacred to *The Education of Henry Adams*. The spirit of exclusion, which served at first to weaken the shadow of those decades, was eventually carried backward into the nineteenth century, and a sustained movement of intellectual history, in which poetry had been among the larger powers, was dismissed as the consequence of a wrong turn—with what success may be judged by Pound's triumphant allusions to the bankrupt firm of "Kelly, Sheats & Co." At this point, Hulme and the others lose credit with us, now that their daring has ceased to be appreciable, but the only alternative to faith in the modernist rewriting of history has often seemed to be an imputation of roughly the same blindness to all the more original minds of the period. In the name of a tolerant historicism, one may reason that some things are invisible to those who invent, and who are as happy to believe lies as they are to sell them if it means more life for themselves. But, after all, an intolerant historicism is more interesting, and the very existence of a critic like Thomas helps to justify it. In his observations on the language of poetry he looks forward to most of the better-known modernist strictures, without their anti-Romantic bias, and his polemic is much finer in its gradations.

It begins in his reviews of contemporary critics but emerges as a consistent argument where one might expect it, in *Algernon Charles Swinburne* (1912), with remarks like this: "Other poets tend towards a grace and glory of words as a human speech perfected and made divine, Swinburne towards a musical jargon that includes human snatches, but is not and never could be speech." By the time he started rereading Swinburne, Thomas had already proposed to himself two maxims: that poetry is what cannot be translated, and that it ought to be at least as well written as prose. The book is a closely illustrated attempt to persuade his readers of the soundness of both. One can see them working together when Thomas observes of some characteristic lines that they "can be translated into prose, and have possibly been translated out of it—not into poetry." But he points out, as a more pervasive fault in Swinburne, a defect of imagination which cannot be blamed on the diction of an age or a century:

> He can astonish and melt but seldom thrill, and when he does it is not
> by any felicity of as it were God-given inevitable words. He has to

depend on sound and an atmosphere of words which is now and then concentrated and crystallized into an intensity of effect which is almost magical, perhaps never quite magical.

Throughout the book Thomas is disposed to recognize the many poems in which Swinburne's ends claim only as much as his means respect, above all "The Forsaken Garden" and "Ave Atque Vale." But the concern with expressive "magic" reveals Thomas's deeper allegiance to Shelley, of whose prophecy he treats Swinburne as an imperfectly satisfying fulfillment. The poetry is deficient not because it is sensational, or republican, or subjective in a style neither hard nor dry, but because the poet has used words as counters, even if not as counters of sense. In a passage of very delicate irony, we are invited to accept Swinburne's lack of valor with words as a cause also of the charm by which he subdues them without protest.

> Perhaps the greatest of his triumphs is in keeping up a stately solemn play of words not unrelated to the object suggested by his title and commencement but more closely related to rhymes, and yet in the end giving a compact and powerful impression. The play of words often on the very marge of nonsense has acted as an incantation, partly by pure force of cadence and kiss of rhymes, partly by the accumulative force of words in the right key though otherwise lightly used.

When he looked at Swinburne lowering his immense press of words onto a half-formed intuition of a subject, Thomas did not say, "This is wrong because some way back the history of poetry went wrong." It was a matter of individual strengths and weaknesses. Thus he supposed that Tennyson no less than Swinburne, though more quietly with his "voluptuous avoidance of excess," had failed to make any but the "entirely personal impression, far different from Wordsworth's, which made of nature a neighbour commonwealth to our own." Yet from the poetry of his youth Thomas turned not to the sixteenth century but back to the first generation of Romantics. In this he resembled Yeats, and the parallel is worth drawing out for contrast.

Symbolism gave Yeats a name for the elements of Romantic practice that he wished to recover, together with a ready-made fellowship of collaborators. But it was Pater's prose that had shown him how the symbolic ramifications of an image could be almost infinite and yet be controlled by the forethought of the writer. A "marmoreal muse" left with each of the words of a Paterian sentence some reminiscence of the pains that had gone to form them. To Yeats this was treating words the opposite of lightly; but Thomas, when he read even the paragraphs of exposition in Pater's lectures, was impressed by a finish like Swinburne's. His objection to such writing was that it could not serve naturally as discourse: in Pater's biographical sketches, there would be times when it aimed to do so and could not, because its success had placed it at too secure a distance from conversational disciplines. *Walter Pater* (1913), generally the most appreciative of Thomas's full-length studies, isolates many sentences like the following, for an exqisiteness that has pared away any suggestion of purpose: "And who that has rested a hand on the glittering silex of a vineyard slope in August, where the pale globes of sweetness are lying, does not feel this?" Here, says Thomas, "The words 'pale globes of sweetness' remind us that grapes are pale, globular, and sweet; they do not vividly suggest or represent grapes, but rather the mind of a man who has pondered the subject of the relation between things and words, and has come to no inspiring conclusion."

Thomas also sees a connection between such traits of style and the special conditions of Pater's solitude. A professor and official mentor to the young, his sense of duty is visible in the mostly somber, but at times arbitrarily heightened, coloring of his style. He writes like a man who must be sure every moment of "professing frankly"—that is, with careful ingenuousness and a careful decorum.

> The most and the greatest of man's powers are as yet little known to him, and are scarcely more under his control than the weather: he cannot keep a shop without trusting somewhat to his unknown powers, nor can he write books except such as are no books. It appears to have been Pater's chief fault, or the cause of his faults, that he trusted those powers too little. The alternative supposition is that he did not carry his self-conscious labours far enough. On almost every page of his writing words are to be seen sticking out, like the raisins that will get burnt on an ill-made cake. It is clear that they have been carefully chosen as the right and effective words, but they stick out because the labour of composition has become so self-conscious and mechanical that cohesion and perfect consistency are impossible. The words have only an isolated value; they are labels; they are shorthand: they are anything but living and social words.

Clearly as Pater may have displayed his convictions, a tutorial relation to his listeners bound him to write English as if it were a dead language. That his words are not fine enough is a criticism Thomas does not make; he argues rather that words used for their "living and social" value feel plain to the writer in that they feel inevitable. This effortless authority was the single grace of style denied to Pater.

Yet the living and social word alone has the effect of somehow modifying the reader's imagination. It can do so because it seems to have claimed the writer's recognition intimately from his life, temperament, and circumstances, and because it commands in turn the reader's own recognition as something more than the name of an object: something *his* life, temperament, and circumstances have to translate. A word of this sort is always mysterious to the reader to the extent that it was familiar to the writer, and nothing is gained by calling it either literal or figurative. Thomas writes of its effect in one of his happiest statements of vocation, "The Word"; the poem describes a spring sound which "Though 'tis an empty thingless name" the poet cannot forget, since

> Spring after Spring
> Some thrushes learn to say it as they sing.
> There is always one at midday saying it clear
> And tart—the name, only the name I hear.

Frost gave a lovely echo of this in "The Oven Bird"; but of the birds which these poems offer as figures of poetic speech, Thomas's is the less flatly antirhetorical: its song is closer to the "tone of meaning" Frost speaks of in another sonnet. The reader who does not know how much a tone can mean will misremember the poem's title as "The Thrush," and that is part of the poem's teaching. Such a reader thinks the word's work is done when the associated object has appeared. But for Thomas the wonder of "the word" that poetry can discover or revive is that it makes all substitutions a matter of question-begging:

> The name suddenly is cried out to me
> From somewhere in the bushes by a bird
> Over and over again, a pure thrush word.

It is not quite the same as a pure thrush's word; indeed, the poem suggests a definition of a poet as someone for whom words and objects have mingled inseparably. By listening for the word a writer joins his names

with ours; and we go on reading him because his society affords as much
hope of renewal as a season.

Yeats for a time considered the Image a fair exchange for words like
this, and he would probably have approved, for he sometimes imitated
the passage about grapes which Thomas quotes as stilted. Imagism in general codified the practice of isolating such passages as the essence of poetry. I think Thomas would have been inclined to reject the movement on
the ground that it was doctrinally unequipped to notice the poetry of "No
motion but the moving tide, a breeze, / Or merely silent Nature's breathing life," poetry not written and not to be valued as naturalistic transcription. But here his graver opinions can only be surmised: all his criticism of
the Imagists he contracted into a joke, with the suggestion that the movement's real source lay less in classical authors than in classical editions.
"The chief influence appears to have been the ordinary prose translation
of the classics—in short, the crib. Burlesqued this had been already by
Mr. A. E. Housman and others. The Imagist poets must have the credit of
being the first to go to it for serious inspiration."

Imagism and Symbolism as Thomas understands them have much in
common: by both movements poetry is identified not with the animating
passion of words but with the ideal distillation they achieve on the page.
Some such effect was Yeats's design when he broke the *as*-clauses of Pater's Mona Lisa into separate lines of free verse. The editor's creation of
discretely vivid pictures, out of a purposeful series interlinked in prose,
made symbolic images of what earlier readers had encountered as allegory. The referent of each clause was expected in consequence to emerge
reliably line by line. But why should the symbolist concern himself with
reference at all? "It is a little unkind to words," writes Thomas, "to suppose that they can be bounded by their meaning, but apparently the symbolist must insist that his words are not only not so bounded, but have a
further significance which is quite precise; otherwise there were no differences between the old and the new." The old reader whom Thomas has in
mind did not assume words were bounded by their meanings, but rather
that everyone interpreted them from a modest consensus about kinds of
meaning, after which everyone built for himself and within his imaginative powers. The symbolist on the contrary grants an independence to
words which they already enjoy, and then returns to guide their interpretation with a new control. Thomas cites as an example Yeats's conscien-
tious notes to *The Wind among the Reeds* for the help they bring to the

poem entitled "Mongan laments the Change that has come upon him and his Beloved." Perhaps "a day will come when the force of Mr. Yeats's genius will have added to common culture the special knowledge through which alone the poem is intelligible. At present [its language] is dead or merely private, and the note, so far from helping the poem, attracts attention exclusively to itself." The poem most fortunate from the symbolist point of view is most opaque to the common culture of meaning.

Poetic language in Thomas's view is everything that may disclose a mind in motion, or a mind occupied with what most concerns it.

> In the mainly instinctive use of [language] the words will all support one another, and, if the writing is good, the result of this support is that each word is living its intensest life. . . . Whatever be the subject, the poem must not depend for its main effect upon anything outside itself except the humanity of the reader.

One may read these sentences, along with Thomas's more straightforward acts of homage to Wordsworth, as a record of how much survived in him of the spirit of the Preface to *Lyrical Ballads,* in spite of the many features of its program he seems to have discarded. There is no claim for purity of diction, only for dramatic propriety. There is none either for the repose of large feelings in rural places, and the poet's difference from other men is no longer measured by degrees of imagination. The difference now comes from an understanding of the conditions of language which the poet alone employs actively and continuously. He is one more person who knows English words. And yet, by picking out an emphasis among the words we use, he touches our habits of thinking and feeling. This he does in a way so commonplace as to be unmeasurable, and in this sense the language of poets is the second nature of men.

According to high-modernist precept, a modern style requires, apart from imponderables like genius, the omission of certain untimely artifices. Syntactical inversions are among these, as well as words of quaint pedigree, "casement" for windows or "lamp" for star; but if one looks for tokens of this sort in Thomas's poetry, he will seem far from sufficiently modern. He appears never to have developed a simple distaste for inversions, and his poems are unsuperstitiously free even with Miltonic orderings of adjective-noun-adjective ("stony square unlit"), or by extension adverb-

verb-adverb ("wisely reiterating endlessly"). These were conscious practices, and not the lapses of an unguarded mood; for Thomas supposed that
being modern was a matter of escaping the belief that there was one preeminently poetic attitude. Some of his changes of heart about other poets
can be traced to his refusal to be charmed when an attitude that once
seemed natural became a self-regarding manner. A 1912 review of Rupert
Brooke's *Poems* is quick to detect the process well advanced by then in
the work of a youthful poet:

> He writes of Helen, of London, of afternoon tea, of sleeping out, of
> seasickness. He experiments in choriambics. He is full of revolt, con-
> tempt, self-contempt, and yet of arrogance too. He reveals chiefly
> what he desires to be and to be thought. Now and then he gives him-
> self away, as when, in three poems close together, he speaks of the
> scent of warm clover. Copies should be bought by everyone over
> forty who has never been under forty.

There is nothing to prevent a poet of whatever age from addressing the
characteristic emotions of readers under forty and producing poems as
lasting as Housman's. But a poet like Brooke, with his pet words and
scenes, wrote partly from sheer irritability at those whom he did not care
to have as readers. Thomas replies by advising them to use the book as a
kind of instruction manual on how to *become* Brooke's readers: the under-
statement here, which turns an ordinary offense into a splendid curiosity,
is a critical tactic both rarer than irony and more versatile. Thomas shows
the same tact for managing imperfect sympathies in his reviews of Pound.

As a fashioner of dramatic speech, Pound had gone further than anyone of the age except Yeats in his plays, and Thomas's first impulse as a
reviewer was to report the cheering news. Of *Personae* he writes in 1909:
"Carelessness of sweet sound and of all the old tricks makes Mr. Pound's
book rather prickly to handle at first. It was practically nothing but this
prickliness that incited us to read the book through a second time. We
read it a third time . . . because it was good the second." Pound's approx-
imation of personality by an unconnected series of negative gestures
would later dictate the structure of "Hugh Selwyn Mauberly," with its
undertone of self-congratulation, its overtones of revolt, contempt, self-
contempt, and the ad hoc satire of its portraits giving an appearance of
consistency to the whole. Even at this early stage, however, Thomas was
annoyed by the cageyness of a poet who never materialized among his

own personae. The steady vehemence of some poems made the unsteady shifts of voice all the more troubling. But in 1909 Thomas preferred to think that "The disdain is the other side of a powerful love for something else."

Yet he came back to *Personae* in a second review, and added several qualifications withheld from the first. "Let us straightway acknowledge the faults; the signs of conflict; the old and foreign words and old spellings that stand doubtless for much that the ordinary reader is not privileged to detect; the tricky use of inverted commas; the rhythms at one time so free as not to be distinguishable at first from prose, at another time so stiff that 'evanescent' becomes 'evan'scent'; the gobbets of Browningesque." Innovation, in which Pound's work is certainly rich, does not impress Thomas as a sign of genuine invention. He had said earlier, in a neutral tone, that Pound seemed to have "practically no extravagance." As he followed Pound's career this began to emerge as a defect. For without natural extravagance, Pound was forced to rely on an unlimited number of mannerisms. And a poet who says of all his devices, "these are provisionally mine and yet not me," may end in a condition of moral weightlessness. Thomas saw this as a danger for Pound, and in a review of *Exultations* later the same year he delivered his warning straightforwardly.

> When he writes in the first person he is so obscure as to give some excuse for finding him incapable of self-expression. And both in personal and detached poems he is, as a rule, so pestered with possible ways of saying a thing that at present we must be content to pronounce his condition still interesting—perhaps promising—certainly distressing. If he is not careful he will take to meaning what he says instead of saying what he means.

The reader of our age, who has lived past the first decade of cantos, the tracts against usury, the broadcasts for Mussolini, the harangue of Pound's speeches and the harangue of his silence, will be equipped to appreciate the depth of the critic who in 1909 found little gravity in a mind so "pestered with possible ways of saying a thing."

Nor can it be objected that Thomas had really failed to comprehend the modernist idea of masks—that he cherished an anachronistic fondness for personality-as-such. He knew the idea very well, not as a modern discovery but from its sources in Keats, and he observed in praise of de la Mare that though his "personal quality is intense and consistent . . . it has no obvious egotism, no significant first person singular, no confession, defiance, lament, or hinted mystery. Mr. de la Mare's work is, in fact, the perfection of personality, and in an impersonal way, without deliberation or obtrusiveness." In the end he saw de la Mare as a personal poet without egotism, and Pound as an egotist without personality, or with one that "rises to the appearance of being positive only by contradiction." His comments on de la Mare bring to mind Eliot's observation a few years later in "Tradition and the Individual Talent," that the aim of poetry is a continual extinction of personality, though only those who have it know what it means to escape from it. If Thomas made his remark more in passing, this was because he took it to express an elementary truth. Poetry since Wordsworth had been the projection of a few intense personal interests as "a neighbour commonwealth to our own." The reader feels at home there because his interests, and for that matter his intellectual activity, are not different in kind from the writer's.

I suspect that what first drew Thomas to the poetry of Frost was its explicit concern with reading. "This," he began his review of *North of Boston*, "is one of the most revolutionary books of modern times, but one of the least aggressive." The language "is free from the poetical words and forms that are the chief material of secondary poets"—here he seems to be thinking of the Georgian movement as a general tendency. As for the rhythms, they avoid "not only the old-fashioned pomp and sweetness, but the later fashion also of discord and fuss"—here unquestionably he has Pound still in view. The sentences that follow are worth pausing over:

> Almost all these poems are beautiful. They depend not at all on objects commonly admitted to be beautiful. Neither have they merely a homely beauty, but are often grand, sometimes magical. Many, if not most, of the separate lines and separate sentences are plain and, in themselves, nothing. But they are bound together and made elements of beauty by a calm eagerness of emotion.

When one considers the range of Frost's tones, from poems like "The Vantage Point" to poems occasional and even ceremonial, like "The Master Speed," that phrase of Thomas's about "a calm eagerness of emotion" seems marvelously precise. But as with *Personae*, he reviewed *North of Boston* more than once, and here again the second article repeats hardly anything from the first. One passage, however, which Thomas does return to is the conclusion of "The Wood Pile": "I thought that only / Someone

who lived in turning to fresh tasks / Could so forget his handiwork. . . ."
One may recall the self-forgetting that Thomas had missed in Pater, and
these lines were probably in his mind when he summed up his estimate
of Frost:

> Mr. Frost has, in fact, gone back, as Whitman and as Wordsworth
> went back, through the paraphernalia of poetry into poetry again.
> With a confidence like genius, he has trusted his conviction that a
> man will not easily write better than he speaks when some matter has
> touched him deeply, and he has turned it over until he has no doubt
> what it means to him, when he has no purpose to serve beyond ex-
> pressing it, when he has no audience to be bullied or flattered, when
> he is free, and speech takes one form and no other.

"With a confidence like genius" expresses a great deal that is finely and
not obviously true about Frost's character as a poet. It does not pamper
the author's self-esteem, but says: this poetry has the kind of intimacy we
are used to seeing earned by genius alone; yet it is remarkable for a *conscious* self-trust which genius has not often been known to display; indeed
it steals a march on our deliberations over merit. The most impressive fact
about Thomas's advocacy of Frost, as even a brief excerpt shows, is the
decency of its reticence. By its refusal of hyperbole, of historical comparisons that merely flatter, of the invention of a new category in which
the poet because he stands alone will stand highest, it leaves the reader to
think further for himself.

About the time Thomas was writing these reviews Frost was telling
friends he had invented a theory of "sentence sounds" which Thomas
would some day expound in an article. As it happened Thomas knew
better than to call it a theory or attribute it to Frost. He quotes the good
terse phrases, "Pressed into service means pressed out of shape" and
"Three foggy mornings and one rainy day / Will rot the best birch fence a
man can build," but he gives them not as instances of a language now forgotten except by Frost, but to remind us that this is the healthy employment of English words in common exchange. Before he saw *North of
Boston* Thomas had written: "Men understand now the impossibility of
speaking aloud all that is within them, and if they do not speak it, they
cannot write as they speak. The most they can do is write as they would
speak in a less solitary world." Frost's sentence sounds made the world
less solitary. But their importance for all writing had been a leading em-

phasis of Thomas's criticism for a decade before he met Frost. He would I think have been willing to accept a generous definition of poetry as anything that created such sounds by design. The point, at any rate, is that between Frost and Thomas the friendship that grew was reciprocal, and included critical thinking no less than poetic practice. Of the temperamental differences that seem to have kept them interested in each other the most vivid evidence is Thomas's reaction to "The Road Not Taken." The poem, as is now generally known, was meant by Frost as a gentle reproof of Thomas's study of self-regret. Yet Thomas failed to see that there was mockery in it; he liked it simply as a Shelleyan poem by Frost and was struck by the pathos of "I shall be telling this with a sigh." When Frost protested against the misreading, Thomas pronounced himself content with the poem as he had loved it first, and ready to forgive but not credit Frost's insistence on a contrary intention. One might turn this into a parable for interpreters, with the moral, "Parody no Excuse for Eloquence."

The story is immediately helpful for what it shows of the more trusting mood in which Thomas as a poet is likely to manage a subject he shares with Frost. He makes a softer approach to the emotions of a poem, or is longer in testing their resonance. The effect in either case is of words used not lightly but seldom quite as emphatically as they are by Frost. The quick pace varied by fluent metrical deviations has its part too in the reader's sense of a decisive voice telling of things not yet decided. Frost conveys the opposite impression, even where his words are most tentative, his step most held by voluntary pauses. He wrote "Spring Pools" with the confidence Thomas knew how to praise as an unconfiding strength, and one wants it nearby to compare with "Tall Nettles," a poem by Thomas similar in theme and movement.

> Tall nettles cover up, as they have done
> These many springs, the rusty harrow, the plough
> Long worn out, and the roller made of stone:
> Only the elm butt tops the nettles now.
>
> This corner of the farmyard I like most:
> As well as any bloom upon a flower
> I like the dust on the nettles, never lost
> Except to prove the sweetness of a shower.

The grammatical complication of the first line and a half is like that of "These pools that, though in forests, still reflect / The total sky"—yet here it brings to the utterance an air of leisure that Frost excludes from the start. This feeling in Thomas, of having always time enough to voice the human sense of a thing, is a poetic trait one has to go a long way back to match, possibly as far back as Cowper. It is what allows him to introduce himself into the second stanza so quietly that we do not notice the change. Whereas the "I" of Frost's poem is all the more powerfully present for being withheld: "The trees that have it in their pent-up buds / To darken nature and be summer woods / Let them think twice." The reflections Thomas cares for are not displaced to the landscape but claimed by the speaker in an unexceptional way: his one imperfect rhyme, *mostlost*, and his eye for "the nettles" in the seventh line, though they cost him an extra syllable, are proof against any charge of obliqueness or cunning. Of the two poems Thomas's is the more modest, and yet it asks no less tact of the reader than Frost's. "Only the elm butt tops the nettles now" is as measured in its bluntness as "These flowery waters and these watery flowers" is measured in its grace.

Thomas's description of Frost as "one of the least aggressive poets" is a curious and revealing testimony to set alongside the anecdotes about Frost at other periods and in other companies. But if one reads these poets together for any length of time one may feel that Thomas after all was describing himself. What is sometimes vulnerable in his poems—to the point of stopping them short of a promised expression—is the poet's conviction of an infinite debt to a nature that was here before him. In *A Literary Pilgrim in England* (1917) the debt was recorded in other writers' names, the study's premise being that imagined landscapes are finer when their prototypes can be traced in nature. It is a scholarly book and a beautiful one, but it goes to extremes: Shelley's childhood haunts are combed for possible clues to "Alastor"; and Thomas suspects that the "deep romantic chasm" of "Kubla Khan" connects it, though tenuously, with the neighborhood of Somerset. He was able to contemplate a nature altogether prior to man and greater by itself, as others have only pretended to contemplate it. So in reading him, and especially his early prose, one now and then enters a realm of primary natural sensibility, without selfish thoughts or fears, which regards nature unaccompanied, not as a nightmare of the earth closing like a dent in dough, but as what "I like most." The result from a human point of view is oddly unreviving. A wise passiveness rewards him with intervals of simple repose; yet these intervals have their own nightmares of listlessness. And Thomas is committed to record in words whole passages of time in which neither mood has quite set, when he stays "listening, lying in wait / For what I should, you never can, remember"—and still more often, the sense of revelations that have passed as if in his absence, when he was offered "truths I had not dreamed, / And have forgotten since their beauty passed." These last are not Wordsworthian epiphanies of "A motion and a spirit that impels / All thinking things, all objects of all thought," but rather ecstasies of the knowledge of intellectual beauty, in a severer tradition: "Sudden, thy shadow fell on me." When he writes of such moments, Thomas as a rule communicates less than he wishes. No reader will doubt the fact of the experience who has not a dogmatic contempt for some part of experience itself. But with Thomas, the report that he has been changed by what happened remains only a report. He is writing in an elegiac mode without any representation of *that time* from which the singer has fallen away. The poems therefore that continue long in this mode, from Thomas's identification with a power beside which he himself is nothing, mark a limit of the uses of sincerity.

His great poems also describe a situation of listening or lying in wait, though in many instances they follow the action to a further stage, when the revelation has come, or when its results are connected with the fate of other men by the poet's conversion to social speech. I will be discussing "Liberty," "I never saw that land before," and "The Owl," with parts of some others, and it is worth stressing that these are composed in the same register as the slighter pieces; what sets them apart, along with "Rain," "Roads," "The Gallows," and "Lights Out," is the ease and distinctness with which they figure the poet himself. Thomas speaks in one poem of his interest in "the ghost / That in the echo lives and with the echo dies," and it has to be said that his poems harbor their echoes with as little worry as any written in this century. The poet's affinities are understood to be a large part of his personal identity: he discloses them with the pride of memory rather than of possession, and quotations are never used as a signal. Since Thomas wrote all his poems in the last three years of his life, the Keatsian echoes of "Liberty" in particular have a special weight with the reader.

> The last light has gone out of the world, except
> This moonlight lying on the grass like frost
> Beyond the brink of the tall elm's shadow.
> It is as if everything else had slept

Many an age, unforgotten and lost,
The men that were, the things done, long ago,
All I have thought; and but the moon and I
Live yet and here stand idle over the grave
Where all is buried. Both have liberty
To dream what we could do if we were free
To do some thing we had desired long,
The moon and I. There's none less free than who
Does nothing and has nothing else to do,
Being free only for what is not to his mind,
And nothing is to his mind. If every hour
Like this one passing that I have spent among
The wiser others when I have forgot
To wonder whether I was free or not,
Were piled before me, and not lost behind,
And I could take and carry them away
I should be rich; or if I had the power
To wipe out every one and not again
Regret, I should be rich to be so poor.
And yet I still am half in love with pain,
With what is imperfect, with both tears and mirth,
With things that have an end, with life and earth,
And this moon that leaves me dark within the door.

It is a poem of intense consciousness, with the check of irony in the halts and false drifts of its many double negatives. "Unforgotten" in the fifth line for example, and "what is not to his mind" in the fourteenth, resist comprehension even after several readings, and half-sentences are in places so loaded with doubt that any affirmation they end in seems intransitive. Yet for all that, it survives as a poem of hope—one of the very few that do not fake a victory—and its success is probably owing to the invention of the moon as a companion. Here one sees the consolation Thomas's naturalism could bring when its subject was not nature. The moon is a circle of light, barely personified, yet for him this little is enough. He speaks from an indecision that to other minds would appear as acedia, but with no prospect of advancing he is cheerful to a degree, for his dread vanishes at the thought of "The moon and I." By remaining in the door, he commits himself neither to suffering nor patience but to a state in which everything once experienced will be known without exemption. Thus the entire poem protracts a mood Keats reserved for the penultimate stanzas of the "Ode to a Nightingale." The *mirth-earth* rhyme belongs to Keats only less notably than "I still am half in love with pain": Thomas, however, had used the rhyme elsewhere with such a range of effects that it joins his melody almost as an impersonal refrain. As a whole the poem feels composed in a single breath. Its uninterrupted lyrical phrases, "Beyond the brink of the tall elm's shadow" and the last line most prominently, break free for only as long as the conditional cast of other phrases permits. Yet it is modern in effect for no technical reason, but because its doubts, connected alike with the poet's circumstances and his period, have refused admittance to a phrase like "pleasant pain." What may be most unusual about "Liberty," and this links it with Owen's "Strange Meeting," is the clarity with which the poet's sense of his vocation pledges him to a life of *thoughts*.

There are poems in which Thomas comes to the brink of self-pity, and one test of his mastery is our certainty that the risk has never been accidental. He writes in his letters of being afflicted with a self-consciousness as far beyond mere selfishness as selfishness is beyond sympathy. This was a subject for poetry. So an autumn poem that begins conventionally, "Gone, gone again / May, June, July," recalls other autumns and alludes to them in a phrase of extraordinary vehemence, as a time before "the war began / To turn young men to dung." Only with this do we realize Thomas's thoughts of autumn have been thoughts of himself; this, and the image of a house, "Outmoded, dignified / Dark and untenanted":

> I am something like that;
> Only I am not dead,
> Still breathing and interested
> In the house that is not dark:—
>
> I am something like that:
> Not one pane to reflect the sun,
> For the schoolboys to throw at—
> They have broken every one.

In a poem entitled "Blenheim Oranges," with as solemn a progression as this has, the view of himself makes a delicately controlled ending. "I am something like that" seems the farthest reach of eloquence that his circumstances will allow. As for the poem's originality with a landscape so traditional, the last line is the only one that would have been recognized as poetry a generation earlier.

Extravagance like this is a matter of surprise. The house, as a feature of the setting, is withheld until the middle of the poem; the poet is compared to it only at the very end; and the oranges we were shown at first, lying fallen in the autumn rains, are touched in retrospect by the poignance of these things. But Thomas is remarkable for surprise of another sort in poems more predictably organized. "Celandine" recounts a story that reminds one in most details of "Surprised by Joy." In that story the poem turns to share a pleasure, and realizes that the person he would have shared it with is gone forever. Yet as the poem begins Thomas has been tranquilly resigned to his loss, until "I saw the sun on the celandines lie / Redoubled, and she stood up like a flame, / A living thing," and the natural vision enchants him. By this confusion he is enticed to pick the flowers, and the reminiscence of death, which he feels in his own gesture, breaks the spell a second time.

> But this was a dream: the flowers were not true
> Until I stooped to pluck from the grass there
> One of five petals and I smelt the juice
> Which made me sigh, remembering she was no more,
> Gone like a never perfectly recalled air.

A visible object both represents the woman he loved and consoles the loss of her: the transition is hardly announced, and yet we share its feeling. Thomas seems to have believed more effortlessly than Wordsworth that death and life inhabit each other through the intercessions of memory and imagination, and the belief gives his last line a quality remote from anything one may have expected of an elegy.

The untitled poem that begins "I never saw that land before" describes a comparable episode of second sight, with objects more nearly consequential for the poet himself. A landscape of great beauty, one of many others as the poet walked in the country, comes back to him in memory with all its constituents, "The cattle, the grass, the bare ash trees, / The chickens from the farmsteads, all / Elm-hidden, and the tributaries / Descending at equal interval," made keener by "the breeze / That hinted all and nothing spoke"—and he recognizes too late that this place possessed him even before he saw it.

> I neither expected anything
> Nor yet remembered: but some goal
> I touched then; and if I could sing

> What would not even whisper my soul
> As I went on my journeying,
>
> I would use, as the trees and birds did,
> A language not to be betrayed;
> And what was hid should still be hid
> Excepting from those like me made
> Who answer when such whispers bid.

"A language not to be betrayed" is a language that both ought not to be betrayed and that cannot be. But this central phrase holds another secret. For "betrayed" has two, almost antithetical, senses, and may suggest *revealed* as much as *given away*. The poem in fact protects the very meanings it affects to disclose.

All this, which baffles a reader or at least halts his progress, affords Thomas himself perfect satisfaction. He has composed what turns out to be a scene of election or self-discovery, and in such scenes cause and effect—voice and inspiration, the poet and the situation with which his poetry is associated—cannot be extricated from each other: if they could, we would know just what to make of the words, and they would cease to be poetry. The poem does not say and we cannot tell whether Thomas only gives the response to "such whispers," or has provoked their "bidding" by his own act of memory. The last stanza of Crane's "Voyages" is so close to the last stanza of Thomas's poem that it seems a natural part of any commentary.

> The imaged Word, it is, that holds
> Hushed willows anchored in its glow;
> It is the unbetrayable reply
> Whose accent no farewell can know.

The syntax of the final line repeats the strangeness of Thomas's "whisper my soul," where the soul may be either giving or receiving. Here the ambiguity of cause and effect, or finder and found, makes two readings equally inevitable: an accent (poetic Word) that can know no farewell because it stays forever; and a farewell (elegiac landscape) that can know no accent because it is imaged only by the Word. There is also the same near-pun on "betray." Crane in his letters mentions Thomas as one of the few modern poets he has read with interest, and this passage feels like one result of his reading.

Such uncanny recognitions by the poet of the place-meant-for-him-alone are interesting to all who believe poetry is the most important fact about the world. But few can hold steadily to that belief, and everything Thomas says about language seems intended to convince us that the poet's situation is *less* special than we ordinarily suppose. Why then should we grant the significance he claims to the search for "a language not to be betrayed"? An answer in keeping with his criticism would be that to grant it, we need think of the poet as nothing more special than a representative of a community of speech, who sometimes recovers a knowledge others repress in order to live. They forget, and he sometimes remembers with a shock, how far we are modified by what we have made, and how far therefore we are at once servants and masters of language. This sort of knowledge is possible to someone for whom words are always both figurative and literal, as they were for Thomas in "The Word," and to someone aware of precisely what is to be defended and what may be betrayed, as Thomas was aware in his writings on Swinburne, Pater, Pound, and Frost. To read "I never saw that land before" with this in mind is of course to read parabolically. But Thomas warns us he is speaking in parable when he refers to those outside, to whom the poet's task must remain unknown: what was hid will still be hid from them.

The gravity with which Thomas accepts his vocation makes him the most satisfying English poet to carry the intelligence of Romanticism into the modern age. In a sentence of prose that recalls the "Defence of Poetry," he speaks of his writing as a pursuit "not of wisdom, but of one whom to pursue is never to capture," an other he may glimpse but not name. It was a generous credo, and he followed it where it led. Often he described what he pursued as a spirit of place, or as a lover. But increasingly in his last years, Thomas seems to have meant by "the other" the interests of other men. For this reason "The Owl" may make the fittest conclusion to a summary essay.

> Downhill I came, hungry, and yet not starved;
> Cold, yet had heat within me that was proof
> Against the North wind; tired, yet so that rest
> Had seemed the sweetest thing under a roof.
>
> Then at an inn I had food, fire, and rest,
> Knowing how hungry, cold, and tired was I.

All of the night was quite barred out except
An owl's cry, a most melancholy cry

Shaken out long and clear upon the hill,
No merry note, nor cause of merriment,
But one telling me plain what I escaped
And others could not, that night, as in I went.

And salted was my food, and my repose,
Salted and sobered, too, by the bird's voice
Speaking for all who lay under the stars,
Soldiers and poor, unable to rejoice.

A very unaccustomed weight falls on the plain phrase "And others could not," and on the plain word "unable." The gesture of sympathy that opens up after the owl's cry has been heard is larger than in "This is no case of petty right and wrong." Yet the unobtrusiveness of the confession ("and sobered, too") serves as assurance that the poet's words are a bearing of witness, and not a declaration of the aim to do so. It is impossible to read "The Owl" for its place in Thomas's career, without thinking of the poetry he might have written after the war in a style like this, "Shaken out long and clear upon the hill." The future of any career that was cut short is of course an idle problem and usually explored in idleness. But in Thomas's case the speculation can have a more specific character. He was the poet of the early moderns who gave some promise of including those unable to rejoice in the words of poetry, and making its words again available to them. He was not likely to succeed altogether, any more than Wordsworth did, but he would not have reversed direction and accused history itself of betrayal. What we made of it always depended for him on how soberly we came to know ourselves in our repose.

What Photography Calls Thinking
STANLEY CAVELL

W HAT I HAVE SO far published on the subject of photography (in *The World Viewed*, 1971, reprinted 1979; *Pursuits of Happiness*, 1981; and *Themes out of School*, 1984) approaches it mostly through motion, through the photographic basis of cinema, and I will mostly continue that approach here. I begin with certain ideas I have recurrently explored concerning the relation of photography and reality. It is around something like a relation to reality—as of the mind to the world—that certain fashionable mottoes concerning the power of photography form themselves. Some notable and, I find, oddly empty examples are mottoes to the effect that "Photographs always lie," or that "Photography has changed the way we see."

To say that photographs lie implies that they might tell the truth; but the beauty of their nature is exactly to say nothing, neither to lie nor not to. Then what purposes may be served, or disguised, in attempting to deny so obvious a fact, in attempting instead to mean that emptiness? If the purpose is to counter those, real or imagined, who bluntly claim that photographs never lie, then the counter only replaces the Village Idiot by the Village Explainer. There must be some more attractive purpose. I believe the motto serves to cover an impressive range of anxieties centered on, or symptomatized by, our sense of how little we know about what the photographic reveals: that we do not know what our relation to reality is, our complicity in it; that we do not know how or what to feel about those events; that we do not understand the specific transformative powers of the camera, what I have called its original violence; that we cannot anticipate what it will know of us or show of us. These matters will be touched on as we proceed.

People who say that photography has changed the way we see, typically, in my experience, find this a good thing, something for us moderns to get excited by, to speculate from. Susan Sontag's *On Photography* stands out within this line of thought in finding the changes introduced by photography to be a bad thing, something to deplore, whatever praises may be due it. But to say that photography has changed the way we see strikes me as something like the reverse of the truth. The remark does not explain the power of photography but assumes it. Photography could not have impressed itself so immediately and pervasively on the European (including the American) mind unless that mind had at once recognized in photography a manifestation of something that had already happened to itself. What happened to this mind, as the events are registered in philosophy, is its fall into skepticism, together with its efforts to recover itself, events recorded variously in Descartes and Hume and Kant and Emerson and Nietzsche and Heidegger and Wittgenstein.

The name skepticism speaks, as I use it, of some new, or new realization of, human distance from the world, or some withdrawal of the world, which philosophy interprets as a limitation in our capacity for knowing the world; it is what Romantics perceive as our deadness to the world, which they understand philosophy to help sustain, and hence to be in no position to help cure. Why skepticism broke upon the mind when and as it did, what succession of guises it assumes, what the roles may be of, for example, the New Science, of the displacement of kings, of the dying of God, are questions I suppose open to historical answer. I find the issues of skepticism fully at play in Shakespearean tragedy and romance. It is perhaps the principal theme of *The World Viewed* that the advent of photography expresses this distance as the modern fate to relate to the world by viewing it, taking views of it, as from behind the self. It is Heidegger who calls it distance; Thoreau rather thinks of it as the oblivion of what he calls our nextness to the world; Emerson preceded Thoreau and Heidegger in calling nextness to the world nearness to it; Kierkegaard and Wittgenstein say, in different contexts, that we are "away"; others speak of alienation.

Since for me philosophy is still—as the names Heidegger and Wittgenstein are meant to suggest—finding its way in this question of skepticism, and since for me the question of photography is bound up with the question of skepticism, I am not likely to regard any proposal as illuminating the one that does not illuminate the other.

Hence I take mottoes about photography's lying, and its changing the way we see, as so many fragments of some pre-Cartesian or pre-Kantian or pre-Heideggerian moment of philosophical surprise or titillation at human vulnerability, or, say, finitude. They may be valuable in pointing to the recesses of the question of photography, but in their empty seriousness, they seem to me efforts to evade the question of what a photograph is. I am likely to characterize this question as asking what a photograph is thinking about, as I have asked, concerning literary and cinematic texts, what the text knows of itself. I am not unaware that these ways of speaking have been found offensive or provocative beyond consideration. Such matters are nowadays sometimes referred to as the text's textuality, or its self-reference. I sometimes speak of the text's self-acknowledgment, and sometimes of its knowledge of others, of *me*. I will not try to provide here any basis for choosing among these descriptions.

It may help to say that by wording my intuition in the form "what the text knows of me" I do not first of all suppose this to denote anything personal. For example, the photograph tells me that I am subject, inherently but impersonally, to some version of hallucination. In writing in *The World Viewed* of the photographic basis of movies I said that film proposes an artistically unheard-of relation between the presence and the absence of its objects. In a photograph we see things that are not, in actuality, before us. You may feel that I am missing the plain fact that what we are seeing is a *photograph,* which *is* before us. But I am not denying that. I am on the contrary asking that we ask what that means, what a photograph is, and I feel you are missing its strangeness, failing to recognize, for example, that the relation between photograph and subject does not fit our concept of representation, one thing standing for another, disconnected thing, or one forming a likeness of another. When I see that child there in the photograph of the group of schoolchildren posing outside the country schoolhouse, the one standing just in front of their teacher Wittgenstein, I know that the child is not here, where I am; yet there he stands, his right arm slightly bent, his collar somewhat disarranged. So, of course, can you point to a figure, perhaps that very child, in a painting, but I think everyone will sense that the words are said in a different spirit about a visual representation than they are about what can be called a visual transcription, a difference registering the fact that in the taking of the photograph the object has played a causal role altogether different from its role in the making of the painting. A representation emphasizes the identity of its subject, hence it may be called a likeness; a photograph emphasizes the existence of its subject, recording it; hence it is that it may be called a transcription. One may also think of it as a transfiguration. Here is one sense of the glory of photography, perhaps due to its power, perhaps to its impotence. It is because I see what is not before me, because our senses are satisfied with reality while that reality does not exist, that in *The*

World Viewed I call film "a moving image of skepticism." This version of hallucination is not exactly mad, but it suggests, as skepticism does, my capacity for madness. (Roland Barthes acknowledges an intuition of derangement as a normal possibility of the experience of the photographic in the closing pages of *Camera Lucida*.)

I said I would proceed to raise the question of the photographic primarily by way of the moving picture, not by way of the still (so it has come to be called) photograph. The principal movie I will interrogate as to its thoughtfulness about itself is Frank Capra's *Mr. Deeds Goes to Town* (1936, with Gary Cooper and Jean Arthur). I choose this example for two general reasons. First, because it is just the sort of popular American film about which it seems most paradoxical to speak of artistic self-reflexiveness, and it may therefore serve to make us wonder whether we know what the concept of the popular means when applied to the art of film. Second, since Capra's own writings about his films are as gullible, sentimental, and, let me say, unintellectual, as he perhaps wishes his audiences to be, this apparently gullible, sentimental, and unintellectual film may serve to emphasize that I am speaking not of the man Capra but of the power and glory of a medium, of what it knows of itself. (That this man Capra turns out to be a master in letting this medium show itself may eventually force us to revise our idea of who or what "the man Capra" is.) I will work toward the Capra film by first illustrating briefly, with two pairs of related films, the kinds of revelation of the medium I expect to find in any significant film—a significant film being one precisely on the basis of which such revelations of the medium are most significantly made. Of course this process of mutual revelation, between a work and the work's medium, being hermeneutic, is circular, global.

The first pair of films are the earliest and the latest of the seven films that, in *Pursuits of Happiness*, define the genre I call "the comedy of re-marriage." In the latest, *Adam's Rib* (directed by George Cukor, 1949, with Katharine Hepburn and Spencer Tracy), an early sequence consists of the depicted screening of a home movie. The enclosing, sophisticated film relates itself to the enclosed, primitive home movie (primitive but complete, like a Wittgensteinian language game) in such a way as to demonstrate the near but not full coincidence of the two films: their framing edges, on reframing, move closer to one another without quite coinciding, creating an effect as complex and illuminating as similar moments in Vertov's *Man with a Movie Camera;* they share the same principal actors and characters and one minor actor and character; they end in the same setting and with the same conclusion (a house in Connecticut for which they have just finished paying off the mortgage). The differences between the enclosing and the enclosed movie—apart from that relation itself, which remains incompletely assessed, and apart from the fact that the enclosed is silent and the enclosing has sound, another incompletely assessed matter—seem to go little beyond a matter of style (which is not to suggest that style is itself a clear matter, but merely that it is not everything). The similarities and differences between the larger and the smaller movies generate a long philosophical story, but in the end I draw a short, multipart moral from that story: the event of film itself is the fundamental cinematic event, not what the filmmaker does to the event, not, for example, whether it was composed in continuity or in discontinuities, which once seemed the fundamental esthetic question of film; the esthetic significance of a given film is a function of the way in which and degree to which it reveals or acknowledges this fact of its origin in the medium of film; the full discovery of the significance of an artistic medium, in the revelations and acknowledgments of its significant works, would be accomplished only by the complete history of an art, I mean by an exhausted art, supposing there is such a thing.

The earliest of the comedies of remarriage, *It Happened One Night* (directed by Capra, 1934, with Clark Gable and Claudette Colbert), specifies "the event of film itself" as an event of censoring. This is how I read the film's most famous prop, the blanket hung across a rope strung between two beds in a motel room to divide the space between the man and the woman. The specification of this division of masculine from feminine space depends on two ideas: first, the idea of taking the blanket as an allegory of the working of a movie screen—it conceals the woman's presence from the man while continuously registering her presence causally by her voice and by the dents and ripples her motions impart to the vertical rectangle of fabric; second, the specification depends on accepting the pertinence, in connection with the ensuing limitation and transgression of knowledge, of invoking Kant's idea of the limitations and transgressions necessitated by human reason in establishing the presence and absence of the world. Again there is a long philosophical story generated by these claims, but the short double moral I draw from this story is that the effect of censoring (as elsewhere) is not to banish but to displace and magnify the sense of the erotic; and that the narrative of remarriage is an account, or rather recounting, of what in the English tradition of philosophy is called the problem of other minds, as studied for example in the final part of my *The Claim of Reason.*

This double moral emphasizes the following points of method in the way I approach the study of film. What you may call the esthetic importance of such a film as *It Happened One Night*—a certain cultural importance may be measured by its having received more Academy Awards than any previous film—is not secured by its position within the genre of the comedy of remarriage, nor by its containing an element that can be understood to allegorize the work of the movie screen, nor by its bearing up under a comparison with the project of the *Critique of Pure Reason.* The conditions of the esthetic power of film, as with the exercise of any human power, cannot be known in advance of a certain criticism, or say critique, of that power, and a conviction in the architectonic of the critique—a satisfaction in the placement of concepts within the structure of importance—is not had apart from its application in individual cases. Sciences call such application experimentation; humanities call it criticism. If we say that what organizes or animates the results of experimentation is mathematical discourse, then we might say that what organizes or animates the results of criticism is philosophical discourse, and perhaps go on to consider the following: a physicist can allow himself/herself to rely on the soundness of a piece of mathematics once for all, and independently of his/her own ability to derive the mathematics; such is the nature of mathematical conviction, or proof. Whereas a critical reader cannot leave it to others to derive the philosophy he/she invokes, because that philosophy is either derived by such a critic in each act of criticism, new each day, or else it is intellectually unanimated, dead, at the disposal of fashion. (Here as elsewhere, one of the best uses of philosophical acumen is to spot and turn aside useless, invasive philosophy.)

The second pair of films I mention in specifying a work's revelation of the photographic medium begins with perhaps the central member of the genre of remarriage comedy, *The Philadelphia Story* (directed by George Cukor, 1941, with Cary Grant, Katharine Hepburn, and James Stewart). The surface narrative of the film has to do with a reporter and photographer who, through blackmail by the unscrupulous publisher of a sensationalist weekly magazine (one that makes news of gossip and gossip of news—it is modeled on *Time* magazine), are insinuated into an upper-class household to do a feature story about a wedding behind this household's commonly impenetrable doors. The film ends with the wedding ceremony about to begin; as it happens, all three principals are standing before the minister. From nowhere the unscrupulous publisher appears at their side and interrupts the ceremony by himself taking the wedding photos. The film then comes to an end with the following events. At the click of the publisher's camera the trio instinctively snap their heads toward it and their startled looks freeze. It is as if *that* is what the still camera captured, a gesture suggesting that no photograph can be candid, that any camera necessarily imposes on its subject its own conditions of capture, and that identifies the publisher's camera and its motives with the camera of this film. Then that still photograph becomes a page which, when turned, reveals a second still photograph in which Cary Grant and Katharine Hepburn appear alone, embracing, beyond the reach of James Stewart. In *Pursuits of Happiness* I read the significance of the turn to stillness in this way: However we understand the provenance of these wedding photos—whether as magazine pages, or perhaps as moments of a wedding album, even perhaps as production stills—the fact of their photographic stillness, after the context of motion pictures, is shocking. It feels as if "we are seeing something after the fact, whereas didn't we just now take ourselves to be, as it were, present at the wedding? . . . What is the difference [between motion and stillness]?"

The fundamental question of the relation between photographic motion and stillness was not one I was prepared to think about very deeply. I let it go once I had located its function in this film, namely that it makes us question the illusion of our presence at these events, and asks us to question the nature of dramatic illusion. I related this, in turn, as I relate other moments in my book, to a problematic in Shakespearean romance, in this instance to Shakespeare's pervasive study of audience.

To take the thought a step further, I want now to pair *The Philadelphia Story* with Dušan Makavejev's 1971 film *Sweet Movie*. As good a way as any of summarizing this immensely complex work, which combines documentary and fictional materials and methods, is to say that it is a psychological-political-philosophical meditation on two themes; first, on a progressive mutual destruction of claims to truth and claims to fantasy which leaves us helpless to believe the one and to take guidance from the other—as if the confusion of news and gossip, depicted in *The Phila-delphia Story* as a matter of distaste to a cultivated sensibility, had now become a global matter of intellectual and emotional poison; second, it is a meditation on the title of the song that underscores the film's opening sequence, "Is there life after birth?" The film is punctuated by, or rather organized around, images and thoughts of birth, and of rebirth, as of exhumation from premature burials—it may be a suffocation in the beds of sugar or the vats of chocolate with which the American and the Russian halves of the globe cloak the failures of their revolutions; or it may be the digging up of the mass graves of the massacred Polish officers in the Katyń forest; or it may be ceremonies of the radical Muehl commune from Vienna, providing a new and bouncing infancy for the bloated grown-up body of one of its group. It is as if the film is asking: Are there ways of thinking, is there a language, in which to speak of such things usefully, nonpoisonously? Is there a form of life, that is, in which such a language may be used? (I have in mind, of course, in this gloss, Wittgenstein's formulation, "To imagine a language is to imagine a form of life"—implying that philosophy needs to take instruction here, that it tends to imagine language as dead, no longer spoken.) Makavejev ponders these questions by subjecting his film to them, getting it to ask of itself whether it creates life or death.

This self-questioning is epitomized and confronted in the final sequence of *Sweet Movie*, as lucid and beautiful an acknowledgment as I have seen of the power and glory of film. The final sequence opens, tinted a monochrome blue, with five corpses wrapped in plastic shrouds and laid neatly on a riverbank. They got there through astounding paths of circumstance which cannot now be retraced. The wrapped bodies begin to stir, and the human beings we knew to be inside—call them the actors—begin removing themselves from these cerements or cocoons, exhuming or metamorphosing themselves. The figure nearest us proves to be the boy who had been the main object of a dance of seduction by a woman who in Makavejev's depiction allegorizes phases of the imagination of the Russian revolution. The boy turns his face toward us, looking past us, as at the invisible camera, whereupon the frame freezes and his looking is thus preserved. Gradually the blue tint gives way, and color returns to the frame, upon which the film ends. Formally this ending is a meditation on film's properties of color or its absence, of motion or its absence, and of sound or its absence. The fruit of the meditation is produced through the interpretation of the plastic shrouds or cerements as visual figures for strips of film. Then, the boy's looking out from the screen, half exhumed from his cocoon of film, becomes Makavejev allowing his own youth to confront the grown-up he has become—touched by the horror of the world he now works within and to that extent consents to—and to pose the question as to whether his film creates life or death. The return of color declares that he takes himself as on the side of life, but the stillness and silence of the frame threaten that answer.

The pair of still and silent frames that end *The Philadelphia Story* are from a different world, and yet the hint of death is also present even there, in arcadia. *Pursuits of Happiness* does not insist on this but it does ask if there is not "some lingering suspicion that the picture of the trio was already a kind of wedding photo?—that somehow, as Edmund madly says in the final moments of *King Lear*, 'I was contracted to them both. Now all three marry in an instant.'" What Edmund means by the three marrying is that he is in an instant going to join them in death. The violence and range of Shakespeare's problematic of marriage, which continues throughout his tragedies and romances, the violence of its creation and its decreation, applies also to the comedy of remarriage, because marriage is there legitimized, authorized, not by state, church, sexuality, or children, but only through the pair's unsponsored willingness to choose one another again, so that the plot will contain the fact or threat of divorce. The ground of this willingness for repetition turns out to be the woman's feeling that she is still in need of creation (as in different ways Nora feels in Ibsen's *A Doll House* and Hermione feels in Shakespeare's *A Winter's Tale*) and that for some reason she has chosen this man to provide the necessary midwifery of this new birth (unlike Nora's case; like Hermione's, but without the full mystery of her choice). "The creation of the woman" alludes in my book to a simultaneity of projects: to the institution of marriage by God in Genesis, creating the woman from the man; to the progress of the feminist movement; to the transfiguration given to or imposed upon particular women of flesh and blood by the camera's power of photogenesis.

The violence of the camera's creation I understand to be declared in another Cukor film, *A Woman's Face* (1944, with Joan Crawford, Melvyn Douglas, and Conrad Veidt), where the power of the photographic may be taken as allegorized by the power of plastic surgery. A related idea is taken up in the film *Gorky Park*, where the medical reconstruction of a head without a face is an emblem for the reconstructibility of a murder, perhaps of history as such, and, at the same time, of the process by which the camera preserves the human figure. Horror films will necessarily hint at the camera's transfigurative power, in their disfigurations, recreations, or decreations, of the human being. In my book this shows the genre of horror film to be adjacent to the genre of remarriage comedy.

After one more introductory word I will propose an application of film's participation in creation and annihilation to the frivolously obvious, I mean the apparently frivolous, *Mr. Deeds Goes to Town*.

Photography's participation in death—as if in preserving its subject a photograph removes it from life, mounts it, like a trophy—is an idea that kept surfacing in *The World Viewed*, where I would have been prompted to it by what I had read of André Bazin, with his recurrent sense of the photographic as a kind of life mask of the world, the twin of a death mask. It occurs centrally as I note that the photograph speaks of its human subjects as distracted from the future awaiting them, hence as blindly facing death, a condition displaced with particular lucidity in shots of candid happiness, where the metaphysical transience of such instants marks their subjects with moral vulnerability; and I close that book with a vision of the world viewed—the world as photographed—as the world of my immortality, the world without me, reassuring in the promise that it will survive me, but unsettling in the suggestion that as I stand now the world is already for me a thing of the past, like a dead star. Romantic writers such as Coleridge and Wordsworth and Emerson and Thoreau mean to awaken us to our harboring of such a vision, and to free us from it. Yet our nostalgia deepens. Memory, which should preserve us, is devouring us. We must, as Thoreau put the matter, look another way. (I should like to cite, in this connection, Garrett Stewart's "Thresholds of the Visible: The Death Scene of Film" in *Mosaic* XVI/1-2, which studies film's presentation of death in connection with recent studies of the presentation of death in written narrative. The idea of the death of the world occurs as a frisson within the vulgar ironies of such settings as those of the *Planet of the Apes* movie series and the television serial *Buck Rogers in the 25th Century*.)

Leaving the issues of stillness and motion so undeveloped, the moments I have described from *The Philadelphia Story* and from *Sweet*

Movie suggest that stillness emphasizes the death in mortal existence while motion emphasizes the life of it. So long as these emphases do not deny that both speak of both, in their particular ways, no theoretical harm is done, if not much good. In turning to *Mr. Deeds* I focus on a feature of human mortality that only the *motion* of photography can capture. It may seem about the most trivial feature of human beings there could be, the fact that they are more or less *nervous*, that their behavior is *fidgety*.

This fact of human life becomes the climactic evidence cited by Mr. Deeds (Gary Cooper) while defending himself in a law court against the charge of insanity. His successful interpretation of this evidence causes general social happiness and wins him the ecstatic embraces of his estranged beloved, whereupon the film concludes. That propositions of such ludicrousness can be seen to illustrate, even to explore, philosophical sublimities is surely part of my fascination with so-called popular movies. About the film's plot, all I will say before looking at a few moments of that trial is that Deeds was arrested for trying to give away his sudden inheritance of 20 million dollars, on the complaint of lawyers—who have their designs on the money—that his behavior shows him mentally incompetent. He has also just found out that the woman he has fallen in love with is a reporter who, using his feelings for her to extract a sensational series of newspaper features, has held his escapades up to ridicule, naming him "The Cinderella Man." In a detention hospital room he has withdrawn into silence.

The trial occupies the last twenty minutes or so of the film, and starts out with Gary Cooper maintaining his silence, refusing to plead further with a world that has erotically and politically ridiculed and jailed him for his utopian fantasies. What causes him to speak again, which means, narratively, what prompts him to defend himself, is an obvious critical question. A less obvious question concerns the participation of Capra's film in the genre of melodrama, in which muteness is a signal feature, and in which the breaking of silence is a climactic declaration of personal identity and the confrontation of villainy. It is an image of ecstasy or exaltation expressed in this instance as the power and the willingness to communicate one's presence, to have one's existence matter, one's own terms taken seriously. (Emphasis on muteness and self-revelation is among the many discoveries in Peter Brooks's valuable study *The Melodramatic Imagination*, 1976.) Less obvious still is what the camera's evidence of fidgetiness has to do with these matters.

Mr. Deeds appeals to fidgetiness as a universal human attribute, if not exactly a normal one, in defense of his playing the tuba at odd hours, a practice taken by the prosecution and its witnesses as a major piece of evidence of madness. Deeds's defense is that his tuba playing is his version of something every human being does under certain universally recurrent conditions. The other versions he cites of such behavior are tics (a man's compulsive nose-twitching, a woman's knuckle-cracking) and doodling (drawing aimless designs, filling in O's). I say he "cites" these instances, but in fact his speech becomes a kind of voice-over narrative as the camera illustrates each of them in close-up, as if it is setting up exhibits of evidence for Mr. Deeds's case. The evidence is, accordingly, not for the depicted judges and spectators, for whom the close-ups are invisible, but for *us*. He does cite two such practices without photographic illustration—ear-pulling and nail-biting—as if to declare that the act of photographing is deliberate. This underscores Deeds's alliance with the camera. It is his acknowledgment that to provide such illustration or evidence is a power and possible glory natural to the moving picture camera, that the most insignificant repetitions, turnings, pauses, and yieldings of human beings are as interesting to it as is the beauty or the science of movement.

Think of this interest or power as the camera's knowledge of the metaphysical restlessness of the live body at rest, something internal to what Walter Benjamin calls cinema's optics of the unconscious. Under examination by the camera, a human body becomes for its inhabitant a field of betrayal more than a ground of communication, and the camera's further power is manifested as it documents the individual's self-conscious efforts to control the body each time it is conscious of the camera's attention to it. I might call these recordings *somatograms* (cf. cardiograms, electroencephalograms), to register the essential linking of the pattern of a body's motions with the movements of the machine that records them. We seem to have no standing word for what somatograms record. "Mannerisms" is partial in its noting of characteristically recurrent behavior; "manners" is partial in its attention to social modification. Freud uses the word *Fehlleistung* (usually translated as *parapraxis*) to gather together something like the stage of behavior I have in mind, but his examples are more selective than mine must be. The plain word "behavior" has the right generality, but in a time subjected to the psychological and philosophical sensibility of behaviorism—in which behavior is reduced to something

outer, from which something inner (call it mind) has been scooped out—
the expressiveness of the range of the restless is more or less incompre-
hensible. Emerson's essay entitled "Behavior," from *The Conduct of Life*,
is an effort to rehabilitate this concept of behavior, along with that of manners, to return the mind to the living body. Here is a sample:

> Nature tells every secret once. Yes, but in man she tells it all the
> time, by form, attitude, gesture, mien, face and parts of the face, and
> by the whole action of the machine. The visible carriage or action of
> the individual, as resulting from his organization and his will com-
> bined, we call manners. What are they but thought entering the
> hands and feet, controlling the movements of the body, the speech
> and behavior? . . . The power of manners is incessant,—an element
> as unconcealable as fire.

Emerson's effort of conceptual rehabilitation constitutes this marvelous
essay as a major contribution to the esthetics of cinema (as well as to the
esthetics of acting, a coincidence hardly coincidental).

Mr. Deeds has a particular name for the condition that causes universal fidgetiness. His name for it is *thinking*. "Everyone does something
silly when they think," he declares. He uses the word "think" or "thinking" repeatedly, and each time emphasizes that each individual does
something different when he or she is in the condition of thinking. Why
he includes playing the tuba as part of his somatogram—not, say, as an
item in his profile as an aspiring American musician and artist—is, of
course, a further question. I want to stay with the question at hand: how
has Deeds been brought to break his silence in order to speak of the connection between thinking and silliness? Why is it now that he is willing to
claim his identity and his happiness against the villainous incomprehen-
sion of the world?

My answer depends on taking his appeal to the concept of thinking
with greater philosophical seriousness than others may be prepared, right
off, to grant it. I have taken Deeds's perception of fidgetiness as disclosing
an essential feature of the human; not a feature of the animal simply, but
of a creature in whom the body and the soul do not everywhere fit together. (I wish to leave open the question whether this may be true only
of the human creatures in our epoch, and especially true of those creatures in the period of capitalism that Deeds's social program of redistribu-
tion defines, one in which a large number of evidently hardworking,
unenvious, independent people are needlessly being deprived of what

they need in order to make a living. "Need" is another recurrent term of Deeds's discourse. His word for those who do not wish to work is "moochers"; he is shown to be indiscriminate in his application of this term.) And I have taken the idea that fidgetiness always accompanies thinking to mean that it proves thinking, or the inclination to think, which, as Heidegger asserts, is part of the possibility of thinking, even its everyday possibility. Hence I see in Deeds's words, and the way he uses them, a recapturing in the everyday of Descartes's perception of what thinking itself proves, namely the existence of the human. So that when Deeds begins to speak, defending his sanity, he is performing, as the climax to be expected in a melodramatic structure, a version of Descartes's cogito, taking on the proof of his own existence, as if against its denial by the world.

Some will be unwilling to grant this degree of seriousness to Mr. Deeds's courtroom lecture on silliness and thinking, and they may wish to protect their sense of the serious by suggesting that Deeds's words are at best a parody of philosophy, not the thing of philosophy itself. But I have shown cause elsewhere to suppose that at some stage serious philosophy may come to manifest itself as—and to exist most immediately as—a parody of philosophy. I have based this idea on Emerson's and Edgar Allen Poe's apparently parodistic adoptions, or adaptations, of the cogito argument. Because Emerson's adaptation will play a direct role in my conclusion about the movie *Mr. Deeds Goes to Town*, I pause here simply to state his observation that we are no longer able to announce the cogito for ourselves, no longer able, as he puts it, to say "I think" and "I am" on our own, for ourselves. I take this to imply that we are without proof of our existence, that we are accordingly in a state or preexistence, as if metaphysically missing persons. Emerson's famous word for lacking words of our own is "conformity." It obviously has precursors in Romantic perceptions of the human as dead, or deadened, and it is a specific conceptual precursor of Nietzsche's "last man," hence of Heidegger's *Das Mann*.

Before we dismiss Deeds as lacking the authority or the circumstances in which to assume the cogito (matters essential to Descartes's broaching of the issue), we had better be sure that we know who this man is and what his circumstances are, know them as well as we must know, for example, who and where one of Poe's narrators is in order to know the spirit in which to take his tales. We have to make up our minds whether we grant Deeds the authority to mean the line from Thoreau that he identifies when he says early in the film: "They built palaces but they forgot to build the people to live in them"; or whether, alternatively, we withhold this grant and thereby rebuke his pretension in voicing it. He says it in his first conversation with the woman, alone at night on a park bench, as part of establishing an initial intimacy with her; a few moments later he seizes an occasion to run from her and jump on a screaming fire engine. Is this what philosophical authority looks like? I note that the line preceding the one about building palaces is also from Thoreau, but not identified as such in Capra's script: "People here seem to have the St. Vitus Dance." (Capra's limitation as a reader of Thoreau and Emerson may show in the circumstances of this line. Deeds says it about New York, with the implication that in small towns such as the one he comes from behavior is radically different. Even I would find it hard to believe that Capra invites this interpretation to show the limitation only of his character Deeds, implying that he has himself a yet more transcendental perspective.) St. Vitus's Dance is the more familiar name for the disorder called chorea, found mostly in children and associated with temporary brain dysfunction. In Deeds's phantasm (and for that matter in Thoreau's) there is no radical distinction to be made between St. Vitus's Dance and human behavior as such, as it has become, as if human behavior is now in general the result of brain damage. When the two comically dotty old maid sisters testify in the courtroom that not only Deeds but everyone except themselves is "pixilated" (controlled by pixies), they discredit their earlier testimony that Deeds is thus affected. Everyone thereupon agrees that this shows the sisters are mentally incompetent. But the only difference between their expressed view of the world and Deeds's view is that he does not clearly exempt himself, any more than Thoreau exempts himself, from the madness of the world. Perhaps this is what philosophical authority sounds like.

To dismiss Deeds as too silly for philosophical thought is to deny him a voice in defining what is silly, one of his characteristic words. And if we deny him this voice, how are we different from the corrupt prosecution, who would exercise an analogous denial by having him declared insane? And how do we understand the muteness that prepares the condition, you may say the seriousness, of his cogito? The woman who loves him screams that he is being crucified. (Frank Capra, like other American artists, finds the figure of Christ near at hand for identifying the posture of his heroes. Some will find this an irredeemably coarse habit, perhaps in the way Nietzsche found Luther's intellectual habits to be coarse.) Without going that far, the question remains how far we credit the grief, the sense of rejection, that this hero's extended muteness bespeaks. Our answer to that question determines how seriously we take this man's intellectual seriousness. If our philosophical sensibility fails us here it may be failing us at any and all times, so that it is we whose perceptions and powers of sympathy will prove to be coarsened and muted.

Evidently, my questions concerning the seriousness with which we grant the intellectual seriousness of Mr. Deeds is some kind of allegory of a more extensive question about whether we will grant to Frank Capra the capacity to undertake a significant artistic response to Emerson and Thoreau. My anxiety about communicating such a thought with due seriousness has waxed and waned since the time, in preparing the chapter on Capra's *It Happened One Night* for *Pursuits of Happiness,* I broached the idea of Capra's filmmaking as incorporating a mode of vision inherited from American transcendentalism, even to the point of sharing American transcendentalism's inheritance, in turn, of German culture (specifically, in Capra's work, of German expressionist cinema). The anxiety tracks my knowledge that lovers of American movies have taken such remarks of mine to be needless and pretentious, together with my sense that professional students of film are often not prepared to credit such company for American movies, colored by my observation of American professional philosophers, for whom, with perhaps a growing number of exceptions, such speculation is fit, at best, for an intellectually frivolous hour. It has been urged upon me that such dismissals should not matter to me so much. But I think one can see in the work of Emerson and Thoreau and of Capra that, in their various American ways, analogous dismissals have mattered as much to them.

To provide a fair test of this question of Deeds's intellectual seriousness, we would need to *place* Deeds in that courtroom, arrive at him, derive him, exactly as he comes to be derived from paths of narrative and cinematic development most of whose contours cannot possibly be accounted for here. I will accordingly end these remarks by returning specifically to the path of the power and glory of photography, asking after the role the camera plays in Deeds's willingness to speak and to claim his happiness with the woman.

I pick up from two ideas already discussed. First, that Deeds will show his awareness that the motion picture camera bears an affinity with metaphysical restlessness, that it has its own imperative to keep moving, and second, that this awareness is, in effect, an acceptance of Descartes's perception that the human stands in need of proof in each case, by each case, together with Emerson's perception that we are mostly incapable any longer of taking on our existence by ourselves. And I take it that Deeds's insight is that a reverse field of proof is available by way of the motion picture camera, so that while thinking is no longer secured by the mind's declaration of its presence to itself, it is now to be secured by the presence of the live human body to the camera, in particular by the presence of the body's apparently least intelligent property, its fidgetiness, its metaphysical restlessness. In Descartes the proof of thinking was that it cannot doubt itself; after Emerson the proof of thinking is that it cannot be concealed.

Am I saying that the camera is necessary to this knowledge? Even if I were, I have also said that the camera reveals something that we recognize as having already happened to us, hence something the knowledge of which we resist. Why, otherwise, would the camera's revelation have been traumatic? Hence the camera reveals what has happened to us together with our resistance to the knowledge of what has happened, namely a new strain in our doubt of human existence. If the price of Descartes's proof of his existence was a perpetual recession of the body (a kind of philosophical counter-Renaissance), the price of an Emersonian proof of my existence is a perpetual visibility of the self, a theatricality in my presence to others, hence to myself. The camera is an emblem of perpetual visibility. Descartes's self-consciousness thus takes the form of embarrassment.

Deeds is accordingly the name of one who sees the stakes in this altered condition and who submits himself to the camera's judgment, permits its interrogation—its victimization—of him. It is an unlooked-for species of bravery. Psychologically, submission to a somatogram—to the synchronization between body and camera—demands passiveness, you may say demands the visibility of the feminine side of one's character. Capra's mastery of the medium of film, or his obedience to it, guides him to make certain that we are aware of the beauty of Gary Cooper's face, and in one instance he photographs him posed as in a glamour shot of a female star, lying on his back across a bed (playing the tuba it happens, as if that mattered), capturing his full length from a vantage just above his head. Cinematically his submission declares what I have called the natural ascendency on film of the actor over the character, so that the rightness of its being specifically Gary Cooper who plays Deeds comes here to the fore, as if Capra is interpreting the embarrassment (say the self-consciousness) of the Emersonian proof—that thinking cannot be concealed—in terms of Cooper's world-historical capacity for shyness; and vice versa, giving a metaphysical interpretation of this American mode of shyness.

Narratively the condition of Deeds's happy ending is that his victimization be interpreted, or redeemed, as his willingness to reverse roles with the woman. We know of his boyish wish for romance, his wish "to rescue a damsel in distress." Jean Arthur asserts once for all her superiority over him in the realm of action, call it the male realm, by pretending to him to be such a damsel. She has ridiculed exactly that wish of his by naming him The Cinderella Man—he is more in need of being rescued than in a position to provide rescue. But this, in turn, is the expression of her own condition of romance: her wish to discover a man for whom she could make it all right that he has been badly frightened by desire and lost a slipper. At the end he shows her this loss, this desire. He has twice run from her, each time at a moment when his desire was importunate. Early, as mentioned, when he runs to the fire engine from the park; then later, elaborately, when, as she completes reading aloud to him the love poem he has composed for her, he races down the night streets, stumbling noisily over visible and invisible garbage cans, in a solo of awkwardness that cinematically registers the falling of an American male in love. In the courtroom his starting to speak is the sign that he has stopped running. He claims the woman's love by acknowledging that the shoe fits, that he was, so to speak, at the ball, that he has desires and can ask her to rescue him from his incompleteness. Narratively the man's willingness to speak, to express desire, comes in response to the woman's courtroom declaration, under cross-examination, that she loves him (a familiar Hollywood topos). I think we are entitled here, further, to understand the man's reading of this woman's declaration of love as a signal of her own distress. Thus, after all, she grants him his wish to rescue, to be active, to take deeds upon himself, earning his name; as he grants her wish to her. So this film participates, with comedies of remarriage, in what I have called the comedy of equality and reciprocity.

The words with which the man had broken his silence were: "I'd like to put in my two cents"—which is still usable American slang for expressing an opinion. Our next step should be to consider why this man, whose adventure recounts the inheriting and attempted bequeathing of one of the richest fortunes in the country, initiates his willingness to quit his silence and to claim the inheritance of his existence, his right to desire, by speaking of speaking as an issue of "two cents." Of course one can bring any number of ideological suspicions to bear here. I think the film deserves also the following line of consideration. The right to speak not only takes precedence over social power, it takes precedence over intellectual accomplishment; no amount of contribution is more valuable to community than the willingness to contribute. Further, unlike 20 million dollars, the contribution of two cents is one that can be responded to equally by others; it leaves your voice your own and allows your opinion to matter to others only because it matters to you. It is not a voice that will be heard by villains. This means that to discover our community a few will have to be punched out, left speechless—one interpretation of Deeds's repeated violence, punching men on the jaw. It is a fantasy of a reasonably well-ordered participatory democracy. It has its dangers; democracy has. If the motion picture camera uniquely helps to keep this utopian idea alive, that is power and glory enough to justify its existence, a contribution somewhere between two cents and the largest fortune in the world.

P. G. Wodehouse

THOMAS R. EDWARDS

W HEN I BEGAN to read Wodehouse, as a Middle American teen-
ager, what attracted me first, as I remember, was not so much his characters and their misadventures as how he *named* them and their world. It
seemed splendid that Frederick Altamount Cornwallis Twistleton, 5th
Earl of Ickenham, of Ickenham Hall, Hants., should be generally known
as "Uncle Fred" and that he should call his unpermissive countess "the
Big White Chief," and his mighty bath sponge "Joyeuse," that the Hon.
Freddie Threepwood should be a brainless young wastrel addicted to
cheap detective stories and movies like *Fangs of the Past* (starring Bertha
Blevitch and Maurice Huddlestone), that the best-known volume by the
surly Canadian poet Ralston McTodd ("the young singer of Saskatoon")
should be *Songs of Squalor*, and so on. Above all, at first, there was
Psmith ("the p is silent, as in 'pshrimp'"), the languid, self-named per-
siflageur and elegant superman whose neo-Wildeian charm, however,
soon enough palled. Psmith was born "Smith," to his dismay; he went to
Eton and Cambridge and belongs to choice London clubs like the Drones
and the Senior Conservative, but his family has lost its money; he went
(briefly) into his uncle's fish business and adopted certain socialist mannerisms, and his self-reinvention into anarchic *flanerie* may have faintly
political implication. But he mainly seems a public-school boy's fantasy of
insouciance as power, the sort of masterful social animal Bertie Wooster
aspires to be but can't, and Wodehouse was wise to drop him in the early
1920s, when the Blandings Castle and Jeeves-Wooster sagas were achieving stronger and purer modes of nonsense. But his name still tells something about what Wodehouse's best nonsense expresses, the exhilarating
power of language to float free of its reputed duties to mere brute fact.

Wodehouse published more than one hundred books of fiction, some
of them marvels, others good enough for idle moments, still others en-
durable only by the compulsive devotee. (I have read maybe half of them
and find that sufficient.) Some of the worst are light romances deriving
from his other career, as a writer of musical-comedy books and lyrics.

Some of his short-story series are much better: the desperate con games of the penniless Stanley Featherstonehaugh Ukridge, whom Robert Graves took to be a gentle caricature of his own brother Percival but to whom other originals have been ascribed; the farcical mishaps of Bertie Wooster's cronies at the Drones Club; the tall tales of those modern Ancient Mariners, Mr. Mulliner and the Oldest Member. But the Wodehouse who matters is the author of two groups of novels and short stories: the Blandings Castle series, centering upon the Shropshire estate of Clarence, 9th Earl of Emsworth, and the famous adventures of Bertie Wooster and his ingenious valet, Jeeves. The earliest Blandings tales are uneven, and both series began to fall off somewhat in the last two decades of Wodehouse's life, when he allowed himself to repeat old jokes too openly and (especially in the Blandings stories) to introduce too many contemporary allusions, disturbing the effect of timeless remoteness that is one of his great charms. But even the weaker books have their moments of comic wonder.

The Blandings books are house party stories, akin to a durable subgenre of Anglo-American detective fiction that Wodehouse loved to spoof. In fact they *are* crime stories of a small and bloodless sort, involving domestic blackmail, theft, imposture, and extortion meant to coerce a parent or guardian into consenting to a socially awkward engagement or marriage. The criminals are usually young and powerless, children or nieces or nephews of Lord Emsworth in love with people as idle and harebrained as themselves. But Wodehouse always sympathizes with their struggles, however illegal, against their stronger but equally stupid elders. Though he's the least revolutionary novelist imaginable, he does seem fascinated by the idea that property is theft.

There are some interesting patterns in the society of Blandings Castle. Lord Emsworth's dead wife is never named or described, but he has at least seven sisters, all highly conscious of rank and eager for rule. They all have married at least once, but none seems to have more than one child, and several have lost their husbands, who one almost suspects were eaten upon completing their procreative task. No sister has married unsuitably—their husbands include a Major General, two Colonels, a Knight Commander of the Bath, and a South African diamond magnate. But the younger generation mostly marry beneath their station, to a land agent, an artist who turns publican, a chorus girl, and various rich Americans of the commercial classes. Though he never stresses it, I can imagine that this infusion of social outsiders gave some pleasure to Wodehouse, a gentleman himself, surely, but descended from clerics and lesser civil servants, educated at what he called a middle-class public school ("Bertie Wooster's parents would never have sent him to Dulwich," he once remarked, "but Ukridge could very well have been there"), unable to enter Oxford because his father couldn't afford to supplement the small scholarship he won, a writer almost by default after a disastrous false start as a bank clerk, always more at home with theater people and Americans than with the British grandees he wrote about. He once ruefully remarked that although he had met Winston Churchill a number of times, Churchill could never seem to remember who he was.

But if the contentions for power at Blandings dimly mirror a kind of generational or even class struggle, they are more clearly modes of sexual warfare. The vague, sweetly idiotic Lord Emsworth (called "Fathead" in his Eton days) wants only to be left alone to oversee the nurturing of the one living creature he truly loves, Empress of Blandings, thrice the winner of the Fat Pig Competition at the Shropshire Agricultural Show. (In the earlier stories his passion is gardening, which is much less funny, especially if one surmises that the Empress is a displaced image of his lost wife.) His overbearing sisters, appalled by his indifference to rank and duty, continually exhort him to assert his authority over his muddled younger relations. His occasional, untrustworthy ally is his younger brother, the Hon. Galahad ("Gally") Threepwood, a roguish survivor of high times in the Gay Nineties, who is even less favored by their sisters. Women, especially young or lower-class women, are often sympathetic figures in Wodehouse novels, but high-born dowagers with a taste for dominion always spell trouble.

Belowstairs, Blandings is abundantly staffed—some dozen or more of the servants are named and characterized. Outside, in the pleasant Vale of Blandings, reside various "local nibs," most notably the sinister Sir Gregory Parsloe, Bart., of Matchingham Hall, Much Matchingham, Emsworth's unscrupulous rival pig-breeder. Close by lies the bustling town of Market Blandings, with its eleven public houses (most notably The Emsworth Arms, G. Ovens, Prop., although some prefer the beer at The Beetle and Wedge); its vicar, Mr. Fosberry; its chemist, Bulstrode's; its hairdresser, Banks; its house agents, Cain and Cooper; its constable, Evans; and its taxi-man, Robinson. Also in the vicinity is Blandings Parva, a village of unnamed and presumably unremarkable souls.

This specificity is oddly comforting. The world of Blandings is densely *there*, in its names if nowhere else, and those who visit it bring their own nominal reality along. Not all of the romantic leads are very interesting, but the outsiders who come there on business—usually private detectives or crooks (or both)—are much more compelling, like Mrs. Maudie Stubbs (alias Maudie Montrose or Mrs. Bunbury), who breathes plebeian vigor into this rather airless place. The niece of Lord Emsworth's monumental butler Beach, Maudie was in her salad days a London barmaid, a dear friend of Gally Threepwood, and briefly the fiancée of the now joyless Sir Gregory Parsloe-Parsloe. Widowed and looking much like Mae West, she now owns Digby's Day and Night Detectives, and her professional visit to Blandings stirs the long-torpid desires of Emsworth himself. Another detective, Claude "Mustard" Pott, an unpleasant card shark and confidence man, teaches Emsworth the joys of Persian Monarchs, a childish card-cutting swindle which the earl always loses at but fancies he can master with just a bit more practice.

Such intimations of a world outside, coarser but full of life and risk, can be conveyed by the briefest narrative vignettes, like the reminiscences of Gally Threepwood about the epic bon vivants of his youth, Major Plug Basham, who went on the wagon by switching from spirits to absinthe, Jack Bellamy-Johnstone, who out of devotion to a Miss Esmeralda Parkinson-Willoughby had her full name painfully tattooed on his chest, only to fall promptly in love with one Mary Todd, and Stiffy Vokes, who for his own good reasons once assumed the name Orlando Maltravers. My own favorite nexus of such stories is yet another detective, Percy Frobisher Pilbeam, once the "nasty little editor" of the gossip sheet *Society Spice* and later the proprietor of the Argus Private Inquiry Agency. The Pilbeam family motto is "Trust nobody," and one sees why as stories about Percy's contentious relatives accumulate. There was Albert Edward Pilbeam, who on declining to pay a fine served seven days in Brixton Prison for failing to abate a smoking chimney; Claude Pilbeam, who once refused to give up his hat and umbrella at the Hornsbeck Natural History Museum in Sydenham Hill; and, most stirringly, Ernest William Pilbeam, of Mon Abri, Kitchener Road, East Dulwich, who sued his neighbor (George Dobson, of The Elms) for throwing snails over the fence into Ernest William's back garden. The tragedies and triumphs of the suburban spirit could hardly be evoked more succinctly, and such stories smile fondly at what connects even a paradise like Blandings with the rest of the world—universal human silliness.

Blandings richly exists in its names and stories, rather as Spenser's

Faerieland does. It offers some of the pleasures, and few of the annoy-ances, of people and places one knows thoroughly in life. Within it, how-ever, little can happen that has not happened before. Various people wish or wish not to marry; someone is plotting to abduct Empress of Blandings or at least put her off her feed before the next Fat Pig competition; Lord Emsworth's repose is shattered by his imperious sisters or by their agent, the earl's infuriatingly capable private secretary Rupert Baxter ("the brains of Blandings"), whose employment the younger generation and Emsworth himself keep plotting to terminate. (Baxter, whose former em-ployer was a Yorkshire baronet given to shooting mice in his drawing room with an elephant gun, understandably likes his present position and vig-orously resists dismissal—"I was happy at the Castle," he says with unex-pected pathos after one of his frequent sackings.) In the end the wrong marriages are prevented and the right ones made, the Empress is pre-served, Baxter is ousted or otherwise humbled, and Lord Emsworth can again lose himself in his sacred text, Whiffle on *The Care of the Pig*, de-lighting in such lore as that a show pig needs 57,800 calories a day to keep in top form.

The effect resembles, just a little, a Jane Austen novel or an Oscar Wilde play rewritten by some more genial and whimsical hand. And a major strain in Victorian fiction, the representing of life through the hu-man negotiations within families or rural neighborhoods, continues in the Blandings Castle stories. The narration is third-person ironic; the chief continuities are of locale and social mood; no single figure, not even Lord Emsworth, dominates the attention; new characters are introduced and old ones dropped whenever it suits convenience. (It seems very Wode-housian that when a new nephew or niece is required for someone to marry, he or she is not simply ascribed to one of the existing Threepwood sisters; a new sister is invented, along with a new husband for her, living or dead, a new address for her to live at, a whole new range of names and details that say just about what the old ones said but are different and make the Blandings world fuller.) Not even the narrative voice is wholly consistent from book to book, though it does stabilize in those written in the 1930s and 40s, after Wodehouse learned what he wanted from con-tinuing characters like Emsworth, Freddy and Gally Threepwood, and Beach the butler.

The Blandings stories are repetitive, almost ritualistic rehearsings of the kind of nostalgic pleasure that old family photographs can give. Lord

Emsworth, we learn, was born in 1859, and Wodehouse, born in 1881, would thus be of an age with Emsworth's sons and their disruptive friends. Though historically later social and cultural data creep in as the author and his readers progress through real time, the world imagined and timelessly held in view is essentially that of upper-class England before the Great War, the world (making all due allowances) of Wilde and Henry James and *The Yellow Book,* of Kipling and Baden-Powell and Cecil Rhodes, of Asquith and Balfour and Victoria's Diamond Jubilee, the lost world upon which writers of Wodehouse's generation—Ford, Forster, Lawrence, Wyndham Lewis, Lytton Strachey, Virginia Woolf—reflect with various admixtures of regret and loathing. Evelyn Waugh praised Wodehouse as a literary world-maker and called the world he made "idyllic"; it seems the right word for Blandings Castle, and one needn't share Waugh's Tory contempt for the world that replaced it to feel the arcadian charm of the place.

Idylls, however, are static pictures of a place in whose perfect sky the boughs hang always heavy, and we come a little (if not much) closer to our own world in the eleven novels and four books of stories Wodehouse wrote about Bertie Wooster and Jeeves, his most famous works and, taken collectively, his best. His practical experience in the theater no doubt contributed to his dramatic powers as a novelist, his fine sense of vocal style as an index to character or social location. His art prospers with first-person narrators—Mr. Mulliner, the Oldest Member, the bemused friend who tells us about poor Ukridge—and the Jeeves books are decisively affected by being told by Bertie Wooster. (The one novel Bertie does not narrate or even appear in, *Ring for Jeeves*—in the U.S. *The Return of Jeeves*—is a hopeless disaster.) It's Bertie's voice that enables us to see just who he and Jeeves are, what social and intellectual space lies between the Young Master and his perfect manservant.

Bertram Wilberforce Wooster, of Crichton Mansions, Berkeley Street, London W. 1, is the child of privilege, but his lineage is otherwise cloudy. His parents are dead—indeed, like Lord Emsworth's deceased countess, they are never even named; of Wooster *père* we know only that he bet on horses and was rich, and of his spouse we know nothing at all. (In being unparented Bertie somewhat resembles Wodehouse, who was largely brought up by aunts and uncles, not because his parents were dead but because they were in Hong Kong during much of his youth.) Bertie is a commoner whose wealth and breeding give him easy access to nobler circles; he was educated, loosely speaking, at Eton and Oxford; he has money by the sackful; he lives the pleasant, idle life of the bachelor clubman; he travels at whim, usually to the Riviera or to New York, which, like Wodehouse, he adores. Though he entirely lacks the panache of Psmith, he too in his way is self-authorized.

The two relatives he is closest to are both paternal aunts. Aunt Agatha, usually not a presence but an approaching storm-front on his emotional weather map, is "the one who kills rats with her teeth," a domineering bully and would-be improver of deficient males like her feckless nephew. Her sister, Bertie's Aunt Dahlia, is a more insidious danger. A bluff, breezy, "county" sort who rides to the hounds and speaks (or shouts) her mind, Aunt Dahlia is scoffingly fond of Bertie, as he is of her, but her strong sense of self-interest—retaining her magical and much coveted French chef Anatole or screwing money out of her tightfisted husband to support *Milady's Boudoir*, the women's magazine she proudly edits— leads her frequently to dragoon Bertie into her nefarious activities.

These aunts outline Bertie's painful problem about women. If he has no discernible interest in sex (no one in Wodehouse really does), still he *likes* girls, often to the point of (brief) infatuations and even marriage proposals. But the young women who attract him are either improvers like Aunt Agatha—Madeline Bassett, a "droopy, sentimental exhibit" who adores bad poetry, Florence Craye, a serious student of modern philosophy, Honoria Glossop, an athletic devotee of Ruskin, all sure that Bertie secretly loves them, and all, to his horror, quite ready to marry and reform him when other prospects look dim—or they are jolly, Dahlia-like good eggs with manly nicknames, Stiffy Byng and Nobby Hopwood and Bobbie Wickham, whose pranks get Bertie in the soup and who are always in love with one of his friends anyway.

Bertie's real enemy is not women but seriousness, self-conscious high culture and moral duty, but this is usually embodied in dominant women or their arty male acolytes, and the serpent in his garden is marriage. (Wodehouse himself, it perhaps should be noted, was contentedly married for over sixty years.) Bertie's pleasures are simple and boyish: eating, drinking, and smoking more than is good for him, wearing flashy new fashions (until Jeeves can get the offending garments away from him), reading cheap fiction, going to nightclubs like The Mottled Oyster, betting, stealing policemen's helmets on Boat Race night, driving fast cars, singing in the bath, playing the "banjolele," dropping literary or scriptural

allusions which Jeeves usually has to correct or finish for him, and devis-
ing hopelessly inept plots to get himself or his friends out of jams. His
natural foes are children, animals, intellectuals, and all figures of authority, be they judges, psychiatrists, politicians, policemen, school-
masters, business tycoons, or aunts. His is a world of unearned freedom,
mindless otiosity, gratification without labor or effort; and yet Wodehouse,
while fully aware of Bertie's triviality and weakness, makes him an object
of fond approval, one who stands for the saving remnant of childishness
within our hopes of being at last responsible, productive adults.

"Mentally, he is negligible," Jeeves is once overheard to say of his
master. The firmness is Jeevesian, but so is the qualification—even to
Jeeves, Bertie may not be negligible in *all* respects. Mentality is of course
Jeeve's own forte. Bertie admires the posterior bulging of his valet's cra-
nium and imagines that he must eat a lot of fish. Jeeves is a student of
psychology, a devoted reader of Spinoza (he finds Nietzsche "unsound"),
and he has a Bartlettian command of familiar quotations. Above all, he is a
master of effective domestic plotting, the Machiavel upon whom Bertie
and his friends rely in times of trouble.

Jeeves is also a mystery, at least to Bertie, which is why having Bertie
tell the stories works so well. Jeeves is the perfect servant: his taste in
dress, speech, books, and everything else is far superior to his master's;
he's an accomplished cook and concocter of a miraculous hangover cure;
he performs his duties so silently and invisibly as scarcely to seem to occupy normal human space, as Bertie notes when he describes him "shim-
mering" into a room or "stream[ing] silently from spot A to spot B, like
some gas." But this angelic creature *is* a servant. He represents a social
area that Bertie, though no snob, knows little about and can be surprised
by. For example, Jeeves too is a bachelor and a clubman, and when Bertie
visits his club for gentlemen's gentlemen, the sublimely named Junior
Ganymede in Curzon Street, he's much impressed by how "extremely
cozy" it seems. If Jeeves often ignores his master's wishes, ill-considered
as they usually are, he does serve his best interests loyally, though with a
deviousness that suggests some relish of Bertie's confusions. But Jeeves
also serves his own interests, promoting the romantic purposes of his relatives, quietly placing winning bets for himself in competitions like the
Great Sermon Handicap that Bertie and his gamester friends lose their
shirts on, arranging that he will be suitably rewarded, in cash or privileges, for saving his betters from themselves.

Oscar Wilde was one of Wodehouse's masters, as the opening scene of *The Importance of Being Earnest* may suggest. Algernon Moncrieff, another affluent and gluttonous bachelor, here jousts with his man-servant Lane:

Algernon	Oh! . . . by the way, Lane, I see from your book that on Thursday night, when Lord Shoreman and Mr. Worthing were dining with me, eight bottles of champagne are entered as being consumed.
Lane	Yes, sir; eight bottles and a pint.
Algernon	Why is it that at a bachelor's establishment the servants invariably drink the champagne? I ask merely for information.
Lane	I attribute it to the superior quality of the wine, sir. I have often observed that in married households the champagne is rarely of a first-rate brand.
Algernon	Good heavens! Is marriage so demoralizing as that?
Lane	I believe it is a very pleasant state, sir. I have had very little experience of it myself up to the present. I have only been married once. That was in consequence of a misunderstanding between myself and a young person.
Algernon	[languidly]. I don't know that I am much interested in your family life, Lane.
Lane	No, sir; it is not a very interesting subject. I never think of it myself.
Algernon	Very natural, I am sure. That will do, Lane, thank you.
Lane	Thank you, sir. [Lane goes out.]
Algernon	Lane's views on marriage seem somewhat lax. Really, if the lower orders don't set us a good example, what on earth is the use of them? They seem, as a class, to have absolutely no sense of moral responsibility.

This bland, mannered glimpse of class warfare in the West End is funny because the forces are so nearly matched. Lane easily deflects the issue from the disappearing champagne to the large philosophical matter of marriage and its erosion of domestic style. (Jeeves would never help himself to Bertie's champagne, but he shares Lane's unstated but evident doubts about the desirability of marriage for masters, which would of course imperil the authority, or even the employment, of valets.) Algernon retakes some of the lost ground with his airy disclaimer of "much" interest in the family life of servants, but Lane strikes back by asserting his own indifference to the subject—his important concerns, like his master's, lie elsewhere. Algernon finally has the nominal victory; his is the power to end such conversations, and he dismisses his man with cool politeness. But Lane too is cool and unruffled, and the outcome is a standoff, leaving teasingly unresolved the Wildeian puzzle of just what "demoralizing" or "moral responsibility" may mean.

Compare the following exchange from "Jeeves and the Yuletide Spirit," in which Jeeves tries to discourage Bertie's infatuation with a lively young lady:

"Jeeves, I insist. This is a time for plain speaking. You have beefed about Miss Wickham. I wish to know why."

"It merely crossed my mind, sir, that for a gentleman of your description Miss Wickham is not a suitable mate."

"What do you mean by a gentleman of my description?"

"Well, sir—"

"Jeeves!"

"I beg your pardon, sir. The expression escaped me inadvertently. I was about to observe that I can only asseverate—".

"Only what?"

"I can only say, sir, that as you have invited my opinion—"

"But I didn't."

"I was under the impression that you desired to canvass my views on the matter, sir."

"Oh? Well, let's have them, anyway."

"Very good, sir. Then briefly, if I may say so, sir, though Miss Wickham is a charming young lady—"

"There, Jeeves, you spoke an imperial quart. What eyes!"

"Yes, sir."

"What hair!"

"Yes, sir."

"And what *espièglerie*, if that's the word I want."

"The exact word, sir."

"All right, then. Carry on."

"I grant Miss Wickham the possession of all these desirable qualities, sir. Nevertheless, considered as a matrimonial prospect for a gentleman of your description, I cannot look upon her as suitable. In my opinion, Miss Wickham lacks seriousness, sir. She is too volatile and frivolous. To qualify as Miss Wickham's husband, a gentleman would need to possess a commanding personality and considerable strength of character."

"Exactly!"

"I would always hesitate to recommend as a life's companion a young lady with quite such a vivid shade of red hair. Red hair, sir, in my opinion, is dangerous."

I eyed the blighter squarely.

"Jeeves," I said, "you're talking rot."

"Very good, sir."

"Absolute drivel."

"Very good, sir."

"Pure mashed potatoes."

"Very good, sir."

"Very good, sir—I mean very good, Jeeves, that will be all," I said.

And I drank a modicum of tea, with a good deal of hauteur.

The fun of this may be slower and somewhat thinner than Wilde's, if only because Bertie is so clearly doomed to lose the battle he thinks he's won. He's touchingly unsure about words like "asseverate" and "*espièglerie*"; he forgets that he solicited, even demanded, Jeeves's reasons for disapproval ("let's have them, *anyway*" is wonderful); he dimly senses an affront in "a gentleman of your description" but, when Jeeves elaborates upon its meaning, assumes that it ascribes to him exactly the qualities it denies him. In the very act of asserting his authority by dismissing his servant, Bertie blunders into a reversal of their roles, calling his valet "sir." And their characteristic intonations of speech show that such a reversal has already occurred. Where Bertie's is the voice of "modern," breezy, socially deracinated neologism ("beefed," "you spoke an imperial quart," "pure mashed potatoes," all of them reflecting his interest in food and drink), Jeeves's is the voice of traditional, conservative social reason. With the "sirs" removed, his longest speech could comfortably be spoken by Jane Austen's Mr. Knightley or Sir Thomas Bertram, and the Austenian effect is bolstered by the name "Wickham," as if to suggest that Bertie's latest heartthrob has somehow inherited her unsoundness from the villain of *Pride and Prejudice*. Wodehouse in fact loves his little echoes of Austen; his books contain, as the names of people, places, or things, "D'Arcy," "Bates," "Willoughby," "Bertram," "Musgrove," several "Bingleys" (one a make of motorcar), and more, and of course he shares his own last name, as he pronounced it, with the matchless Emma.

Where Wilde's Lane holds his own on a social-linguistic ground he would once have been barred from competing for, Wodehouse's Jeeves is

the secret master of that ground. And his power is all the funnier for being
so invisible to his nominal master. Mere historical accident has made Bertie the one with the money and the rank. He usually concedes *mental*
superiority to Jeeves, to be sure; but braininess is scarcely the hallmark of
the born aristocrat, and even Bertie's claim to the role's more essential
attributes—style, taste, composure, the right to be obeyed and to do just
as one wants—is a transparent illusion which only Jeeves's forbearance
and self-interest sustain.

At the same time, Bertie is lovable and funny, and Jeeves, apart from
Bertie, really is not. (His one recorded venture at telling a joke involves
men named Nichols and Jackson who are dismembered when their tan-
dem cycle collides with a brewer's van; their remnant parts are surgically
reassembled into one man, who is henceforth called "Nixon.") For all his
privilege, Bertie is a born victim, continually tricked, shamed, or coerced
into doing things for others that leave him embarrassed, insulted, cozened,
arrested, or physically hurt. In his small way, he's open to experience,
vulnerable to life rather than shielded from it by social advantage as are
the people at Blandings Castle. His vanities—in his instinctive good taste
and musical talent, in having had an article ("What the Well-Dressed Man
is Wearing") published in *Milady's Boudoir,* in once having won the prize
for Scripture Knowledge at his private school—are touchingly modest in
scale, and his ability to endure and forgive the most awful abuse by his
friends and relations is almost saintly. He's by far the most authentic fool
among Wodehouse's endlessly foolish heroes (the exception being Psmith,
whose folly is only feigned and so is not lovable), and his unwisdom, like
Don Quixote's or Tom Jones's or Huck Finn's, is what redeems him.

One of the best novels of this series, *The Code of the Woosters,*
shows how this kind of comedy centers upon Bertie's haplessness.
Wodehouse's plots are usually intricate and finely tuned, and here he
makes everything flow from three parallel actions, each focused upon an
object of larcenous desire. First there's an eighteenth-century silver cow
creamer, recently bought by the sanctimonious Sir Watkyn Basset, of
Totleigh Court, Glos. (where the story takes place), but coveted by Aunt
Dahlia's husband, himself a collector; to put her spouse in good spirits
so that she can get money from him for her magazine, Dahlia demands
that Bertie steal the creamer for him. Then there's a pocket notebook,
in which Bertie's old friend Gussie Fink-Nottle, a timorous, fish-faced
dullard now engaged to Sir Watkyn's imposing daughter Madeline, has

recorded his scurrilous views of his future father-in-law and others. Gussie, who much prefers his research into the mating habits of newts to any human converse, has been terrified of having to speak at his wedding breakfast, but Jeeves has emboldened him ("Mussolini could have taken his correspondence course," Bertie admiringly observes of the new Gussie) by suggesting that fear of one's audience is dispelled if one cultivates absolute contempt for them, a theory that may provide an insight into Jeeves's own unshakable public composure. But the inept Gussie has lost the notebook, and he implores Bertie to steal it back from Sir Watkyn's headstrong niece and ward, Stiffy Byng, who threatens to disclose its explosive contents unless Gussie and Bertie assist her own romantic purposes. Finally there's a policeman's helmet, reluctantly stolen from the local constable by Stiffy's fiancé, the Rev. Harold Pinker, at the insistence of Stiffy herself, who seeks vengeance on P. C. Oates for his collision with her unruly, bicycle-chasing dog Bartholomew, an event which Bertie memorably observed:

> A smeller—and amongst the finest I have ever been privileged to witness—was what this officer of the law came. One moment he was with us, all merry and bright; the next he was in the ditch, a sort of *macédoine* of arms and legs and wheels, with the terrier standing on the edge, looking down at him with that rather offensive expression of virtuous smugness which I have often noticed on the faces of Aberdeen terriers in their clashes with humanity.

In all these plots and counterplots, Bertie is an essentially innocent bystander, accused of everything but technically guilty of nothing. At the start he tries to steal the creamer but is interrupted by Sir Watkyn and his intimidating friend Roderick Spode, who have him under close surveillance and blame him when Aunt Agatha finally steals the thing herself. Knowing that if Madeline can't marry Gussie she will surely marry *him*, Bertie begs Stiffy to give up the notebook, but she refuses unless he steals the creamer for her, so that Pinker can restore it to Sir Watkyn and win his grateful consent to their marriage. When Bertie and Jeeves search for the notebook in Stiffy's bedroom, the dog Bartholomew intervenes, and a rare moment of pure accord between master and man ensues: "At the exact moment when I soared like an eagle on to the chest of drawers, Jeeves was skimming like a swallow on to the top of the cupboard." Thus perched, Jeeves openly declines to endeavor to give satisfaction:

"Are you afraid of a tiny little dog, Jeeves?"

He corrected me respectfully, giving it as his opinion that the undersigned was not a tiny little dog, but well above the average in muscular development. In particular, he drew my attention to the animal's teeth.

I reassured him.

"I think you would find that if you were to make a sudden spring, his teeth would not enter into the matter. You could leap up to the bed, snatch up a sheet, roll him up in it before he knew what was happening, and there we would be."

"Yes, sir."

"Well, are you going to make a sudden leap?"

"No, sir."

Bertie's transition from "you" to "we" is delicious, but for once Jeeves is shown to share some of his master's imperfection of spirit.

Bertie's technical innocence does not exempt him from suffering, as the incriminating objects uncannily gravitate toward his presence. (And toward each other—at a crucial moment the notebook gets hidden in the creamer, and both creamer and helmet show up in Bertie's suitcase just when he seems safely out of danger.) For a time the chief threat is Roderick Spode, the one character whom Wodehouse has not used in earlier books. Spode is a gigantic figure ("It was as if Nature had intended to make a gorilla, and had changed its mind at the last moment"), much given to threats and acts of mayhem. He's also a very topical figure for the late 1930s, being the Mosley-like founder and fuehrer of a gang of domestic Nazis, the Saviours of Britain (familiarly, the Black Shorts). His fierceness, however, like Hitler's, contains a streak of smarmy sentimentalism; he worships Madeline Bassett from afar and is determined to mangle any man who, like Gussie and Bertie, seems to be trifling with her affections, though when it gets down to action they best him by not playing the game—Gussie stuns him with an oil painting and Bertie enmeshes him in a sheet and conks him with a vase.

But the key to controlling Spode is not physical but psychological force. Jeeves finds an embarrassing secret about him in the confidential club book of the Junior Ganymede, to which members contribute intimate facts about their masters, for mutual entertainment and guidance to future employment possibilities. (Bertie is stunned to hear that he himself plays a prominent part in these scandalous records.) Though Jeeves is pledged not to disclose the secret itself, he does reveal that mentioning the name "Eulalie" should have an arresting effect on Spode, as indeed it does when Bertie tries it. The intimidated fascist is in fact the agent of the book's happy ending. When Sir Watkyn finds Bertie with the stolen helmet and locks him up, and Bertie (remembering Sidney Carton) nobly refuses Aunt Dahlia's offer to yield Anatole to Sir Watkyn in exchange for his freedom, Jeeves plays the Eulalie card to make Spode falsely confess that he himself stole the helmet. At Jeeves's suggestion, Bertie then threatens Sir Watkyn with a suit for wrongful arrest unless he permits his daughter and niece to marry Gussie and Pinker, and all ends well, although in *Stiff Upper Lip, Jeeves* we learn that Madeline did *not* marry Gussie but, much more appropriately, the egregious Spode.

Finally, after Bertie promises that they may go on a world cruise, Jeeves discloses the secret. Spode is the owner of Eulalie Soeurs, a Bond Street emporium for which he designs ladies' underwear, and Bertie is prompted to a fumbling political reflection that may be shrewder than it sounds:

> "Good Lord, Jeeves! No wonder he didn't want a thing like that to come out."
>
> "No, sir. It would unquestionably jeopardize his authority over his followers."
>
> "You can't be a successful Dictator and design women's under-clothing."
>
> "No, sir."
>
> "One or the other. Not both."
>
> "Precisely, sir."

No cheap snicker about unmanliness is invited, only a quiet smile at the frequent discontinuity of our public and private selves.

Spode's presence in *The Code of the Woosters* points to what generally distinguishes the Jeeves stories from the Blandings Castle ones. Both series were begun during World War I and kept going until Wodehouse's death in 1975. Both draw on traditional country-house farce, with exaggerated caricaturing of upper-class folly, stagily intricate plots and timing, and that extraordinary idiom, compounded of old and new slang, quasi-realistic social mimicry, and shopworn literary allusion, which is his greatest literary invention. If the conversion of English society is at most a faint aura somewhere around the edges of his stories, the conversion of English speech into something less routinely indicative of class and personal possibility is an exuberant enterprise of his writing.

But where the Blandings stories are retrospective, almost wistfully Edwardian in setting and mood, dominated by elderly gents Gally Threepwood, Uncle Fred, even Lord Emsworth himself who have heard the chimes at midnight, the Jeeves stories are Georgian, *entre deux guerres*, tinged with the new excitements and social recklessness of the 1920s and '30s. (The earlier novels of Waugh and Anthony Powell may owe as much to Wodehouse's literary example as to the real-life escapades of the "bright young things" of their own generation.) Like his author, Bertie Wooster is a somewhat Americanized Englishman, and though most of his adventures occur in Blandings-like precincts of old wealth and landed ease, he's more at home in livelier, theoretically more democratic circles like those Wodehouse preferred, in London, New York, Hollywood, the south of France. Only Jeeves speaks at all cogently for older orders and forms, but he also indicates a radical shifting of authority; it is now up to servants, not sprightly old aristocrats, to help the young survive their own salutary unruliness.

This, however, had better not be put too solemnly. Wodehouse's is a delicate, fragile comic art, almost as remote as Wilde's or Waugh's from sober and routine notions of value. Spode the fascist, for example, is ludicrous and distasteful, but he's no more evil than the bedraggled parlor Bolsheviks found in a few of the earlier stories, or than Orlo Porter in the final Jeeves book, *Aunts Aren't Gentlemen* (U.S. title *The Cat-Nappers*), a ranting CND activist who's also a go-getting insurance salesman hungry for Mayfair flats and Rolls-Royces.

In Wodehouse's world, distinct feelings and views, moral or otherwise, are always limited by the pressure of other considerations:

> "Jeeves," I said, "don't try me too high. Not at a moment like this. Who was it you were telling me about the other day, on whose head all the sorrows of the world had come?"
>
> "The Mona Lisa, sir."
>
> "Well, if I met the Mona Lisa at this moment, I would shake her by the hand and assure her that I knew just how she felt. You see before you, Jeeves, a toad beneath the harrow."
>
> "Yes, sir. The trousers perhaps a quarter inch higher, sir. One aims at the carelessly graceful break over the instep. It is a matter of the nicest adjustment."

"Like that?"

"Admirable, sir."

I sighed.

"There are moments, Jeeves, when one asks oneself 'Do trousers matter?'"

"The mood will pass, sir."

One agrees with Bertie that in life even the nicest adjustment may fail to meet the case, but also with Jeeves, that long views are often what makes life tolerable. When Wodehouse while living in France was interned by the Germans in World War II, he got himself into serious disgrace in England by doing radio broadcasts to a then-neutral America; these were not even remotely treasonous or propagandistic but simply tried to remind everyone that a sense of humor helps even in very unpleasant circumstances. It was far too nice an adjustment for many of his embattled countrymen, as a less innocent soul might have foreseen; but forty years later my own sympathies lie with him, and with the government's decision to make official amends by giving him a knighthood before he died.

"Innocent" seems the right word for him and his talent, as it surely does not for many of the English comic writers he learned from or who learned from him. Some of them—Congreve, Fielding, Austen, Peacock, Wilde, Shaw, Beerbohm, Waugh, Powell—were simply smarter than he was, with powers of wit that could fuse contradictory possibilities in a word or phrase or gesture. His humor, like Dickens's or Thackeray's or Trollope's, or for that matter W. S. Gilbert's or Lewis Carroll's or Noel Coward's, is less a matter of single dazzling strokes (though such do occur) than of narrative accumulation, *building* rather than suddenly revealing significant absurdity in familiar places. But there is no need to dignify him by supposing him the equal of greater writers whom he in some way resembles. Alexander Cockburn's introduction to the Vintage edition of *The Code of the Woosters* is one of the good commentaries on him, but Cockburn's claim that "the Wooster-Jeeves cycle is the central achievement of English fiction in the twentieth century" sounds wrong unless you define "central" very carefully indeed.

My claims for the books have to be smaller. They do make an instructive case for whimsy in a world that has been taught to prefer the intensities of high wit or social realism or intellectual fireworks in literature. They remind us that formulistic writing, if the formula is a strong one, needn't always be less alive than writing that strives to reconstitute itself and the word upon every new occasion. His popularity, in itself, ought to be no embarrassment. There is of course a Wodehouse cult, enthusiasts who know every detail of the books and season their speech with quotes and allusions; Cockburn tells a charming story of an imitation Drones Club his father found in Budapest in the 1920s, where "ruined aristocrats and adventurers of every description" wore spats, threw rolls in the dining room, and generally sought the consolations of the Woosterian style. Consolation, though of a different sort, may be what that style gives me, too—consolation for having grown up, for living in a difficult time and place, for needing (often) to be very serious about art and life. Though I don't plan to join the Wodehouse cult or any other, I do take some comfort in knowing that there is one, that my own pleasure in him resembles that of other people whom I may not otherwise much resemble, and that they too must like him, in their own terms, for giving language a holiday from its important struggles with the real.

There's a photograph of him posing in academic regalia with Sir Herbert Grierson, when both men received honorary D. Litt. degrees at Oxford in 1939. Grierson, the great editor and scholar of Donne, stands partly turned away from his companion, and his lean, thought-worn countenance wears what seems to be a wry, puzzled expression. Wodehouse, in what looks like the wrong suit and tie for such occasions, confronts Grierson squarely, arms akimbo under his gown, his round hearty face beaming with companionly delight and pride. On intellect's own ground, it's the unserious intruder, the popular farceur, who looks the more at ease and gives the picture its comic, human point.

Beginnings, Balanchine
ROBERT GARIS

FOLLOWING George Balanchine's career has been so much my most pleasurable and absorbing experience of the arts that I have come to believe I could learn something important by following my own following of this artist: describing how I got to know his work, became attached to it, watched its development, and revised my conception of it as it changed and I changed. What follows is the first step of this project, an attempt to describe what I was like when I saw *Apollo* at the age of twenty, and what that experience was like.

When I first became aware of Balanchine and of ballet in general, at about the age of eighteen, I had already been seriously interested in the arts for about four years. I followed music and fiction and the movies closely, and discussed my artistic experiences in great detail with my best friends. These interests in fact formed my chief bond with these friends, and the whole enterprise formed the center of my life.

This is perhaps an unlikely adolescent identity to have formed itself in Allentown, Pennsylvania, in the late 1930s, and I must try to account for it. My family was not particularly cultivated, though both my parents liked music and my mother read a lot of novels. There was pressure on me at home to do well in school but apart from that little encouragement toward any intellectual pursuit. But there was a piano, a big upright—with the brand name of Hensel, which I've never encountered since—and when I was about eight I taught myself to play it by trying out hymns from our Baptist hymn book. This turned out to be an ideal way of learning how to follow different musical voices at the same time. Because a C-Major hymn like "Jesus Is Tenderly Calling Me Home" is so easy, with so many repeated tonic and dominant chords, I learned to play it pretty quickly, and this immediate gratification led me to attempt the easy Mozart, Haydn, Beethoven, Schubert, and Bach to which my repertory at the piano is still limited. Wanting to teach myself to play the piano shows some love for music, which may have had a relation to my lack of interest in sports; likewise my ability to teach myself to play the piano shows some musical gift, which was perhaps related to my lack of gift for sports. I was hunting for something of my own to be interested in and good at.

This part of my history seems relatively easy to understand. What may perhaps need more explanation is the degree of concentration, even semiprofessionalism, I had reached relatively early. I owe something of this to the curriculum of my junior high school, where I could get out of certain "shop" courses I dreaded by choosing to take extra art or music courses in ninth grade. The hymns had made me a good sight reader, and at the age of twelve I already knew some piano pieces pretty well—not just the Beethoven Minuet in G, though I remember playing that a lot— and so I felt able to choose music, and nothing was clearer than the fact that I *had* to escape auto shop and advanced mechanical drawing. And so my ninth grade music major brought my interest in music to focus by allowing me to make it a conscious choice.

I owe even more to some of my public school teachers, who gave special attention to students with special interests and abilities. I was one such student for two energetic, gifted, and generous English teachers. (Had the eighth and ninth grade music teachers showed equal interest in me, I doubt that I would ever have centered my interest, and my professional work, in literature.) But the most gratifying and influential attention came not from an English teacher but from my French teacher in high school. With a generous intuition for how education happens, she gathered together and invited to her apartment a group of students interested in music. This teaching succeeded, it now seems to me, because we all had just about the same degree of interest and expertise she herself had—if not, gratifyingly, even a little more. She had an enviably grand floor-model Philco radio-phonograph—the phonograph part tilting toward you as you opened it, as I can still vividly see—and I seem to remember that she bought it during my sophomore year of high school, which would make it 1939. She didn't have an immense number of records—78 RPM records still cost two dollars apiece—but there were enough for some real variety, and she simply began inviting to her apartment, once a week, at 7:30 in the evening, a group of between six and ten boys and girls to listen to her records and talk about music. These gatherings gave a kind of public extension to my interest in music and the arts. They established my sense that part of one's love for music and one's interest in it took the form of hearing it in the company of other people and of describing one's experience to them. Miss Swope must have chosen me and the other members of this group—some of whom already were my friends—because we had shown at school that we liked to talk about music; the formation of the group wasn't actually the first public ratification of my interest in talking about art. But being in the group brought what had been desultory and inchoate into continuous form and into consciousness.

Our group didn't cut much of a figure in the world of the whole high school, which was in fact rather a big world. Allentown was then as now a city of about one hundred thousand, but it had only one high school, a large one with more than three thousand students, among whom this group of six to ten music lovers couldn't and didn't have much impact. Yet I don't remember missing this kind of public acknowledgment. The fact that a teacher had formed a group helped us to believe that it represented an elite, and it now seems clear that it actually did represent that.

Music was only the center of the discussion; plenty of time was spent talking about plays and novels. The level of the music we discussed was fairly high, since Miss Swope's records were those of the standard orchestral repertory of the day, with too much Tchaikovsky—plus the Franck symphony—to be highbrow, but enough Beethoven to be serious. The level of our discussions of drama and fiction was very much lower, though, because it somehow worked out that in these fields we discussed not the classics but current popular works—the recent plays on Broadway which might or might not come to Allentown on their road tours, and the novels which were reviewed week by week in *The New York Times Book Review* and appeared on its best seller list—which, sad to say, was a respected guide. In a stern view of things, then, our group was an adolescent version of those notoriously midcult women's club discussion groups endemic to exactly the kind of provincial city I grew up in. If, as I think true, our group was better than that, it must have been because we were young. And the group wasn't our only intellectual connection. We all had a few close friends who weren't in the group, with whom we had other discussions. I had a not-quite-friend (we have since become close friends) whom I saw in the library at night, and when we took walks after the library closed, we talked about Dostoevski and, as I remember, German lyric poetry. And my closest friend was a tremendously difficult, brilliant, sad, furious, unclubbable, overweight, strong, and bullying young student of physics with whom I discussed everything. We had an intricately structured symbiosis which gave us great power over each other's minds— what comes back to me now is the time he forced me to spend what felt like hundreds of hours soldering with infinite ineptitude the relatively few connections in the primitive hi-fi set that he had designed for me but made me build for myself.

By the time I was eighteen I had developed a special angle on all this. I was still "interested in the arts," but in my case a more distinct motive linked all these concerns and ways of spending time: running through my interests in the arts, bringing them into focus, giving form to my discussions with my friends, and giving the whole enterprise its central motive and energy, was a preoccupation with the very act of making aesthetic judgments. I thought of myself quite consciously as someone who did that, and I was aware that in this respect I differed at least in degree from most of my friends and from most of the members of my group. I didn't want to be a passive, submissive appreciator; I wanted to be an active judge. Another way of being active, of course, would have been to make works of art, and I had some hopes in that direction. But these were rather dim, and if what Pound said is right—that the way to find out whether you are a poet is to write lots of poems—then I didn't really seem to want that. On the other hand, the judging I did instead of making art didn't seem negative or a pis aller. Many of my judgments were enthusiastically and excitedly favorable, and I was eager to express and defend them. And the intensity of my negative judgments and the pleasure I took in expressing them made them, too, seem active, alive, essentially positive.

I was of course making something in this procedure, though I wasn't making art—I was making my self, I was judging art in order to form and express my identity. And though this must have been a response to some uncertainty about the identity I feared I had or didn't have, there seemed to be a positive side to this too. For while this self-making was certainly to a degree compensatory and imitative, it was not entirely that. It had the energetic, hopeful feel of a real project of living.

What now seems problematic and a little awkward about all this is the relation between my preoccupation with judgment and my pleasure in the arts. With so much—my very identity—riding on it, each separate act of judgment became a test not only of my powers of judgment but of myself, and so all my experience of art was infiltrated by an anxious self-consciousness which, though it didn't destroy the pleasure I got from works of art, certainly complicated that pleasure, as for instance in my early dealings with Mozart. I had become interested in opera very early—

in seventh or eighth grade when I was eleven or twelve—through a boy whose own interest came from the unworthy circumstance that he was a fan of Jeanette MacDonald. Although this friend became a member of Miss Swope's group when that got formed three or four years later, I didn't think him nearly as smart as the other members of our group, and I don't really associate him with the way in which the group was important to me. I got to be rather ashamed of having him as a close friend, in fact, but it had been a crucial relationship. He not only went to the movies, which I wasn't allowed to do, but went all the time and, even more important, went to the same ones over and over again, so that he knew the dialogue of a lot of movies absolutely by heart. This was irresistible: he could give me exact, detailed information about a world I was denied access to. Our talks, as I remember them, had mostly this as a subject—which was hardly a subject, and they were hardly talks: what went on between us was his recital, with the appropriate descriptive commentary, of the scenarios of the movies he knew by heart, while I listened and imagined. His favorites were the operetta movies of MacDonald and Eddy, a taste held in complete contempt by my other friends later, and I betrayed my movie friend shamefully and often by never acknowledging, really, how well I knew the MacDonald-Eddy movies. I knew them very well, because my friend knew them completely, and he also knew something about opera because Jeanette MacDonald sang parts of operas in these operetta movies; the Jewel song from *Faust* was the first operatic aria I remember hearing, simply because it was the first operatic record he bought. Soon after I got to know him he singled out the Puccini operas as the ones he liked best. Jeanette MacDonald had sung parts of *Tosca* in *Rose Marie* and he had found that immensely exciting; so he began buying *Tosca* record by record, and I got to know it, record by record. I still know it by heart. He followed this with *La Bohème* and *Madame Butterfly*, and even made contact with the exotic world of the Gramophone Shop in New York to buy the imported Decca records of *Turandot*.

While I was learning and very much enjoying the Puccini operas through my friendship with this fan, I was at the same time beginning to learn from many other sources that this was a low taste, not the right judgment at all, and when I was earning enough money from working in shoe stores on Saturdays to buy opera recordings, in 1940, it was *Don Giovanni* that I chose. And my next acquisition was *Cosi Fan Tutte*. I find these operas completely beautiful and valuable today, and I believe I did so back then when I was fifteen. But what stays in my memory about these choices has little to do with pleasure in the music and much to do with pleasure in making the right judgment. I have negative evidence for this. I didn't buy the records of *The Marriage of Figaro* at that time, and though I can't remember why, I'm pretty sure it had to do with making right judgments. I somehow picked up the idea that the singing wasn't as good on *Figaro* as on the other two sets, and I imagine I was thinking about the fact that the least gifted Glyndebourne singer, Audrey Mildmay, sang the important role of Susanna—and I remember knowing that Mildmay was the wife of the director of the Glyndebourne Opera, and I remember too the scorn I felt at this nepotism. Now I realize that all the singing in the ensembles, even Mildmay's, is perfectly integrated, and it is of course as an ensemble performance that this Glyndebourne *Figaro* has remained unrivalled. This judgment against Mildmay's singing wasn't really a bad one; it was merely incomplete. But I was also making a judgment about the music itself. I didn't know much of the music of *Figaro* at this time, though I had gathered from reading B. H. Haggin, one of my authorities, that it was a great work. But *Don Giovanni* figured more excitingly as "the world's greatest opera" in the writing of Shaw, Kierkegaard, and W. J. Turner, who were also important voices for me; and *Cosi Fan Tutte*, I knew, had a very special cachet because only people of the highest taste realized that it wasn't a lapse into artificiality and triviality after *Figaro* but a triumph of art through convention—so ran Turner's powerful advertisement. My friend had bought *Tosca* because he had loved the scenes from *Tosca* that Jeanette MacDonald sang in *Rose Marie*, but I bought *Don Giovanni* and *Cosi Fan Tutte* because I knew they were the best and I wanted to get to know and like them.

The upshot was that I knew only bits and pieces of *Figaro* by the time I knew *Don Giovanni* and *Cosi Fan Tutte* literally by heart. And then an extraordinary thing happened. I encountered in *Figaro* my first really intense aesthetic pleasure in the music of Mozart, and I still remember that this took me by surprise. It was in 1944, I believe, during a performance under Bruno Walter at the Metropolitan Opera, and what astonished and delighted me was not, as I would have expected, Steber's "Dove sono" but Albanese's "Deh vieni non tardar." Albanese, though very popular in all quarters, was not one of the most highly approved singers, and she rarely sang Mozart, so one way of describing my response, and in particular my surprise, is to say that I simply hadn't been programmed by any of my authorities for this experience. But so invidious an account is inadequate to what happened to me. I had had an encounter with the true enchantment of art. I can still remember Albanese's touching byplay with a rose as she sang. I remember her utter conviction, and I remember too the summer night atmosphere of the woodwinds and the plucked strings: it was ravishingly beautiful. Which is to say that it took me by surprise because "liking it" felt so little like "making a judgment": it felt more like being seduced.

Figaro, as it happens, has come to seem to me greater than *Don Giovanni* or *Cosi*, but that is because, say, of the Act II Finale rather than because of things like "Deh vieni." And I have since felt equally enchanted by things in all of Mozart's operas. I have come to love Mozart's operas as well as to admire them, and in fact without this coming together of love and judgment I could feel no authority or authenticity as a critic. And yet my surprised reaction to Albanese's "Deh vieni" still seems to me important, a signal of an advance in my experience of music, and it is relevant to my present theme, because the same kind of thing was soon to happen with Balanchine. Before seeing any of his ballets I was ready to approve and like his work, and even ready to fight for it, since I had conceived of him from my reading of criticism as a great artist whom it took unusually fine and bold and unconventional taste to admire. But my first experience with Balanchine, which was of *Apollo* in 1945, was as enchantingly seductive as my first experience of *Figaro*, and I was similarly surprised. I had anticipated approving and loving this ballet, but I had not expected to be helplessly overcome by it, to the point of shedding tears at the apotheosis, as in fact I did.

I felt this kind of enchantment and surprise fairly seldom, I believe, and the instances are correspondingly vivid in my memory. It had also happened a couple years earlier than the *Figaro* event, when I first saw Preston Sturges's *The Palm Beach Story*. Here my surprise took the form of hardly being able to believe that I could be watching something so dazzlingly witty and inventive, so sophisticated, in the Rialto Theatre in Allentown. Orson Welles's *The Magnificent Ambersons* was a tremendous event too. Then there was my first *Toscanini* concert in Studio 8H at Rockefeller Center.

I am glad to remember such experiences because I am proud of them as judgments, and no doubt there are less happy and wise enchantments that I have suppressed. But I believe I had relatively few such moments, and my surprise at them shows that my dealings with art and judgment took place in an atmosphere less characterized by pleasure in art itself than I like now to realize. I spent a lot of time learning to like what I knew I ought to like. There was much anxiety and some hypocrisy in this whole endeavor. But my dealing with the arts took place mainly not at these extremes but on some middle ground between enchantment and that degree of anxiety or pretense that would have inhibited pleasure altogether. As I now remember it, I was always sort of "at work" at this judging business, but I felt that it was a fine business; I never doubted its worth to me and never tired of it; I always regarded it as my special business, thought myself good at it, and knew I would succeed in it. Success—the hard word, for this was a goal, in a fairly familiar American way, despite the supposedly disinterested nature of the aesthetic pursuit. I wanted to be, I hoped to be, and I pretty much knew I was going to be successful at this business of making judgments about art, and this was the center of my pleasure in the arts at that time—this, and the anticipated pleasure of seeing and hearing myself acknowledged as a good judge and of seeing my judgments carry authority and influence others' tastes.

My early experience with the work of Willa Cather shows how much I wanted acknowledgment and how curious a form acknowledgment could therefore take. When I was about fourteen, I learned, first from one of those influential English teachers and then from the whole phalanx of middle-brow American literary journalists, to identify Willa Cather as a writer of special excellence. Looking back, I now see many things working together to give this artist, now firmly identified as minor, such stature. The teacher and the critics I was following had themselves followed Cather's career with a quite conscious sense of dedication, and I believe they thought of her as working with a peculiarly strong and pure sense of dedication: this accounts for the note of tribute in much of the writing about her. All my authorities, as I remember them, accented Cather's style, never her insight or vision, and this was the way I too described my judgment of Cather to myself. I admired *A Lost Lady*, for instance, because it was "beautifully written." Exactly what I may have meant by that isn't easy to recall. *The Song of the Lark* appealed to me much more in my teens because of my interest in opera, and I still remember vividly my initial response to Thea Kronborg's operatic career in New York, her apartment on Riverside Drive, and other details. But this didn't mean that I found this novel better than *A Lost Lady*. I wholeheartedly subscribed to the view that the later work was the best. And yet the beautifully written element in this work, its famous style, wasn't in itself an object of my attention. Although I am sure I could have performed creditably if asked to specify what was distinguished about this style, I don't seem to remember savoring it or even thinking about it much. I would barely have had time. What I remember doing is something quite different: savoring Cather's style indirectly through the medium of critical praise. I read about her more than I read her own work; I got more pleasure from seeing her art acknowledged than from experiencing the art itself, and when I saw her art acknowledged I felt acknowledged myself.

To put it concretely, I spent really hundreds of hours during my teens in the periodical section of the library going back through the bound volumes of *The Nation, The New Republic, The Atlantic Monthly, Harper's, The Dial,* and a few others to find the early reviews of Cather's novels. When those reviews were favorable, I was pleased, but I required more than this, since the novels always were in fact praised. I required that special note of tribute to Cather's rare distinction as a stylist, and when I encountered that—by no means seldom—I felt a sense of unmistakably personal gratification. I had transferred the artist's power and worth to myself, in a process as ordinary and as easy to understand in its psychological motivation and mechanism as it is now faintly shameful to contemplate.

I remember making such a transaction at this age with two other artists, Mozart and Shakespeare, and their immense stature helps expose the central dynamics of this need for acknowledgment. It's hard to imagine any critic not praising the work of Mozart and Shakespeare in the highest terms, so it was a more intense kind of acknowledgment than mere praise that I hungered and hunted for and transferred to my own account. What I wanted to read was aggressive praise of the artists I admired, along with an equally aggressive detraction from their rivals. I conceived Mozart as in rivalry with Bach and Beethoven, and when I saw his superiority to these rivals explicitly acknowledged I felt quite simply that I had won. Such anxious adolescent competitiveness (in my case transferred to a safer realm from the gym or the debating society) is callow enough, to be sure, but familiar too. And such singling out of favorites to cherish and to follow with personal investment and identification sounds pretty much like following athletes or movie stars.

As it happens movie stars were indirectly involved in the business. My parents' fundamentalist religion led them to forbid me to go to movies or plays, though books and music were allowed. It's because of this that I valued my movie-fan friend so much and that I still feel such different degrees of excitement about the arts I am interested in. Literature is an abiding and professional interest, and I have always thought of myself as destined to deal with it somehow—in fantasy by being a critic at least, a novelist at best, but in reality always by being a teacher of literature. But I am sure that my parents' prohibition of movies and plays and their licensing of books is the reason why I have always felt literature to be the least glamorous of the arts. And there is a kind of logic, then, in the way the excitement I might have felt about movie stars, had I been allowed to watch them, was transferred to other "stars," the great people in the arts I was allowed to experience.

My parents' prohibition of movies and plays had the further effect that my knowledge of movies and plays before about the age of thirteen consisted entirely of hearing my friend recite *Rose Marie* and the rest of those movies, and of reading reviews in newspapers and magazines—my introduction to the periodical room in the library that made possible my later Cather research. I was an excited, in fact an involved, participant without firsthand experience, and my guess is that a lot of my sense of participation came from the aggressiveness and competitiveness with which I practiced critical judgment of plays and movies that I hadn't actually seen. The reviews I enjoyed most at first were in a theatrical magazine called *Stage*, and I can remember exactly why I loved them. The editors of the magazine had a system of summarizing reviews by little preliminary cartoons of a theater-goer who could take four possible poses: standing up applauding, sitting down applauding, sitting down doing nothing, and leaving his seat in boredom or dejection—you saw only his back, so this wasn't completely clear. These cartoons seemed to me at thirteen an absolutely dazzling way of representing judgment, and the cause of this overestimation has to have been my vicarious pleasure in the assertiveness of the "statements" being made by the cartoon figure. And these were matched by an equal assertiveness, a verve of judgment, in the style of the writing elsewhere in the magazine. I fear this would all seem pretty crass if I were to read it today, but I have been reluctant to check, out of self-protective generosity toward my former self.

After discovering *Stage* I looked elsewhere for similar opportunities to participate in the experience of art through sharing aggressive judgment-making. I wandered through the various magazines available in our library in Allentown, and in due course, I no longer remember exactly when, I encountered the critic who was to prove decisive in so many ways. B. H. Haggin, the music critic of *The Nation* from the mid-thirties to the mid-fifties, brought the assertiveness, the aggressiveness, the competitiveness of the act of critical judgment to a height, strength, and unremittingness that I hadn't encountered anywhere else. And in his seriousness, his power of intellect, he entirely, or so it seemed at the time, removed all taint of the merely aggressive or assertive from the whole process. With Haggin it was all a matter of the utmost public urgency. And his anger, which I didn't at that time consciously hear in his writing although I must have responded to it with alert intuition, was the anger of the righteous, if there were ever such a thing in the world. For this critic expressed his judgments with a force that made the little man in *Stage* seem just a joker; Haggin meant business, serious public business. He didn't just leave his seat in disapproval; he fought back. He identified and attacked his critical enemies by name, and he identified their disqualifications by name—their inability to hear what was virtually *palpably* to be heard, their vulgarity, their log-rolling, fantasy-spinning, system-mongering. And it was from Haggin that I heard about ballet and about Balanchine.

The terms of Haggin's recommendation gave it unusual power even from this critic who always spoke with emphasis. A music critic, not a dance critic, he acknowledged his lack of special expertise in recommending certain dance artists, the exciting point being that it was the sheer power of what he was calling to our attention that made him risk the charge of amateurism. The dancing of Danilova and Markova, and the ballets of Balanchine, had given Haggin such pleasure that he couldn't restrain himself from writing about these things for readers who had found his views persuasive on musical matters. These were marvelous conditions under which to encounter Balanchine. I was being invited, by someone whose taste I trusted by virtue of the power and accuracy of his critical assertiveness, to enter an entirely new language in order to experience works of art of great value.

Haggin's invitation to learn the language of ballet in order to appreciate a great artist wasn't quite as intimidating a challenge as it might have seemed, because reading Haggin had prepared me for such challenges. He was not only a fighter, he was a teacher, the best I have ever known. In his music criticism I had already encountered, and been converted to, a mode of dealing with art as if one were dealing with a language. In this mode, which has remained central with me ever since, one conceives oneself to be making contact with a mind that is carrying on a line of expressive thinking by making choices between the various directions in which its thinking might move. Art so conceived is a structure of movements which one becomes aware of because one is aware that there might instead have been different movements; as one gathers experience in the medium, one develops a sense of the range of its vocabulary, a sense of what is probable, and therefore one can measure the effect when what is probable happens and the different effect when it doesn't. With this sense of what following an artist's thinking was like, I went to see Balanchine prepared to find an artist whose artistic thinking was interesting to follow, and I was ready and able to learn the new language I needed to appreciate him because I had already been trained to conceive of an art medium as a language in which a mind could embody, at the very least, its movements, its choices, and thereby become expressive.

Haggin's conception of the artist as a choice-making mind embodied in a medium had further implications about what made art interesting. For Haggin the most important kind of artist seemed to be the kind who made, to put it as plainly as possible, a lot of choices. The kind of art Haggin seems to have found most intensely enjoyable exists in a linear dimension and takes place in time and with a kind of narrative logic. And this narrative movement is enclosed in a kind of frame, the known vocabulary and syntax of a language, and, on a larger scale, the conventions of a certain art form. Inside this frame the movement of the expressive thinking is particularly visible because it can only go so far, and one can pretty accurately gauge the distance the mind has moved because of one's sense of the frame. To gauge this distance, and to feel the impact of that movement of mind, is thereby to sense a value—a force of imagination, a power generated by the distance the mind had moved, and a precise power controlled by the precision of the movement—using "distance," of course, to stand also for other factors such as direction, angle, and momentum. Haggin's interest in sheer quantity of choices and in precise framing of the choice-making activity in order to enable precise measuring of the distance of the mind's movement—these predilections showed themselves in his pedagogical choice of the variation form, Bach's Passacaglia in C Minor, to be specific, as an introduction of the very concept of musical thought to his reader, that "man who loves *Hamlet*" but doesn't know how to connect with music. It's relatively easy to get your bearings while listening to variations—keeping track of where you are by remembering where you've been, getting the point of the minor mode you're hearing by remembering the major mode you recently heard, noticing the adagio of one variation by remembering the allegro of the one before. The exceptional legibility of these choices is due to the fact that alternative choices—the other variations—are immediately or almost immediately present in your mind.

In this way of experiencing art, the artist is seen as making choices all the time; but some of these choices are of a dramatic power of unexpectedness that makes them into events. Identifying these events is of course the key process in this understanding of art, and it rests on the primary assumption underlying the whole concept: the assumption that you can derive (and that all people seriously and sensitively interested in an art will certainly derive) a fairly secure sense of the normal choices available to an artist, a sense of the kinds of sentences the artist usually makes at this juncture or that, a sense of the good activity of a good mind. In the framework of this sense of good normal procedure, you can get an intense pleasure in recognizing that a particular choice just made by the mind you're following is an extraordinary choice. The upshot is that you not only *want* to measure and judge the brilliance of such choices, but that the procedures of the art, and of the way you are following it, make you able to judge it and take pleasure in doing so. In this way your participation in what Haggin would call the "operation" of the artist's mind combines judgment with pleasure.

Thus prepared at the age of twenty in 1945, I saw *Apollo*, my first Balanchine ballet and a particularly fortunate one to have lit on. My good fortune was half-accidental, for *Apollo* was available to be seen only because Ballet Theatre chanced to have revived it in 1943 for Eglevsky—and the capriciousness of such chances in the world of ballet is not exaggerated in the legends about the intrigues in this world. But another reason why *Apollo* was my first Balanchine ballet was that since it was one of Haggin's favorites, I went out of my way, down to New York, especially to see it. There was good reason for its being one of Haggin's favorites. Though I don't remember his explicitly saying so at that time, *Apollo* happens to be a particularly legible instance of the choice-making artist's mind at work in a medium. This work was capable of playing in ballet the role that Haggin had assigned the Bach Passacaglia in music, that of demonstrating the nature of the medium in itself, what expressive thinking in that medium was like, the range of the vocabulary possible in that medium and the brilliant choices actually made by a great artist in a particular work—all at the same time. *Apollo,* more than any other ballet, is full of events.

The other critic whose work prepared me for *Apollo* was Edwin Denby, whom I learned about, significantly, through Haggin. For Haggin's aggressive and angry judgment-making proceeded not only by attacking bad critics but also by praising good ones, those from whom he had himself learned, and in the field of ballet there was only one such figure, Denby, to whom Haggin repeatedly, then and since, has paid tribute. When I saw *Apollo* I was equipped by Haggin to follow its thinking, and I was also equipped in a different way by having read Denby.

A key word in Denby's writing about *Apollo* and about many other Balanchine ballets in those days is "modesty." In 1945 he called *Mozartiana* "another of his unassuming pocket masterpieces." He was not coincidentally thinking about the kind of modesty one finds in Mozart. And when he wrote about *Apollo,* his accent on its modesty implied that Balanchine, like Mozart, could create art of profound spiritual value not only with nongrandiose resources and in a nonheroic genre, but also with qualities of grace, charm, and wit that don't often accompany or achieve profundity or spirituality.

The other key idea in Denby's writing about *Apollo* was that the deepest meanings in the ballet don't come through narrative or dramatic gesture or paraphrasable idea or motive, but rather through the gradually increasing primacy, as the work goes along, of the formal devices and vocabulary of classical ballet. Denby completely accepted the fact that *Apollo* meant something about the birth and the triumph of the poetic impulse: a natural enough thing for a ballet called *Apollo* to be about. But this special claim was that the ballet got to be a profound and powerful expression of this meaning by becoming more overt and explicit in its deployment of ballet vocabulary and structure. Instead of choosing rhetorical afflatus, emphatically noble gestures, and explicitly high purpose, Balanchine had chosen the different road of conventional formal art, and

Denby was implying that this didn't just happen to be the mode Balanchine had chosen for this profound ballet, but that it had been the necessary mode.

In this account of *Apollo* Denby was arguing (implicitly as always—for unlike Haggin his rather Byzantine sense of courtesy forbade direct argumentation) against the view of *Apollo* offered by John Martin, who therefore also had a certain kind of effect on my first experience of Balanchine. Martin, who wrote for *The New York Times*, was the best-known dance critic in America in the thirties and most of the forties, and his views on dance had considerably wider circulation than those of Denby or Haggin. Denby had written for the small audience of *Modern Music* in the thirties and had come to greater prominence only when he substituted for Walter Terry as dance critic on *The New York Herald Tribune* for a couple of years during World War II while Terry served in the armed forces; Haggin's audience at *The Nation* was never large, and in any case he didn't present himself as a dance critic. Martin's judgment was that *Apollo* was decadent: chic, trivial, and artificial—a contraption of empty formalism. This view now seems absurd, and it wasn't easy to account for back then. One saw easily enough that a generally negative response to *Apollo* was part of Martin's campaign for his own interest in expressionistic modern dance and ballet, such as the work of Martha Graham and Anthony Tudor. Though this interest in dance expressionism seems somehow peculiarly boring and faded today, there is no reason to doubt that Martin actually felt it, and therefore it doesn't seem surprising that he should have been antagonistic to *Apollo*. Not that this was a sensible judgment, but this is the way people's tastes do work: only exceptional critics can really see what they're fighting against, much less give it justice. But Martin's tone was another matter. There was a note of waspish, weary, Clifton Webb outrage in the way he deplored Balanchine's ballets, as in his response in 1948 to *Symphony in C*: "Balanchine has once again given us that ballet of his, this time for some inscrutable reason to the Bizet symphony." Martin was so committed to Graham and Tudor and Humphrey that he just couldn't like Balanchine, one could see that. But something impure in his commitment to these artists showed up in the nastiness with which Balanchine was being not so much judged as reviled.

But whatever his motives, Martin's hostility to *Apollo* in the early 1940s was useful to me, for it fed into my sense that making critical judgments was an excitingly aggressive and competitive business. Martin on

Apollo proved that everybody was involved in a battle about its value, not just the habitually quarrelsome Haggin. And so in this respect too I was lucky in having encountered *Apollo* as my first Balanchine ballet. Its disputed status made it the subject of the important controversy in its field— just my meat, and I certainly knew which side I was on.

John Martin's hatred of Balanchine was also part of his pro-Americanism. First and simplest, Balanchine just wasn't American—what do we need these imports for anyway? Balanchine stood for RUSSIAN BALLET, which Martin thought American ballet companies had to get out from under, and he represented the late rather than the heroic early period of the Diaghilev Ballets Russes and therefore was a more dangerous influence to have around than Fokine or Massine—more Parisian, less exotically Russian, and therefore, in the logic of this sort of thinking, still less American. I remember thinking that this objection to Balanchine was foolish, but my lack of interest in Americanism in ballet can't count for much, since I had had virtually no experience with the American dance scene before my encounter with Balanchine. It seems unlikely that I would have been more interested then than I am now in Doris Humphrey or Martha Graham, and I turned out to be uninterested in ballets with Americana subjects, such as *Billy the Kid* and *Rodeo*, when I got to see them. On the other hand, I was something of a chauvinist in my proud pleasure that the great Willa Cather was an American, and there was Preston Sturges too, among others. And one of the facts I knew first about Balanchine was that he had worked successfully both on Broadway and in Hollywood, and for me today this aspect of his talent—the way he has been able to incorporate American dance impulse into his classical vocabulary—seems immensely important, even crucial and central, and that's a way of saying that I find Balanchine to be a particularly American kind of artist. But I didn't at all understand this in 1945. I think I believed Martin's campaign for American ballet simply provincial—and I still do.

There was an anti-Wagnerian angle to the *Apollo* battle that fitted in with many of my other tastes. In loving Mozart and hating the *Ring* I was flashing my credentials as a person of advanced taste as I had come to conceive it from my various authorities: I was against rhetoric, against high lyric or heroic afflatus, against the overt intentionality of the expressionistic aesthetic. Through Denby's suggestions I thought of Balanchine as sharing this taste and therefore as on my side of this battle. I was on the periphery of what I am calling anti-Wagnerism, so much so that Wagner

himself—fifty years after his death!—was still at the center of the battle as
far as I was concerned. I had not yet read Eliot and I didn't have that central interest in painting which would have made me question the importance of subject matter; and I was utterly unaware of the "no more
masterpieces" cult in Paris and other aspects of modernism. What I really
had a feeling for on this issue was music. I thought *Parsifal* at the Met at
Easter was boring and hollow and intolerably tyrannical over its audience,
and I regretted having missed what sounded like the best opera of the
twentieth century, *Four Saints in Three Acts*, with its libretto by Gertrude
Stein, music by Virgil Thomson, choreography by Frederick Ashton, performed in 1934, in cellophane costumes by an all-black cast, very few
times and to a select and knowing audience.

The bravado and uncertainty of this advanced taste of mine shows
up in the way my anti-Wagnerism extended to a denigration of middle-
period Beethoven. I was running all of Mozart against Beethoven, but I
was also committed to the correct idea that late Beethoven was virtually
supreme, and perhaps it was as a way out of this dilemma that I chose to
single out middle Beethoven for detraction. I claimed to find this music
overextended, uneconomical, too rhetorical, too overtly expressive, too
earnest, too provincially "heroic," too naively individualistic. So foolish a
mishearing and misjudging of art that seems to me now incontestably
major and beautiful is hard to credit, and in fact I hardly know what I
meant by it. I suppose I was thinking about the *Eroica* and the Fifth Symphony, yet I remember no specific dissatisfaction with these works. Practically the only thing I do remember about the Fifth Symphony in those
days is being amused by Oscar Levant's calling the way the last movement
winds up a "Roxy finale"—and the reason I was amused by this was that it
made me hear for the first time the joyous extravagance in this "overextended" passage. It is true that something a bit thick about the texture of
the *Appassionata* Sonata still keeps me from admiring it completely. But
that's all I can think of on the negative side, and my memories of the ex-
pansiveness and extendedness of, say, the first movement of Op. 59, no. 1
are entirely positive. My anti-middle-Beethoven campaign had no real
substance to it, but as a negative gesture I think it had a stimulating and
clarifying effect way back then. More to the immediate point, it certainly
played its role in making me welcome Denby's preview of the modestly,
sweetly, wittily sublime *Apollo* and in recognizing these remarkable
qualities when I experienced the ballet myself.

When I saw *Apollo* for the first time after having been prepared for it by my critics, I saw with the greatest satisfaction most of what I had expected. I saw a multitude of extraordinary, surprising dance images which represented striking movements of Balanchine's mind, brilliant choices on his part, which is to say that I saw what Haggin had prepared me for; and I also recognized that wonderful combination of modesty and profundity that Denby had prepared me for. And then there was something else that seemed to exist in another realm: I was enchanted, ravished with pleasure by what I saw; and in the apotheosis, when Apollo and the muses ascended to Parnassus, my eyes filled with tears. I was weeping not only for the beauty of the moment but for its tragic meaning, Stravinsky's special tragic note of eternal loss that Balanchine had corroborated so simply and affectingly in his choreography. Apollo and the muses represent our art, our capacity for expression, and therefore they are ours, and their immortality is ours; but in the lamenting phrases of the music at the end and in the movements of the dancers at that point, these presences seem to be leaving us behind, alone in our mortal human situation, as they ascend into an ideal realm. So this was not only one of my first enchantments; it was I think my first intense experience of tragedy.

What I don't remember recognizing at this first encounter is the increasingly explicit formal organization as the piece proceeds, which Denby had also prepared me for. I was of course a novice in this language and had little sense as yet of what explicit formal organization in ballet might look like. But my lack of experience with ballet might have made it equally hard for me to judge Balanchine's dance imagery, the boldness of his choices, the distance of the movements his mind was making throughout the ballet. Why could I see the one but not the other? The answer, I think, is that the events, the brilliant choices I was aware of, were not quite, not exactly, embodied in the vocabulary of ballet classicism. They were strokes of wit and fancy which were embodied in the movements of ballet dancers, and they took place in a classical ballet and in a mode not antithetical to ballet classicism—but they were not exactly classical ballet.

These strokes are everywhere in *Apollo*, and they form its mode. Let me name some of them. There is the maypole dance in which the nymphs unwind Apollo's swaddling clothes; the way Apollo frees himself completely by his own bold balletic pirouette; the way two nymphs turn themselves into one nymph and a wheelbarrow when they bring the lute to Apollo; later in the *pas d'action* there is Apollo pushing the three muses off on a little train ride; in the variations for the muses there is Calliope's stomachache of poetic inspiration, Polyhymnia hushing herself into mime with her finger to her lips, Terpsichore pawing the ground like a horse before she begins to dance; in Apollo's variation there is the clenching and unclenching of his hands in time with the music's pulse (the gesture Balanchine says he picked up from the signs in lights in Picadilly Circus); in the pas de deux there is the Michelangelo imitation—God touching Adam's finger metamorphosed into woman inspiring man; then Terpsichore sitting on Apollo's knees, the game with hands and elbows, the swimming lesson; in the coda there is the charioteer figure, and at the end of the coda there is the muses' sudden hand-clap and Apollo falling asleep for a second on the palms of their hands; before the final procession, there is the ritual blessing of the toe shoes; and in the apotheosis, there is the sunburst figure passing before your eyes like a cloud formation (rather than what it has become in the current version, a brilliant Apollo-logo to ring down the curtain).

These events must have been what John Martin particularly hated in the ballet when he saw it first. In 1957 he said that the recostuming of the ballet in practice clothes had at last revealed its beauties (the invidious but I think correct reading of this revelation is that Martin took the occasion provided by recostuming as a pretext under which to change over to the side the money was on); but he continued to say that "some of the invention remains self-consciously over-inventive." This is a wrong judgment but not a foolish one, for these inventions seem directly offered for pleasure and admiration, and admiration is what they got from me in 1945. The fact that Haggin has chosen to record so many of them in his recent *Discovering Balanchine* and that Denby referred to several of them in his pieces at the time of those performances suggests that they were important for both writers, and it seems likely that they still are. They were important for Stravinsky too. In the official, diplomatic language of the *Autobiography* (essentially a ghosted work, to be sure), he had said that "Balanchine had arranged the dances exactly as I had wished—that is to say, in accordance with the classical groups, movements, and lines of great dignity and plastic elegance." But one of the Craft conversation books, *Dialogues and a Diary*, shows that what he seems actually to have remembered from Balanchine's dances is not the classical movements or lines but two of these images—the wheelbarrow and the charioteer—which he naturally calls a troika.

These strokes of fancy get noticed and described because they are particularly noticeable and describable, to be sure, but they form the special mode of *Apollo* in a very special way. Perhaps not the essential mode—terminology is a problem here, and I don't want to seem to be saying that *Apollo* is not a classical ballet. But classicism is not the distinguishing feature of its identity, nor is it what seized my interest in 1945. *Apollo* was a lucky first Balanchine ballet for me, then, because it captured my attention by these not-essentially-balletic strokes of dance imagery; meanwhile, beneath the level of my consciousness, it was beginning to teach me how to read ballet by getting me to follow, and therefore gradually to understand, the logic of its formal dances. I don't remember anything else in Terpischore's variation from 1945 but Alicia Alonso pawing the ground like an elegant horse. Now the wide fourth position, tremendously *contraposto*, from which Terpischore begins her dance proper seems to me almost the most eloquent moment in the whole ballet. I have come to understand the way ballet language works.

My education in ballet proceeded rapidly enough so that within just a few months, as I remember, I was able to follow the expressive thinking in *Concerto Barocco*, a work of 1940, twelve years after *Apollo*, in which there is almost no vestige of this witty and fantastic dance imagery which had so seized my mind in *Apollo*. Since *Serenade* in 1934 Balanchine had gradually been abandoning the special mode of wit and fancy in *Apollo*, which had also been the mode of *The Prodigal Son* (1929) and apparently of *Cotillon* (1933), a lost Balanchine masterpiece which I have never seen. And there is a lot of evidence that this change in style amounted to a deliberate self-criticism. (He seems after the 1972 Stravinsky festival to have lost interest in *Apollo* if not in fact turned quite violently against it, mostly because of its narrative elements, I am sure, but conceivably also because of these strokes of wit and fancy which his taste had long before discarded.) At any rate, the distinctive imagery of the great neo-classic masterpieces made in America is quite different. In his 1945 review of *Concerto Barocco* Denby describes one of its most powerful images: "the final adagio figure before the coda, the ballerina being slid upstage in two or three swoops that dip down and rise a moment into an extension in second—like a receding cry . . . another image that corresponds vividly to the weight of the musical passage. But these 'emotional' figures are strictly formal as dance inventions." This kind of image, figure, movement, choice, event was to become the essential vocabulary of Balanchine's language, and it will be perfectly clear how different it is from the muses' hand-clap in *Apollo*. The image in *Concerto Barocco* is arguably greater, and Balanchine's choice to work almost entirely in the mode of this imagery is probably what made possible the extraordinary breadth and depth of his development as a classical artist. But the imagery of *Apollo* is as beautiful as art can be, and the invitation it extended to me was irresistible. When I first saw *Concerto Barocco*, I was able to experience what Denby had promised I would find at this eloquent moment. But it had taken a lot of learning of ballet vocabulary before I could do so, and my learning was hastened and made exciting by my first experience of *Apollo*. And for this reason this marvelous work has kept a special place in my love—not only for what it is but for what it made possible.

Slide Show:
Evans-Pritchard's African Transparencies
CLIFFORD GEERTZ

THERE ARE some voices that are very easy to imitate, whether for mockery or social climbing, but almost impossible to describe, so particularly inflected, exactly displaced, precisely off-common are they. The East Indian manner in English is perhaps one such; so is Humphrey Bogart's or Louis Armstrong's or Franklin Roosevelt's. They linger in the auditory memory, once heard exasperatingly difficult to forget. Among those which have been significant in anthropology, that of the Oxbridge senior common room is far and away the most important, and there has been no greater master of it than Sir Edward Evan Evans-Pritchard: "E-P."

Because it is so difficult, especially as a written style, to characterize—such adjectives as "assured," "limpid," "measured," "equanimous," "effortless," "superior," "conversational," but beat around its edges—it is necessary to quote a fair patch of the stuff to convey the maddening brilliance of it. Almost any line of E-P, stylistically one of the most homogeneous writers the world has seen, would do—from the opening one of his first major work, the 1937 *Witchcraft, Oracles, and Magic Among the Azande* ("If I seem to have been overlong in publishing a monograph on Zande culture I would plead that I have done my best to write preliminary and partial accounts of Zande customs during the intervals between my expeditions"), to the last of his last, the 1956 *Nuer Religion* ("At this point the theologian takes over from the anthropologist"). But rather than to quote from any of his anthropological writings (more than 350 items, including five major works) I want, in the first instance, to take us into his prose-world by means of some fairly extended excerpts from a fugitive, out-of-category, little noticed piece of his describing his activities as a bush-irregular in the Sudan during the early phases of the Second World War: "Operations on the Akobo and Gila Rivers, 1940–41," published in *The Army Quarterly*, a British military journal, in 1973, the last year of his life.

I do this not just to be perverse or cute nor to unmask him as possessed, as he certainly was, and even defiantly possessed, of a colonial mentality—let he who writes free of his time's imaginings cast the first stone—but because the piece, some nine printed pages overall, displays virtually all the characteristics of E-P's way with discourse in a text in which his substantive and methodological arguments as an anthropologist do not, save glancingly, figure. Nevertheless, "Operations on the Akobo" gives a nutshell image of the limits of E-P's discourse that are, as are anyone's, the Wittgensteinian limits of his world.

But apologies are easy, especially for sins not yet committed; let me get on with it. E-P, then thirty-seven and in the Middle of the Journey, both as to his career and his life, was posted, so the Major-General who introduces the Akobo piece to its military audience instructs us, to one of the least known parts of what was then the frontier between Italian-occupied and British-held territory in East Africa, six hundred miles south of Khartoum, four hundred north of Lake Rudolf, five hundred west of Addis Ababa. E-P himself relates, with customary briskness, how this came to happen in his opening passage:

> Perhaps I should begin by explaining how I became caught up in the events I describe. When war broke out I was at the time a Lecturer in Oxford University and I made an attempt to join the Welsh Guards. The regiment accepted me but I was prevented from training by the university on the grounds—pointless as it seemed to me—that I was in a "reserved occupation". So I went to the Sudan on the excuse of continuing my ethnographical researches there and on arrival joined the Sudan Auxiliary Defence Force. This was just what I wanted and what I could do, for I had made researches in the Southern Sudan for some years and spoke with ease some of its languages, including Nuer and Anuak.

He had, uniquely, ethnographically "been there," and once there again his expertise came rapidly into play:

> Captain Lesslie [the Royal Scots officer in command of the sector, whom, E-P manages to make clear, he did not much care for] attached me to the Gila Force, with instructions to patrol the upper Akobo river and keep an eye on the Anuak of the Adongo region, for no one knew what was happening there. I should explain at this point . . . that the Anuak are a Nilotic people, on a rough estimate 35,000 in number, living along rivers in the Sudan and Ethiopia. They are almost entirely agricultural, tsetse fly preventing the keeping of cattle in most of their country. They have somewhat complicated so-

cial and political institutions, and all that need be said here is that in the eastern . . . part of the country, where the minor operations about to be described took place, there is a king, who keeps his pre-eminence so long as he can retain the royal emblems. If a noble kinsman attacks him and can deprive him of them he loses his crown to the attacker. The . . . Anuak country is remote and difficult to reach, and it can scarcely be said to have been administered . . . in more than name, either by the Anglo-Egyptian . . . or the Ethiopian Government[s]; and its people are warlike and independent.

Arrived, signed-on, his bona fides presented, he collects his guns and his natives and is away immediately from parade-ground captains to the liberty of the bush:

> At Akobo I was issued with fifteen rifles of a last century model and 50 rounds apiece, and told to recruit a force of irregulars from among the Anuak. I took with me . . . seven of the local Anuak as I knew the men personally, though I had little confidence that they would remain with me for long. I decided to recruit the other eight from the . . . Anuak to the east because they knew the area in which we were to operate, had more sense of discipline than the local[s], and had some regard for the opinion of the man who at that time was the Anuak king. . . . Fortunately all Anuak could handle rifles and were fairly accurate shots at very close range, and they did not object to living on the country. With so small a force everything obviously depended on mobility and good intelligence. We moved mostly at night as is the Anuak custom in war. I had the great advantage of having been through the country before . . . and of knowing also the people and their language. I gave a very liberal interpretation to my instructions. . . .

Both British and an anthropologist, he heads directly for that king (though it is the rainy season and the route is largely under water), who is very glad to see him, "for he thought that the Italians would be persuaded by his kinsman and rival . . . who lived in Ethiopia, to attack him and seize the Anuak royal emblems." He recruits eight "lads" from the king's homestead, including the king's brother, later king himself, and sets off to conduct his "minor operations."

> [On 6 November] I started with my force of fifteen Anuak for the upper Akobo. We got through the swamps and high grasses with the utmost difficulty. I received a warm welcome from the inhabitants of

these upstream villages for they remembered me well from my earlier visit. [We intended] to return downstream on the following day, but we learnt that there was a small picquet from the Boma force at Ukwaa. I sent a message to it saying I intended to pay a visit next day, but shortly after the message had gone I received intelligence that an Italian force was advancing toward Ukwaa to attack the picquet so I left for the village at once, arriving opposite it about midnight. The picquet's information, later confirmed from Italian sources, was that a force of native irregulars with a good number of Somali regulars under two Italian officers, probably round about 200 strong, was just outside the village near a rock called Abula, a well-known Anuak landmark. I told the picquet to evacuate Ukwaa and join me on the Sudan side of the river.

He attempts at first to ambush the Italian force, all two hundred of them, and when that fails he trails it as it moves back and forth along the opposite bank, exchanging a few shots with it now and then. Tiring of this, "The Italians sent a message to say that if we did not clear off they would attack us. I sent back a suitable reply." The greater part of the Italian force then departs for its base, leaving a detachment of thirty men or so on the Akobo, which E-P and his band of fifteen then promptly attack. "There was much wild rifle and from the Italian side some machine-gunning and throwing of hand grenades, the total result of which was one Italian casualty. They reported this as an important engagement. They packed up at once . . . and we never saw them again."

His force exhausted from trekking about in the rain on insufficient food and himself down with fever, E-P establishes a camp alongside the river, a break in the action that is matched with one in the narrative as he reflects on the sort of men he was leading and on his manner of leading them:

> I may say here something of the qualities of the Anuak as fighters. They are brave, but become very excited and expose themselves unnecessarily. They like to fire from the hip and when firing from the shoulder do not use the sights, so to conduct a successful skirmish it is necessary to take them right up to the enemy and let them shoot at point-blank range. They must be led. They will go with you anywhere and will not desert you in a scrap if things go badly, but they will not go without you. I found too that it was necessary to consult them before any action and to lead by example rather than by command, for they are rugged individuals and very obstinate. I learnt

that if, after discussion of the course of action I proposed they refused to agree to it, I could attain my object by proceeding to carry out the proposed operation myself, whereupon all eventually followed suit.

Soon recovered, E-P wants to take his little band, now risen to a couple dozen, and capture the Italians' headquarters at Agenga—manned by a force several hundred strong—so as "to break [their] prestige on the Gila." ("I was confident that Agenga could be taken by surprise without much loss of life.") But Lesslie forbids it, sending E-P a few Anuak foot-police "to compensate me for my disappointment." A few days later, some local Anuak tell him that about thirty men from Agenga under an Ethiopian N.C.O. have entered a nearby village:

> This seemed too good an opportunity to be missed. I sent my Anuak to start an attack on the village on the land side while I and the foot-police moved up to it on the river side. The enemy had the advantage of the village ramparts and were assisted by the Anuak population of the village. My Anuak drew enemy fire and enabled the police and myself to get close to the village without being spotted. They afterwards worked round the village to join us in a frontal attack. We crawled under heavy but very wild fire to within point-blank range. Some of my Anuak got into the village and fired the huts and in the confusion created . . . we rushed the position. We had contacted the enemy at 7:30 in the morning and took the village just three hours later. Enemy casualties were eight dead and two wounded. We had no casualties. The Italians reported they had been attacked by fifty [colonial soldiers] and 250 Anuak. . . . The taking of [the village] was a blow to Italian prestige in that part of Anuakland where it was the strongest [and] an encouragement to our supporters among the Anuak, especially as in Anuak fighting among themselves the great object is to take a village from its defenders and destroy it, as we had done.

I will not follow the story of E-P's adventures any further, though the Black-and-White-in-Color charm of it all makes it difficult to resist. The tone, which is what I am after, should be clear, and I will just append, *presto staccato*, a few more quotations, out of context, concerning his view of the Anuak and of himself among them to round out the picture. On the inability of the Italians to get information from the Anuak:

> The Anuak did not like the Italians even though many of them took Italian pay and joined their irregular bands, and they let my force

through the country without warning the enemy, whereas the slightest move in our direction was at once reported, the civilian population acting as self-appointed scouts, sentinels and spies. The Italians tried to get information by threats and promises of rewards and only got nonsense. They did not know how to obtain information from the people by treating them decently.

On the difficulty of disciplining the Anuak ("who were prepared to march and fight but not just to march") away from an immediate scene of action:

> On the way I had the worst trouble I ever had with the Anuak. They said they were completely fed up with this constant marching about the countryside to no purpose and would not go to the Gila again unless I could promise them that there would be a fight when they got there. For security I felt I could not tell them about [a planned air attack there]. Finally I told them that they could come with me . . . or not as they pleased but that I was going there in any case. In the end they followed.

On their courage in action, when properly led:

> For some reason . . . the Italian officer in charge of this detachment withdrew after a short skirmish and left the garrison [Galla tribesmen from southern Ethiopia] to its fate. We killed seventeen irregular troops . . . and wounded a considerable number of those who got away. Unfortunately five women, wives of Galla, and a child, who were in the trenches, were killed also. Two of my Anuak were wounded . . . when we charged the trenches. The Anuak had fought very courageously. They were a dreadful nuisance most of the time but they were good to have around in a fight.

And on the superiority of British officers (never mind Italians) who understand the natives over those who do not:

> Lesslie and I did not see eye to eye about the best way of attacking the post. The Anuak, whose point of view I expressed, thought the venture was a bad bet but that it might come off if we approached the enemy position by night and attacked at dawn, extending when the fighting began. Lesslie wanted to act more in accordance with textbook tactics and attack by daylight. As he was in command we had to do things his way.

This, of course, ended badly, and the Anuak, "who protested strongly," were ordered to withdraw. The center sections, "who had no British officer with them . . . bolted," and the British were surrounded. "Without the Anuak we would, I think, have been lost, but following their guidance we bolted into the long grass away from the river and taking our wounded with us [escaped]." Lesslie himself is killed, we are informed in a clause, a short time later; but the Italians are finally cleared out of the Akobo-Gila area, and E-P, tired, three stone lighter, and plagued by unhealing wounds, is dispatched, against his inclinations, on a six weeks' march up the Gila into Ethiopia to demonstrate British domination.

> My instructions were to show the flag so I decided to do so in the most liberal sense. My column was preceded on the march by a large Union Jack at the end of a pole and this was planted in all the villages where we camped.

They are, as usual, glad to see him wherever he goes—save in the village in which Italian headquarters had been, where the people flee into the bush. "Coming back through the swamps," he concludes his tale, in his finest *Boy's Own Paper* manner, "was a real hard job, but on the whole the trip was interesting."

It would be as unwise to assume that Evans-Pritchard was anything less than intensely aware of the figure he is cutting here as it would be to swallow him or his story whole; the tale has clearly been through too many pub-recitals to be the offhand account it so industriously pretends to be. What is interesting is how that effect, something common to all of E-P's work whatever the subject or the intent, is accomplished and why it is sought. This easy certitude of perception is a difficult thing to bring off rhetorically, especially when one is dealing, as E-P was and knew that he was throughout his whole career, with precisely the sort of materials that most gravely challenge it. It is one thing to write about the fenced-off gardens of English poetry in sentences that all end, as Denis Donoghue has written (in *Ferocious Alphabets*) with respect to another votary of this sidelong approach to prose, Dame Helen Gardner, with an implied "of course." It is quite another to write in such sentences about witchcraft or anarchy, or for that matter about scrambling around minor tributaries of the White Nile with pigheaded Scotsmen, clownish Italians, and mercurial Blacks.

It is, again, very difficult, simply because they are so backgrounded, blended into the familiar "between us" hum of educated speech, to isolate the means by which this in fact quite elaborate text-building strategy is pursued. But it is clear that it rests most fundamentally on the existence of a very strictly drawn and very carefully observed narrative contract between writer and reader. The presumptions that connect the author and his audience, presumptions that are social, cultural, and literary at once, are so strong and so pervasive, so deeply institutionalized, that very small signals can carry very big messages. As Donoghue goes on to say, regarding Dame Helen and what he calls more generally "gunboat linguistics":

> The reader doesn't need to have the point explained, a nod will do, and he's expected to be gratified by the evidence that he's deemed worthy of this attention. The sentence has the inflection of a glance. It helps if the writer is an Oxford don; better still if he gives the impression of being such a person by birth, class, nature, and nurture, as well as by notable academic achievement and the publication of such a work as the one the reader is now holding. Then you can appeal to shared values, good taste, fine discernment, which make communication a privilege congenially offered and accepted.

In line with my anxiety not to be seen as seeking to unmask, demystify, deconstruct, or otherwise belittle my "authors," all of whom, and E-P especially, I hold in high regard, whatever our differences in social attitudes, I must say immediately that I do not share what Donoghue cheerfully admits to be his Irishman's dislike of this mode of discourse. (Though I see what he means about Dame Helen, who has raised the preemptive "We" to unsuspected heights.) Indeed, it seems to me a theater of language of enormous power and, in ethnography, the most powerful yet constructed. Certainly, with the appearance of the so-called British school of social anthropology, which is held together far more by this manner of going about things in prose than it is by any sort of consensual theory or settled method, it has become the most prominent. (What Radcliffe-Brown, E-P, Fortes, Gluckman, Leach, Firth, Richards, Nadel, Lienhardt, Douglas, Peters, Mair, and Needham share, aside from rivalry, is tone—though naturally, some of them are greater masters of it than others.) Even most Americans sound, by now, a bit like "Operations on the Akobo."

In any case, no matter how carefully the species markings of this sort of "of-course" discourse are camouflaged by a studied air of unstudiedness (that is one of the major markings: everything—those Galla women and children, for example—is too casual by half), once one realizes that they are in fact there, they are not all that difficult to spot. Some, like the extreme simplicity and regularity of subsentence punctuation (as few commas as possible, mechanically placed, and hardly any semicolons at all: readers are expected to know when to breathe) are only visible in the written texts. Others, like the related avoidance of clause embedding, amounting almost to a phobia, can perhaps be sensed even aurally. In the writing there is now and then a dash or a parenthesis, but they are also rare, as, apart from their use in introducing quoted text, are colons. The passion for simple subject-predicate-object sentences, unmodified and undecorated, is intense. ("For you," as Clemenceau is supposed to have instructed his amanuensis, "there are only nouns and verbs; I will take care of such adjectives as may prove necessary.") Though E-P spoke at least French and Italian fluently, there are virtually no foreign phrases— aside, of course, from native vernacular—in his ethnographic writings; though he was very broadly educated, literary allusions play little role; and though he was the professional's professional in self-presentation, the absence of jargon, anthropological or any other, is so nearly total as to seem ostentatious. The only speech act of any frequency is the flat declarative. Quizzical interrogatives, hedging conditionals, or musing apostrophes simply don't appear.

On higher levels of organization, the mechanisms are equally apparent and even more powerful. The homogeneity of tone I have already remarked upon—a point-blank rifle exchange is described in the same unheightened language, the famed "middle voice" of educated England, as is a tramp through high grass. There is always a clear and fixed point of view even—no ventriloquism here—when it represents other outlooks that are at issue: "In Anuak fighting among themselves the great object is to take a village from its defenders and destroy it." "It would be quite contrary to Nuer thought [this from *Nuer Religion*], as I have remarked, and it would seem even absurd to them, to say that sky, moon, rain, and so forth are in themselves, singly or collectively, God." There is the suppression of any sign of the struggle with words. Everything that is said is clearly said, confidently and without fuss; verbally, at any rate, there are no blanks to fill in or dots to join, what you see is what you get, deep reading is not encouraged. And there is the pervasive personal distancing by means of a constant play of the lightest of light irony: nothing really matters enough, not even the Union Jack, for which all this fighting and dying is taking place, to be fully serious about it. Or, more accurately, it is precisely because it does all matter so much that one must not be fully serious about it. Even the strange is more interesting and amusing than it is disturbing or threatening. It bends our categories, but it does not break them.

It is this last, so it seems to me, that this text-building strategy—shall we call it "Akobo Realism"?—and the delicate tactics that relentlessly subserve it, are all about. The point, the overriding point of every image, every elegance, every nod, is to demonstrate that nothing, no matter how singular, resists reasoned description.

"[The] history of social anthropology," E-P writes toward the beginning of his lecture for the BBC, "Fieldwork and the Empirical Tradition," perhaps the most explicit statement of his view of his vocation, "may be regarded as the substitution, by slow gradations, of informed opinion about primitive peoples for uninformed opinion, and the stage reached in this process at any time is roughly relative to the amount of organized knowledge available." The informing of informed opinion (those discerning readers, with whom the "as you will see" contract is in force) in the matter of primitives is anthropology's appointed task, as other disciplines inform it about Homer, Italian painting, or the English civil war; and though it is an extraordinarily difficult task, it is only practically so.

There are language barriers to be crossed. ("Many primitive languages are almost unbelievably difficult to learn," as E-P points out.) Taxing conditions of work must be endured. (The anthropologist is "all alone, cut off from the companionship of men of his own race and culture, and is dependent on the natives around him for company, friendship, and human understanding.") And personal biases are not wholly eradicable. ("One can only interpret what one sees in terms of one's own experience and of what one is.") But the barriers can be crossed. ("[When] one has fully understood the meaning of all the words of [the natives'] language in all their situations of reference one has finished one's study of the society.") The conditions can be transcended. ("Anthropological fieldwork . . . requires a certain kind of character and temperament. . . . To succeed in [it] a man must be able to abandon himself [to native life] without reserve.") The biases can be neutralized ("If allowances are made for the personality of the writer, and if we consider that in the entire range of anthropological studies the effects of these personal differences tend to correct each other, I do not think that we need worry unduly over this problem in so far as the reliability of anthropological findings is in question.") We need not, indeed, worry unduly much about anything, except sticking manfully to it: "It is almost impossible for a person who knows what he is looking for and how to look for it, to be mistaken about the facts if he spends two years among a small and culturally homogeneous people doing nothing else but studying their way of life."

Transferred to the ethnographic page this attitude leads to a string of clean, well-lighted judgments, unconditional statements so perspicuously presented that only the invincibly uninformable will think to resist them. One can find this sort of first-strike assertiveness almost everywhere in E-P's work. In *The Sanusi of Cyrenaica*: "The Bedouin certainly have a profound faith in God and trust in the destiny He has prepared for them." In *The Nuer*: "In a strict sense, the Nuer have no law." In *Witchcraft, Oracles, and Magic Among the Azande*: "Azande undoubtedly perceive a difference between what we consider the workings of nature on the one hand and the workings of magic and ghosts and witchcraft on the other hand." In *Nuer Religion*: "Certainly one cannot speak of any specifically religious emotion among the Nuer." In *Kinship and Marriage Among the Nuer*: "With rare exceptions, I found Nuer women well content with their station and that their husbands and other men treated them with respect."

The question here is not the truth of such statements (though I have my doubts about those Bedouins and those women), nor does Evans-Pritchard fail to support them with extensive and detailed evidence, carefully weighed. They are not obiter dicta, however much they may sound like them when torn from context. The question is how does a constant rain of such promulgatory declarations (for one encounters, literally, a half-dozen per half-page) produce (as, particulars aside, it clearly does) a believable account of Lybians or Nilotes, or, in other hands, perhaps not quite as sure, Australians, Polynesians, Burmans, or East Africans. How (why? in what way? of what?) does all this resolute informing inform?

Let me first answer this compound question in the E-P manner, with a pair of flat, unshaded assertions—one concerning how he does it, the other concerning what he does—and then, in my own manner, unflatten these assertions, and shade them, with tendentious references to his work. How he does it: The outstanding characteristic of E-P's approach to ethnographical exposition and the main source of his persuasive power is his enormous capacity to construct visualizable representations of cultural phenomena—anthropological transparencies. What he does: The main effect, and the main intent, of this magic lantern ethnography is to demonstrate that the established frames of social perception, those upon which we ourselves instinctively rely, are fully adequate to whatever oddities the transparencies may turn out to picture.

Though it has not, so far as I can discover, been explicitly commented upon, and certainly never analyzed, the intensely visual quality of Evans-Pritchard's style is so apparent to anyone who has read much of him that a few allusions to particular images is sufficient to call up entire books of his.

There is the most famous of all, the collapsing granary scene from *Witchcraft, Oracles, and Magic*—those hapless Zande forever taking refuge from the sun under a storehouse precisely at the point at which termites have finally eaten their way through its supports—fixing in our minds the whole colliding causes and unfortunate events theory of witchcraft E-P develops there. There are the ox and cucumber, and the twins and birds ideograms from *Nuer Religion* that virtually every writer on sacrifice or totemism or "primitive thought" seems obliged to conjure with. There are the endless cattle celebrations, the flooding grasslands with homesteads perched on mounds or strung along sand ridges, and the "tall, long-limbed, and narrow headed" spear wavers "strut[ting] about like lords of the earth, which, indeed, they consider themselves to be" of *The Nuer* that makes theirs perhaps the most seeable society in the whole of ethnography. Leopard-skin chiefs, rubbing boards, dance duels, beehive cattle byres . . . hip-shooting, fired huts, and paraded flags: they all flip by, driving the argument home.

And again, E-P is himself quite conscious of all this, as aware as we are (or would be if we paid more attention to such matters than we usually do) that his natural idiom is, so to speak, optical, his "being there" signature passionately visual:

> When I think of the sacrifices I have witnessed in Nuerland [this from *Nuer Religion*] there are two objects I see most vividly and which sum up for me the sacrificial rite: the spear brandished in the right hand of the officiant as he walks up and down past the victim delivering his invocation, and the beast awaiting its death. It is not the figure

of the officiant or what he says which evokes the most vivid impression, but the brandished spear in his right hand.

Even when it is not a question of direct experience the language remains intensely visual, as in his account, based on informant memories, in "Zande Kings and Princes" of a nineteenth-century king:

> Gubudwe was a short man, though not excessively short. . . . [He] was stout also, not, however, unpleasantly stout. He was stout with the stoutness of a man whose flesh is loose with it. His breasts protruded like those of a woman, but not altogether like a woman's for they were a man's breasts. His wrists were wrinkled with fat, and his forearm was like a man's shank. His eyes were little protruding eyes and they sparkled like stars. When he looked at a man in anger they were terrible; then they went grey like ashes.

And this penchant, not to call it something stronger than that, for a seer's rhetoric is hardly confined to his verbal text, as anyone who looks into his works will be immediately aware.

There are, in the first place, those astonishing photographs, which though they may seem initially to be your standard, "note the clan marks" ethnographic snapshots—"initiation ceremony," "natives fishing," and so on—are, with few exceptions, not so much illustrative as emblematical. Frankly, even ostentatiously posed, so that they seem almost like still lifes, objects arranged for ruminant viewing (a tall, naked cowherd leaning negligently, legs crossed, against the tension of a tether; a similarly negligent, similarly naked, standing girl, sucking on an elaborate pipe; a seated blind man, hands folded, cradling his spear between his elbow and his neck), or when that is not possible, meticulously composed (tensed warriors flashing spears at a wedding dance; massive cattle, clustering, bovine, in a downpour; a boy, arms raised like great curving horns, singing praise songs to his ox), the photographs stand irregularly among the word paintings, unreferred to, barely captioned ("Youth," "August Shower," "A Maiden, Smoking Pipe"), and for the most part singly, making points of their own.

There are, too, the line drawings. Evans-Pritchard is one of the few modern ethnographers—quite possibly he is the only one—who seems to have grasped the fact that the photograph has not only not rendered the sketch obsolete but, as moving pictures have done for the photograph, has pointed up its comparative advantage. His books are set off by, again, self-standing, unexplicated sketches ("cupping horn," "neck rests," "instrument used in wedding invocations"), rimming, like visual footnotes, the edges of the text. (There are very few verbal footnotes and, notoriously, virtually no professional citations at all. "The literature" is another thing one is expected already to know.)

And there is, finally, the diagramming; the representation—especially in *The Nuer,* that anthropological geometry book—of social structure in terms of a set of elementary plane figures: squares, rectangles, triangles, trees, circles, arcs, rays, matrices, plus of course the more standard kin charts, graphs, and sketch maps, which also take on, in his hands, a Euclidean look. The blurred edges of social things—villages, tribes, seasons, cattle claims, war, bad magic and good—are drawn onto the page as straight lines and angular shapes, firmly bounded, thoroughly definite. As Ivan Karp has pointed out, the argument of *The Nuer*—essentially that society is an enmeshment of relational systems—is importantly held together by the repetition of a single figure, an equilateral triangle, first as a representation of the space-time system, then of the lineage system, and finally of the political system. A similar point could be made about the subsectioned (and sub-subsectioned) rectangle, which is used to represent tribal organization, intertribal relations, and the feud.

The vignette, the photograph, the sketch, the diagram, are the organizing forces of E-P's ethnography, which moves by means of decisively imaged ideas, coheres more as a landscape coheres than as a myth does, or a diary, and is dedicated, above all things, to making the puzzling plain. His world is a noonday world in which sharply outlined figures, most of them more than a little singular, act in describable ways against perceptible backgrounds. If he is "the Stendhal of anthropology," as Mary Douglas suggests in a book which otherwise takes a rather different view of him than mine (she thinks of him as a kind of homemade social psychologist), it is not because of his "penetrating" sense of "the delicate strain and balance between desires." (I do not see that he had such a sense.) It is because, like la Sanseverina, his Anuak, Zande, Nuer, Dinka, Shilluk, and Bedouin, and in his texts he himself, subsist in an absolute light.

All this drastic clarity—luminous, dazzling, stunning . . . blinding—is, to drop the other shoe of my argument, not just an adjunct of Evans-Pritchard's ethnography, a stylistic quirk or a bit of rhetorical decor added on to make the facts less wearying; it is the very heart of it. Here is, not a world of equatorial shadows and jungle darkness, as for example, that of Lévi-Strauss's *Tristes Tropiques*. It is, rather, one of manifest vitality, distinct and immediate; recognizable, strangely reminiscent, familiar even, if but looked at steadily enough.

As Ernest Gellner has remarked, the abiding concerns of E-P's work, the puzzles to which he again returns—the maintenance of cognitive order in the absence of science, the maintenance of political order in the absence of the state, and (though Gellner doesn't mention it) the maintenance of spiritual order in the absence of a church—are aspects of a single concern: how what we take to be the foundations of genuinely human life manage to exist without the assistance of our institutions. E-P's classic studies all begin with the discovery of a lack of something cultural we ourselves have: our distinction between natural and moral causation, among the Zande; our structure of state-enforced law and management of violence, among the Nuer; or, in *Nuer Religion*, "dogma, liturgy . . . sacrament . . . cult and mythology." And they all end with a discovery of something—witchcraft, segmentary organization, or a modalistic image of divinity—that works well enough instead.

It is this, finally, that Evans-Pritchard's text-building strategy, "Akobo realism," accomplishes, or anyway seeks to accomplish. It seeks the disenstrangement of apparently bizarre, irrational, anarchic, heathenish ideas, feelings, practices, values, and so on, not by setting fanciful cultural representations of them out in formal universal orderings but by talking about them in the same equanimous, "of course" tone in which one talks about one's own values, practices, feelings and the like. Powerful for "including out," it is, that tone and the assumptions and judgments it projects, equally powerful for including in, and indeed for doing both at the same time. In E-P's hands, that is precisely what it does for his various sorts of Nilotes. Depicting them as not other but otherwise—sensible enough when you get to know them, but with their own way of doing things—causes them to appear to differ from ourselves only in things that do not really matter. "Dreadful nuisance[s] most of the time but . . . good to have around in a fight."

The marvel of this rather dialectical approach to ethnography is that it validates the ethnographer's form of life at the same time as it justifies those of his subjects, and that it does the one by doing the other. The adequacy of the cultural categories of, in this case, university England to provide a frame of intelligible reasonings, creditable values, and familiar motivations for such oddities as poison oracles, ghost marriages, blood feuds, and cucumber sacrifices recommends those categories as of somehow more than parochial importance. Whatever personal reasons E-P may have had for being so extraordinarily anxious to picture Africa as a logical and prudential place, orderly, straightforward, and levelheaded, firmly modeled and open to view (and there is some reason to believe he did have some fairly powerful ones), in doing so he constructed a forceful argument for the general authority of a certain conception of life. If it could undarken Africa it could undarken anything.

This bringing of Africans into a world conceived in deeply English terms, and confirming thereby the dominion of those terms, must, however, not be misunderstood. It is not ethnocentricity, except in the trivial sense that all views must be someone's views, all voices come from somewhere. In contrast to what has sometimes been said of him, E-P did not make "his" Anuak, Nuer, and so on into black Englishmen. They exist as fully realized as any peoples in the ethnographic literature, having their own weight in their own space. It is not "they are just like us" that E-P is telling his appointed audience waiting respectfully for informed instruction; it is that their differences from us, however dramatic, do not, finally, count for much. On the Akobo as on the Isis, men and women are brave and cowardly, kind and cruel, reasonable and foolish, loyal and perfidious, intelligent and stupid, vivid and boring, believing and indifferent, and better the one than the other.

"The least He that is in England," it has been famously said (though we should want now to add an explicit "She") "has a life to live as the greatest He." The extension of that sentiment beyond England to Africa, and further (perhaps even to Italy, though the matter is difficult), is the purpose of Evans-Pritchard's slide-show. And whatever this is—presumptuous, romantic, or merely wildly inadequate ("the English Ideology rides again")—it is neither smug nor ungenerous nor uncompassionate. Nor, for that matter, is it untrue.

———————

But the question may not be so much what is true as what is doable. The confidence that Akobo realism gave to Evans-Pritchard seems less and less available to many anthropologists. They are confronted by societies part modern, part traditional; by fieldwork conditions of staggering ethical complexity; by an army of wildly contrasting approaches to description and analysis; and by subjects who can (and do) speak for themselves. They are also harassed by grave inner uncertainties, amounting almost to a sort of epistemological hypochondria, concerning how one can know that anything one says about other forms of life is as a matter of fact so. This loss of confidence, and the crisis in ethnographic writing that goes with it, is contemporary and is due to contemporary developments. It is how things stand with us these days. It is not how they stood for Sir Edward Evan Evans-Pritchard.

Writing at the Computer
REGINALD GIBBONS

THE SUDDEN availability of microcomputers in only the last few years seems to bring with it a discernible change in what might be called the psychology of composition. Computer technology is characterized by extreme rapidity of change: in the months in which I have worked on this essay many new sorts of both computers and software have appeared, and more will appear between my finishing this essay and its publication. I want, however, to discuss those aspects of writing at the computer that are fundamental and not likely to change greatly.

It's a temptation to call my thoughts "Writing in the Age of Electronic Reproduction," to echo Walter Benjamin's prescient essay, published in 1936, "The Work of Art in the Age of Mechanical Reproduction." Replacing the noun "work" with the gerund "writing" may seem a slight change, but it hints that the parallel is only apparent. Benjamin argued that the technological ability to reproduce works of art in quantity not only had affected our way of perceiving unique original works but also would influence future social and political life, through a largely irrational and destructive substitution of image for substance. His essay remains a more telling commentary on recent American television politics than much that has been written subsequently:

> Since the innovations of camera and recording equipment make it possible for the orator to become audible and visible to an unlimited number of persons, the presentation of the man of politics before the camera and recording equipment becomes paramount. . . . Radio and film not only affect the function of the professional actor but likewise the function of those who also exhibit themselves before this mechanical equipment, those who govern. Though their tasks may be different, the change affects equally the actor and the ruler. The trend is toward establishing controllable and transferable skills under certain social conditions. This results in a new selection, a selection before the equipment from which the star and the dictator emerge victorious.

Benjamin's essay and the present topic might suggest an analogy between the way the technology of modern printing, photography, and film has changed our perceptions of original works of art, and the way in which the computer has changed our perception of the printed (or, more generally, the mechanically preserved) word. But the analogy turns out to be false for three reasons. First, the written word had already been transformed before the coming of the computer by the sheer quantity of words that modern bureaucratic and commercial society produces. This flood of language can in itself be regarded as the progenitor of the computer's application to words and texts, for the computer is from this point of view merely a technological response to the need for a faster way of processing information; that is, of producing and disseminating new written material quickly enough for it to ride that flood, and, conversely, of searching the flood for the particular floating bits that are wanted at a given moment so that they can be manipulated. By contrast, earlier there was no analogous artistic flood which called photography and film into being, nor an analogous flood of nonartistic images. It seems significant to the current state of the written word that the largest publisher in America is reputed to be the Citibank corporation.

Second, an analogy with the "mechanical reproduction of the work of art" is false because, while the computer certainly changes the manner in which written works are accessed by readers, for the most part it has only affected the productive methods of those persons already immersed in the flow of information involved in industrial production, sales, management, governing, research, and so on. The rest of us have been affected in our roles as consumer, voter, and so on. Most people don't employ the computer to generate or manipulate information; rather, they read information that has already been manipulated, often by computer. I mean first of all manipulated in the simply mechanical sense, in newspaper offices, for example. But also, inevitably, the manipulation of texts follows from the manipulation of meaning. This was no less true, after all, in the age of scribes and copyists. Whatever the computer's usefulness as a writing and editing machine, it does not materially create a new sort of writer, as photography and film created new kinds of artists.

Third, Benjamin concerned himself with how the reception of works of art was affected by mechanical reproduction. Photography certainly did influence how paintings would be conceived (as, for instance, in Caillebotte's famous *On the Europe Bridge*, which, like a cropped photo or a photo of persons in motion, truncates the left-hand figure of a man), and it called into profound question the value of representational painting. But Benjamin's point is that mechanical reproduction drastically changed the accessibility of painted works to audiences by making the original almost unnecessary and by changing the accepted view of what was valuable in a painting—making it the evidence not so much of the work of the artist's own hand or the historical circumstances of a work's creation and preservation, as of those visual qualities least affected by mechanical reproduction: theme, motif, pictorial and narrative interest, ideological content, and so forth; not of uniqueness but of wide emotional or ideological applicability, let's say. The painting not only was influenced by the photograph, but also itself became a kind of photograph, since it subsequently became quite well known in reproductions.

Since the computer's development into a small form that is powerful and not remarkably expensive, it has indeed affected both the production and the distribution of written texts. And if it has not in fact created a new kind of literary artist, it has affected the way in which one artistic medium, language, is manipulated. But to complicate matters, the written works disseminated by computers tend to be valued most for their factual, statistical, or rhetorical (promotional) nature; few if any persons use computers only in order to read literary works. And while the computer permits manipulation, especially through creating a false authenticity for documents, it is mostly with the process of writing, not the dissemination of written works, that my remarks are concerned. (It would lead far, if interestingly, afield, to meditate on the startling fusion of falsified computer memoranda and distracting, meretricious TV-screen celebrity in the recent case of Lieutenant Colonel Oliver North, who testified before a joint Congressional committee.)

I once borrowed a technologically ancient portable typewriter whose huge black cabinet unlatched and ingeniously unfolded to make a typing table with short legs, on which the tall narrow black typewriter itself, unbudgeable and iconic, sat as if on an altar. The friend who loaned it to me had dubbed it "John Reed's typewriter." The appropriateness of his tying the typewriter to the observer of social and political revolution, and even to change generally, seems all too apparent. Now I see also that this typewriter was a transitional device between the earliest typing machines and the portable computer. Or, as Borges might have said, the portable computer has changed the portable typewriter into its precursor. The portable typewriter reflected the writer's desire to carry his writing machine with him everywhere, into the field—to bring the convenience of the machine and, perhaps more important, the validation of mechanized script to the immediacy of the process of composition.

It's interesting to recall the reactions of the poets T. S. Eliot, Ezra Pound, or Charles Olson to using the typewriter, and their work habits at it. They broke with the earlier habit and image of the poet; they seem to have enjoyed the relative ease of composition and the freedom apparently conferred by the rapid producing of an intelligibly scripted draft. Pound's and Olson's poems and letters depend dramatically on the typewriter, which Olson thought would revolutionize the process of writing. His definition of *process* in his famous 1950 essay "Projective Verse" associates it with such impulses as

> get on with it, keep moving, keep in, speed, the nerves, their speed, the perceptions, theirs, the acts, the split second acts, the whole business, keep it moving as fast as you can, citizen. And if you set up as a poet, USE USE USE the process at all points, in any given poem always, always one perception must must must MOVE, IN-STANTER, ON ANOTHER!

Perhaps here the significance of using "writing," a gerund, as opposed to Benjamin's motionless substantive "the work of art," is clearer.

The typewriter worked on an expanse of paper of a given size; Olson, surely not coincidentally, conceived the poet's work as one of composing, as he put it, in a "field," which I take to be in part a backwards reflection, a retroinfluence, on the creative imagination, of a mechanical requirement of the machine. While poems composed in the memory or by hand may have suffered various constraints, the size of standard paper was not one of them: Keats and countless others scribbled on any available scrap; Poe glued sheets end to end to make possible a continuous manuscript of a long poem. With the typewriter also came a difficulty in throwing off the expectation of seeing printed works mostly in books—which can be inferred from the passing mention in the 1911 *Encyclopaedia Britannica* of an early typewriter designed to type in the pages of a blank bound book. This is a kind of late, fleeting echo of the perceptual limits of the first printers and their readers, which required the earliest printed books to resemble manuscripts. Olson's ideas show us another moment of transition, from the manuscript to the typescript.

Olson's metaphor of the field suggests both movement through a defined space and the placement of objects within that space. He describes the typewriter's advantages this way:

> From the machine has come one gain not yet sufficiently observed or used, but which leads directly on toward projective verse and its consequences. It is the advantage of the typewriter that, due to its rigidity and its space precisions, it can, for a poet, indicate exactly the breath, the pauses, the suspensions even of syllables, the juxtapositions even of parts of phrases, which he intends. For the first time the poet has the stave and bar a musician has had.

But it was even more than precision and the notion of writing as process that seemed to attract Olson. Some of the evident pleasure Olson and Pound got from their frequent use, in poems and personal letters, of slang, nonce spellings, and other linguistic high jinks, suggests a boyish delight in the little shock of seeing these words typed at the very instant they are used, because, even as late as the 1950s, such orthographic exuberance still implied defiance of the conformity of correctly spelled words in published work. This revolution was meant to be fun, a highly significant contrast to the accepted use of the typewriter as an office machine.

The barest history of the typewriter is itself revealing. The pre–World War I, Eleventh Edition of the *Encyclopaedia Britannica*, with an amenable tone that suggests a mild fascination with mechanical ingenuity and even a slightly exasperated but affectionate familiarity with the machines, devotes three columns of history, description, and illustrations to the subject. While patents for typewriters of some sort appear as early as 1714, it was not until the mass-produced Remingtons appeared in America after 1878 that the machine could be regarded as an available technological reality. (The same company manufactured guns.) The encyclopedia article gives no explicit information about the alteration of social and economic life—business and law, for instance—by the typewriter. And in 1975 *The New Columbia Encyclopedia* summarizes the same history and adds an approving comment on the electric typewriter, which dates from 1935, but also says nothing about the effects of this extraordinarily momentous invention on modern life. Can we expect the microcomputer to occasion no more pondering than this in future reference works? A contrast is provided in any number of magazines and books on the personal computer, where the question of the machine's influence on its user often arises, if not exactly within a context of critical analysis. For, of course, owned and transported like a typewriter, a microcomputer— with powers which only a few years ago were not possessed by individuals but only by institutional mainframe computers—brings with it an even greater shift in the habits of writing and reading than the typewriter ever caused.

The anonymous *Britannica* writer, apparently with firsthand experience at the typewriter, noted with a tone of knowing superiority that although the machines then in use did not always make it possible to see immediately what one had typed, "to the practised operator it is not a matter of great moment whether the writing is always in view . . . for he should as little need to test the accuracy of his performance by constant inspection as the piano-player needs to look at the notes to discover whether he has struck the right ones." This passage suggests two observations on both the typewriter and the personal computer.

First, the machine imposes change on the writer. The *Britannica*'s analogy, depending on the word "keyboard," is perfectly false. Appropriate verbs are necessary: I play the piano and I use the typewriter, not vice versa. If I perform music, it is the performance of a piece of music; if I perform at the typewriter, I am judged by my bare mechanical competence in the accurate typing of words, while my performance at the piano, if it is to have any value, must amount to considerably more than not playing wrong notes. The typewriter sounds no audible notes, and the gradual mastery of it does not depend on the operator's immediately seeing, as the pianist immediately hears, the error of an individual key, or note, when it is struck, but on his perfecting a routine positioning and use of the fingers. The piano, vehicle of an art of interpretation, has as its end the presentation of a perfectly performed work experienced in time; the typewriter has as its end an increased speed in the accurate recording of information for the sake of some future moment of reading. Olson's comparison of poet to musician, with regard to a standard notation available to each, is not so far from the *Britannica* writer's false analogy, even though Olson is comparing notation, not performance.

The encyclopedia writer's attitude is that of one who would exhort operators and, as likely, their bosses to fulfill the utilitarian purpose of the machine with no reference to the person using it except his or her accuracy. That is, the mechanical precision of the machine is transferred backward, by analogy, to become the operator's responsibility for accuracy. The person's utility in the workplace becomes an adjunct to the machine's capabilities, rather than the other way around. Historical improvements in the pianoforte made possible richer composition and performance; improvements in the typewriter made possible greater speed. While changes in the piano created new possibilities of playing, the changes in the typewriter imposed new ways of fulfilling the jobs of scribe and clerk.

Of course the computer in its turn seems to promise great savings in labor for the operator. Yet one of the most common conclusions of those who work with personal computers is that they do not always accomplish what was hoped for by those who developed or disseminated them: that they would improve efficiency—at least, not as efficiency is most simply envisioned. For the first aspect of the personal computer is that, while it does save mental and physical labor in some impressive ways, it also creates labor: the labor of learning to use the machine and its changing software, and the labor of learning and performing a variety of computer housekeeping tasks necessary if what has been written and analyzed and computed is to be identified, organized for ready retrieval, prepared for transmission over phone lines, "encrypted" and "decrypted," updated, copied, sorted and otherwise manipulated, transformed into other forms, protected against loss, and so on.

Like the typewriter, then, the computer not only imposes a certain amount of machine-specific work on its operator, but also demands a certain alteration in work habits, an adjustment to the machine—even though the machine does not depend entirely on the manic exigencies of office or factory for the authority to enforce such changes, but enforces them itself, through its operational requirements, even on the solitary writer. If the early typist was chided for wanting to see the letters he had typed, then the computer user may be chided—by those more familiar with its use and more influenced by its nature—for wanting to be able simply to speak to the computer and get it to do what is wanted. Indeed, programs and equipment that allow the computer to respond to spoken commands, and to issue spoken responses, already exist, but they cannot yet be applied to any but the most basic computer tasks. Instead, the operator must learn much: the computer responds to programs and, within these, to typed commands or possibilities designated with an electronic pointer manipulated either with the keyboard or with a movable "mouse" beside it, the animal designation (it's Mickey!) intended to make the device as welcome as a helpful little toy attached to the more ambiguous—half helping, half threatening—machine.

We might have noted, above, that it took a surprising number of years from the invention of the typewriter and its widespread use in business and government for the phenomenological implications of this writing machine to come fully to consciousness in Olson—who, as a poet, saw its usefulness in fulfilling a need of no consequence to office workers. One may suppose that this long delay was imposed by the very thoroughness of the typewriter's subordination of its operator. It was Olson, a poet but one who knew offices, who conceived in theoretical terms a higher purpose of usefulness for the typewriter. One wonders whether the computer will find its Olson—not only a creative writer who will link his or her work inextricably to the nature of the machine, and whose habits of composition will thus in some fundamental way be determined by the machine, but also one who produces work of substance whose essential nature validates such a link. And even Olson's peculiar esthetic of typography seems to have died with him; later poets who acknowledge his effect on their own work have not had much to say about typewriters.

***

The design of office machines responds to a desire for efficiency. Tied to the development of talking computers, the recent development of "user-friendly" "artificial intelligence" programming that enables the computer to respond to simple typed English commands and requests seems to be an acquiescence to the partial failure, so far, of the inefficient "interface" between computer and user. For now, if the many different available interfaces are to be successful, some shift in the human operator's attitude is required, and it involves a new vocabulary. The common substitution of *word-processing* for *writing* may be meant to suggest only the computer's ability to manipulate words and texts in various ways. But the neologism establishes languages as a kind of quantifiable material to be manipulated by computation. *Compute* comes from Latin roots that pertain to mental operation, whereas *write* derives from roots—which we will look at in a moment—that suggest a materiality, a physicality, a kind of action. Thus efficiency has its own nomenclature, which redefines both things and language itself.

In Western industrialized cultures, efficiency is one of what Douglas Hofstadter, citing the biologists Jacques Monod and Richard Dawkins, calls *memes* (the word is Dawkins's). A meme is a "self-replicating idea" that survives by causing itself to be imitated and thus established successfully in many "host" minds; the analogy is to a virus. Hofstadter quotes Dawkins's book, *The Selfish Gene:*

> Examples of memes are tunes, ideas, catch-phrases, clothes fashions, ways of making pots or of building arches. Just as genes propagate themselves in the gene pool by leaping from body to body via sperms or eggs, so memes propagate themselves in the meme pool by leaping from brain to brain via a process which, in the broad sense, can be called imitation.

The meme of efficiency—an entire set of related concepts and goals that in our society is powerfully tied to machines—has been extraordinarily successful in establishing itself. As one of those infected by it, I can at once diagnose and even disapprove of my infection and yet continue at the same time to benefit from and even occasionally enjoy it. After all, I *am* infected, which means that efficiency has found a hospitable spot in my mind.

Monod had written that the success of certain memes comes from "preexisting structures in the mind, among them ideas already implanted by culture, but also undoubtedly certain innate structures which we are hard put to identify." The quest for artificial intelligence, the desire to create computer programs that will produce such refined computational responses and inquiries that their aggregate will resemble what we call intelligence in ourselves, is one of several powerful memes in the computer culture, including notions revolving around complex efficiency, speed of calculation, and miniaturization. These are the very memes that most touch the writer at his or her computer, too, and may well require an adjustment which, for all its lightness or subtlety, substantially alters how one writes, and at some deep level, what one writes. (I have heard a public relations person complain about what was in reality a decent piece of writing by saying that it needed to be more user-friendly, and I suppose this evidences a thoroughgoing acceptance by the unwitting flack of a quality desired properly only in a machine.)

A second observation follows from the *Britannica* author's comment on typist and pianist. In what *manner* does the computer alter the computist? It frustrates a routine expectation by denying to the unhabituated user something he or she would certainly have taken for granted: physical access at any time to the tangible body of what has been typed. First of all, the writer is no longer typing the document; it is not the purpose of typing at the computer keyboard to produce a legible, nice-looking copy of a document. Neither metal nor ink nor paper nor even plastic comes into play. That task has been automated and at a later moment is directed by the computer itself, and called *printing out*. Rather, the writer who is a computer operator (now *user*) is composing a text to be held in a device analogous to memory, so that at a future moment it can be printed out and presented physically upon demand.

Thus the user must adjust the idea and action of typing to a different physical reality, to some extent at the keyboard, and certainly when viewing the screen. At the computer, one cannot see everything one has already written; it is recorded on a disk or held in the computer's electronic memory, and while one may have nearly instant access to any portion of it, one cannot, except on special and very expensive equipment, see more than about twenty lines of it at a time. All the rest of the already composed words remain invisible. Not written, one might say, but digitized, numericized, some such word as that: encoded as binary numbers, along with all punctuation and custom of the written word; although the vocabulary of computing includes *write*, as in to "write a file to disk," this *write* has become a metaphor, perhaps one already dead. There is no stack of typed sheets lying next to the typewriter as one works, but instead a disk (floppy or hard) spinning out of sight inside the computer.

Not only do computers necessarily transmit all forms of data, including text, through the tiny window, if I may call it that, of the binary number system (which of number systems is the most bland, the most lacking in texture and historical evolution both as idea and as script). More apparent is the fact that computers, unlike any other common form of transmittal of written information, also deprive the writer of any sense of the accumulated physical bulk of a piece of writing, and require the work to be viewed as if through another window, the glowing screen. No lamp is needed to see one's work; one writes by one's own electroluminescent light.

The feeling of this is quite strange to the habituated reader or writer, as perhaps it may not be to those who have grown accustomed to personal computers without much previous habit of reading or writing. One can easily adjust to scanning bibliographic records on a computer screen; but imagine reading a novel that way. Even if one's eyes could accomplish it without failing, one would have no sense of the size of the book, nor of the size of each chapter in relation to the whole (except by estimating, also on screen but at another moment, how large the file is, given its size in bytes). This proportion, for all its obviousness, is very important, and in itself conveys something of the place of that novel in the tradition of novels and in the history of writing, publication, and reading. Question: What sort of novel would the computer make possible? Answer: since the computer's forte is the manipulation of data, then the sort that allows the reader to choose among prescribed options how the narrative will branch, develop, and conclude. Such "novels" already exist.

Another example: on the computer one can keep notes in such a fashion that finding the word, idea, or reference one wants to recover somewhere in their midst is only a matter of an electronic event of a few seconds—but one can never see, all at once, the bulk or heft of them or the number of pages or index cards, or handle them, sifting through them half randomly, becoming familiar again with their contents, with the sequence and circumstances in which one took them (pencils, different pens, more or less wear or smudging, at the library, at home, at night, etc.).

Finally, imagine writing a work of book length, working away on a digitized version of it. (Not to disallow the possibility of printing out a complete version and then working at this with pen and pencil, but first such a complete version must be created electronically.) For both the writer and reader, the written work is a kind of vital materialization of language. This is not a notion owned by Marxists; the poet Karl Shapiro put it a little differently: "Poetry is the materialization of experience; philosophy the abstraction of it." The materiality of language is the opposite of the experience of writing at the computer, which instantly transmutes the material effort of writing into innumerable, infinitesimal, and invisible electronic changes—any perceptible material result is absent. The level of the infinitely small, at which multitudinous computer calculations take place, has an uncomfortable symbolic correspondence to the tendency of modern government and corporate business to envision persons as statistics. The aggregate of words becomes a *file*, which can be manipulated in many ways; the aggregate of persons becomes a market to be manipulated, too—a population, a number calculated for the purpose of analysis and active influence: marketing or persuading or informing, to make us buy or vote or believe.

But the changing of a single byte of electronically recorded information can alter all the rest or destroy it, while one purchase or vote or prayer has no such effect. We cling therefore to our individuality, even as we sit at our personal and even pleasurable computer screens; we do not willingly become ciphers. In "The Poet and City" W. H. Auden wrote disparagingly of the many young people he encountered who wanted to be writers; but he understood their attraction to the role of the artist. It was not because they felt they had innate talent, but because they admired the artist as one who still had personal responsibility for what he or she made. The young person's "fascination is not due to the nature of art itself, but to the way in which an artist works": unlike other labor in industrial society, the artist's solitary work seems sufficient to itself and thus personally meaningful, while the work available to most people is not. In offering a substitution, welcome to many, of unarguably satisfying computer skills for more arduous writerly ones as the goal of one's learning, the computer and its boosters extend the egalitarian illusion that anyone can become a writer. (It is an illusion not because many more people could not indeed become writers, but because their work would never find an audience.) But is the cost, even to the serious writer, partly in the unavoidable and paradoxical dematerializing power of the machine? Is what is produced with its aid deindividualized in some subtle way? Does all writing thus produced become merely a product and thus begin to be drawn, however reluctantly, into the realm of skills readily acquired for industry and service corporations?

That is, are the physical aspects of the work of writing negligible? I don't mean only psychologically, in the moments of writing, but also with respect to one's personal history as a reader and writer, and the evolution of one's thoughts and feelings. The physical textures of the tangible world and of lived time are transformed, in electronic note-keeping, into a form as clean and instantly mutable at any moment as at the precise instant of one's first recording or annotating. An original cannot be said to exist, for it is continuously changed without trace and so has far less historical dimension in the author's life, none of what Benjamin defined as *aura*.

Thus to transform the first stages of one's thinking is partly to remove both the thing studied and one's studying it to a kind of physical abstraction, a state corresponding, if only imperfectly, to mental abstraction.

Note-taking and scribbling and revising and second thoughts and re-minders become in a way pure and thus less profound. That is, until and unless the piece of writing is printed out (the prepositional tag used in the computer phrase suggesting the necessity to get the electronically pre-served information out of the computer or off the disk and into the per-ceptible realm), it seems to have no concrete existence; its form is so volatile and remote from unaided human perception as to seem vaporous, illusory.

Without this physicality, notes or longer texts lose certain character-istics which I think must be considered essential. No searching at a com-puter, whatever its electronic speed, can stimulate the mind to make unanticipated connections in the same way as looking through notes physically recorded (even if, contrarily, no physical form of recording can equal the computer's speed in finding already-known quantities, such as key words). One has to ask for what one wishes to see; otherwise, the only alternative is to look through the small twenty-line widow as the informa-tion moves by.

This necessity introduces another aspect noticed already by some who ponder the interface between the person (who does have a face) and the machine (is it thus implicitly humanized by the implied metaphor?). There are two distinct ways of conceptualizing the viewing of information on a computer screen, neither of which corresponds to how the informa-tion is recorded electronically and spatially on the disk. One way is to imagine the information as if it were on a continuous imaginary sheet of paper that is moving up or down inside the computer screen window (*scrolling*—a word of exquisite historical irony in this context). The other is to imagine the information fixed in place on its imaginary page, and the computer screen moving, like a diver's face-mask, over it. Either the in-formation moves, or the window does. But in each case one of the ele-ments is always fixed and stationary, and the other moves along rigid vertical and horizontal axes.

Of course, the practical reality of reading—with all the attendant, unperceived and unknown psychic reverberations of our having learned to read and write and our habits of continuing to do so—has no such rigidity except the customarily rectangular shape of the book and the page itself. Flipping back through a typed draft of an essay while lying on one's back on a couch, one's head at an angle and the pages not quite vertical, to find a page where one had written in the margin, so as to connect that annotation, by writing another note, to a fresh one on a subsequent page—nothing truly like that is possible on the computer screen. Instead, one scrolls backward or electronically leaps to the page one is looking for, and then adds the note between lines or in brackets or otherwise, so that the passage can be found later; then one returns to one's point of departure, again either by scrolling steadily or by leaping. There are no true margins on the computer screen. Most word-processing programs do not permit a large scrawled question mark over a point one has come to doubt, or an urgent "EXPAND THIS" to one side; even when they allow the superimposing of windows containing other text, they require that all words in the document or file, however spontaneous or however much they may usefully represent counterarguments, contradictory intuitions, doubts, negativity, and critical thinking, be formatted—that is, be formally incorporated into the rigid rectilinear parameters of typed text, and, so far as possible, naturalized there—made a part of the text, not allowed to exceed its margins, however much it is precisely the marginalia's violation of the typed format that conveys the value of thoughts running counter to the text. That a few recently released, elaborate and expensive word-processing programs will allow some kind of marginal notes only emphasizes this supreme difference from writing, for this particular feature of the program—touted as a great advance—is in fact a retrograde action against the inherent tendencies of such programs, and answers not to the dominant meme of efficiency at the screen but to hankerings for the former ways of handwriting.

Some thoughts on the physicality not only of writing, but of all the attendant thought-work and hand-work that leads to it:

The spatial, three-dimensional (more accurately, four-dimensional!) randomness of one's desk, on which books, papers, notes, pencils, notebooks, paper clips, pads, are spread, is far different from the succession of reordered instances of sorting of, or random access to, data on computer disks. The pen or pencil leaves on paper the traces of the movement of the human hand: it seems to me that every element of this description is of supreme significance, even if at a subliminal level, to writing. The typewriter creates a mild fiction of finish, of *print* (from root words meaning "to press," thus conveying a physical operation). The typewriter and even computerized printing-out are instances of the universal intelligibility of standard letters, no matter who formed them first by hand, or who would utilize them in any way, rather than the individuality of handwritten words (or, by implication, the individuality of their source). Handwriting is not only a precious token of that individuality but also a record of an individual's time at work writing; its uniqueness reinforces, recreates, and represents individual identity and thus substantiates the writer. Handwriting is proof of the writer's existence. Typing and printing make these letters universally intelligible—thus acceptable, decodeable—and so substantiate, validate, and encourage the reader. They are proof of a written work's existence in the historical time of readers.

We bring forth a text with our writing; we lead the pen or pencil over the paper, and thus we produce the work. The stages of the computer's mediation between writer and finished text are multiplied several times beyond those of writing by typewriter. The computer copies what is electronically transmitted from the keyboard, and then writes it to the screen and the volatile Random Access Memory (RAM), whence it writes it to disk, thus saving it; finally it sends the text electronically to the printer.

Further, writing by hand or typewriter produces, in the stages of the evolution of the work, a set of documents attesting to the process of composition over time. Thus writing leaves evidence; it preserves an essential condition or aspect of a written text, which is its authorial historical dimension, its existence in the writer's time and space. And to remove such evidence requires physical intervention, whether inadvertent or deliberate—a suppression, a destruction, or a loss. It requires a destruction of the earlier stages, the drafts—which are the "drawing out" of the words and sentences, as a plow is drawn across a field (again, an act in time). The etymology of *draft* suggests movement, even movement accomplished against resistance; thus the blank page finds its analogy not in the emptiness of the void, as Mallarmé conceived, but in the waiting physicality of the bare field. The very word *verse* derives from Latin *versus*, "a turning of the plow." Olson's "composition by field" is in this light a very appropriate conception.

But writing with the computer means not that the successive stages of composition scribe a field repeatedly, but that each stage in the sequence of revisions obliterates its predecessor (in some cases, depending on the computer program, the last stage but one). The computer breaks a historical chain of association, moves away from the kind of activity suggested by the word *palimpsest*, with all its physical connotations. What now remains is the finished document or file. Most important, the removal of the evidence of each earlier stage can be accomplished not only by deliberate effort or an accidental loss, but also by an automatic and intentional electronic routine to which the program defaults unless prevented from doing so. (It was only the failure of such a routine that preserved the lieutenant colonel's memoranda for later embarrassing discovery, when they became not only evident but also evidence.) One can of course preserve each electronic version (by giving each a different name), but this preservation of the earlier stages would require an effort beyond the ordinary. In fact, the computer term for preserving on the disk what one has written is to *save* it. An elementary computer prompt might be: "Have you saved your work?" A novice might understandably ask in reply, "From what?"

The implication, clear to everyone who has worked at a computer, is that computerized work must be guarded, even rescued, from threat. This threat is the complete loss, the material abolition, of one's work before it has become tangible. If the machine is turned off or the power fails, what's held in the memory chips becomes a dead stillness. Those historians who would study the drafts of treaties (including what we might call postmodern treaties: the contracts of international conglomerate corporations, the stipulations of the International Monetary Fund, etc.) or speeches, letters, and memoranda of public figures, have already expressed dismay that the use of computers to write and revise such documents routinely destroys—or rather, fails to save, in a way not always inconvenient to the modern industrial state or statesman—all evidence of the differing stages of composition. The final draft, then, serves not to represent the evolution of a complex moment in history, but to conceal it or overwrite it with a single and in many respects unreliable image, one that may be unassailable in the absence of conflicting evidence.

I mentioned naming a piece of work. More precisely, one names a file. This file name is required for the electronic identification of the work stored on the computer, an identification apart from true titles. This necessity introduces a small, unaccustomed formality into the relation between writer and written word. Sensing an entrepreneurial opportunity here, some companies have produced computer programs that allow the writer to imitate the production of hurried notes, the titling of which would be absurd. Since such programs must be added onto one's word-processing program, they require another round of learning program commands. This would seem the farthest thing from spontaneous writing, and in fact even when the preservation of impromptu notes is possible, they are of necessity limited to those created while sitting at the computer, or transcribed there.

The enforced formality of the writer's behavior is not in the civil sense, regarding other persons, but in the sense of procedurally precise with relation to the machine. In most word-processing programs the smallest independent hint or fragment of an idea, in order to be saved, must be given a file name; because the computer organizes information and instructions in files, the writer must do so too. Therefore an inflexible sequence of actions at the keyboard must be followed to produce and save the text, in some programs, before the writer can even begin to write. It is a kind of ritual, but of sequence, technicality, and procedure rather than of invocation, inspiration, or gratitude. It is practical rather than intellectual or spiritual.

If, in the old way, you are writing and you stop work, and later you return to it, then—barring catastrophe—you find your desk, your typewriter, and the sheets of paper where you left them. You sit down and try to begin again. But if you want to return later to your work on the computer, you will have to leave the humming machine on and running all the time. Otherwise you must submit to the full routine of starting again: booting the computer, starting (loading) the program, calling up the file, and moving to the right spot in it. It is not the small inconvenience that is most striking here; rather it's the technical mediation between writer and work—a necessary gateway through which the writer must always pass before even the first words can be composed and preserved.

If you need to consult a dictionary, the computer is available for this purpose, but the present limitations of its usefulness are revealing. Computer dictionaries may flag one's typing errors and suggest synonyms, but most are not really dictionaries at all. They contain no etymologies, meanings, or notes on usage. They are merely word lists or thesauruses. So even though the astonishing capacity for helpfully manipulating such information exists, it has so far been used instead to serve a smaller convenience—so as not to misspell a word, or to jog one's memory for a more appropriate one. The need to know something is subordinated to the need to save time. Inevitably, the utility of the computer is primarily determined not by writers but by business and governmental scribes and the computer-industry entrepreneurs who wish to answer their needs. From their point of view and that of their employers, there is no pressing need for knowledge of a word's roots and past usage; that is a luxury whose consumption of time is precisely what the use of computers avoids. If you're the sort of person who is going to use a dictionary to look up a word you already know, then you'll use a dictionary in book form anyway.

The "John Reed typewriter" prefigured another aspect of the quest for efficiency, or rather of the quest by the meme *efficiency* for further substantiation: the portability and self-sufficiency of a writing device that can transform the words in one's head into a kind of finished, communicable product—preserved with ink and paper and carried by hand or mail, or preserved in the arrangement of electrons and either sent on a disk by mail or transmitted over telephone lines. Even the astonishing present computing power of the small lap-top microcomputers fails to impress everyone; many are longing for a six-pound machine the size of a big book that will do what now requires a machine of desk-top size weighing forty or fifty pounds, and only five years ago was inconceivable. Because, you see, if only we could carry it around like a big notebook, then we could write something down anytime we wanted, we could recover our spontaneity, we could work in a remote cabin or a motel room, we could get around the irritation of taking notes in the library and then transcribing them at the computer, and all these mechanical formalities and civilities would be easier, and we would really be the free creators of our work!

Olson, in the passage that immediately precedes his praise of the typewriter, wrote, "What we have suffered from [till now], is manuscript, press, the removal of verse from its producer and reproducer, the voice, a removal by one, by two removes from its place of origin *and* its destination. . . ." He saw, with a sense of irony, that the modern invention of the typewriter—a personal possession of the writer—could restore a preindustrial intimacy to poetry. But precisely because the computer's efficiency brings with it a concomitant abstraction or etherealization of the antiquated ink and noise of the typewriter, and because its final product, even when printed out, can look provisional and ugly, it's not easy to argue that the lap-top answers Olson's desires more fully.

His wish to be in control of the material production of his poem suggests how keenly the writer may feel an insufficiency, even under the best of circumstances, of material involvement in his art. Since William Morris, some modern poets—and small publishers—have allayed this feeling by looking backwards technologically and producing books whose type is set by hand and whose pages are printed by letterpress. The desire is for the anti-industrial, for the physical stamp of individuality, Walter Benjamin's *aura*. The computer now promises to make every man a publisher, despite the obvious difference between letterpress books and those designed on a microcomputer and printed offset from laser-printer copy. This latter procedure may be the next logical step in taking control over the material production of the book, but it is irrelevant, even inimical, to the desire to savor the very materiality of highly deliberate language which the carefully made book embodies.

This account of the difference the computer brings to writing would be insufficient if it did not also mention that there is pleasure in it. The pleasure comes partly from the satisfaction of being able to control and use an extremely complex machine—a feeling otherwise denied to most of us. Given our sex-role socialization, this particular satisfaction has so far been mostly the privilege, if it is a privilege, of men. This is decidedly a luxury of the personal computer more than the office computer: do those who are required to sit at the screen all day and perform data entry—most of whom are women—enjoy it? (While, for example, cold type and hot lead were set by men, most computer typesetting is being done by women.)

One of the pleasures is sheer speed: Olson's pusuit, with the lumbering typewriter carriage, of the speed with which perceptions follow one another in the mind, would have been signally rewarded by the computer. And not only, nor even primarily, in simply recording the desired words as they first come: an electric or electronic typewriter can do this also. It's another order of writerly perceptions that the computer can foster and abet, those of revision and refinement. One can only be grateful for the ability to start a thought six times in succession, refining it rapidly as one goes, without retyping very much; for the ability to leap into the middle of a paragraph or page and add as much as one wants and not retype the rest; to delete anything, instantaneously, and watch the paragraphs perfect their shape again, automatically; to perform the otherwise onerous task of reordering sentences or paragraphs, again nearly instantaneously, by touching a few keys a few times; to format and reformat part or all of a written work (that is, to change it from single-spacing to double, or to narrow the margins or widen them, without retyping anything); to index it without setting pencil to a single index card or ever alphabetizing anything one's self; and so on. The computer can retrieve and reorganize stored information in immensely fruitful ways. It can search one's work for a desired word, number one's pages and footnotes, compose one's bibliography, transport the library card catalog to one's home, and so on.

But just as Olson's use of the typewriter placed essential value on what, for business users of the machine, had been its incidental value (his prizing of expressive flexibility, where they prized accuracy, legibility, and speed), there is a radical opposition between the serious writer's use of the computer and the ordinary paperwork world's use of it: the writer seeks the perfection of expression and argument, and the perfection of the finished copy is secondary, though not without value. The paperwork world seeks the perfection of the copy and perfectly accurate entering of data, and it accepts, but does not at all seem to require, the perfection of argument or expression.

It happens, too, that what for Olson was the typewriter's most important feature, the exactitude of its placement of typed characters on the page—a kind of musical scoring—is for the computer the most flexible and thus least protected aspect of the written word: what is called the *formatting* of a document. While some word-processing programs include impressive formatting powers—and indeed cannot preserve anything that is not formatted—this very flexibility gives formatting a decorative rather than essential status. The powers of the programs are a twofold response to software creators, not to a desire for exact and minute aspects of formatting that are meaningful, but to procedural necessities and a desire for a merely visual variety and attractiveness in what is printed out. Here image, while it need not oppose the substance of words, at least achieves a status independent of the meaning of words. Contradictorily, the ever more common electronic transmission of text commonly requires that formatting be stripped away to leave a simple string of words. If any illustration were wanting, this will serve to show the computer's relative lack of utility for poetry, whose formatting since the invention of printing has been rigid and must be protected, for it does indeed create a portion of the meaning of the poem. Thus the computer favors by its nature the content of written works, their illustration with image (graph, chart, etc.), and their reduction to easily transmissible form regardless of the specificities of their appearance in any given hard copy or electronic version.

This bias may work little loss or hardship on most prose texts, but it clearly diminishes or eliminates the machine's potential as a device that creates artistic possibilities as opposed to reducing them (compare the piano, the synthesizer, the typewriter).

The volatility of the written word housed in the computer, the ready malleability of the written text, and even the repeated loss of the record-in-time of the evolution of a written text, all suggest a connection between the swerving of print culture, or writing culture, toward the computer, and a narrowing of the gap between the written word and the mass image. The mediation of electronic machinery smooths out and removes important differences between the individual writer's labors at his or her work and the creative director's team's universally broadcast images and texts. The computer screen is, after all, technically the same as a television screen, not a piece of paper. I have read of a university dean having said that English departments are museums, that our Shakespeares are in Hollywood, and he said it with enthusiastic approval. I do not think that print culture will ever be dead in the way he wishes it were; indeed, now there is more paper in offices than before computers were introduced. But already it's clear that information of economic importance, when available instantly and over great distances through computers, is in fact far less freely available than printed works. After all, a book or a page requires no electrical current or other connections, weighs little, is cheap to produce, has very efficient RAM, and can be used gratis in the public library.

Such a swerving of print culture also seems to coincide with many things: the vulnerability of journalism, both print and electronic, to contentless but influential images, and to simply too much information; an increase in the number of books that are vapid and obsolescent commodities; the ease of creating false intelligence (disinformation), especially with an aura of technological authority; the control of politics by the techniques of public relations and advertising, with correspondingly vast increases in the cost of running for office, and all too often a rate of success according to the amount spent; the growing proportion of workers in service industries rather than manufacturing; and other notable and troubling changes in our industrialized, televised, heavily armed, and computerized society. There is a great and justified clamor among Third World countries that

the control of important information flowing from the industrialized countries to all the rest—even, and perhaps especially, information about all
the rest of the countries—is an arbitrary, unchecked manipulation of
power. This is true both of factual information to which access is limited,
and of cultural information, such as television programs whose broadened
access is tied to commercial markets for products and whose control of
news is effectively a control of public awareness and opinion. The control
of financial information is clearly evident in many contexts—such as the
influence of computer speed on the newly deregulated London stock exchange or on the Black Monday crash in America in 1987. All these developments have to do with the computer's manipulation of information to be
read. Many librarians are aware of the new way in which information is
sought more frequently than learning, and they have already warned that
access to electronically disseminated information is becoming limited to
those who can pay for it (mostly corporations), and cannot be delivered by
libraries as a free service to the general public.

Thus is a portion of even the imaginative writer's work at the computer bound up with such vague pervasive influences as world political
rhetoric and world economic relationships, for the writer's participation is
now in a medium not only of composition but of electronic communication
ruled by the economic exigencies of speed and transmissibility. There is,
after all, a computer publication named *Infoworld*. The so-called information age, of which writers are a part, leans quite noticeably toward words
and figures whose political and economic value is not conclusive but
simply up-to-the-minute. Instant assessment by computer of rapid and
anonymous telephone polling has come largely to define the tactics, and
perhaps even the strategies, of national political candidates, who may
thus tailor pronouncements and actions to statistical samples of opinion
rather than to elections at which people registered by name and address
cast individual ballots. Polls quite obviously have as much real power as
the ballot to influence public policy and government action.

What belongs to yesterday is devalued; speed, convenience, and manipulation of the mass of consumers are values on which technology and
American politics converge, even while older or former politicians and
historians repeatedly point out the mistakes caused by haste and historical
ignorance. Some recent print advertisements for AT&T emphasizing personal computers purport to state a corporate belief that information belongs in the hands of the little guy; yet the power and profitability of the

corporation must depend on the very opposite, on a continuous rapid out-flanking of such information as the little guy must base his decisions on. If poetry, and by analogy any creation of the imagination such as novels, plays, and essays, is "news that stays news," in Ezra Pound's phrase, then present-day information is in this sense a kind of antipoetry, and the manipulation of information is a kind of antireading and even antithinking. It is this flood, as well as a sense of the enforced insignificance of self in the infonuclear age, that Auden's hopeful young writers were resisting, and continue to resist, however ineffectually.

The informational bias is nowhere more apparent than in a comparison of the preferred vocabulary of two distinct intellectual groups: literary critics and computer programmers and users. Critics are given to speaking of literary works as texts. The term is now neither honorific nor exclusionary; indeed, critical preference for it stems in part from a desire to widen the category of literary work so that the objects of literary-critical study will include many more than those already accepted and preserved as the canonical works. Etymologically *text* comes out of Latin *texere*, "to weave," and this conveys the writer's and the (professional?) reader's sense of a literary work as a thing woven of many strands, perhaps revealing several meanings, appearing to conceal some, and tied by those strands to the culture around it, the history before it, and the future, as well as to other works. The text is thus a complex object of scrutiny, a made thing-in-itself, a noun of meaning. The literary-critical term emphasizes the value of a written work.

In contrast, the most common computer-world term for a written text, *document*, emphasizes the use of a written work. Document derives from the Latin word for a lesson, an example, a warning, which in turn derives from *docere*, "to teach." I think the present-day connotations of document are often procedural, if not actually legal, and so the implication available here is that a document is not first of all a thing-in-itself, much less with a complicated historical and cultural existence, but a transparent item that is used. It offers a utility-value and then is needed no longer. Also, a technical writer documents a computer program, writes the documentation for it—which is to say, provides information about it. This is not to disparage utilitarian communication but only to point toward the significant difference in the attitudes of two intellectual groups toward writing. More vividly, perhaps: one can document, but one does not text. If one were to text, this verb would translate as "write a poem," "write a novel," "write a play."

If I were myself perfectly acclimated to the information age, there would be no private record of this piece of writing except the final one: no holographs, no typescripts, no hard copies. But because I am not a wholly naturalized citizen in the realm of the computer, the completion of this piece required me to pass many times through the intermediate stages of printed-out versions and to add to each a variety of afterthoughts and changes in the form of marginal and interlinear scrawlings. Revisions and revisions of revisions, jammed in everywhere, do reassure me of myself: these very sentences were blue scratchings down the right-hand margin of the last page of one hard-copy draft.

Whitman wrote in and of his *Leaves of Grass* that who touched the book touched him. But who touches these pages, and most others, these days, touched the work of both person and machine. I wonder if any author is likely to express thanks in a book's preface to a computer instead of to a person, however indispensable the former. It has forced unwanted changes in my methods, yet I take pleasure in some of its careful, minutely correct ways, even as I wonder about the precise nature of what I am participating in. Serious computer adepts refer disparagingly to computer games as "mind-candy"; that there is an appetite for such sugar is itself a troubling clue to what it is, exactly, that happens when one is sitting at the machine, one's eyes only a few inches from it, in order to write. That's closer than you'd ever want to get to your television, closer than you would want to let it get to you. But that's where I'm sitting, right now, and there I am, on the screen myself, my words, neat and glowing.

Cinema, Language, Film Theory
MIRIAM HANSEN

TEN YEARS AGO Ernest Callenbach, in an editorial in *Film Quarterly* first voiced his concern over the disintegration of "the film community." A hypothetical entity, but one in which people believed, the film community "comprised all those dedicated souls who took the medium seriously—who wrote about it, taught about it, or used it conscientiously as artists." Despite variations in taste and differences of opinion, according to Callenbach, the devotion to the art, the love for the medium, ensured "a curious sense of a shared world." This Edenic state, flourishing under the benign rays of the California sun, was being threatened by an intruder from the East: the name of the beast was Theory, its nationality French. The same issue of *Film Quarterly* featured a translation of Jean-Louis Baudry's influential essay "Ideological Effects of the Basic Cinematographic Apparatus," with its Lacanian-Althusserian premises clearly marking it as an instance of the new Gallic heresy.

Subsequent developments in the field of film studies have more than confirmed Callenbach's fears, though not necessarily his nostalgic preferences in defense. What we witness today is indeed a shattering of the mythical film community—not into theory ("abstract," "cold," "dead") on the one hand and practical criticism ("at the pulse of the liveliest art") on the other, as Callenbach predicted, but into fundamentally different attitudes toward talking about film. Traditional film criticism, from journalism to academic auteurism, implicitly had assumed a role analogous to that of literary criticism since the early eighteenth century, as a medium through which individual sensibility and experience could be communicated socially, thus constituting an instance of the public sphere. The public sphere that crystallizes around the cinema, however, has come a long way from the ideal of the classical public sphere which based its claim to

This article originally appeared as a review essay of *Cinema and Language*, edited by Stephen Heath and Patricia Mellencamp, The American Film Monograph Series, volume 1, 1983.

legitimacy on its putative independence from the sphere of interests, the liberal marketplace. The experiential values offered by the cinema are being manufactured and distributed on a corporate scale; the equality and classlessness of the film viewer are those of the mass-cultural consumer. Scorned by the more "serious" cultural authorities, film scholars and popular reviewers were hardly distinguishable from each other. And more often than not, film critic, film buff, and film establishment were engaged in forming a mutual admiration society.

New directions in film theory and criticism seem to be characterized, above all, by a rejection of this compromise, the fiction of a public sphere encompassing critic, filmmaker, and "common" viewer/reader as equal, disinterested participants. I am thinking in particular of semiological and psychoanalytic approaches that made their way into film studies during the 1970s. Motivated by a political goal—the critique of Hollywood as an agency of dominant partriarchal-capitalist-imperialist ideology—these approaches promised to advance a systematic analysis of how ideology functions in and through films, how cinema as a social institution succeeds in binding and realigning the spectator's desire. Taking its impulse from French critical movements in the wake of May '68, new film theory entered discussions in this country largely via the Paris-based American University Film Center as well as the British journal *Screen*. The influence of French film theory coincided—and certainly prompted to a considerable degree—the emancipation of film studies as a discipline in its own right, with its own set of theories, methodologies, and critical vocabulary. The growing professional self-awareness among academics working in film involved a deliberate break, not only with the nostalgic notion of a film community but also, in most cases, with the traditional disciplines under whose auspices film was (and continues to be) taught at colleges and universities. Suffice it to recall the "film appreciation" courses offered by English departments all over the country, the notorious "gut" course whose intellectual respectability was usually figured in inverse proportion to its degree of popularity while the teacher was left to his or her own devices, in a dubious balance of repressive tolerance and complicity.

Now a new generation of film scholars, with degrees from film departments such as Iowa, Wisconsin (Madison), or NYU, are competing for teaching jobs, and an increasing number of colleges offer film studies as a possible concentration within a humanities curriculum; film appreciation has been superseded by segmentation exercises or syntagmatic analysis. A rather specialized discourse, both more technical and more theoretical, seems to have become the lingua franca at film conferences and in avant-garde journals (*Camera Obscura, Ciné-Tracts, Wide Angle,* et al.), marginalizing other approaches if not dismissing them as part of an outmoded liberal-humanist esthetic.

One might interpret this development as the formation of a separate, oppositional public sphere, resisting the assimilation by the mass-cultural one, insisting on a language of its own. But to reduce the situation to such a polarity would be overly simplistic; positions of resistance and attack do not always divide that neatly along predictable lines. Debates are launched in unexpected quarters—thus, for instance, Noël Carroll's seventy-five-page review of Stephen Heath's *Questions of Cinema* in *October,* a journal that usually considers itself in the forefront of fashionable theory. Mobilizing Western philosophy from Aristotle to Hilary Putnam, ordinary language plus common sense against Althusserian-Lacanian assumptions in film theory, Carroll's "Address to the Heathen" succeeded in provoking Heath into writing a fifty-three-page epistle in response, "Le Père Noël," a piece more forcefully, wittily, and clearly argued than most parts of the book under attack. (Rumor has it that Carroll is gearing up for another invocation of the "San'ty Clause.") The apparently interminable exchange deserves attention—partly for its discussion of basic concepts ("subject effect," "ideology," "cinematic illusionism")—but more significantly because it throws into relief the problematic status of film theory as theory, urging us to rethink its relation to other disciplines, its intellectual standards, its pragmatic functions, its own language.

In recent years, film theory seems to be moving into a phase of revision, reintroducing issues strategically neglected in the early seventies, in particular issues relating to history and culture. *Cinema and Language,* a collection of essays edited by Stephen Heath and Patricia Mellenkamp, could be described as a snapshot of film theory on the threshold of this revision from the 1970s to the 1980s. The essays are based, in part, on a conference held in March 1979 at the Milwaukee Center for Twentieth-Century Studies, an institution that has been singularly active in promoting new film theory in this country. (That this volume—along with three others of similar orientation—is published under the auspices of the American Film Institute, an organization funded by the NEA and based in Washington, is in itself a remarkable event; this should not, however spark any hopes for a possible reintegration of the "film community": immediately after publication the AFI Board decided to discontinue the series and to abolish its Education Department.)

The book explores the relationship between cinema and language from a variety of angles, e.g., verbal language as an analogy, a material component, a function in filmic signification; the role of language in the interaction of conscious and unconscious processes in spectatorship; language as a structural framework for analyzing the ways in which film participates in the social production of meaning. In exploring such questions, *Cinema and Language* also illustrates the significance of linguistic premises for current directions in film theory, especially the blending of semiology with Lacanian psychoanalysis. While most contributions to the book confirm Heath's observation that film theory today seems to be "emerging from the hold of [the linguistic] impetus," not all of them are ready to reconsider the assumptions inferred from it. Rather, they might be viewed as symptomatic of certain difficulties and shortcomings of the linguistic approach, thus helping to sharpen the focus for questions that film theory needs to address. I see these questions centering on two major problems: (a) the hierarchy implicit in the linguistic approach, i.e., the universalizing of "language" and the concomitant low status assigned to non- or preverbal forms and materials of signification; (b) the mistaken ambition to confer upon the study of film the status of a science, borrowed from the discipline of linguistics and supported by scientistic claims in Marxist and psychoanalytic thought. The latter, I would tentatively argue, may account to some degree for the alienating—as well as alienated—quality of much of current scholarly writing on film.

The current dissociation of discourses on film appears all the more ironic if we recall that the invention of film was hailed, not as yet another language, but as an essentially new language, one that would overcome all contradictions and conflicts of opinion. "Finally, the universal language has been found," the first spectators of the Lumière films (1895) were said to have exclaimed. And in this country, two decades later, D. W. Griffith announced: "A picture is the universal symbol, and a *picture that moves* is a universal language. Moving pictures, someone suggests, 'might have saved the situation when the Tower of Babel was built.'" More than a witty remark, the allusion to the biblical confusion of languages goes to the core of Griffith's conception of the cinema—and his own mission as a filmmaker. As Lillian Gish reports, "Mr. Griffith once heard one of his actresses call a film a 'flicker.' He told her never to use that word. She was working in the universal language that had been predicted in the Bible, which was to make all men brothers because they would understand each other. This could end wars and bring about the millennium. We were all to remember that the next time we faced a camera."

Far be it from anyone living in the age of Falwell to make light of millenarian media politics. Nor does the concept of film as a new universal language appear as quaint and innocent when considered in its function for the film industry of its day. Between 1905 and 1912, when the majority of moviegoers were urban working-class, in large part immigrants from southern and eastern Europe, the universal accessibility of moving images seemed more than obvious—at least in comparison with traditional cultural activities that involved spoken or written language. The universality of the new medium was extolled as the condition of its democratic, emancipatory function, meaning, for most writers, its function as an agency of acculturation ("democracy's own theater," "the laboring man's university," etc.). Such idealist visions might suggest, in Judith Mayne's words, "that movie houses and nickelodeons were the back rooms of the Statue of Liberty." The average program offerings, however, suggested otherwise, consisting mostly of knock-about humor, pornographic sketches, prizefights, and war and disaster films.

Moreover, the universal language slogan ("the Esperanto of the Eye"), complete with democratic trimmings, gained widespread currency only around and after 1912, when the industry's systematic efforts to "kill the slum tradition in the movies" (Adolph Zukor) began to show signs of success, displacing the lower-class clientele for whose benefit it was supposedly working. The independent producers' bid for the more lucrative middle-class trade could generously advertise itself as universal, since it was promoting the absorption of all class, ethnic, and psychosocial difference into the insatiable melting pot of mass culture. Carl Laemmle, like Zukor one of the leading independents, boosted his recently founded "Universal" Film Manufacturing Company by listing an encyclopedic range of themes and locations made available by this studio, reaching out to "millions of people in every clime." According to this ad, "Universal Moving Pictures are Mightier than Pen or Sword" because they speak to everyone, "not in cold, unspeakable type, but in the universal language of pictures—moving, animated pictures that transport one to the very scene, defying time and distance." A metaphysics of presence par excellence, using metaphors of voice to sell the fictions of the silent screen.

The notion of a visual Esperanto, as Christian Metz first pointed out, is a contradiction in terms, since it yokes the concept of a totally conventional and organized language with a medium as relatively indeterminate as moving images. In its unacknowledged metaphoric makeup, the conception of film as universal language was to become a powerful staple in Hollywood's mythology about itself, sanctioning not only worldwide economic expansion but also the particular ideology of representation that characterized its products. Griffith, for one, did not publicize his notions on film's God-given universality until he came under attack for the racist tenor of *The Birth of a Nation* (1915), the first American film epic. Griffith defended his dramatization of the Civil War and Reconstruction period (actually based on a novel and a play by Thomas Dixon, Jr.) by claiming only to have rendered visible history "as it really happened." With the enthusiasm of a nineteenth-century positivist, he prophesied the imminent displacement of all historiography by motion pictures. "Instead of consulting all the authorities, wading laboriously through a host of books, and ending bewildered, without a clear idea of exactly what did happen, you will merely seat yourself at a properly adjusted window, in a scientifically prepared room, press the button and actually see what happened. There will be no opinions expressed. You will merely be present at the making of history." In other words, film would eliminate once and for all the problems of interpretation inherent in textual sources; its "truth" would emerge automatically from the photochemical basis of cinematic representation; the obvious similarity between image and object represented would lend history the force and facticity of natural events.

To everyone who remembers sitting through *The Birth of a Nation*, feeling simultaneously fascinated and appalled, this line of defense may seem a rather peculiar one. Yet for all his naiveté, Griffith was prophetic of an ideology that was to become a formative tendency in American cinema—the tendency to present its images as natural, transparent, self-evident, as "speaking by themselves." The editing style that became the trademark of Hollywood's "classical" period (roughly 1930–1955) used to be called "invisible"—for good reasons, since it involved complicated conventions (the continuity system) designed to efface themselves in their very application. Along with other techniques, this type of editing works to absorb the viewer into a story coming from nowhere, telling itself through the actors and actions on the screen. The fiction thus produced is a temporary and tenuous one, to be sure, yet in most cases pleasurable enough to make us suspend disbelief, indulging in the illusion that we ourselves are the authors of these visions. Ideology—like the camera, the director, the studio—participates as an invisible guest, thus delivering its messages all the more effectively. As Horkheimer and Adorno put it in their critique of the "Culture Industry" (1942 draft): "no shepherd but a herd."

Considering these formal mechanisms of mystification, the introduction of semiology into film studies marks a necessary step—even if the cinema had remained silent. When sound was added in the late 1920s, it predominantly served to enhance the "reality effect," the naturalness of cinematic representation. The heterogeneous matters of expression that make up a film—the moving photographic image, written titles, recorded speech, music, noises—tended to get thoroughly fused, amalgamated under the primacy of effect, subordinated to the "truths" of the image track. A critical analysis of classical American cinema therefore had to attempt a systematic disassembling of this effect, an emphasis on film's construction as a text. In political terms, this involved a shift from the question of *what* kind of images and social-sexual roles were assigned to people historically excluded from authorship (like racial and ethnic minorities, like women), to questions of *how* these images were constructed, *how* meaning was produced in film, *which* codes and conventions were at work in the process of signification.

Such questions could not have been posed without the framework of semiology which developed into a kind of discipline only in the 1960s. The pedigree of semiology lists Ferdinand de Saussure and the paradigm of structural linguistics—another ancestor being Claude Lévi-Strauss's structural anthropology. Language, the "most complex and universal of systems of expression," as Saussure had proposed in his *Course in General Lingusitics,* could become the "master-pattern" for all branches of semiology, "a science that studies the life of signs within society." Important here is Saussure's insistence on the arbitrariness of all signification, prefigured by the unmotivated, conventional relationship of signifier and signified in the linguistic sign. Meaning is produced, neither on the level of inherent essences nor that of individual intention, but on the basis of the position of the sign in relation to other signs, i.e., its structural values within a system of minimal oppositions. The radical implication of Saussure's theory clearly lies in its proposition that meaning is not natural or God-given but a matter of social and historical practice.

While film theory received a major impulse from the Saussurean paradigm, it also inherited a number of problems—problems first addressed by Christian Metz in his influential essay of 1964, "The Cinema: Language or Language System." Metz confronts the cinema with the Saussurean model and concludes that the cinema is *a kind of language,* a language lacking a specific system comparable to Saussure's notion of a "langue." For one thing, the cinematic sign is not primarily arbitrary—to the degree that it is a photographic image—but "motivated" by the analogy between signifier and signified; it participates in the category of signs Charles Sanders Peirce has termed "iconic." This iconic bias makes it difficult to determine a "minimal unit" of filmic signification (the shot already implies the status of a sentence); likewise, it precludes a structure of "double articulation" comparable to the phoneme/morpheme distinction in verbal language. Finally, the cinema represents a system only in a rather rudimentary way in that it has a very limited number of paradigmatic structures, such as, for instance, the use of light and dark costumes signifying "good guy/bad guy" in the classical western. Even in highly formalized narratives like American genre films, however, the meaning attached to these oppositional values is rather unstable, and like all generic conventions subject to constant revision.

Despite such caveats, Metz himself reintroduced the model of structural linguistics in his subsequent work (especially in *Language and Cinema*), with its emphasis on the formal codes operating in the cinema, especially the syntagmatic structures (shots in their spatio-temporal order) of narrative films. Focusing on the systematic articulation of cinematic discourse, Metz suppresses the element of selection, the possibility of temporarily derailing the codes by means of figurative expression; in true structuralist style, he declares that cinematic grammar and rhetoric are identical, since film does not have an "ordinary" language against which to construct a figurative meaning. With the submersion of rhetoric into a linguistic notion of grammar, film studies seemed to have banned, once and for all, the parent specter of literary criticism.

In recent years, however, the problem of figuration in cinema—which can be traced back to Eisenstein's project of a "rhetoric of montage"—is re-emerging as an important concern. A number of essays in *Cinema and*

Language illustrate this: Mary Ann Doane on irony in Hitchcock's *Spell-bound;* Laura Oswald and Linda Williams on surrealist metaphor; Dudley Andrew on "The Primacy of Figure in Cinematic Signification." The shift in focus from the systematic organization of cinematic discourse (code, syntagma) to the particular textuality of films seems largely motivated by the "historical switch" in semiology, its embrace of psychoanalysis. In his introductory essay, "Language, Sight and Sound" (reprinted from *Questions of Cinema*), Stephen Heath describes this displacement of the "first" or "classical" semiology as a shift in emphasis from structure to the formation of the subject, in particular the role of language in the interaction of conscious and unconscious processes.

The critique of the "subject" as a sovereign, self-identical agent in history is as old as Nietzsche; its particular impact on recent literary and film theory, however, derives from positions associated with the names of Althusser, Lacan, and Kristeva. Film theory's adaptation of Lacan focuses on primarily two concepts: the claim that the unconscious is "structured like a language" (and, by the same token, is nothing but "the discourse of the 'Other'") as well as the concept of the "mirror stage" and the concomitant distinction between the "imaginary" and the "symbolic." The latter concept links the child's awareness of sexual difference (recognition of "lack," threat of castration) to his access into the realm of language. If ideology "interpellates" (Althusser) the individual as subject, "suturing" (Lacan/Miller/Oudart) him/her through the dialectics of imaginary and symbolic, then there is no place like the movie theater for studying these processes. The cinema represents an unparalleled instance of the "imaginary signifier"—as Metz sets out to show in his recent collection of essays under this title—it lures us into an imaginary coherence and plenitude of perceptual identity while realigning our desire again and again with the structures of the symbolic, the regime of the lack.

Metz's turn to Lacan ultimately repeats his earlier equation of cinematic codes and language, rephrased in terms of the symbolic as the vanishing point of desire. Not surprisingly, the most powerful critiques of Lacan have been formulated by feminists who—like Teresa de Lauretis in her contribution to *Cinema and Lanuage*—argue that he further entraps us in the "procrustean bed of phallic signification." In de Lauretis's analysis, structuralist hierarchies (implicit in Lévi-Strauss's conception of symbolization on the basis of kinship structures that require woman as an object of exchange) reenter in Lacan through the back door of the link between language and the order of the symbolic, which effectively conflates linguistic and sexual difference. This link is further compounded, I would add, by Lacan's concept of negation which—unlike Freud's—is Hegelian in spirit and thus rules out the coexistence, albeit in a hierarchical relationship, of earlier (preoedipal) and later (oedipal) stages of psychic development as well as of verbal and nonverbal modes of signification. Until we acknowledge a diversity of signifying modes, in their material and historical specificity and perhaps even deviating forms of subjectivity, de Lauretis concludes, the psychoanalytic vision of the cinema will relapse into the same phallic hierarchies it sets out to undermine.

Most contributions to *Cinema and Language* reflect an increasingly critical stance toward Lacanian categories. This seems to coincide with a renewed "return to Freud," a rereading not necessarily through the lens of Lacan. Freud obviously would have had no use for the Saussurean concept of the sign as a stable, intelligible relationship between signifier and signified. Nor would he have reduced the a priori collective determination of the unconscious to a preestablished symbolic order derived from the model of structural linguistics. Rather, we find in Freud a variety of approaches to signification, from the conception of dream work in terms of rhetorical figures, through the analysis of discursive transformations in jokes and fantasy, to his late remarks on the "mystic writing pad."

The coexistence of word-representations and thing-representations ("hieroglyphs," "pictographs"), of different degrees of figuration and hybrid forms of signification in the interplay of conscious and unconscious processes, provides a link between Freudian psychoanalysis and the concept of "inner speech," a concept elaborated in the 1930s by Eisenstein, Eikhenbaum, and psycholinguists associated with the Bakhtin circle. Both Stephen Heath and Paul Willemen relate this concept to cinematic signification which similarly involves distinct and unevenly developed layers of consciousness, as in C. S. Peirce's characterization of inner speech, "a dialogue between different phases of the ego." The "frontier" status of this "creature" leads Willemen to propose that "inner speech is the discourse that binds the psychoanalytic subject and the subject in history."

If such a proposition could be developed further, it might help overcome one of the major problems in current film theory, namely, the difficulty of conceptualizing historical and cultural differences within a psychoanalytic-semiological framework. This problem is addressed, in *Cinema and Language*, by Phil Rosen in an essay on "Subject Formation and Social Formation" as well as by Noël Burch, Don Kirihara, and David Bordwell in essays dealing with Japanese cinema. In his discussion on deep focus in the films of Mizoguchi, Bordwell points out some crucial differences in comparison with American uses of that technique, notably in the films of Welles and Wyler. At the same time, he cautions against an ahistorical celebration of the "otherness" of Japanese modes of signification, linking semiological approaches (Roland Barthes, the *Tel Quel* group, Noël Burch) to a longstanding fascination with the "Oriental sign" on the part of Western avant-garde artists and intellectuals (Eisenstein, Artaud, et al.). Bordwell draws attention to the historical mediation between Japanese and Western styles of representation and suggests that the mutual discourse on the "other" plays a significant part in the development of a national film tradition.

As much as history and cultural difference have to be reconsidered within film theory, so too should film theory begin to understand itself historically. Not coincidentally, the linguistic impulse in current film theory began in France, a country with an overwhelming fixation upon language, particularly its own. In 1784, Rivarol published his *Discours sur l'universalité de la langue française*, demonstrating the unique role of the French language for the nation's cultural, economic, and political superiority. Two centuries later, the patriotic pathos may have evaporated, but the faith in the universality (supremacy, priority) of language remains. The assertion that there is nothing outside language could be questioned on Humean grounds; nonetheless, it has a pragmatic—political, polemical—validity in film theory as long as mainstream cinema continues to exploit the reality effect of iconic (photographic, analogic) representation, the ideological truth of the visible as first invoked by Griffith. But to acknowledge that all signification is mediated by language does not necessarily mean that the diversity of cinematic signification can be explained in terms of linguistic structures, albeit unconscious ones. Rather than submerging the differences between the cinematic and the linguistic sign in the Lacanian concept of the imaginary (with its implicit inferiority vis-à-vis the symbolic), film theory should elaborate its focus on the material qualities of image and sound in their production of meaning, should explore the relative indeterminacy and essential impurity of cinematic signification in its potentially subversive function towards dominant symbolic structures. In this connection, Peirce's theory of "semiotics" (introduced into film theory by Umberto Eco and Peter Wollen, among others) offers an important alternative, since it allows us to conceive of signification without the constraints imposed by the heritage of structural linguistics.

A more distanced attitude toward linguistic paradigms (such as is already emerging in some contributions to *Cinema and Language*) may also move film theory to a greater awareness of its own critical language. Writing on film involves a complex process of translation from one medium into another, from heterogeneous sensory perception defined by movement into a text that can be deciphered and rewritten. An increased awareness of this activity would involve a shift in focus from *the* "subject effect" produced for *the* spectator to the process of reading engaged in by a particular reader and writer, and thus would urge film theory to reconsider its relationship to other disciplines of textual interpretation. Such a move has been initiated by critics like Thierry Kuntzel and Marie-Claire Ropars with recourse to modes of deconstruction (the Barthes of S/Z, Derrida). While semiology emphasized the constructedness of cinematic signs, the degree of discursive determination that is masked by the ideology of visual immediacy, the critical impulse of deconstruction aims at the basic indeterminacy (*différance, Nachträglichkeit*) of textual meaning, thus redefining the task of reading as one of rewriting. A deconstructive approach to film, however, divides into critical writing and the practice of filmmaking, thus involving textual revision on two distinct but interacting levels. Film criticism ultimately has to go beyond the exemplary reading of individual films towards an analysis of the ways in which all films—with radical intention or without—are necessarily revisions of other films.

The development of more speculative modes of reading and writing in film theory and criticism encounters a major obstacle in semiology's implicit aspirations towards the status of a science. An unreflected endorsement of Lacanian theory as "the elaboration of the science of linguistics within psychoanalysis" appears dubious enough from the point of view of either discipline; when it occurs, as in *Cinema and Language*, in an essay on the Marx Brothers, it becomes outright parodistic. Semiology as a science makes as little sense as psychoanalysis as a science or, for that matter, the study of film as a science. Linguistic structures may—and indeed have proven to—shed light on filmic structures, to borrow Phil Rosen's image; but the relationship between film and language has never been anything but a complex metaphor, itself a figure requiring textual interpretation. Any theoretical analysis of cinema and language that does not acknowledge its activity as a textual one ironically returns to the cinematic positivism that it set out to undermine—to the tradition inaugurated by Lumière, Laemmle, and Griffith.

How to Say *"Fetch!"*
VICKI HEARNE

If you do not teach me I shall not learn. —Beckett

Terms that have histories cannot be defined. —Nietzsche

I F W E F O C U S on the nature of the social space created by the language shared by two or more creatures, if we describe the integrity of a language as the physical, intellectual, and spiritual distance which talking enables the speakers of a given language to travel together, then it looks very much as though the dog and the horse (who are neurologically simpler organisms than chimpanzees, and whose linguistic codes certainly appear simpler) have a greater command of language than chimpanzees do. There is even a sense in which a well-trained dog or horse may be said to have a greater command of language than a human being whose code is infinitely more complex. The dog/dog-trainer language is perhaps more primitive (in the sense Wittgenstein has in mind when he criticizes Augustine or invites us to consider primitive language games) than the chimpanzee's language, or the schizophrenic's, or the president's, but I can go a lot farther with my dog than I can with a schizophrenic, or a Nazi, or the president, if only because my dog doesn't bore me.

Does this matter? Or is it just a sentimentalization of the enslavement of the domestic animal? Well, dog trainers and horse trainers insist that training—teaching animals the language games of retrieving, say, or haute école—results in ennoblement, the development of the animal's character, the development of the dog's *and the handler's* sense of responsibility and honesty. This is either hopelessly corrupt, in a sense that *The Genealogy of Morals* might unfold, or else it can tell us something not only about what goes on in training, in the sense that I am trying to get at, but also about what it might mean to respond fully as human beings to "character," "responsibility," and "honesty."

It is worthwhile, then, to describe part of one of the language games of training, namely, retrieving, hoping to discover what sort of moral cosmos is revealed thereby. I am going to begin from William Koehler's

159

work, not only because Koehler is one of the great trainers in a tradition whose locus classicus is Xenophon's *Cynegeticus*, but also because his method is formally the most complete one I know. That formal completeness, together with his muscularly asserted freedom to talk anthropomorphically, gives his theory—his theology, if you like—a clarity and comprehensiveness rarely found since the collapse of the world views that made obedience a part of human *virtù*. We may read Spenser with pleasure, but how can we imagine ourselves obeying anyone or anything the way his knights do?

Koehler holds, against the skepticism that in the last two centuries has become largely synonymous with philosophy, that getting absolute obedience from a dog—and he means absolute—confers nobility, character, and dignity on the dog. Dignity? This is such a repugnant notion in a world still reeling from the shock of the Third Reich that his books and his methods have had to survive serious legal challenges from animal lovers confused about what cruelty is. Now, even though the courtroom battles have been largely won, a serious segment of the dog-oriented population still can't say his name without attaching to it epithets like "devil" or "monster." This is not a response to his methods. Very few people who think that it's right to train a dog at all are repulsed when they actually see a dog being worked in the way he teaches. It is not his tactics but the morally loaded language in which they are embedded that repels his critics.

So in order to consider the counters, gestures, or utterances of retrieving-language I am forced to consider a seemingly tangential issue, and a larger one, which can be phrased here, "What could possibly give us the right to say, 'Joe, sit!'—ever?" In thinking about this there is a grave danger of wittingly or unwittingly invoking some sort of calculus of suffering—of saying, for instance, that although obedience training is painful, it certainly isn't as bad as the fate that awaits the vast majority of untrained dogs, under the wheels of cars, in the decompression chambers of the Humane Society, or in laboratories. Circumstances may force us, rightly, to apply such a calculus, but that is an emergency procedure irrelevant to a fundamental discussion of rights, including the right to the pursuit of happiness. (I take *happiness* to have at least the range of significance Aristotle saw in it.)

What sense does it make to speak of a dog's having a right? It may help to begin by asking what sense Koehler makes of it, in what sense, that is, he uses the term "right." He says that the dog has the "right to the consequences of his actions." What does this mean? Or what does it mean to be *able* to mean such a remark?

To be able to mean the remark, to take the responsibility for meaning it, is to be committed to imagining the nature of the commitments involved, or at least to acknowledge the possibility of such imagining; otherwise the remark is as deeply incoherent as the double-bind tyrannies of much preaching, including academic preaching. I believe that the remark is coherent, and that we can see a little of what it might mean to mean it if we consider the job "consequences" is doing here for Koehler, and for any trainer who uses the conception well. The trainer has occasion to be aware, as few people are, that human authority is corrupt to the core, and that any trope of ascendancy—especially the trope of nobility—stinks of the immodest, the self-righteous, and the sadistic. Yet the trainer must get on with training the dog. The dog is compellingly present.

In order to get on with it, Koehler makes a sharp distinction between correction and punishment, understanding that punishment may irrevocably be born in the taint in our authority. This is not a distinction between lenience and harshness, although it is part of a distinction between kindness and cruelty, or maybe between rightness and cruelty. A sharp, two-handed, decisive upward jerk on the training lead, performed as impersonally as possible, is a correction. Irritable, nagging, coaxing tugs and jerks are punishments, as beatings are. The self-esteem of the handler gets into them, with the result that, by obeying or failing to obey, the dog takes on responsibility for the handler's emotional well-being, as we can make children, or spouses, responsible for our souls. This is the sort of obedience Lear wanted from his daughters. With some dogs, exacting a pretense of such obedience is as dangerous as it was for Lear with Goneril and Regan.

Corrections, in Koehler's vision, are administered out of a deep respect for the dog's moral and intellectual capacities. Punishments on the other hand are part—and this matters tremendously—of the demeaning repertoire of so-called trainers who propose babbling at the dog as sweetly as possible. Cooing "Oh my goodness, what a G O O O O D doggie!" is, for Koehler, profoundly cruel, dishonest, and dishonorable, the flip side of a beating. Even moderately self-respecting humans grab their hats when addressed in such a fashion. And although dogs are on the whole surprisingly tolerant of our specious doctrines, many of them will, in effect, grab their hats or else, like Cordelia, attempt through precisely administered bites to turn the rhetoric. It is usually a diet of syrup, bribery, and choked rhetoric, rather than physical abuse, that creates in dogs character disorders such as viciousness and megalomania. Biting is a response to incoherent authority.

It is difficult to see this through the tangled and sprawled rhetoric of the informal training most pets receive, but highly trained animals have sufficient control of trope to make the point with, sometimes, telling cogency. I am thinking now of Hans, a Doberman, one of the most talented and competent dogs I have known. His response to the command "Fetch!" was so instantaneous, accurate, and powerful that it sometimes seemed the air must ignite as he leaped forward from his handler's side. Among his more spectacular performances was the Drop-On-Recall. In this exercise, as performed in competition, the handler tells the dog to stay and moves some thirty to fifty feet away and then turns and, facing the dog, commands, "Joe, come!" When the dog has travelled some distance, usually about half way, a drop command or signal is given, and the dog must drop to the ground and wait for a new recall command. With Hans it was generally necessary to say, "Hans, come down!" in one breath, for by the time the handler had finished pronouncing "come," Hans was already halfway home. And it was risky to perform the exercise on blacktop, since Hans responded to the command by simply flattening out in midair and sliding, accepting like a base-runner the ripping of skin and joints the game of being a great dog entailed.

Even insensitive and inexperienced observers were impressed by this dog. But unfortunately, it was possible to be moved by Hans without understanding that you might have to earn the *right* to say, "Hans, down!" A person called Uncle Albert accompanied Hans and his handler one day. Uncle Albert decided it would be nice to have Hans do his "tricks" for Uncle in the absence of his handler, who had gone off to fetch some training equipment. Uncle Albert held out some liver snaps to Hans while saying, "Come to Uncle," or some such folderol. Hans looked at him for a moment in disbelief, and then, with a stiffness expressive of deep disgust, got up and walked slowly away, thus disobeying both the "stay" command his handler had given and Uncle Albert's phony recall command. His handler, returning in time to witness disobedience of a sort that hadn't been possible for years, refrained from correcting Hans. (The complications of *that* moment require separate consideration.)

Koehler puts the bribers and the coaxers together under one heading—he calls them "humaniacs." (To be distinguished sharply from people who devote themselves to the prevention of genuine cruelty, even though these can often be irritatingly blind to the differences between bearbaiting or bullfights and Grand Prix dressage.) Koehler calls humaniacs

> "kindly" people, most of whom take after a "kindly" parent or an aunt "who had a dog that was almost human and understood every word that was said without being trained." . . . They often operate individually but inflict their greatest cruelties when amalgamated into societies. They easily recognize each other by their smiles, which are as dried syrup on yesterday's pancakes. Their most noticeable habits are wincing when dogs are effectually corrected and smiling approvingly at each other when a dozen ineffective corrections seem only to fire a dog's maniacal attempts to hurl his anatomy within reach of another dog that could maim him in one brief skirmish. Their common calls are: "I-couldn't-do-that—I couldn't do that," and "Oh myyyy—oh myyyy." They have no mating call. This is easily understood.

This Nietzschean-sounding anger may in fact have one of its sources in Nietzsche, via Jack London, but exactly how Koehler got so angry is not my present subject, but what he is angry about, what vision of dignity and significance is at stake, is.

Another trainer, Jack Kersley, in *Training the Retriever*, writes:

> When a dog is corrected, perfect justice may be administered. There is no question of making an example so that others may be deterred, nor as in human crime must the penalty be made so heavy that the public is protected. Least of all must punishment be administered to satisfy the sadistic irritation of the trainer. . . . In nature, there are no punishments, only consequences. . . .

Here "nature" of course means something like "paradise," a region of clarity in which language never refers beyond ourselves and our intentions. Something very like a myth or story of expulsion from such a paradise stands behind the trainer's attempt to make sense of a life in which we must say, "Joe, fetch!" or at the least "Joe, sit!" I hear a story that goes like this: When God first created the Earth He gave Adam and Eve "dominion over the fish of the sea, and over the fowl of the air, and over every living thing that moveth upon earth." Adam gave names to the creatures and they all responded to their names without objection, since in this dominion to command and to recognize were one action. There was no gap between the ability to command and the full acknowledgment of the personhood of the being so commanded. Nature came when called, and came the first time, too, without coaxing, nagging, or tugging.

Then Adam and Eve themselves failed in obedience, and in this story to fail in obedience is to fail in authority. Most of animate creation, responding to this failure, turned pretty irrevocably from human command. The tiger, the wolf, and the field mouse as well as, of course, the grasshopper refuse to come when called, to recognize our naming. One may say that before the Fall, all animals were domestic, that nature was domestic. After the Fall, wildness was possible, and most creatures chose it, but a few did not. The dog, the horse, the burro, the elephant, the ox, and a few others agreed to go along with humanity anyway, thus giving us a kind of second chance to repair our damaged authority, to do something about our incoherence. Training, in this story, can, through its taut catharses, cleanse our authority, for varying stretches of time, of Nietzschean *ressentiment*. Without that catharsis, dogs very properly withhold full obedience. Hence Hans's disgust with Uncle Albert, hence "wild and uncontrollable" collies, and hence, of course, Fido's being perfectly happy to *play* fetch while refusing to bring the stick all the way back. The gap the dog insists on between us and the stick represents the gap between our ability to command, give advice, and so forth, and our ability to acknowledge the being of others. This is the taint in our authority. And the dog or horse trainer's special interest in "wild and uncontrollable" animals assumes that the degree of violence in a dog's resistance to incoherent authority may indicate the depth and power of response such a dog might give when the gap between command and obedience is closed. Hence the mythology of Buck in *The Call of the Wild*, or of the dog, Lion, in Faulkner's *The Bear*.

It is the full acknowledgment of language that closes the gap. Except for complete isolation, only such acknowledgment can deprive authority of its power to render false, filthy, stinking, and sadistic the operations of our relationships. It won't do to suggest that the dog can just live peacefully around the house while we refrain from giving any commands that might deprive him of his "freedom," for that simply doesn't happen. We are in charge already, like it or not, and when a dog is about, everyone involved is going to be passing out advice and giving commands whether or not they've earned the right to do so. One might as well suggest that we leave off keeping toddlers out of the street, or teaching anyone anything at all. We do assume authority over each other, constantly, or at least we had better do so if only to be able to say "Duck!" at the right moment. If our authority is weak, if we haven't taken responsibility for it, we *won't* say "Duck!" at the right moment, or the person addressed may not duck. A refusal to give commands, or to notice that commands are being given, is often a refusal to acknowledge a relationship, just as is a refusal to obey. The syrupy, nagging punishments that require the dog to "want to please," to be responsible for the handler's feelings, fail to get authority out of the relationship by refusing to take the dog's position into account, or to bear the consequences of speech. I am echoing Stanley Cavell's discussion (in *The Claim of Reason*) of "Knowledge and the Concept of Morality," and I'd like to summon Cavell's aid further to say that Koehler's rage against humaniacs is the rage of someone who, knowing what the full acknowledgment of a dog demands from a trainer, must hear the for him unbearable "tone of one speaking in the name of a position one does not occupy, confronting others in positions of which one will not imagine the acknowledgment."

A practical consequence of the trainer's knowledge of the significance of command is that trainers say things like "Hans, down!" far less frequently than most people, or at least to fewer dogs, and that they dream of a world in which they could say "Down!" or "Fetch!" more often, a world in which dogs had civil rights as a matter of course. If it sounds queer to talk this way, to suggest a connection between commanding and granting rights, that is only because we have failed to be sufficiently anthropomorphic. We don't imagine we can grant civil rights to human beings without first assuming authority over them as teachers, parents, and friends, but we have lately supposed, strangely, that rights can be granted to animals without our first occupying the ground of commitment that training them instances. The dog trainer isn't willing to occupy that ground with every dog he or she meets—can't, in fact, do so (just as there are certain responsibilities it is logically impossible to assume toward someone else's spouse). And with this goes a refusal to pretend to occupy such a ground, knowing that such a pretense is a debasement and deception of the dog as any fraudulent behavior is.

It is important to say that "the trainer" I am talking about is, like the poet or the philosopher, an invention of our minds. I have met people who think and act in relation to animals in a way that is very nearly as coherent as the way of the trainer I am here imagining, but not even Bill Koehler is that trainer. However, there are facts that can be known about this imagined object, just as there are facts about the mathematician's omega that can be known, although the animal trainer is in some ways more difficult to know than the mathematician's omega, because the trainer speaks. In order to investigate this trainer further, I am going to tell a story in which I am the trainer and the dog is a year-old pointer bitch named Salty.

Salty is a bird dog, and a good one, which means that the chance of her biting me is so remote that we won't have to discuss that. Not that Salty is a "soft" dog. She is a hard-core pointer, birdy and geared to travel all-out for miles, the heiress of an unsurpassable tradition that includes Algonquin who was (according to Dion Henderson's *Algonquin: The Story of a Great Dog*) "very gallant, sir. I think perhaps he would pity his brace-mates if he were not enough of a nobleman to know that they would rather die than be pitied." For a true pointer admirer, the pointer's fire, speed, precision, and power is the central good in the universe, the rest of which is judged by its ability to honor and celebrate the pointer. "Mr. Washington felt that any bird you didn't hunt exclusively with pointers was unfit to associate with gentlefolk."

So Salty, in my story, has it in her to be staunch to wing and shot, to hunt wholeheartedly where lesser dogs lose spirit, to work with full courtliness and gallantry, to become so dedicated to the perfection of finding and pointing birds that the sort of hunting where the art is adulterated by actually shooting the birds is uninteresting. Unfortunately, her wonderful qualities may look to the uninitiated remarkably like wildness and uncontrollability. She's a year old, and she hasn't even had puppy conditioning; the only part of the noble rhetoric she has gotten down is the part about going hard and tirelessly. This she does everywhere, as indifferent to obstacles like the kitchen table or the bedside lamp as her forebears were to unleapable gullies and impenetrable thickets. Her former owners had only known the sort of dog who is more accommodating of cooing and bribery. Salty was not so much intolerant of the cooing as she was indifferent to it—it had no meaning, literally, to her. She thought she was doing a fine thing when she went through the picture window to point some meadowlarks in the backyard, and the cries of "You bad dog, how could you do this to us, you're supposed to be our precious baby, look at my potted Chinese palm, all ruined!" deterred her no more than the gashes on her neck and shoulder. But she was tolerant of the fussing, even if she was unresponsive. Proof of her tolerance is in her not having bitten anyone. A German shepherd or a Doberman, or any of the breeds for whom the forms of companionship can be as deeply visionary as the forms of hunting are for Salty, might very well have responded to this particular incoherence with hostility.*

When Salty enters my life she's been talked at a lot, but she knows virtually nothing of talking with people who mean what they say, so I don't say much of anything to her at first. I take her out of her kennel and am silent except for a calm, "Good morning, Salty." I put her on a fifteen-foot line, attached to a training collar, and I begin to go for a little walk. Salty stays at my side for about one and one-quarter seconds, which is how long it takes her to spot something huntable—in this case, my motley-coated cat, Touchstone, who is idly watching the progress of the ten o'clock shade of the pepper tree toward his sunny spot, contemplating as is his wont the curious ways the shadows move round and round, forcing him to change napping places as the day wears on. Salty heads all-out for Touchstone, at proper field trial speed. I say nothing—nothing at all. Instead, I drop all fifteen feet of slack into the line and turn and run in the opposite direction. Salty hits the end of the line and travels, perforce, some distance in the direction I am going, tumbling end over end.

This thoughtless behavior elicits no hysterics from her, as it might from a lesser dog who is used, as Salty is, to being coaxed and tugged away from kitty cats instead of having to deal with a handler so clumsy and impolite as to fail to check first on what Salty is doing before dashing off. She is startled, of course, but she forgives me and romps toward me to let me know it. On her way to forgiving me she catches sight of a leaf moving in a way that might mean *bird* and spins out after it. Again, I head swiftly in a direction opposite to hers and again she tumbles end over end, correcting her story about who I am.

The third or fourth time it dawns on Salty that there is a consistency

---

*It is impossible to say enough in defense of the deeply civilized hearts possessed by members of these breeds, especially Dobermans. The fear of Dobies is all too easy to understand in light of the bad press they've had, which hasn't so far been offset by tales as powerful as those of Rin Tin Tin. I shall content myself by saying that the bad press started with Hitler's charge that they were of impure blood and therefore unstable in temperament, and that perpetuating the myth of the vicious Doberman amounts to perpetuating a Nazi line.

in my inconsiderate and apparently heedless plunges. She sits down to think this over, cocking her head in puzzlement, trying to work out the implications of my behavior. She suspects that they are cosmic. I respond by heading purposefully toward an open gate. She decides she'd better keep an eye on me, and follows. Then the sight of the gate standing there open in such an *opened* way tempts her, and, forgetting the new cosmology, she charges for it. I turn again to do my routine, but this time she remembers before she's in high gear that I can't be counted on to follow, and she brakes and turns, loping in my direction and avoiding hitting the end of the line.

By the end of the first session she is more attentive to me, more willing to follow—to try, that is, to understand—than she has ever been to anyone in the whole course of her life, and I've said *nothing* to her. When the session is over, I utter the first command—"Salty, okay!"—as I release her to think things over. The "okay" is essential. It means something like "You are free to walk about, sniff things, take a nap, have some lunch, initiate a conversation with Touchstone on the mysteries of time, but you are *not* free to commit any crimes, dig holes, chase Touchstone, leap into the middle of my morning tea, or generally buzz around at low altitudes." If she does any of these things I correct her by jerking sharply on the line while hollering " O U T!" in my most terrifying voice, sounding as much as I can like a clap of doom. Since she is neither a wild animal nor a hardened criminal but a true dog, she is able to grant fairly quickly the reasonableness of my demands, and since neither "Okay!" nor " O U T!" requires her to love me or nourish my soul, her willingness to cooperate need not be contaminated by questions about whether she loves me better than she loves the vision of herself as a mighty huntress. There can't in any case be much talk of love between us at this point, though we do find each other likable enough. Love will follow on shared commitments and collaboration, on a mutual autonomy that is not now possible.

The mastery of the "okay" command is not about love, but about the simultaneous granting and earning of some rudimentary rights—in particular, Salty's right to the freedom of the house, which, like my right to the freedom of the house, is contingent on not making messes, respecting other people's privacy, refraining from leaping uninvited onto furniture and laps, and making the right distinctions between mine and thine, especially in the matter of food dishes. I have managed to grant this right only by becoming inflexibly in command about certain things. It is a matter of authority, not love—I don't even have to like a dog in order to accomplish this. In most adult human relationships we don't have to do quite so much correcting in order to grant each other house privileges, but that doesn't mean that house privileges don't depend on the possibility of such corrections. Try putting your ice cream cone on my typewriter and you'll get the idea. Freedom is being on an "okay" command.

Love, of course, is getting into things, but at this point I love, not Salty, but the literary tradition that has produced her. She doesn't know this tradition, but she has it in her to respond to and enlarge on my response to it, in the way that a talented young poet has it in him or her to respond to a mentor's response. That is an important part of a talent for anything. In Salty I see echoes of the great field trial dogs of the past and the paintings and tales of them, in the way I see in a student's work and manner of thinking echoes of the authentic energy of Stevens or Dickens. The better I am at responding with great accuracy—at for instance not making mistakes about which great tale or painting is being invoked—the greater the likelihood that this dog's particular qualities will be realized.

After about a week of work on the longe line (*longe* is a term for a certain piece of equipment, and for certain sets of exercises, in both the dog and the horse worlds) it is time to introduce a piece of linguistic behavior whose syntax is more like the syntax of the imperative mode than "Salty, okay!" is. I spend a while in an activity called "Teaching the dog what 'sit' means," although that phrase captures very little of what teaching anyone anything is like. Briefly, I gently place her in a sitting position at the same time that I say, "Salty, sit!" This is not what "sit" will come to mean, but an incomplete rehearsal of it. I do this for several days, without giving any corrections, not because a dog needs more than one rehearsal to learn *that* the utterance means a certain posture, but because it *is* a rehearsal, and more than one rehearsal of more than one kind must precede genuine performance. There are, as I said, no corrections. Attending to me, refraining from biting and leaping about, is the only obedience required at this point.

Then comes the moment when I give the command without placing her. If she refuses to sit, or just doesn't think to sit, I give her a harsh, emphatic sit correction. The meaning of sit has now changed, been projected into a new context. Salty says to herself, "By God I'd better sit when she says to, or the world will keep coming to an end!" The imperative mode has at *this* point, *this* form.

Someone may be wondering about all that glorious dashing about, full expression of creaturely energy and so forth. It may seem that I've destroyed that, broken Salty's spirit. It is possible to do this, though quite difficult especially in this particular case. With some dogs, syrup and cooing will do it, especially if there's a full-blown emotional blackmail system in operation. That didn't work on Salty, but if I fail now not only in respect for her but in love of the literary tradition that taught me to want to train Salty, I can in fact "break her spirit." The danger here is that most of the stories we know about authority are about people getting, as it were, stuck in a parental or imperative mode. So with Salty I must be prepared to drop that instantly and to respond to every true motion with awe. If my "Way to go, kid!" or "Good dog!" invokes for me what I know and feel about the great dogs of the past, then what we are doing will lead in time to the second inheritance, for the dog, of her running gear. Dog training is one of the arts concerned with the imitation of nature, which is to say, the second inheritance of nature.

At this point in Salty's training it is not clear whether the utterance, "Salty, sit!" is language, even though there is plainly a looped thought involved: Salty is sitting in response to her recognition of my intention that she do so. But it's not clear how interesting or useful it is to *say* that it's language, or that anything much is known that we couldn't know just as well if the anecdote avoided terms like "meaning" and "intention" and used instead a Skinnerian or a Cartesian vocabulary. The situation is far more complex than my account of it, but those complexities don't further illuminate the issue at this point. We have a looped thought, but the flow of intention is, as it were, one way. In my account the dog doesn't initiate anything yet. She obeys me, but I don't obey her.

One day, though, and quite soon, I am wandering around the house and Salty gets my attention by sitting spontaneously in just the unmistakably symmetrical, clean-edged way of formal work. If I'm on the ball, if I respect her personhood at this point, I'll respond. Her sitting may have a number of meanings. "Please stop daydreaming and feed me." (Perhaps she sits next to the Science Diet, or her food dish.) Or it may mean, "Look I can explain about the garbage can, it isn't the way it looks." In any case, if I respond, the flow of intention is now two-way, and the meaning of "sit" has changed yet again. This time it is Salty who has enlarged the context, the arena of its use, by means of what we might as well go ahead and call the trope of projection. Salty and I are, for the moment, obedient to each other and to language.

Understanding has been enlarged by enforced obedience! How queer, one may want to say; surely this is a borderline case having very little to do with understanding as we usually talk about it. But our concept of obedience is larger than we admit in certain discussions, as when we're concerned to talk about the importance of autonomy, or the power of the individual imagination. *Obey* itself comes from a word meaning "to hear." We covertly recognize that this may not be an irrelevant etymology by using expressions like "I don't follow you," or "I'll go along with that." It is a certain spookiness about the *word*, together perhaps with the terror of being suggestible and therefore weak, that makes us forget that no one is more suggestible (more responsive to a text) than the great critic or philosopher, no one more obedient, more fully surrendering of the self, than the master of an art. *What* we surrender to matters, of course. Salty appears to have no choice about surrendering to me, but to say that as though it distinguished her from us is to overlook the degree of choice any of us has about surrendering to our native tongues. My training methods, like any teaching method, depend on her willingness to cooperate,* which is one of the reasons the chimp trainers so insist on the word *teaching* to refer to what they do, and there are contexts where they are quite right to do so. Salty's surrender, I would like to say, is not entirely helpless. She can't know ahead of time how fully I will follow through on the commitments commanding another being entails, but she has (unlike the wolf) something like the rough-and-ready criteria we use frequently in judging when to surrender. She has a million tiny observations of my tone and manner to go on, and her recognition of them is not entirely unlike the recognition that leads me to attend more closely to a book I have

---

* Since most housecats would rather die than obey a direct order, some people have been led to elevate the cat in their estimation. "A dog's an easy going lout / He'll answer any hail or shout. . . ." The belief in the independence and pride of cats is an example of what has been called anthropomorphism but is not. It is the attributing to animals, not of traits that we possess, but of traits that we wish we possessed, or are afraid that we possess, or that someone possesses. Pure savagery, unending and impersonal sexuality, unshakable love, etc. In this case, the mythical emotional independence of the cat. It is imaginative failure that obscures our view of the ways the housecat cooperates deeply in the domestic enterprise.

picked up idly. Of course, I can always decide I've made a mistake and put the book back down (or at least I like to think this, though even when I can there are tiny increments of loss even in so trivial a repudiation), but Salty, too, can always decide to bite me and split. I have known this to happen. She is free, or rather she is not free, in the way babies aren't free.

Now, though Salty is not yet the master of anything, and I am not yet her master, some more rights have been granted to her, or she has earned them, whichever you prefer. If my behavior has been just, as in Kersey's quotation above, then Salty has the right to a certain attentiveness or responsiveness. We stand on the threshold of a discipline that can free us from some ancient and troublesome trespasses against language, and the resources of consciousness have been renewed.

There are a lot of things we don't have yet. Among others, we don't have a subject—a grammatical object, that is—for our primitive language to engage. Even Salty's creative management of the food dish and the garbage can doesn't enable her to name the garbage can. Naming is an advanced activity of language and not the prior, essential act our allegories about ourselves and matters such as signing chimpanzees make it out to be. Names for anyone or anything but the speakers of a language are not necessary for knowledge or acknowledgment, not until we actually do name objects, and then they will be necessary.

But we can now say something about how the story the behaviorist brings into the laboratory not only affects his or her interpretation of what goes on, what will count as part of the authorized literary canon, but also how it affects what actually does go on. To the extent that the behaviorist manages to get free of any belief in the dog's potential for believing, intending, meaning, etc., there will be no flow of intention, no meaning, believing, hoping, going on. The dog may try to respond to the behaviorist, but the behaviorist won't respond to the dog's response; there will be between them little or no space for the varied flexions of looped thoughts. The behaviorist's dog will not only seem stupid, she will be stupid. If we follow Wittgenstein in assuming the importance of assessing the public nature of language, then we don't need to lock a baby up and feed it by machine in order to discover that conceptualization is pretty much a function of relationships and acknowledgment, a public affair. It takes two to conceive.

It turns out that saying "sit" requires a lot of detailed work on various cases, for Salty's idea of the conceptual boundaries is as annoyingly rigid as the philosopher's idea of the conceptual boundaries of truth. She'll sit in the middle of the yard, but she won't sit a foot away from the fence. Sitting-on-grass is one thing, sitting-on-blacktop quite another. Sitting when she's calm is not sitting when another dog is inviting her to play, nor sitting when the Mailman Monster is approaching nor sitting when she'd rather eat. I make her sit in as many different situations as ingenuity and luck will provide, with some exceptions. For most dogs, for example, sitting in a puddle of water is at this stage of training deeply unacceptable. There just isn't in the language yet available to us any way to make that a coherent demand. It can become coherent if we develop a story about hunting birds, or trailing lost children to the kidnapper's den, a story whose domain includes the possibility of the articulation of a reason. (When is it coherent to give the command, "Read Aristotle's *Metaphysics* by Wednesday"? or "Take up battle stations"?) A great variety of projections of "sit" are going to be required, and these are by and large projections into new moral contexts.

Similar projections of the meanings of terms will give the other novice commands a wide variety of uses. They are all unique in significance, but I only want to look at part of one of them, the command, "Stand." In this exercise, the dog learns to stand and stay while a complete stranger examines her (painlessly). This is the only exercise in which the dog must allow someone besides me to touch her, and the only one in which I must commit myself to staying within range for the duration—the other stay exercises are eventually performed with me out of sight, and I will eventually call her from out of sight. In the out-of-sight exercises, the dog makes her own decisions about her safety, not being corrected, for example, for moving from a stay because someone touched her. But in the stand-for-examination, she gives over to me all of the responsibility for judging the danger of the situation. This is an extremely important exercise for, say, dogs in police work, because it greatly increases the dog's reflectiveness in judging situations.

At first I must be able to judge character as minutely as the dog does. In particular I must be careful not to ask anyone who is a "natural bitee" to approach and touch her. Natural bitees are people whose approaches to dogs (and perhaps people as well) are contaminated by epistemology. They attempt to *infer* whether or not the dog will bite, jump up on them, or whatever. Instead of "reading" the dog, as handlers say (Heidegger might call it listening to the dog's being), they cast about for some premise from which they can draw an inference that will give them certainty about the dog's behavior. They are—sometimes only momentarily—incapable of beholding a dog. It is not that the required information will follow too slowly, but that they *never* come to have any knowledge of the dog. And dogs read this with the same uneasiness we feel when we walk into a room and find that our spouse, or a friend, has plainly been sitting around inferring something about us—welcome has been withheld. This creates in dogs and people an answering skepticism, an answering terror. The dog starts casting about for premises, making inferences back, tries to reach certainty, fails to reach certainty, and sometimes bites, just as we do. Most dogs, however, express this uneasiness by trying to reassure us with affection, and dogs are astoundingly good at demolishing skeptical terror, which is why they are so often effective in therapy even when the therapist doesn't suspect that epistemology is the disease. Dogs are in general more skilled at belief than we are. In a culture which so commonly conflates skepticism about others with dignity, the maintenance of personal worth, and professional and intellectual integrity, the dog seems, as T. S. Eliot has it, "frequently undignified" and "much inclined to play the clown." The dog's clowning breaks through our murderous skepticisms something like the way Dickens dealt with the tyrannies of "reason" and "fact" that kept the poor poor and dehumanized.

However, Salty's clowning will be more effective and significant when she asks herself when it is appropriate, so I teach her the stand-for-examination. Salty, as a pointer, has (as is evident in the still, brown-gold gaze she turns on fools) a bit more contempt for epistemologists than, say, most Airedales do, but she has no hidden premises from which to draw logically sound bites, so she is likely to break her stand by offering to romp, and she will be corrected. This will not only make company manners possible, it will mean that if the chips are down I can expect her to be more rather than less effective at biting when there's some reason to bite. If it sounds surprising to say that learning to refrain from attacking or romping is part of courage, that may be because we tend to forget that it does take courage for dogs to attack, and that both submission and discrimination are aspects of valor in most of the stories we've told about the various forms of life in which human heroism is possible.

This wonderful ability to distinguish between good guys and bad guys is related to a faculty I mentioned earlier—dogs have a highly developed sense of what does and does not belong in the dog/human world.

With this faculty goes a tendency toward sometimes rather tiresome opinions, whose degree and form of expression will vary from breed to breed as well as from individual to individual.

Salty isn't especially opinionated, at least about, as it were, hearth matters (quest matters look different), and she expresses her sense of the forms for the sake of wit. It comes about, for example, that I am in the front yard with her one day, working on recalls on a fifty-foot light line. She is doing beautifully simply because the increasing distance she travels back to me has brought with it a transformation. Her earlier pleasure in running to greet me when not distracted by philosophical cats, together with her glee in the use of that transcendent running gear, has been troped into a love of the exercise for its own sake. She now performs recalls with passionate energy and precision. She is a pretty sight indeed. My friend glimpses this from the study window and comes out to watch her work. Salty, the next time I call her, performs a flawless recall, straight sit, and an unbidden but accurate finish—but to my *friend,* who is idling about smoking his pipe. This is an ancient form of animal humor (horses do it too), but there are some dogs who wouldn't at this late stage debase what to them are sacred forms, especially some members of the working breeds, who take the domestic virtues more solemnly. I knew, for instance, a German shepherd who grumbled noisily at the other dogs when they didn't obey—a female, as it happens. My Airedale is another matter. When, in training him to retrieve, I begin placing the dumbbell in odd ways, he enjoys the play on form. When, for instance, I first set the dumbbell on its end, he scoops it up happily and tosses it in the air a few times on his way back with it, to show his appreciation of the joke. A very fine, very serious German shepherd I worked with, confronted with the same situation, glared disapprovingly at the dumbbell and me, then pushed it carefully back into its proper position with his paw before picking it up and returning with it, rather sullenly. The Airedale's enjoyment of oddity and ingenuity makes him a good candidate for movie work, whereas the shepherd is better suited for something like tracking.

All of this, it seems to me, bears on the question of animal rights, on what we have to notice when we project the incredibly complex syntax of rights, duties, and the like into our various ways of discoursing with and about animals. The trainer welcomes the attempt to make the notion of "speciesism" coherent but wants impatiently to say something like, "Look: when we have said, 'for all x such that P, where P is the ability to feel physical pain, etc.,' we have said virtually nothing, haven't taken the tiniest step toward imagining the personhood of any animal." There's something deeply appealing about, for example, the Australian philosophers confronting the scientists about what goes on with animals in laboratories, as there is something appealing about arguing that whipping slaves is wrong, or that women ought not to suffer. Without opposing such activities, I yet want to digress for a moment in order to take a small look at a small corner of the sort of thing that springs into a trainer's imagination when "speciesism" talk gets going.

Most people are taught that, when confronting a strange dog, the thing to do is to hold out your hand invitingly for the dog to sniff, and not to pet the dog until you're sure the dog is not going to bite you. This sounds innocent enough, especially when we first hear it, generally as toddlers. But it can be dangerous advice, since many dogs interpret the motion of the arm as a threat. (They are less likely to do this if the proffered arm actually does belong to a toddler.) Beyond that, it amounts to a discounting of the dog's dignity that is flabbergasting for a trainer. We have come lately to recognize the assumption that you have the right to touch and speak to any member of a certain class of human beings as part of an oppressive rhetoric. And if I were to offer to shake hands and initiate conversation with anyone who came within reach, I would be regarded as insane.

Most dogs—not all—are more forgiving of this than most people, partly because they tend to take a lightheartedly opportunistic view of us anyway, and partly for something like the reasons women may go along with a story about women not having strength of mind, or whatever. It relieves you of the responsibility for your own soul, or seems to, and more to the point it's usually rather difficult to figure out how the new story would go. When some "kindly" person interrupts a dog I am working by petting and yammering, I feel the jolt of rage on the dog's behalf you might feel if a stranger or even a friend were to interrupt your concentration in the library and start telling you how pretty, or handsome, or whatever, you are. And in some moods I want to say that the failure to imagine why there might be such rage is one way of characterizing my sense of the failure of the philosophy of animal consciousness.

Most people, of course, are as innocent of the intention to, say, violate the animal's privacy or deny the animal's right to meaningful work as they are innocent of any knowledge of the principles of animal training. In practice, however, trainers have come up with some unfriendly responses, such as "Watch out, he's had attack training," or "Don't do that, he's not your dog." Educating-the-public is one pious possibility, but if one goes about all day expounding the principles of animal training, one gets no training done. Besides, there aren't any principles of animal training, only some aphorisms, dog stories, and what not, just as there don't seem to be, if one looks closely, any principles of philosophy, just insightful epigrams and some philosopher stories.

Perhaps I ought to return to the story I'm telling. Trainers distinguish between hard and soft dogs. Size and strength have very little to do with this; these are qualities of the soul. A hard dog is one who will give you a proper time of it in training, testing the coherence of your right to command at every turn. This hardness is very different from the wolf's resistance, which springs from the general inappropriateness of training a wolf in the first place. (A wolf is most unlikely ever to use the sit exercise in the way Salty already has, to expand the possibilities of discourse between us. Thus, the possibility of granting rights to a wolf is highly attenuated, but the wolf isn't especially interested anyway.) Salty's hardness springs rather from the courage to insist that it really matters how we talk. It looks hostile in places, just as Wittgenstein, writing out of stunning courage, looks a bit hostile in places. It is the hardness we see in the lives of people for whom a certain sort of coherence matters more than the conventions of approval. Someone might want to say that people of that sort risk madness or the exile of criminal status. So do hard dogs who don't find the right person to talk to.

From what we've seen of obedience so far, to say that it can be understood as a way of building a society of dogs and humans doesn't capture my sense of the difference between saying, "Joe, sit!" and "Joe, fetch!" The difference isn't absolute, but it's profound, and I want to explain to myself why there are people who can learn to say "Joe, sit!" pretty coherently, but who never learn to say "Joe, fetch!"

It may help to summon a distinction Auden felt like making, in his essay "The Virgin and the Dynamo," between societies and communities. A society is comprised of a definite number of members

> united in a specific manner into a whole with a characteristic mode of behavior which is different from the modes of behavior of its members in isolation. A society cannot come into being until its component members are present and properly related. . . . [A] society is a

system which loves itself; to this self-love, the self-love of its members is totally subordinate. Of a society it may be said that it is more or less efficient in maintaining its existence.

A community, on the other hand, is united, not by a system of relations, but by a love of something other than itself:

> In a community, all members are free and equal. If, out of a group of ten persons, nine prefer beef to mutton and one prefers mutton to beef, there is not a single community containing a dissident member; there are two communities, a large one and a small one. To achieve an actual existence, it has to embody itself in a society or societies which can express the love which is its *raison d'être*. A community of music lovers, for example, cannot just sit around loving music like anything, but must form itself into societies like choirs, orchestras, string quartets, etc., and make music. . . . Of a community it may be said that its love is more or less good. . . . A perfect order, one in which the community united by the best love is embodied in the most self-sustaining society, could be described as science describes nature, in terms of laws-of, but the description would be irrelevant, the relevant description being, "Here, love is the fulfilling of the law." . . . [T]he traditional term for this ideal order is Paradise. In historical existence where no love is perfect, no society immortal, and no embodiment of the one in the other precise, the obligation to approximate to the ideal is felt as an imperative "Thou Shalt."

So, the imperative "Joe, fetch!" commands the dog (and the handler) not as Newton's laws were understood to command the behavior of falling bodies, but as God's laws command some. "Fetch!" cannot be said meaningfully unless it is said with reverence. Its coherence requires that retrieving be sacred for both members of the community. But here is a paradox: the trainer must speak as if the sacred spoke through him or her, like a prophet, even while knowing that that is mostly impossible, that the gap between the sacred and our knowledge of it is ineluctable. This recognition is part of the responsibility incurred, and so a trainer seldom says, "Fetch!" and often tells (true) stories about the dog's being the ultimate authority as to the rightness of our methods. And if retrieving training becomes profane for a trainer, then that is that, and retrieving training either stops or becomes incoherent. One may say that Germany fell in love with Hitler, and beyond that, terrifyingly, that Hitler fell in love with Germany, that he was sincere, that he was able to command as a master commands a student of painting. Hitler, however, seems to have been less sensitive than trainers are to the importance of realizing that the ability to exact obedience doesn't give you the right to do so—it is the willingness to obey that confers the right to command. I suspect that people with this understanding so seldom end up in charge simply because with it goes an awareness of the immense imaginative burden of authority.

In the case of dictatorships, Auden might want to remind us that there is also this consideration: "Of a community it may be said that its love is more or less good." Perfect love doesn't exist; perhaps our sense of uneasiness in the presence of what we call fanaticism may be expressed, not only as Stevens had it, by talking about the "logical lunatic," the "lunatic of one idea / In a world of ideas," but also by saying that fanatics don't seem to have noticed that the world really is fallen, and that acknowledgment of this is as essential to our lives as that acknowledgment of human separation which, in Cavell's words, "can be accepted, and granted, or not" is to the prevention of tragedies in human love. Political tragedy, perhaps, comes about through failing to acknowledge imperfection in our apprehension of the sacred, what Cavell calls "the separation from God." Perhaps, too, this is why we feel that teaching a child to play the piano or (as in *Nicholas Nickleby*) to speak French, *for profane reasons*, is such a repellent travesty. The resulting noise offends more than good taste.

Another glance at the wilderness: It happens that wolves have more emotional and physical armor against incoherent teaching from humans than either dogs or children do, so that incoherent piano lessons are much more common than attempts to get wolves to fetch. This doesn't mean that the wolf is any better at preventing in himself the attendant soul muddles, but just that the trainer, faced with the wolf's teeth and the tenacity of his opinions, has more trouble convincing herself that any real training is going on. It is possible to form some sort of society with a wolf, but forming a community with one is at the outer edge of the likely.

So when I have taught Salty the novice obedience commands, we have formed a society. There is some community as well, for it is in the nature of things that the precision of formal work stirs the Primary Imagination. But a curious thing has happened along the way. Salty has taken to digging holes, partly in order to occupy herself in the yard while I am at my typewriter, but also because hole digging is sacred; in the activity the secret significance of everything reveals itself. Here, corrections won't work. I may yell, scream, deliver out-corrections all I like, but these will have little or no effect. She learns to make sure I am distracted, perhaps by listening for sounds of the typewriter, and has her hole-digging fix as often as she can. Any corrections and punishments are just part of the fun, accepted as a dedicated athlete accepts aches and injuries. I don't mean she *likes* being walloped, but she is not deterred by walloping as she was deterred when the matter of puddling on the rug came up: puddling on the rug wasn't sacred.

So I submit myself to the holy discipline of hole digging. Dressed in gardening clothes, I go into the backyard and discover the Hole. I rejoice. I dance a jig around the Hole in celebration of the Mystery. I congratulate Salty on the Hole and, still dancing, get out a spade and shovel, with a view to making this perfect thing even more perfect. Salty is delighted, and helps me dig the Hole. We perfect its form, making it diamond or heart shaped. I dance another jig when we're done, and, still dancing, I go get the garden hose and fill the Hole with water. Then, still rejoicing, I put Salty's head in the Hole. She emerges quite quickly (she's a very strong, agile dog) gasping in astonishment and outrage. I am surprised and say, "But I thought you loved hole digging!"

I do this every day for three weeks. If there is no new hole, I redig the old one. It is not long before Salty starts hanging back as far as she can when I start humming my hole-digging hymn as I get out my overalls. Her face begins to express something like, "Christ, she's crazy! Hole digging is not fun!" And she stops digging holes and devotes herself to preventing the very thought of holes from coming into my mind. *This has nothing to do with punishment or authority,* and if it is corrupted by either then it becomes cruel. I just am, or have become, the sort of animal who has this crazy, incurable response to the sight of a hole; the only way to handle it is to keep me away from holes. (The spouse of a dedicated sailor may feel similarly about bodies of water.) An important aspect of this hole-digging cure is that it won't work unless I really do get excited in just this way about holes. Going through the motions won't compel the dog's belief. Holes must become sacred for me. This means that unless some other object, such as tidy lawns and flower beds, is stronger in my imagination than hole digging, I will lose my ability to disapprove of holes, and in the future chances are quite good that unless the foundations of the house are threatened I won't cure any more dogs of hole digging, and will instead stop and admire their holes.

One day Salty and I are going for a walk through an abandoned orange grove. We come upon a hole made by some burrowing animal. Salty glances at me nervously, hoping I haven't noticed, and when she thinks I am distracted, reaches out a nervous paw and scoops some dirt and leaves over the hole. Then she frisks off, inviting me to play elsewhere.

Trainers tend to talk about the importance of corrections being impersonal, especially the out-corrections I discussed above. That is to say, they should be expressions, not of opinions, but of the trainer's nature. You simply become the sort of animal who, as it were, helplessly gives certain corrections in the face of certain crimes. This is something like the impersonality of the law, having to do with our sense that the law ought to be sacred to judges, but it also has to do with our sense that a good judge, or a good teacher, is not so much someone who is good at slipping into the imperative mode as someone who does it without expecting that with obedience can or ought to come obeisance as well. Alas, the law is administered, and music appreciation is taught, by and to people for whom they are not sacred. There are ways of diminishing the resultant incoherence, but no way of eliminating it. Kurt Vonnegut pointed out the extraordinary power of denial the ghetto student acquired simply by thinking to say, "Whaffo Ah wanna read no *Tale Of Two Cities*?" It was not that there was no meaningful answer to this question but that most of us, living in the complacency Nietzsche tried to reveal for what it was, had forgotten that there could be such a question and that having an answer to it, or as many answers to it as there are people to whom one assigns reading lists, is part of the obligation taken on. Frequently the only answer that can be given *ahead of time* is: "Because you have to if you want to pass this course. You may also fall in love with Sydney Carton, or learn something useful about the necessity and tragedy of revolution, or you may come to love Dickens's language. Or none of this may happen." A teacher may or may not be willing to accept the further commitment of entering into the student's reality to see what meaning Dickens might have there. Not much else can be said, perhaps.

So, when I go to teach Salty to retrieve, I don't speak to her of the greatness of Algonquin, although I need to remember it myself in order to respond appropriately to the minutest motions of such greatness in what goes on. They will be pretty minute for a while. First, I command her to sit and stay. I gently place a dumbbell in her mouth for a moment as I say, "Salty, fetch!" I remove it instantly and praise her. She tightens her chops and regards me dubiously, perhaps swallowing to get the taste of the wood out of her mouth. *This* has nothing to do with the passion that led her to tear through brambles in order to chase balls for her former owners. At this point she can't even say, "Whaffo Ah wanna fetch?" because the word doesn't mean that yet. All it is, is part of a distraction from the stay command. For about a week I place the dumbbell in her mouth several dozen times a day, saying the command. Not because it takes her that long to "know" in some abstract sense *what* I mean, but because she has to know that I mean it. She can ask, "Whaffo ah wanna let you put that dumb thing in my mouth?" and I can say, "Because if you resist you will inevitably break your sit-stay and the earth will open up and swallow you." That's all we can say. She can't believe formal retrieving language at this point, in something like the way I can neither believe nor doubt Maxwell's equations. Anyway, even if I could explain things, the explanations would no more put truth into the commands if it wasn't already there than the word "true" will put truth into propositions if it isn't already there. Frege, the founder of modern mathematical logic, remarks in an awesomely lovely essay, "Thoughts," that "assertoric force does not lie in [the word *true*] but in the assertoric sentence form; and where this form loses its assertoric force the word 'true' could not put it back again." This is perhaps truer of commands than of declarative sentences, or more obviously true. I had better be right, that is.

There is now an object in our language, the dumbbell. After requiring Salty to allow me to open her mouth and place the dumbbell in it, I require her to open her mouth herself. Then I demand that she actually reach out one full inch and cover the dumbbell herself, and so forth. At each stage I get "Whaffo?" All I can say is, "Because I'll pinch your ear if you don't." My praise is another matter. When she does accept the dumbbell, I must respond with the awe that consists in honoring the details. Here the contaminations of approval (as opposed to Recognition) will be worse in their effects on the language than with the novice exercises. Salty may be willing and able to sit in order to please me, but even if she wanted to she couldn't retrieve in order to please me. Even if I wanted to I couldn't write philosophy in order to please you. If I am writing philosophy I must be prepared, as Wittgenstein said, to discover something completely new, and this completely new thing may not be—probably isn't—among the things that already please you. Hence no matter how large and wonderful and full of glorious creatures your philosophy already is, and no matter how much you love me and approve of me, and no matter how much this love and approval is returned, it will be impossible to do philosophy in order to please you. I may, of course (will be, in fact), deeply enabled in my writing by the conviction that you are able to recognize what I have done or am trying to do, or at least that you are able to acknowledge without demanding proof that I am trying to do something that will count as philosophy. This is the sort of praise I must be able to give Salty if we are ever to trope this or any other version of retrieving into a full-blown true story about her independence of mind and greatness of soul. Full-blown retrieving demands grown-up love of the activity itself. Salty doesn't (can't) retrieve *for* me, she can only retrieve *with* me. This is a mentor relationship. I am not denying that encouragement is essential to achievement; we do take heart, are encouraged by, each other. However, the sort of encouragement that leads to a novice working with a nervous eye out for a teacher's approval is a distraction from the business at hand. In practice it is probably not possible to be interested in what the novice is doing without being interested in the novice, or being willing to be interested if that becomes appropriate, but that is not to the point.

I should notice at this or at some point that one of the things that might lead someone to wonder about what looks like the wildest sort of anthropomorphizing is the sketchiness of the tokens of this language game. For one thing, I'm not filling in all of the details (this isn't a language primer). More to the point, a reason for trying to get a feel for a dog/human language is that it sharpens one's awareness of the sketchiness of the tokens of English. Wittgenstein says, "It is as if a snapshot of a scene had been taken, but only a few scattered details of it were to be seen: here a hand, there a bit of a face, or a hat—the rest is dark. And now it is as if we knew quite certainly what the whole picture represented. As if I could read the darkness." When we learn a language game, we learn to read the darkness.

Retrieving makes possible a new sort of truth between Salty and me. It also makes new sorts of deception possible and, in fact, the new truth is possible against the possibility of the new deception. The day comes when I lay the dumbbell on the ground, move about a leash-length away from it, stand with Salty sitting at my side, the two of us facing the dumbbell, and, without my hand on the dumbbell, send my dog. She leaps out eagerly, with every appearance of sincerity, swiftly covers the dumbbell with her chest, lying on it, and then sniffs around in all directions industriously as if to say, "I'd love to bring it to you, Boss, but I just can't find it!" It is unlikely that she doesn't know where it is, so I get on her ear and correct her. Suddenly she "remembers" that it's under her chest and picks it up. This is a moment when Koehler would be especially disgusted by any hesitation to correct, and the word he uses to express his disgust is "dishonest." Why? Salty's dishonesty is clear enough, but why would it be so wrong to fail to correct her? Why wrong to say something like, "Well, the poor thing is just so upset by the newness of everything that I'll wait a while before insisting"?

By now I'm saying a great deal when I say "Salty, fetch!" Not everything I will come to say, but a great deal, and one of the things I'm already saying is "I promise that something is going on here that is worth doing right, and I am deeply committed to getting it right, and I know that it is appropriate for you to pick up the dumbbell when I command you to." So in failing to correct I'm going back on my word, as I would be doing if I corrected angrily, righteously, or pettishly, as if I were personally offended. Similarly if a student-poet performs some anxious evasion of form and if I know (this is knowing *a lot*) that for this particular poet a full surrender to this particular form will be fruitful, and if I then accept the evasion, fail to correct, perhaps because I have a headache that's making it hard for me to concentrate or to care, then the teaching relationship will have moved toward incoherence and may disappear. This happens all the time, of course, and I very seldom know enough about any student to be that certain of my corrections. The moral of this story, however, is not that we ought to lessen the demands we make on poetry itself.

I do know enough about dogs, and about this dog, to feel confident about my corrections and my manner of praise. Soon, Salty explores yet another form of dishonesty, whose syntax is more like the syntax we have in mind when we think of lying as opposed to deception or evasion. Now I am throwing the dumbbell out as far as twenty or thirty feet, and it lands between Touchstone and a stick from the pepper tree. Salty picks up the stick rather than the dumbbell. This is almost like saying, "It's not this one but that one," although there are some queer things about it. For one thing, I assume that Salty doesn't imagine that *I* don't know the difference between the stick and the dumbbell. (Perhaps Saul Kripke, or some other wunderkind of Western puzzlement, could wonder about this, but Salty can't.) Salty is lying about *herself*, not about the dumbbell. She wants me to believe that *she* believes I meant the stick rather than the dumbbell. A curious thing about dogs is that the more talent they have for retrieving the more they tend to think of inventive variations of this maneuver. Salty is very talented indeed, and she tries to retrieve Touchstone, rocks, the tires to my car, the lawn. She looks a bit sullen when I don't accept these "retrieves." It is as if the forms of retrieving are so deeply if inarticulately felt for her that she must test my commitment to them thoroughly. That, at any rate, is a story that will enable me to get on with my training. Another story is that she is playing around with the story I am trying to tell, is curious enough about it to be willing to risk the corrections. What I want to do is note the nature of this "lying." Since she doesn't know yet the honesty of a proper retrieve, because she hasn't experienced it, she can't very well lie about that, and not much is being violated, by her at least, though a great deal is violated if I accept her lies as truths.

One day I notice that the nature of her retrieving has changed. I can tell, by the knowing way she sails out, the purposefulness of her movements, the wholly gay seriousness with which she scoops up the dumbbell, the addition to her performance of a degree of precision and fire I hadn't asked for (since no one can ask for *this*), that It's Happened. She has walked, or galloped, into real retrieving. She is transformed, I am transformed, and the world is transformed, for now I am able to mean all of *this* when I say, "Salty, fetch!" Now there are all sorts of new ways our language can be projected. I have her retrieve things besides her dumbbell. Perhaps I have her retrieve Uncle Albert. Retrieving can become carrying messages. I can teach a directed retrieve, having her retrieve things I haven't thrown. I can, that is, use "Fetch" to name things, in somewhat the way we use "this" and "that" to name things.

If Salty and I proceed to scent work, then many other moral, syntactical, and theological complexities will enter the situation, including a more advanced syntax of deception and hence a more advanced syntax of truth. Now, when sent to select one of two or more indicated articles by scent, she can say, "It's this one (rather than that one)." "The child went this way." "This is the criminal." The investigation of how this comes about belongs elsewhere; I mention it in order to point to what I have been hoping to make clear all along. The investigation of animal consciousness, like the investigation of human consciousness, is centrally an investigation of language, and this ought to remind us of what an investigation of language is.

The beginning of scent discrimination involves having the dog look for hidden objects whose location the trainer knows. So in scent work it becomes possible to give *advice*, and to give advice about something we are mostly ignorant of (scent). "Look for the criminal's tracks over there, to the west of the sycamore tree," or, "The way the wind is today, we'll do better if we move down river." This is what generally spoils scent work. Once in a while the advice is right, but it almost never is, and it almost always discounts the dog's possibilities as an autonomous, trustworthy, responsible creature. Knowing nothing about scent, people give their dogs advice about it anyway because, I think, we tend to do this with each other, and it's just that the "irrationality," as Cavell puts it, of the way we give advice—"As though advice operated on others at random, like a ray"—is generally more obvious in scent work.

How advice comes to be possible isn't my present concern. That advice is given brings me to notice that in the natural history of this language I am looking at, the possibility of giving a command is prior to (both historically and in terms of the unfolding of the syntax) such things as naming, referring, advising, and full trust. (I now trust Salty enough so that although the general rule is no-dogs-on-the-furniture, I know that if she should once in a blue moon get up on my chair, she would be making some sort of joke.) Trope is possible, too. (One day I absentmindedly fail to respond when Salty brings her feed dish. I put the dish on the desk and continue my work. Now she brings me a wastepaper basket, wriggling so hard with gleeful appreciation of her own wit she drops it on her way. I don't know what trope it is.) There is a great deal to say about this, but all I want to say here is that I am struck by a new wonder at the priority of the commands and also at how the coherence of the commands depends on my ability, my willingness, to hand authority over to Salty, in the case of the wastebasket by acknowledging the possibility of her saying something I haven't taught her to say. (An extraordinary number of failures at formal tracking trials happen when the handler pulls the dog away from the trail, which may be why bigger, stronger dogs do so well at tracking.) If I can't say to you, should the occasion arise, "Duck!" or "Put the broom in the other closet when you're done," or "Write your name on the top right-hand corner of your paper," or "No mayonnaise on mine," or "Lower down. Ah, that's it," then it's not clear what sort of relationship we can have. What if I can't give the command, "Stop!"? In dog training commanding is made possible because dogs and people are domestic, and this is true without formal training, too, of course; there are all sorts of gestures and commands pet dogs respond to. Those are the commands being imitated in formal training, imitated in some of the ways that poetry imitates utterance, which is part of why trainers have the impulse to speak of the *art* of training.

In cheerfully suggesting that authority is essential in our relationships, that talking depends on the possibility of command, I haven't forgotten the taint in authority I began by worrying about. If commanding is essential and if the untainted expression of authority is well nigh impossible, since we can never fully know another's cares and interests, never fully share the sacred and profane objects in their world, then how *are* we to command each other? How say, "Turn in your papers on Tuesday," or "Take one pill after each meal," or "Practice an hour a day," or "Pay your taxes by April 15"? What gives us the right to say "Fetch!"? Something very like reverence, humility, and obedience, of course. We can follow, understand, only things and people we can command, and we can command only whom and what we can follow.

The Naming and Blaming of Cats
JOHN HOLLANDER

M ORE THAN THIRTY years ago, Professor John Clive announced
the formation of a new Mozart Society along old European scholarly lines.
All candidates for membership had to submit papers, and for his own,
Clive proposed one on the subject of *"Frau Köchel: Ein Lebensbild."* I
believe that I was provisionally admitted for a projected talk, of adequate
irrelevance and tedium, on "Sussmayr's Descendants in America." Now,
at the end of the T. S. Eliot centenary year, I am moved, this time without
frivolity, to engage the heavy *Wissenschaft* of the penumbral and peripheral yet once more, having left the poet's central work to those literary
scholars with professional claims on it. I shall also allow myself some personal reminiscence.

I met Mr. Eliot only once, at just about the time of the founding of
Professor Clive's learned society, one Monday evening in Cambridge,
where he was a guest of the Harvard Society of Fellows, and where I got
(the truth must lie somewhere between "got" and "arranged" . . . perhaps "arranged to get" will do) to sit next to him at dinner. Despite my
youth and audacity, I think I had the good sense not to mention any of his
poetry or criticism that I had grown up with, lest I say something boring
to, or ask something irritating of, a writer who had heard it all. (I still feel
that serious discourse about a serious writer's work had best go on behind
his or her back.) But we did talk of (*a*) cats and (*b*) Sherlock Holmes and
his fictional world. Having read and reread the Conan Doyle stories since
childhood, I was aware that there were societies, not unlike John Clive's,
devoted to the study of the details of the Holmesian canon, what has since
become known as "trivia"—the Baker Street Irregulars was one such
group—but I had not yet met more than one person for whom the prose,
the very phrases of the fiction, resounded with an almost scriptural
power. Thus I was delighted to find that the Great Man delighted in
these. I remember one moment at which the crucial distinction was
drawn among the epithets "the most dangerous man in London" (the
arch-adversary, Professor Moriarty, of course), "the second most danger-

ous man in London" (his exec, the infamous Colonel Sebastian Moran, so designated in "The Adventure of the Empty House"), and "the worst man in London" (the vile blackmailer, Charles Augustus Milverton, in, yes, "The Adventure of Charles Augustus Milverton"—he is *so* bad that he gets to have a tale named just for him.) I mention this now because my text for this occasion concerns both Holmes and cats, even though it is not by Eliot himself, but by his fascinating "heteronymic" author (the great modern Portuguese poet Fernando Pessoa having given us this concept), Old Possum.

I remember when, at the age of sixteen, I was handling for the first time the yellow-backed (or, at least, jacketed) old *Collected Poems* of Eliot, giggling with a friend over the juxtaposition of the last two titles of the other books by the same author listed on the back of the jacket: *The Idea of a Christian Society* and *Old Possum's Book of Practical Cats*. But I would not begin to understand for decades, I think, the relation between the two bodies of work. Is the poet Eliot playing possum by playing at being Old Possum? Or is he truly Old Possum, and thereby—is the banking, criticizing, Arnoldizing, de-Emersonizing, famous-barding T. S. Eliot playing dead? In that case, he might come to full poetic life only in the protected, unobserved realms of poetic minority. Like the grand superseded gods of old Ireland, who survived the hegemony of Christianity only by going underground, shrinking and becoming the "little people," the fairies, wielding their daemonic power from behind a screen of apparent triviality, the poetic imagination often goes underground during the imperium of mere Literature. Prose romance, after the rise of the novel and the triumph of lyric over narrative in verse, goes underground in the nineteenth century, and survives in certain great books written for children, or in America. The American "possum," the opossum, derives its name from the Algonquian *aposoum*, itself deriving from an earlier word perhaps meaning "white beast." But playing dead inside the American word a poet would perceive the punning etymon from Latin, *possum*, "to be able, physically or morally." The naming of selves is a difficult matter (as is naming versions, masks, portions, or subsets of selves), and *Old I'm Capable*, whose "Effanineffable / Deep and inscrutable singular Name" may have been True Poet, is singularly well-so-called. Old Possum's corpse may have been part of T. S. Eliot's life, while the poet played dead under apparent diminution.

I should like to argue that he comes closer, as Old Possum, to coping with the deep sources of poetic power than he does as the poet even of *Four Quartets,* and that the Muse of Childhood—of pre-Freudian and post-Wordsworthian, *special,* nineteenth-century childhood—surely empowered the poem on the naming of cats. This was the private muse of those other romantic imaginations blocked by the *lyra dentata* (or whatever) of the major one, such as Lewis Carroll, Edward Lear, and Hans Christian Andersen; among other things, she allowed Old Possum to be far more loving to, say, the Gumbie Cat named Jennyanydots than T.S.E., in propria persona, could ever be to the unfortunate females (save for Shakespeare's Marina) condemned to haunt his poetry: the wretched Fresca (whose name Pound wisely excised from *The Waste Land* perhaps with the prophetic prescience that it would return decades later as the name of a nasty diet soft drink); all "the ladies of the corridor"; Grishkin and Rachel née Rabinovitch; the nervous lady; Lil and her unnamed friend, and so on.

Then, too, there is the matter of The Cat. In modern discourse, cats have been objects of contemplative meditation (Montaigne, Schopenhauer) and ecstatic contemplation (Christopher Smart and Baudelaire—although the latter seems always to be pursuing some essential Felinity rather than considering a particular cat we could think of as having a *name*). Their deaths have been mourned by poets, and their lives moralized upon. Eliot may have considered Baudelaire one of his precursors in modernity, or, at least, appeared to want to. But Old Possum's roots are more authentically revealed in his own work. Possum's allusions are forthright, direct, uncoy, and above all not set up, as they conspicuously are in *The Waste Land,* as a means of screening the allusive truth, a hiding of the sources of his echoing as if even from the poet himself. The very flavor and tone of Possum's verse affirm its awareness of what we hear in it: W. S. Gilbert, Kipling, Chesterton, and particularly, I should say, that grand master of light verse, Charles Stuart Calverley (1831–1884), whose soliloquy of a tomcat, "Sad Memories," is itself full of loud poetical echoes—of Milton, Shakespeare, Thomas Hood—and, as in the opening of this passage (the falling china coming from *The Rape of the Lock*), of Alexander Pope:

> Should china fall, or chandelier, or anything but stocks—
> Nay, stocks when they're in flowerpots—the cat expects hard
>   knocks—
> Should ever anything be missed—milk, coals, umbrellas, brandy—
> The cat's pitched into with a boot or anything that's handy.

In these lines the cat is himself complaining about the eternal scapegoat condition of his mode of Being-in-the-House. (Even that pioneering naturalist Buffon remarks—and I quote a late eighteenth-century English translation—"They are naturally inclined to theft, and the best education only converts them into servile and flattering robbers.") Old Possum's visionary transumption of this passage filters it through the lens of Conan Doyle. It takes Calverley's cat's complaint about the infelicity of essential catness—that it is always under suspicion for all household mischief—and refocuses it on Possum's own exemplary objective correlative, "the Napoleon of Crime" Macavity. (It was of course Sherlock Holmes who identified Professor Moriarty as "the Napoleon of crime, Watson!") Moriarty-Macavity is a strong figure who transforms the condition of being falsely blamed into a position of power. The cat, abstract, general, who in Calverley is "pitched into with a boot or anything that's handy," is reenvisioned by the capable Possum as having been *really* responsible all the time. The other forces at work on the milk, coals, umbrellas, brandy (a splendid list in itself) are, in Possum's words, "nothing more than agents for the Cat who all the time / Just controls their operations." So, too, we remember, for Macavity:

> And when the larder's looted, or the jewel-case is rifled,
> Or when the milk is missing, or another Peke's been stifled,
> Or the greenhouse glass is broken, and the trellis past repair—
> Ay, there's the wonder of the thing! Macavity's not there!

But if it is the Holmesian voice, in particular, that is heard in the matter of Macavity, what are we to say of the profound and pointed, the sage and serious poem which is my central text? Old Possum's vitality (*Katzenleben* in obscure German usage, I believe) here encounters the deeper poetic matters of names and naming. The first poem, the Original one, as Renaissance writers liked to think, was God's literal *poesis* of the world. The first poem as modern poets think of it was Adam's naming of the animals. (Proust's remark seems to conflate these: "*Si Dieu le Père a créé les choses en les nommant, c'est en leur ôtant leur nom, ou en leur en donnant un autre que l'artiste les recrée*"—if God created things by naming them, the artist re-creates them by unnaming, or renaming them.)

In the poetry of everyday life we continue to be able to name things in a realm in which it is not only poets who effect original poems. "The naming of cats is a difficult matter," avers Old Possum at the outset. At first, the history of poetry would seem to belie this. We can think of so many poetical cats with names that sound as though they had been easily and naturally given, without any epistemological, logical, or even metaphysical struggles. Consider the nineteenth-century American poet Christopher Pearse Cranch's cat Tabitha Jane, who ends her little monologue with a simple and not unsurprising confession that

> I don't care much for the people
> > Who are living with me in this house,
> But I own that I love a good fire
> > And occasional herring and mouse.

Or Marianne Moore's very puzzling Peter ("Sleep is the epitome of his delusion that one must do as well as one can for oneself"); Gray's "pensive Selima," whose "conscious tail her joy declares"; Christopher Smart's Jeffrey and George Herriman's Krazy, not to speak of Krazy's relative, Don Marquis's Mehitabel, "*toujours gai, toujours gai*" or even Du Bellay's possibly anagrammatic Belaud. (Wordsworth, Cowper, and Keats, I'm afraid, come up with nothing more than "Puss," "Tabby," and "Cat" in their feline verses.) In any event, it is significant that even the preceding sample contains the names both of actual pets being mourned or celebrated in poetry, and of purely notional creatures: the names of persons and of fictions, too, are of one linguistic substance.

A linguist might classify names by genre, by tradition, or convention—for example, English Christian names can be those of saints, of Old Testament personages (in more radically Protestant traditions), Anglo-Saxon animal names (often in apparently arbitrary combination), and so forth. But for the poet, there are apparently three conditions of naming, "which often look alike / Yet differ completely." With the unfettered power by which Eliot speaks of cats, he can clearly assert that "a cat must have THREE DIFFERENT NAMES":

> First of all, there's the name that the family use daily,
> > Such as Peter, Augustus, Alonzo or James,
> > Such as Victor or Jonathan, George or Bill Bailey—
> All of them sensible, everyday names.

(It might be observed here that this first list ends with the totally American and powerfully allusive "Bill Bailey"—the apparently errant cat whose owners have named him from the famous 1902 ragtime song, "Bill Bailey, Won't You Please Come Home." It might also be observed that the cats they name are, like Mr. Eliot, all Toms.) But these names turn out not to exhaust the first category, even though if we think merely of surface representations rather than of deep onomastic structures, the next list of high-classical names would seem to manifest a second mode:

> There are fancier names if you think they sound sweeter,
>   Some for the gentlemen, some for the dames:
> Such as Plato, Admetus, Electra, Demeter—
>
> —"But all of them sensible, everyday names," as well.

What then would the second way of naming involve? Firstly, since "a cat needs a name that's particular," "peculiar," it would have to avoid the difficulty we all experience on discovering that we share our given names, and our surnames, and sometimes both, with many other people, so that even our social security numbers are more distinctive, in a strong but—we feel—trivial sense, than our names are. Those numbers don't *mean* anything: they do designate each of us uniquely, but that is almost all—they are all *Bedeutung* and minimal *Sinn:* a social security number could be treated as a ten-digit number and thus as odd or even, prime or composite, I suppose, but that would provide less matter for contemplation than whether one's name was that of, say, a flower, a month, or a virtue. (Conversely, if everyone in a community were named "Beautifulperson," the name would provide lots of lovely *Sinn* and insufficient *Bedeutung.*) But now imagine a name, totally and comfortably and even enjoyably utterable in English (unlike, e.g., "Shtrutzpflk"), but as singularly denotational as a twelve-digit number and uniquely intentional as well. The giving of such names is the second way:

> Of names of this kind I can give you a quorum,
>   Such as Munkustrap, Quaxo, or Coricopat,
> Such as Bombalurina, or else Jellylorum—
>   Names that never belong to more than one cat.

These purely ad hoc names would partake of the primal quality of the Original ones given, scripture tells us, by Adam, proper names that, immediately upon being conferred, became common nouns.

But the final way of naming must transcend even this merely linguistic mode of uniqueness, with its applicability to ordinary selfhood. It is utterable only in the phonemes of silence, lest that utterance of it even sound like other language. This is a far more serious hedge around verbal performance than even the muffling of the Tetragrammaton, the name of

God in Hebraic tradition. If Peter, Augustus, Alonzo, or James seem too common; if Plato, Admetus, Electra, and Demeter, in my demotic at any rate, are names just like the other ones; and if Coricopat or Jellylorum are full parts of words and reek of things, then what name—pure of the bodily decrepitude of language, even, sheer name without linguistic form— could designate any cat as representing the highest form of unfallen, still emparadised, selfhood? Possum's moral essay concludes with this third stage:

> But above and beyond there's still one name left over,
>   And that is the name that you never will guess;
> The name that no human research can discover—
>   But THE CAT HIMSELF KNOWS, and will never confess.
> When you notice a cat in profound meditation,
>   The reason, I tell you, is always the same:
> His mind is engaged in a rapt contemplation
>   Of the thought, of the thought, of the thought of his name:
>   His ineffable effable
>   Effanineffable
> Deep and inscrutable singular Name.

But here the interpreter is on dangerous ground, for, as Wittgenstein reminds us at the end of the *Tractatus,* "Whereof one cannot speak, one must remain silent," and I shall not for a moment presume to consider the nature, substance, or accidence of the name that "THE CAT HIMSELF KNOWS." Even to suggest that it is like a *mantra*—a concept perhaps beloved of the poet of "What the Thunder Said" or "The Fire Sermon"— would be a profanation. It should be added that calling out a name can be very like some Heideggerian sort of acknowledging, or attributing—and that naming itself is perhaps even a conferring—of Being. Naming cats, as I have previously observed in these pages (*Raritan,* Fall, 1981), is a poetic matter, in that a cat will almost always not respond to its name the way a dog will. Its knowledge of its own name is in fact a very deep and inscrutable knowledge, immune to human testing; and even as we ascribe names to cats, we ascribe an effanineffable mode of knowledge—knowledge "of" those names—to them as well. Thus in summoning up for itself—not calling out—its own unutterable name, its own private but transcendent Tetragrammaton, the cat is continuing to acknowledge, and perhaps even to intensify, its own Being.

The end of the poem thus gets to the heart of the poetic matter, and it is only appropriate to observe here that the great poetical skills of Old Possum are fully at work in these lines, and in an exemplary fashion. The splendid resources of the jingle and sing-song of light verse are usually employed to frame a joke, to set up or deliver a punchline; at the very best, they can also make ancillary jokes about patterning, about prominent rhythm and speed in verse itself, and often about language and its bits and pieces. In sing-song, we take for granted repetitions of word or phrase at points of chorus or refrain. Nobody could seriously suggest that the threefold repetition of, say, "For he's a jolly good fellow" encoded a trinitarian message, or that each iteration applied to body, mind, and soul successively. But when Possum tells us that the cat "in profound meditation" is directing himself to contemplation "Of the thought, of the thought, of the thought of his name," the jingle song pattern, an ordinarily superficial repetition, doubles with a logical designation. A cat is a cat; the word "cat" names any particular present cat, here, now, furry, as well as all other such cats. But we can progress onward, to the name of a name, putting alternate single and double quotation marks around the inscribed letters. (For example, Boston is a city in Massachusetts with roughly 700,000 inhabitants; "Boston" is a word naming it with precisely 6 letters; "'Boston'!" I answered [when you asked me for an anagram of "Snobot") is a citation with a high probability, under the circumstances, of being deployed.)

So, too, there is a recursion of "thought of a thought of a thought" that hides beneath the casual, refrainlike repetitions of singsong. And yet finally even this logical progression vanishes into an ultimate and elusive domain. The closer the cat gets to the knowledge of his name, the more distant he is; the more it is contemplated, the more terms must be added to "thought of the thought of the thought of the thought . . ." The deeper, the farther out. The naming of cats is indeed a difficult matter, and should be considered a dangerous one. So is the writing of true poetry. Karl Kraus said about aphorisms something that all good poets know about poetry, and I shall conclude with the appropriate form of it here:

> A last comment that I hope Old Possum's ghost will still allow,
> That to name a cat is easy if you DON'T KNOW HOW.

Hannah Arendt:
Alienation and America
GEORGE KATEB

Fᴏʀ ʜᴀɴɴᴀʜ Arendt the spiritual condition of modernity is marked
by loss, which she calls most generally alienation. She finds in alienation
not a specific horror, but a pervasive mentality that is often painful to endure and that is part of the direct or ultimate source of the specific horror
of totalitarianism and the source and also the intensified outcome of
smaller wrongs and evils. I would like to propose that by seeing only the
horror in alienation, and the horrors that may be connected with it, she
fails to deal properly with the heroism and greatness of modernity, which
are at the source of alienation. Even more important, she takes little account of the benign effects and implications of a moderate, everyday
alienation, the kind of alienation that helps to define the self nurtured by
modern constitutional representative democracy. I do not think that this
benign sort of alienation could have come into existence unless the acute
sort had also. Thus, Arendt is at one with all those who lament alienation,
even though her analysis contains some novel elements. It may be, however, that lamentation is not the right response, or at least not the solely
right response. Unless alienation inspires more than lamentation in the
political theorist, the theory cannot be fully adequate to the work of confronting modernity.

By *alienation* Arendt means two things: first, world alienation, and
second, earth alienation. Words like *homelessness* and *decenteredness*
catch most of the content, as does the more common synonym, *estrangement*. She is trying to conceptualize the condition in which the rightly
expectable is taken away or has always been felt as missing. Quite without
elaboration Arendt assumes this condition is in some of its manifestations
painful, and will, painful or not, necessarily issue forth in social and political aberrations, large and small. But aside from the pain and the consequences, alienation is to be lamented as the wrong condition to be in. The
largely unargued premise is that the human race exists in order to be at
home in the world and on the earth, that our humanity is tied to the absence of alienation—at least, the radical alienation of the modern age.

196

The hope that humanity could be fully at home is dashed by modernity, by the growth of human capacities to master and use nature. In the perspective of *world* alienation, the great series of events that comprise the European "discovery of the globe as a whole," and the emergence of a global economy spurred by economic ambitions retrospectively called capitalist, are decisive. In the perspective of *earth* alienation, the splitting of the atom and the exploration of space are decisive. These two related sets define modern alienation. Because mankind is just beginning to explore space, and because the full consequences of splitting the atom are not yet disclosed, we are in a better position to know the meaning of world alienation than of earth alienation. Nevertheless, Arendt says that world alienation is of "minor significance" in comparison to earth alienation.

What is world alienation? Arendt's discussion suggests a dynamic, remorseless process of economic growth, accompanied until fairly recently by immense human suffering. She says:

> Expropriation, the deprivation for certain groups of their place in the world and their naked exposure to the exigencies of life, created both the original accumulation of wealth and the possibility of transforming this wealth into capital through labor. These together constituted the conditions for the rise of a capitalist economy. . . . What distinguishes this development at the beginning of the modern age from similar occurrences in the past is that expropriation and wealth accumulation did not simply result in new property or lead to a new redistribution of wealth, but were fed back into the process to generate further expropriations, greater productivity, and more appropriation.

The essence of the process in its earlier phases was the uprooting of many people from their land and their conversion into "free" laborers. At the same time the very notion of property as rootedness, and as an inviolable private place and shelter, was transformed. "Society" replaced the family as "the subject of the new life process," while national solidarity was supposed to make up for the weakening of family solidarity. The ultimate logic of the system is a global society in which cultural singularities fade and the human race experiences the same experiences and is affected by the same happenings.

Arendt could therefore be expected to worry about the unitary world state as a proposed remedy for the problem of nuclear weapons. Abhorrence of a nearly undifferentiated global society in which all people exist, so to speak, in the same time and on the same plane, is part of the worry.

The fact is that Arendt *defines* the core of world alienation as precisely the loss of group differentiation, which is not only the loss of mediation between the individual self and everything else, but the loss of elements that help to compose a self and sanely enlist its energies. The unchecked movement to a global society would consummate world alienation. To be in the world one must be in only a part of it; and a part is what it is only because there are distinct other parts. Individual identity depends on group life, which depends on group identity. Every identity, whether individual or collective, requires otherness, not for the sake of developing itself through opposition and awareness of contrast, but because it is real only when perceived and acknowledged by something outside itself and different from itself. The world as a whole is not a world for any person.

In a large sense, then, *world* here means the common life of a group fixed in a place, and extending over the generations. We can add that in a narrower but deeper sense the public realm—the realm of political action—is also the world. The human condition of modernity is characterized by loss of the world both in the large and in the narrow sense: the loss of cultural rootedness and of a proper public realm. In another formulation, she says, "The rise of society brought about the simultaneous decline of the public as well as the private realm." The rise of society is the rise of capitalism as a global political economy. She insists, against Marx, that "World alienation, and not self-alienation . . . has been the hallmark of the modern age." She accepts Weber's thesis concerning the spiritual origins of capitalist conduct, and transforms it into "his demonstration that an enormous, strictly mundane activity is possible without any care for or enjoyment of the world whatever, an activity whose deepest motivation, on the contrary, is worry and care about the self." Exploiters alienate the exploited from their roots in the world: that is the worst fact about exploitation. But the exploiters themselves are also alienated from the world, precisely because their work is heedless of the world. It is done for a totally self-regarding purpose: otherworldly salvation.

What is earth alienation? *World* alienation is, above all, the process whereby the many are ruthlessly made into one; whereby peoples and groups are drawn together in ways that weaken or abolish their identity, which cannot exist except in the world. *Earth* alienation, on the other hand, is, most generally, the ruthless transformation of the indefinite into the enclosed, the transformation of the whole earth into just one more object in the universe. In *The Human Condition* and a later essay, "The Conquest of Space and the Stature of Man," Arendt tries to show that the basic meaning of modern science has been to adopt the universe rather than the earth as its true standing-point and frame of reference. The intellectual animation behind the ability to make nuclear weapons derives from an intensification of moral and intellectual passions that first emerge clearly with Galileo and Descartes.

> Without actually standing where Archimedes wished to stand (*dos moi pou sto*), still bound to the earth through the human condition, we have found a way to act on the earth and within terrestrial nature as though we dispose of it from the outside, from the Archimedean point. And even at the risk of endangering the natural life process we expose the earth to universal, cosmic forces alien to nature's household.

She deploys the notion of the Archimedean project as a metaphor for the whole sustained effort to repeat the processes of aboriginal nature through deliberate human capacity, and to define man as no more than an observer of the universe. She refers not only to reproducing "cosmic processes" but also to the will to "create or recreate the miracle of life" by the advance of biological knowledge. Writing in 1958, she mentions the recent fact of artificial satellites: humanity was "creating as it were . . . new heavenly bodies." This fact she calls "second in importance to no other, not even to the splitting of the atom."

Earth alienation became literal; it became earth departure with the commencement of the exploration of space. Not only could men use and exploit nature, not only could they imitate some of its fundamental processes, they would soon be able to employ their inexhaustibly unsettling science and technology to leave the earth itself. But to be able to do so much, to be able to take leave of the earth, is to signify a disposition to a general abandonment of the earth as sufficient place, as the only home. She says:

> The most radical change in the human condition we can imagine would be an emigration of men from the earth to some other planet. Such an event, no longer totally impossible, would imply that man would have to live under man-made conditions, radically different from those the earth offers him. Neither labor nor work nor action nor, indeed, thought as we know it would then make sense any longer.

The greatest number of surprises in Arendt's reflections on alienation, especially on earth alienation, are found in her essay on the conquest of space. Among them is her finding alienation in a condition that at least formally resembles the one theorized by Hegel and Marx as the *end* of alienation. For Arendt, to be totally immersed in a situation in which everything is man-made and recognizable as the result of human effort successfully achieved is to be cut off from nature but not to have found oneself or man. It is to be lost in a possibly "self-defeating" enterprise. Not only does the short life span of any human being set strict limits to his ability to be an agent of space exploration, but beyond that, the exploration of space seems in Arendt's understanding to substantiate with ever greater force the uncertainty principle of Heisenberg. This principle has often been made to lend itself too nicely to literary uses, but we must grant Arendt her moment. She is persuaded that the loss of "the very objectivity of the natural world"—which Heisenberg himself inferred from the ideas that observation is dependent on theory and that incompatible theories may be used to explain the same events—is incurred ever more steeply as modern technology proceeds indefatigably. Space exploration is one of the great instances of technological genius, and as such, it makes an unsurpassed contribution to spreading an overall sense of the loss of objective reality. At the same time it epitomizes earth alienation. On the loss of objective reality she says:

> All of [technology] makes it more unlikely every day that man will encounter anything in the world around him that is not man-made and hence is not, in the last analysis, he himself in a different disguise. The astronaut, shot into outer space and imprisoned in his instrument-ridden capsule where each actual physical encounter with his surroundings would spell immediate death, might well be taken as the symbolic incarnation of Heisenberg's man—the man who will be the less likely ever to meet anything but himself and man-made things the more ardently he wishes to eliminate all nonanthropocentric considerations from his encounter with the non-human world around him.

The extreme of the human is thus unnatural; the abolition of otherness in its otherness, in its strangeness, is the *triumph* of alienation. The further prospect is that once arrived at the Archimedean point with respect to the earth, once having acquired manipulative control over the whole earth, man would "need a new Archimedean point, and so ad infinitum. In other words, man can get lost in the immensity of the universe, for the only true Archimedean point would be the absolute void behind the universe."

There is worse yet, by Arendt's account. She uses a formulation of

Kafka's for her purpose. Kafka wrote that man "found the Archimedean point, but he used it against himself; it seems that he was permitted to find it only under this condition." She turns this grim irony into a futurist conjecture toward the end of the essay. In this culminating expression of pessimism concerning earth alienation, there is an uncharacteristic rhetorical unsteadiness. The literal and the figurative mix confusingly:

> Without as yet actually occupying the point where Archimedes had wished to stand, we have found a way to act on the earth as though we disposed of terrestrial nature from outside, from the point of Einstein's "observer freely poised in space." If we look down from this point upon what is going on on earth and upon the various activities of man, that is, if we apply the Archimedean point to ourselves, then these activities will indeed appear to ourselves as no more than "overt behavior," which we can study with the same methods we use to study the behavior of rats.

"Seen from a sufficient distance," mankind appears to undergo a mutation: to become one with his methods of movement and communication, indistinguishable from his technological creations, and rid of "speech and everyday language." Thus would man's "conquest of space and the science that made it possible" have approached destroying the stature of man. She thus hazards an answer to the question of what man is, a question she suggests in *The Human Condition* only a nonhuman entity, only God, could answer. She has the confidence to say here what man is not.

But what does "seen from a sufficient distance" mean? The literal seeing of the earth from space yielded different emotions from those Arendt mentions. The metaphorical seeing—the imagining—is already present in a good deal of social science even when the laboratory study of human beings and the study of animals with human behavior in mind are not pursued. Behaviorism and the statistical handling of human data already imply the wish for an Archimedean point, even if the point has not been reached, or can never be reached. It could also be argued that the metaphorical seeing is merely illusion. Close up—that is, understood properly—the human being remains intact, and survives all theoretical reduction.

Yet if Arendt stirs up more matters than she manages to shape coherently, her reflections help to give some freshness to the subject of modern alienation. She weakens, perhaps breaks, the Marxist connection between the achievement of human mastery and the overcoming of alienation. Nevertheless, because she specifically repudiates the Nietzschean concept of will to power as the secret of human aspiration, rejects the notion of power-drive, "the passion to rule or govern," as the secret of politics; and insists that totalitarian genocide was not explainable by reference to the lust for power or the rational accumulation of power; we cannot say that she performs a simple reversal. She does not suggest that the *search for mastery* is the great cause of alienation (rather than being the key to its overcoming). Nearer to her meaning, I believe, is the supposition that mastery is a main consequence of some other drive, though certainly present itself in particular instances, as a drive itself. The passion for mastery, with its irrepressibility that resembles or counterfeits joy, gives way in Arendt's analysis to something darker: resentment against the several conditions of existence which she proceeds to itemize.

They are "a free gift from nowhere (secularly speaking)." Arendt lists "life itself, natality and mortality, worldliness, plurality, and the earth." She does not systematically tie any human endeavor to resentment of any particular one of the conditions, as she ties political action to joy in natality. Nor does she give primacy to any—say, resentment of mortality. The net sense is that humanity (or at least Western humanity) resents limitation as such. (Perhaps Camus's "metaphysical rebellion" is a similar conceptualization.) Its resentment induces extremist, excessive, unsatisfiable aspiration, exertion, and accomplishment. The result is world alienation and earth alienation as a general condition.

If we can say that Arendt's thought contains a dialectic of alienation, it moves from resentment to extremism to alienation. The pains of alienation may then issue in pathology or help cause it. (It is not the sufficient cause of totalitarianism, but totalitarianism takes advantage of it, intensifying it by the very methods that promise to alleviate it.) But it would seem that the experience of alienation and of its consequences does not press humanity to give up the extremist project (of which the Archimedean point is perhaps the most dramatic form). Sickness is perhaps driven to seek its cure in more sickness. Resentment dominates, and modern science and technology give it ever greater instrumentalities, thus strengthening their own source and inspiration. At one point, to be sure, Arendt describes alienation as the basic *cause* rather than the basic *result*. She says that it is "a basic condition of our whole life because out of it, and partly at least out of its despair, did arise the tremendous structure of the human artifice we inhabit today, in whose framework we have even discovered the means of destroying it together with all non-made things on earth." Still, I think that her most consistent meaning is that the root of alienation is human extremist exertion, and the root of that, in turn, is resentment of the human condition.

The question arises as to whether Arendt theorizes a complete acceptance of the facts of the human condition (as she itemizes them). If she did, we would find a quite remarkable combination of elements in her thought: an uninhibited celebration of political action and a deep suspicion of all other human activities insofar as they show resentment of limitation. She would seem to bless only the political uses of human energies (to the point of not always showing theoretical care for their moral cost) and to desire restraint and self-restraint everywhere else. Restraint and self-restraint would come from *acceptance* of the human condition and would lead to less alienation. She sometimes speaks as a humanist, and as one who hopes to see humanism revived by being made adequate to modernity in its capacity to engender horrors. Quite clearly her humanism would not consist in the affirmation of human powers displayed and employed indefinitely and in diverse modes. Her humanism is a humanism of limitation, of confinement—except for political action.

I believe that, in truth, Arendt's tendency is to counsel acceptance of the facts of the human condition. She does not do so as a theologian. She does so as a philosopher, even though she is prepared to endorse the Platonist view that "the true philosopher does not accept the conditions under which life has been given to man." I suppose she would rather have resentment lead to extremist exertion than to the characteristic philosophical distillation of resentment which offers the judgment that until you die "withdrawal into a sect is the second-best cure for being alive at all and having to live among men." In any case, there is no paradox involved in her granting all of her favor to political action while theorizing the desirability of accepting the facts of the human condition and submitting human activities, in general, to the discipline of such acceptance.

The basic proposition is that in the absence of concerted and efficacious resentment of the human condition and in a corresponding acceptance of the facts of the human condition, there emerges the chance for an *individual's* reconciliation with other facts: the events and experiences, the suffering, in his or her life in the world. Where resentment of the human condition is not a cultural drive, all those activities that grow out of it and work to alienate humanity from the world and the earth would perhaps abate, and the possibilities for a positive commitment to the world, both in the broad cultural and social sense and in the specific political sense, would increase. The way is then prepared for political action to establish itself as the focus of human energies. One measure of the greatness of politics is that it is, far more than any other human activity, implicated in the hope that each person can be reconciled to his own life. That is why Arendt can release politics while reining in everything else. Everything else tends to alienation and thus to, among other undesirable things, the foreclosure of reconciliation. Modernity makes reconciliation ever more difficult.

Experience exists for the sake of language. "We can no more master the past than we can undo it. But we can reconcile ourselves to it." Reconciliation consists in acceptance. There is nothing to regret or excuse. There is, instead, "consent." Quoting Isak Dinesen's words, "My life, I will not let you go except you bless me, but then I will let you go," she adds: "The reward of storytelling is to be able to let go." In "Truth and Politics," Arendt expands the point:

> It is perfectly true that "all sorrows can be borne if you put them into a story or tell a story about them," in the words of Isak Dinesen. . . . She could have added that joy and bliss, too, become bearable and meaningful for men only when they can talk about them and tell them as a story. . . . The political function of the storyteller—historian or novelist—is to teach acceptance of things as they are . . . this acceptance . . . can also be called truthfulness.

The notion of acceptance unites her thought on Being, the human condition, one's existence. Even the freest and most creative activity—political action—is finally consecrated because it is the truest road to acceptance.

But, as I have said, unless alienation inspires more than lamentation, modernity's greatness cannot be seen clearly or given its due. All the more so is that the case when alienation is conceptualized by reference to acceptance and hence to the connected themes of resentment (which is the source of alienation) and reconciliation (which is the greatest prize for individuals when humanity is not alienated). Arendt's philosophy is inhospitable to modernity through and through. She converts almost all its leading phenomena into horrors or sees them from the perspective of their contribution to horrors. She comes close to doing what Jaspers warned against doing: letting fear of the worst preclude taking risks for the best.

In response, let it be merely an act of faith to say that the existential opportunities as well as some of the achievements of modernity deserve praise. We can say that and still believe that no amount of greatness can outweigh or weigh as much as the horrors. There is no commensurability, no wish to strike a balance. The horror of totalitarianism is unforgivable. It is incommensurate with other evils and with all greatness. Other evils are also horrors, and also incommensurate with all greatness. Still, there is a life, a life in modernity. Political theory must try to take it in, in its vast indefiniteness. All I can do is to raise certain questions about Arendt's work—questions that she enables and inspires. I hope to suggest that resentment and alienation may be commendable, and that reconciliation is not. Thus, acceptance as the unifying idea must be indicted in behalf of modernity.

Is resentment of the human condition as significant for modern extremist aspiration, endeavor, and achievement as she says? We must acknowledge that though she deplores resentment, she never makes it a small passion or sees it at the service of envy, or of the will to undermine or tarnish. It is not Nietzsche's *ressentiment*. On the contrary it drives those who feel it to overreach. She sees its largeness of spirit but is offended and dismayed by it. At the same time she beautifully imputes to the scientists who worked on the space program, for instance, an utterly disinterested submission to the task of understanding nature—a submission not totally dissimilar from the disposition to be a spectator, free of all interests, whom she follows Cicero in calling "the most noble group of the free-born men, for what they were doing: to look for the sake of seeing only was the freest, *liberalissimum*, of all pursuits." She is also fully aware of the heroism of space feats. Yet for all these contrary motions against herself, the force of her theory is to see resentment of the human condition behind the dynamism of modern life.

She does not give a sufficient place to motives other than resentment. Disinterestedness added to resentment still does not make a complete enough picture. The effects, of course, are what they are, whatever the motives may be. Nevertheless, such matters as the exploration of space, the development of biological knowledge (on the one hand) and the pursuit of wealth on a global scale (on the other hand) show delight, virtuosity, perfectionism, restlessness, a sense of craft, and a fearlessness that are humanly admirable, even though streaked with cruelty and rapacity. They show that disdain for the merely utilitarian which Arendt herself expresses when discussing art or political action.

Yet even if resentment were the major animating energy, perhaps that is the way it should be. She says in *On Violence:* ". . . rage and violence that sometimes—not always—goes with it belong among the "natural" *human* emotions, and to cure man of them would mean nothing less than to dehumanize or emasculate him." One could say, analogously, that without resentment of the human condition humanity would become dehumanized or emasculated. To give the last word to acceptance of the human condition is to court cowardice or sterility. The celebration of political action is not adequate to rid her theory of this danger. Not all heroism is political heroism. Political action cannot exhaust the best human energies and capacities. It leaves too much out of the spectrum of human nature for it to be considered the definitively human activity— even if it were not as morally problematic as in fact it is. Indeed, if it really is the best means by which each person may honestly reconcile himself to the events and patterns of his life, then perhaps we should question the very idea of individual reconciliation.

For a more adequate and savvy account of the projects of modernity we can turn to the Emerson of "Circles." At the beginning of the essay he writes:

> Our life is an apprenticeship to the truth that around every circle another can be drawn . . . every end is a beginning. . . . This fact, as far as it symbolizes the moral fact of the Unattainable, the flying Perfect, around which the hands of man can never meet, at once the inspirer and the condemner of every success, may conveniently serve to connect many illustrations of human power in every department.

Thus, the energy to try to complete a project is in itself a warning that every completion is only temporary. The will to perfection guarantees that in spite of every effort, no achievement will ever permanently satisfy us. Following Emerson, we could say that perhaps the deepest resentment is not of the human condition but of human imperfection: what is operative is not the will to be *superhuman* but to be human. The will is unappeasable. The dignity is in the self-rejection by the species. If that quasi-Emersonian thought is plausible, we can say either that resentment is philosophically defensible or that resentment, looked at through an Emersonian prism, is not rancor but mobility. Correspondingly, the hope for reconciliation with one's own life may be a matter less of exaltation than of a certain kind of individual self-rejection. "Don't you see," Arendt says, "if you want something better, and better, and better, you lose the good." No thought could be more foreign to modernity, or, for that matter, to Emerson, than this one.

The Emersonian perception by no means requires loyalty to a current of thought in Heidegger, which Arendt knew and detested. I refer to the eager fatalism that consists in wanting to see every extreme tendency go its length with the philosopher's blessing, so that in its full expression it will do what it must, and by so doing, help prepare for its supersession. In a letter to J. Glenn Gray Arendt speaks of Heidegger's "grotesque idea" that National Socialism was "an encounter between global technology and modern man." Heidegger's idea is worse than grotesque; but Emerson's idea, Emerson's blessing of extremist aspiration, is not Heidegger's. Emerson could say in "Circles" that "'Blessed be nothing' and 'The worse things are the better they are' are proverbs which express the transcendentalism of common life." But this is an expression of defiant will, not of metaphysical resignation to the excesses of others. At the farthest edges of his view of "compensation," Emerson could not have lent himself to seeing the highest good as the "saving power" in relation to the greatest evil. At most, he is urging that a seeming evil may not be a real evil but a blessing. The highest good must be a good defined apart from evil, even if the energies of good are intertwined with those of evil. The evil cannot be willed or wanted or philosophically tolerated, whatever good it may lead to unintentionally. Emersonian innocence consists in its entire lack of that historicism which sometimes tainted Heidegger.

On the question of resentment of the human condition, one last thing can be said. If it is possible that resentment is not wrong in itself, even when it is what Arendt says it is, and that many phenomena that seem to stem from it (if only partly) are not to be condemned but praised, it may also be the case that it is compatible with wonder at and gratitude for Being. Only that wonder and gratitude would have to be somewhat different from those proposed by Arendt. They would have to have room for the Weberian sentiment, "In spite of all." This sentiment is caught by Emerson's carefully phrased answer, in "Compensation," to Hamlet's question: "it is worse not to be than to be." To have that sentiment is not to wish that there had never been anything; it is only to work very hard to keep feeling gratitude. The wonder would survive the strain; actually, it is severable from gratitude. Despite its risks of passivity, wonder may be the superior passion.

When the young Marx tried to imagine a life in which social conditions were so right for man that the human condition was no longer resented, he foresaw the evaporation of God. He said, "the question about an *alien* being, about a being above nature and man—a question which implies the admission of the inessentiality of nature and of man—has become impossible in practice." These words suggest that a perfect acceptance of the human condition seems to be quite capable of strangling wonder at and gratitude for Being. What is at stake is not rescuing belief in God but, to the contrary, adhering to "the inessentiality of nature and of man." As a matter of course, unbelief goes better with the sense of inessentiality than belief. I think that wonder and gratitude are keenest when one is smitten by that sense. Arendt has no wish to overcome inessentiality. To say that man (to leave aside nature) is essential is first to assume the propriety of the degrading question, Why is it necessary for man to exist at all? and then to answer it theologically, or as Marx does, humanistically. Both answers are as degrading as the question. Both presume to be able to say, finally, what man is, and thus to cure him of his indefiniteness. Arendt does not think, however, that some kind or degree of resentment may help to keep the sense of inessentiality alive. Yet if it does, we may conclude that the ideal of acceptance of the human condition is an obstacle to the wonder and gratitude that Arendt cherishes. And if resentment of the human condition is understood with Emerson's help, then one might say that it is the very expression of gratitude, because it radiates a greater trust in the way things are.

Let us turn again to alienation. Modern resentment of the human condition engenders attempts and achievements that alienate humanity from the world and the earth. The feeling of being at home is weakened. Masses of people feel disoriented, lost, cut off from coherence and meaningfulness, which require stability and boundedness. For the time being, world alienation is the more actual and widespread experience. (We are only at the beginnings of earth alienation.) The question arises as to whether the condition of world alienation is, in itself, as clearly lamentable as Arendt says. Not only may resentment and the achievements spurred by resentment be praiseworthy, but so also may resentment's ultimate consequence, alienation.

As always with her, there are contrary moments. Most impressively, the essay on Lessing contains a noteworthy distinction (present elsewhere, but not as vividly). She speaks there of the fraternity of persecuted or enslaved peoples, using as an example European Jews before their emancipation in the nineteenth century. She says that the persecuted may manifest their humanity in "dark times," in the darkness of their exclusion and maltreatment, by bonding together, huddling, treating each other compassionately. Indeed, these "pariahs" can develop "a kindliness and sheer goodness of which human beings are otherwise scarcely capable." In describing their response to life, Arendt even employs a formulation she normally reserves for the ecstatic thinker's relation to reality. She says that pariahdom can be "the source of a vitality, a joy in the simple fact of being alive, rather suggesting that life comes fully into its own only among those who are, in worldly terms, the insulted and injured." But she insists that this state shows loss of the world; it is not another way of being at home in it. Pariahdom, in its intense humanity, signifies a radical absence of those qualities which are created only by having a world to be at home in and take care of. The persecuted and enslaved suffer an "atrophy of all the organs" which people use to engage with the world: common sense as well as "the sense of beauty, or taste, with which we love the world." The humanity of the pariah is thus dearly bought. The "great privilege of being unburdened by care for the world" sponsors their humanity.

Thus she makes it clear that the world (understood as a culture that has a politics) is not meant to be a warm place, any more than it is meant to be a place of oppression. It is cool and hard, a place of struggle. It must be made a home, and can be kept a home only precariously. A home is what necessitates sacrifice. Likewise, it is not a place of intellectual uniformity or certainties: politics works on opinions; its food is disagreement growing out of human diversity. Yet all these characterizations do not suffice: for a people, to be at home in the world is to be free, to be responsible politically for the cultural totality. To be alienated from the world may not always mean oppression or even physical or mental hardship. Pariahs can be comfortable, though usually they are not. What matters finally, however, is to have a world: the place of the highest existential opportunities as well as the greatest dangers. It gives individuals identity and the chance for reconciliation; but it may ask that not only comforts but life itself be given up.

When therefore we say that Arendt dreads alienation from the world, we do not mean to suggest that she falls for one of the worst modern temptations, that of pining for an intimate community, for some anthropologically induced tribalism. Her antimodernism is free of this excessively modernist antimodernism. She theorizes the need for distance between peers, not only their need for mutual presence and common undertakings. Yet is there not something more to be said in behalf of world alienation—something other than what she has said about the vitality and warm humanity of certain excluded or exploited groups of people?

We may begin negatively. We say something in behalf of alienation when we try to tally the cost of being at home in the world. Obviously Arendt's strong sense is that by arming resentment scientifically and technologically, modernity fosters alienation. The conclusion must be that all the achievements that are thus tied to alienation should, ideally, have never come to be. In fact, whatever the role of resentment in their making, humanity would be better off without them. I do not know how one can talk sensibly about undoing, but I suppose many would prefer a world without the human ability to create nuclear weapons. Going back to the time we now call the dawn of modernity—the time of European global exploration, the Reformation, the Renaissance, the start of the system of capitalism—we cannot wish all this undone. Not even the most feudal Catholic could, except in an insubstantial mood. To undo the productions of later capitalism? We do not have to be Marxists to repel the thought. It is not that I seek here to transfer the sentiment of acceptance to precisely the one area from which Arendt withholds it. Rather, I am saying that humanity is no longer imaginable without these and related happenings. Who would we be without them? Their costs have been and will continue to be stupendous. They are costs of the sort that Arendt keenly theorizes about and others as well. But we cannot undo five centuries except in fantasy, not even in imagination. Then, too, it is hard to resist the feeling that the fruit of the science and technology of these centuries has been such an enhancement of human experience that perhaps the true response is, after all, the sentiment of acceptance. We are not at home; we have too much at our disposal merely to construct a home. There must therefore be some metaphor other than home for the desired condition, even when home is as richly difficult a place as Arendt conceives it. The metaphor cannot be architectural. The modern world is not solid but misty or particulate.

The costs of alienation are great; so would be the costs of trying to insure its absence. It must be emphasized that Arendt's idea of being at home in the world involves hostility toward other things besides those that pertain to capitalism and to modern science and technology. First, Arendt expresses a continuous guardedness toward modern subjectivity. Second, she speaks approvingly of Greek friendship and Roman *humanitas*, both of which she says rested on the deliberate exclusion of various human endeavors, especially the search for knowledge. Third, in her last intended book, she brings thinking itself under extensive indictment as a force for alienation. In effect, the world is always threatened; so much of what human beings try to do conflicts with the health of the world; modernity is not alone in threatening it. Nor does Arendt say that resentment is the source of everything that alienates. By the time we survey all the things that must be suspected because they contribute to alienation from the world, we might be dismayed by the variety. Not only are the great achievements of modern science and technology regarded with a cold eye, but so is much of the long-standing human effort to gain ever more truth and experience.

Note in passing that her pages on the Cartesian *cogito* in *The Human Condition* try to trace subjectivism to a distrust of the senses and hence to a distrust of everything outside one's mind. Though she realizes with an exemplary acuteness that the great early astronomers had given sufficient reason to distrust the senses as invariable sources of truth concerning the natural world and the universe, she meditates on the Cartesian project with remorse. But there is another possible source of her antagonism to modern subjectivity. I say *possible* because while I have no explicit evidence, I think my point is consonant with the urgencies of her thought. I suspect that when she says that the heart is a dark place and means that it is not fit to be explored or lived in, she is also saying that intensive self-analysis will always discover filth. Modern psychology in its relentless truth-seeking excels at discovering filth. The cultivation of subjectivity thus flows into the ungovernable search for knowledge.

I think she feared the disclosure of too much psychological truth because by catching the individual in a trap of loneliness this truth enfeebles commitment to the world. In a chapter added to the second edition of *The*

Origins of Totalitarianism, she says that the loneliness of modern masses makes them receptive to totalitarian domination because loneliness disposes a person to seek relief in the rigidity of an ideological system. But her discussion includes the comment that there is some underlying complicity between the dominated and those who dominate. She says, following Luther, that a lonely man "always deduces one thing from the other and thinks everything to the worst." I infer here that the worst means the worst about oneself: loneliness facilitates self-discovery which nourishes self-loathing. She says also that the "extremism" of totalitarian regimes consists in "this deducing process which always arrives at the worst possible conclusions." She had already remarked on how totalitarianism prepares each individual equally well to be executioner or victim. In short, from this perspective, the secret resource of totalitarianism—and perhaps of all forms of political cruelty—is guilt induced by self-analysis of the sort that modern loneliness promotes. The distance between self-analysis and the institutionalization of analysis by psychological experts is not great. The latter heightens the danger. I take D. M. Thomas's novel *The White Hotel* to be saying what I think Arendt would have accepted completely. Self-analysis combined with psychoanalysis can always either find or plausibly construct reasons for self-accusation of the most searing kind. The premonition of destruction is a yearning for punishment. But the person, for all the filth inside, is still innocent, even if self-convicted. Arendt could have said that unless the darkness within remained unapproached, a ruinous loneliness would grow, the world would be lost, and the acceptance of victimization prepared. These are the bitter results of cultivated subjectivity. Self-knowledge, not just self-absorption, is self-alienation. The courage of self-knowledge is perhaps the one kind of courage she refuses to insist on.

Even without this uncertain example in which increased knowledge and the cultivation of subjectivity are in each other's baleful service, Arendt unmistakably links the search for cognitive truth, for knowledge of every kind, to world alienation. It is not a matter only of such knowledge as can be converted into world-alienating and earth-alienating technology. She never says that she wishes such a search and such knowledge had never existed, but she does persist in admiring what she thinks they have made altogether less likely, if not impossible. She certainly does not locate human dignity in the endless accumulation of knowledge. The level of abstraction (or degrees of vagueness) of the question as to just where to locate human dignity is so great that one can scarcely say a relevant word.

Still, she does want us to see that a determined philosophy of the world-as-home, and of political action as the exemplary relationship to the world, is continuously at odds with the project of indefinite knowing. This tension is not the immemorial one between the alleged requirements of order and stability and the corrosive effects of inquiry; nor is it the other immemorial one between the commitment to action and the commitment to reflection. The latter certainly figures in Arendt's thought; the former concern would not have suited her natural rebelliousness. The issue is related to the immemorial ones, but nevertheless distinct from them. Knowledge, in the period of modernity, makes the world more and more strange and thus cultivates estrangement from the world. The effect of the accumulation of knowledge may paradoxically increase uncertainty about the ability of humanity to know; or contrastingly, by establishing certainties it may freeze the play of opinion. In either case, her implication is that there may be such a thing as knowing too much for the good of the world.

Arendt finds antecedents for her attitude. She tries to recover Greek, but especially Roman, notions of humanness, all of which demand limitations on the pursuit of knowledge (and beauty). She deploys several considerations. First, she proposes that the very political notion of friendship present in Greek thought—personal friendship as linked to public citizenship; citizenship as a kind of friendship; and friendship as in itself political because, like citizenship, it is made from the discourse of equals—provides a starting-point for thought about which matters are fit for utterance. She says that there can be no "humane" world unless it is "the object discourse." Talk with others is what creates the world, which "remains 'inhuman' in a very literal sense unless it is constantly talked about by human beings." Similarly, we learn to be human in the course of speaking. Yet if the world is to be humane and its inhabitants are to be human, the very idea of the human must be delimited. She extends the Greek idea: "Whatever cannot become the object of discourse—the truly sublime, the truly horrible or the uncanny—may find a human voice through which to sound into the world, but it is not exactly human." With the phrase "not exactly human," rather strict limits are placed on the publicly expressible. The public realm undergoes a purification. But the powers of human expression, thus confined, may, in turn, undergo atrophy.

In the same essay, she praises Lessing not only for seeing that "single absolute truth" would mean the end of human discourse, but for taking pleasure in this insight. She joins him in exulting in the fact that "the truth, as soon as it is uttered, is immediately transformed into one opinion among many, is contested, reformulated, reduced to one subject of discourse among others." She also exults in the "distress" this vicissitude caused Plato and Parmenides. But this point is preliminary to a more radical one that she finds unhesitatingly present in Lessing's work. *Nathan the Wise* is her text, and the point which she makes her own is that "Nathan's wisdom consists solely in his readiness to sacrifice truth to friendship." Once again the political notion of friendship works to discredit truth. Truth, here, is not knowledge but moral or metaphysical truth. The trouble is that Arendt does not distinguish between the fallacy of thinking that in every particular case submitted to disinterested judgment there is one and only one right answer instead of a range of equally or almost equally eligible answers and thinking rightly that a basic principle can be accepted by all participants. The latter condition is usually the necessary precondition for meaningful and robust dispute of the sort she idealizes as the talk of the world. Thus, the search for the principle, or for greater clarity about it, is surely compatible with the well-being of the world, as it is indispensable to the health of a friendship. Only a rigidly Kantian notion of moral truth, extending from the principle to all cases that arise under it, works with the devastating effect on the world that Arendt feared.

She finds other antecedents for her desire to limit the pursuit of knowledge or truth in a formulation from Pericles' funeral oration, and in Cicero's views on truth in relation to culture. The Periclean formulation in Alfred Zimmern's English is: "We are lovers of beauty without extravagance, and lovers of wisdom without unmanliness." She calls the formulation untranslatable, and offers a paraphrase: "We love beauty within the limits of political judgment, and we philosophize without the barbarian vice of effeminacy." She interprets this text to mean that "it is the polis, the realm of politics, which sets limits to the love of wisdom and of beauty." The gist is that "a kind of overrefinement, an indiscriminate sensitivity" is barbarian; while "the lack of virility, the vice of effeminacy, which we would associate with too great a love of beauty or aestheticism, is mentioned here as the specific danger of philosophy." She suggests that the danger of philosophy is that it may lead to contemplative inactivity, as it begins in wonder and ends in "the speechless beholding of some unveiled truth." She seems to endorse the descriptions of inactivity as effeminacy. There is the slightest hint in Arendt's discussion that Socrates was not a citizen, as if there were only one way of being a citizen.

The cause of truth is assaulted another time in her discussion of Cicero. She once again takes hold of a formulation and expands its sense. She quotes Cicero from the first book of the *Tusculan Disputations:* "I prefer before heaven to go astray with Plato rather than hold true views with his opponents." Though she thinks this remark "an outrageously bold statement," she interprets it with an entire sympathy. Her thesis is that Roman humanism, as incarnated in Cicero, gave ascendancy to the faculty of *taste*. Taste is "the political capacity that truly humanizes the beautiful and creates a culture." It is a political capacity because its principle is "to take care of and preserve and admire the things of the world." Of course, taste does not operate brutally as censorship. The method of exclusion is subtle. It insists on one's freedom as a man of the world (and hence as a citizen). She says: "This Roman *humanitas* applied to men who were free in every respect, for whom the question of freedom, of not being coerced, was the decisive one—even in philosophy, even in science, even in the arts." Worldliness is a rejection of the absolute claims of any art or discipline, in behalf of the preservation of the world as home. There is no home, only unsettledness, when human creativity strains toward autonomy.

The costs, in sum, of the lamentation of alienation and the affirmation of being at home in the world are immense. Every human struggle against limitation, or every aspiration to perfection, except the political one (rightly understood), comes under scrutiny or indictment. As Arendt's political theory unfolds, the full cost of avoiding alienation so that groups of people may aspire to be at home in a culture with a politics is demonstrated. The cost seems immense in the cultures which may be said to have lived for politics—the Greek and the Roman. The costs are nearly total for modernity. I mean to say that I do not think the cost would be worth paying, even if it were possible to pay it.

Now, we do not praise alienation in itself when we point out that its abolition has a prohibitive cost. At its worst, it is a condition that must be endured for the sake of our humanity, even though it is sometimes implicated in appalling events. However, it is possible to imagine a good form, a *moderate* alienation. There exists an idea of a culture in which events and achievements cause alienation in its gross form. They help to prepare us for it but do not define it. There is a way for a people to be at home by not being at home, and consequently a way of achieving individual reconciliation that does not depend on living a life that lends itself to a "properly narrated story."

The true beneficiary of all the dislocations and uncertainties of modernity is the democratic individual living in a culture of moderate alienation, and himself sharing in that alienation. Arendt (and others) are probably right to see individualism in general as a symptom and expression of alienation. The theory of democratic individuality, however, is the conversion of this distress and loss (whether felt as such or not) into a great good. Each individual becomes individual because the general condition of moderate alienation provides the opening. More than anyone else, Emerson, Thoreau, and Whitman have shown how that may be so. I cannot do anything more than point in the direction of their ever-fresh teaching.

The moral unit in any discourse on the rightness of moderate alienation is the individual, not humanity or masses of people heaped together traumatically. The individual is the democratic individual, not some unconditioned and unsituated ghost. The key to his stature is self-consciousness carried to the point of what Emerson calls, with mixed feelings, the "double consciousness" in "The Transcendentalist" and "Fate," and what Thoreau calls "doubleness" in *Walden*. Its essence is self-objectification: to be ready to treat oneself as another. It is a form of practiced alienation. This doubleness is conceptually related to the Socratic "two-in-one" that Arendt makes paradigmatic for the experience of thinking and fundamental to the avoidance of atrocity, but is not altogether the same. Nor is it altogether the same as the Kantian "enlarged mentality" that allows one to understand how another person looks at the common world, and when alone, to "think in an anticipated communication with others," by thinking in the place of everybody else. It is also far removed from the late Stoic conceptualization, as found in Epictetus and Marcus Aurelius (and borrowed by St. Augustine), which counselled a *double life*. The Stoic doubleness consists in following the rules of society outwardly, but inwardly thinking one's own thoughts and managing one's impressions. The double life is like living a lie: you act as if the rules you were following behaviorally were good, or not to be questioned, not at all changed. The world and the self are separated and left untouched. Thoreau explicitly calls such a life a "failure."

The American Romantic doubleness is most radically present in Whitman's *Song of Myself* (section 4):

Apart from the pulling and hauling stands what I am,
Stands amused, complacent, compassionating, idle, unitary,
Looks down, is erect, or bends an arm on an impalpable certain
    rest,
Looking with side-curved head curious what will come next,
Both in and out of the game and watching and wondering at it.

The capacity being invoked in these lines is that by which one becomes all the more active because detached; all the more active because
constantly enlarging one's passivities and receptivities; all the more active
because one knows of certainties that underlie the futilities and impreci-
sions of action. There is no *social* identity worth holding on to. The self is
loose-fitting. There is no chance that bad faith will substitute itself for reconciliation. There is restlessness, contradiction, bursting all confines.
There is serious play, without winning and losing. Taste is put down, because everything is allowed in, everything can be poeticized. There is no
pretense that the classical understanding of excellence or virtue is being
reproduced in a democracy; nor is there the lesser pretense of "cultured"
personalities issuing from that process of self-improvement which Arendt
scorns as philistine, but which is not, in any case, the aim of democratic
individuality. Emerson's and Whitman's "spontaneity" also scorns the deliberate putting together of a beautiful self. The enlargement of human
powers is an enlargement of the power of *each* individual to experience,
and to poeticize experience. Modernity stands for such enlargement.
Courage and generosity accept and require alienation in *each*. Modernity, when it is benign, or can be made benign, or can be twisted into
benignity, supplies this good alienation. Modern democracy is the unset-
tled "home" of moderate alienation. The risks are great, of course; so are
the costs; so are the perversions and failures. If, however, one does not
find in the culture of moderate alienation the best of modernity, where
then?

In exasperation Arendt says of America:

And this body politic has at least endured to the present day, in spite
of the fact that the specifically modern character of the modern world
has nowhere else produced such extreme expressions in all nonpolitical spheres of life as it has in the United States.

She also complains that modern (especially American) society "introduces
between the private and the public a social sphere in which the private is

made public and vice versa." In both cases, I believe, she has decried tendencies that actually are signs of the vitality of the democracy: the will to extend its spirit throughout the society and not restrict it to the public realm. American democracy is expressed in, and thrives on, "extreme expressions in all nonpolitical spheres of life," and the mutual moral permeability of public and private. (And so, to a degree, did Athenian democracy.)

To wrest something fine from modernity requires sympathy with the ideal of democratic individuality. We have seen that Arendt finds individuality, serious or not, unserious and even repugnant. Naturally, she will not be able to do for the best of modernity what she is able to do for the worst: present its innermost meaning. For her

> The true forerunner of modern mass man is this individual, who was defined and indeed discovered by those who, like Rousseau in the eighteenth century or John Stuart Mill in the nineteenth century, found themselves in open rebellion against society.

With such a coarse reduction, her political theory of modernity exposes its shortcomings.

The curious thing is that when she writes about "men in dark times"— the men and women who are courageous and generous in the gloom—she articulates the ideal of individuality with an exceptional clarity and, what is more, sympathy. The trouble is that she confines its possibility to a few; and these few are writers (and include one pope and one revolutionary). She cannot contemplate an idealism, like that of the American Romantics, which aspires to the encouragement of a poetical or a philosophical relation to reality on the part of all, to some significant degree. Democratic individuality is the doctrine of every person a poet or philosopher, not as writer, but as one who sees beauty everywhere, even in the commonplace or ugly; as one who spends himself in the service of the desire to understand otherness, even when it is supposed to be hateful or despicable; as one who, emptied of self-interest, is liberated all the more for strenuous exertion. Modern democracy finds its highest justification in the sponsorship and protection of this ideal. It rests on the belief that more than a few can see, imagine, and act, like the best few, and that the extension of the ideal enhances rather than cheapens it. One may say that the Romantic poetical or philosophical relation to reality is the democratically refined sense of wonder at and gratitude for Being.

We should notice some of Arendt's formulations because they are serviceable for a doctrine she does not want us to embrace. It is not accidental that they all come from *Men in Dark Times*, which turns out to be a book of reflections on defiant individuals. She refers to Jaspers's "high-spirited independence" that does not so much make him rebel against conventions as keep his distance from them: the conventions are always recognized as such, never taken seriously as "standards of conduct." He was always capable of resisting enlistment; he was "inviolable, untemptable, unswayable." This independence was sustained by confidence: "the secret trust in man, in the *humanitas* of the human race." She also praises Waldemar Gurian for his lifelong decision "never to conform and never to escape, which is only another way of saying that it was built on courage." With all these words we are suddenly in the world of Emerson's "Self-Reliance." He makes us see that democracy robs convention of its majesty by reinforcing its citizens in the idea that political authority is constructed and artificial, and so must be most of the laws that come from it. What is true of laws must also be true of social conventions. To see such truth is the beginning of emancipation into democratic individuality. But Arendt writes as if only someone of Jaspers's genius could possibly live a life with such a tenuous connection to convention.

In summarizing Jaspers's theory of the "axial" period between 800 and 200 B.C., she ascribes to a few "great personalities" virtues that Emerson and Thoreau endeavor to make commonly available: ". . . great personalities appear everywhere who will no longer accept or be accepted as mere members of their respective communities but think of themselves as individuals and design individual ways of life." When Thoreau says that "we should be men first, and subjects afterward"—"afterward" can only mean not at all—he is speaking to his neighbors in the democracy. The scorn in Arendt's phrase "mere members" could have come from Thoreau.

She praises Lessing because "Lessing never felt at home in the world as it then existed and probably never wanted to, and still after his own fashion he always remained committed to it." She insists that "special and unique circumstances governed this relationship." But why must they? Why cannot his relationship to the world be envisaged as the norm, as the aspiration, as approachable by democratic individuals who redefine the notion of world and of being at home in it?

Arendt speaks of Rosa Luxemburg as one of those persons "whose genius forced them to keep the world at a certain distance and whose significance lies chiefly in their works, the artifacts they added to the world, not in the role they played in it." But why the restriction to two choices, works or role? The *vita activa* is not exhausted by labor, work, and political action; the sole alternative to the *vita activa* is not the *vita contemplativa*. There is the unstructured immensity in which people idle, observe, ruminate, imagine, move about, encounter, travel down the open road; in which, in short, they experience. For them, too, the world with its commitments must be kept "at a certain distance," if the unstructured immensity of possible experience is to be entered. The modern technologies of communication and travel, the modern technological media of art and entertainment, and the modern methods of reproducing and disseminating art and the works of culture all transform the very nature of experience, as well as its content. The achievements of modernity have made individuals more able to see, have given them more to see, have devised new ways of seeing. They have created utopia as vision. The key to the modern transformation of experience is to be found in the emancipation of sight more than in the emancipation of all the other senses (to use Marx's early formulation). This is an unmeasurable advance.

In her great essay on Brecht, Arendt pictures him wandering through Germany, as a young man, after the horrors of the First War:

> As it appeared to Brecht, four years of destruction had wiped the world clean, the storms having swept along with them all human traces, everything one could hold on to, including cultural objects and moral values. . . . It was as though, fleetingly, the world had become as innocent and fresh as it was on the day of creation. . . . Hence it was life that the young poet fell in love with—everything that the earth, in its sheer thereness, had to offer.

She abandons, for Brecht's sake, the view that being at home is necessary if one is to love the world. The very feeling of strangeness—a kind of *Verfremdungseffekt* for the theater that life in society is—tightens the tie to the world and one's life in it. This is not the same as moderate alienation, which does not presuppose a literal calamity. Rather, the condition of democratic individuality is as it were the regularization of the *Verfremdungseffekt*, both as a continuous and domesticated perspective (Whitman's "in and out of the game"), and as an exceptional possibility, now and then made actual and ecstatic, as Emerson, for one, describes it in the famous passage in *Nature* about crossing the common.

For Brecht she even lets go her religiousness. She thinks that no one has excelled him in conveying "the clear understanding that what Nietz-sche called 'the death of God' does not necessarily lead into despair but, on the contrary, since it eliminates the fear of Hell, can end in sheer jubi-lation, in a new 'yes' to life." The doctrine of democratic individuality, on the other hand, goes beyond this jubilation, great as it is. It is Emerson who best sounds the note. In the "Divinity School Address" of 1838, he says, "men have come to speak of the revelation as somewhat long ago given and done, as if God were dead." The assassin of the old God is de-mocracy, the culture of human self-positing, out of which emerge values and projects, the culture in which everything becomes a subject for un-sponsored, self-conscious discussion. Emerson knew that the traditional God was dead, but such knowledge is preliminary:

> Heartily know,
> When half-gods go,
> The gods arrive.

Religiousness is restored, but altered, and understood as the spiritualiza-tion of democratic individuality. This is the "new 'yes' to life," and be-speaks a cultivated alienation, which builds a saving doubt into the "yes."

Finally, in an exuberant passage in her memoir of Waldemar Gurian, Arendt seems to break away from the disposition to confine individuality to a few. In doing so, she comes to the center of the doctrine of democratic individuality. She says:

> . . . it remains the greatest prerogative of every man to be essentially
> and forever more than anything he can produce or achieve, not only
> to remain, after each work and achievement, the not yet exhausted,
> sheer inexhaustible source of further achievements, but to be in his
> very essence beyond all of them, untouchable and unlimited by them.

Oddly, these words were written more than ten years before the contrast-ing words quoted above from the essay on Rosa Luxemburg. There is an untypicality in them, not because they are charged with hope, but be-cause they do not go well with a concentration on the world as home, as the object of devotion and sacrifice. Neither do they merely repeat her idea of freedom as unpredictable action. These are words, instead, of indi-vidual transcendence. Their expression is full of unintended echoes of Emerson, Thoreau, and Whitman. They comprise the faith of modernity. How startling is their appearance in the work of this great antimodernist.

Loomis: A Memoir
LINCOLN KIRSTEIN

---

for Edward Mendelson

W HO WAS Loomis? He was the first genuine enigma I had encountered. He was six years my senior at a time when such a discrepancy is
significant. I ran into him when I was an infantile fifteen, he a manlike
twenty-one. I was still at boarding school; he'd graduated from Yale. Usually, it was athletes I idealized. Prone to hero worship, it was brawn not
brain I idolized. Loomis breathed all mind. He showed no outstanding
physical aura, yet he incarnated an atmosphere of intellectual or even
moral self-sufficiency. I judged he knew exactly what he wanted from
life, yet customary reticence, which could have been diffidence, spelled
wisdom, or at least some distillation of extremity. He was accustomed to
thinking as an analytical exercise. What one might come to call metaphysics occupied his waking hours. Coolness and corporal remoteness distanced him from the mute enthusiasms, simple greeds of most young men
I chanced to know.

Who was Loomis? The yearbook of his preparatory school told me all
I would ever need to know.

PAYSON WALKER LOOMIS
"Pays"
Yale

"I have no mockings or arguments, I merely witness and wait."
(No. I don't like that at all. Signed P. W. L.)

1918–19   St. Luke's and Pythian Societies. Second Honor Roll Fall
          Term. Second Class Football Team. Second Choir.
1919–20   Second Class Football Team. Dramatic Association, Cast of "It
          Pays to Advertise". Lit. Board
1920–21   Musical Association. Banjo Club. Debating Union. Lit. Board.
1921–22   Third Honor Roll Fall Term. Second Class Football Team.

Musical Association. Banjo Club. Dramatic Association, cast of "Grumpy." Debating Union. Lit. Board.

He was neither supercilious nor epicene. His sorcery for me lay in an attachment to the concrete ordinary, rootedness in the quotidian, his use of everyday happenings as research in the typology of the normal. No thoughtless incident of daily life failed to demonstrate some significance in his measured analysis of the inescapably fabulous continuum of habit and incidence. Layers of meaning accrued in just how one brushed one's teeth, had one's hair cut, changed one's socks, washed one's hands. These were digested in heartless analytical exercise.

A common kitchen garden of what was plainly granted by God required daily maintenance; techniques for teeth and nails lurked behind custom. He could invest the choice of a shirt—if indeed it finally transpired that he possessed, or there existed, any choice—with lucid significance. He had long since vowed to "save time" by eschewing any color in clothes save black and white. When I figured roughly that he'd accumulated two or three-quarters hours a year by such economy, he smiled gravely and asked me if I had read Rainer Maria Rilke's *Journal of Malte Laurids Brigge*. I had not. Well, Rilke's mysteriously bland young intellectual Dane had kept a time-bank, but at the end of twelve months he had slight notion as to how to use the unspent minutes.

Loomis had read "everything," particularly in comparative religion: the Gitas, *Gilgamesh*, Apocrypha, Quran, Confucius, and Madame Blavatsky, whom he particularly defended when I had risked thinking she was the fraud that her contemporaries often claimed. To him, she had brought to the West the wisdom books of a sequestered Orient. I had a rooted resistance to our Testaments, Old or New. They were, to me, dead sources of vindictive orderings, useful for Sunday chapel, but otherwise unfriendly and benighted. But Loomis told me of Bible sources and other books that raised demons, which caused me to smile and shiver.

What did he look like?

To be art-historically accurate, his was the skull structure of a Ptolemaic diorite portrait, cut in Alexandria early in the first century after Jesus. His was the head of a long-dead atavistic ancestor in the last secondary room of the British Museum's recently rearranged galleries. His skin was parchment stretched over thin steel; a fullness in the lips denied any deprivation of the sensual. Sandy hair cut short but not cropped; his flesh

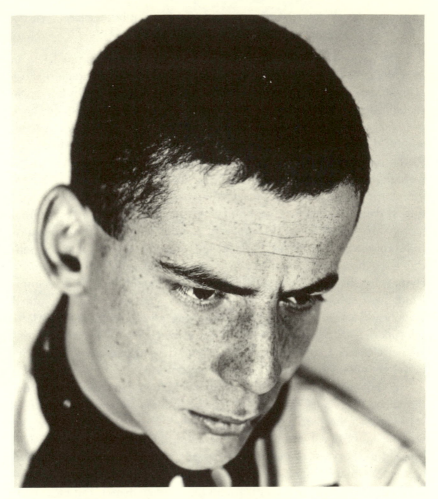

Lincoln Kirstein in 1928—photograph by Walker Evans

had a dull blush, a dusty rosiness, not precisely "pink," but with the unemphatic bloom of absolute health. His was an immaculate deliberate freshness without the priggishness of ostentatious puritanism. A single adjective will do: "clean"; but his was a forest freshness, nothing hygienic, nothing scrubbed. All this amounted to an extra aura of fantastic normality, a level of existence which elevated the ordinary into the exotic.

Loomis's magic for me was a distillation of given but hardly vivid characteristics. I admired him, was physically attracted to him, but I don't think I said, even to myself, that I loved him. His self-sufficiency, dignity—yes, "integrity"—was not warming. Being as young as I was when we first met, physicality, enthusiasm, expenditure of reckless energy were gross magnets. Loomis had gone through all that, if, indeed, he was ever prone to it. He'd come out on the other side, and elementary hedonism was, to him, wasteful or in poor taste. His principle was purpose; his aim an unstated matter of perfectability. He didn't lack a "sense of humor"; his fun was dispassionate irony, a harsh presupposition that nothing under his microscope or telescope was as it might first appear. His essential misprision of every manifest phenomenon that loosely presented itself was that most men and their makings were false and also cor-

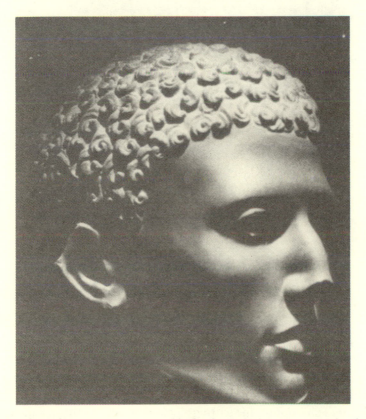

Graeco-Alexandrian portrait head in black schist, 1st century A.D., *a head which the author found reminiscent of his friend Loomis—British Museum (photograph by Michael Leonard)*

Payson Walker Loomis from the Hotchkiss School Yearbook, 1918

rupt, harmful though absurd. Naturally this dialectic pitted him against his fellows, who were at first ready to curry his disdain, almost as if to be noticed by him were a compliment. But when it was discovered that his lack of personal interest was indeed genuine, the reaction naturally turned to something like frightened contempt.

His endemic doubt, his putting all circumstance to the question, was not cynical. Who was this accidental "*he*" to judge chance, injustice, cruelty, violence, greed, vanity, or the cold wind of the world? Accepting the horrors of this planet never robbed him of curiosity or appetite.

Where did he come from, and how did he get his odd way? Supposedly his family owned woodlands in Oregon; I never met any of them. He graduated with honors from Yale in Russian and Arabic, with a parrot's charm for vocables. His friends, those few I met, were a loose confraternity of White Russian exiles, disinherited scions of tsarist officials who had found a haven in Harvard, Yale, or Dartmouth. I assumed he was aiming at diplomatic service; he fulfilled my notion of one of the cub second-secretaries at some Near Easten imperial mission vividly sketched by Harold Nicolson in *Some People*. Actually, nothing could have interested him less. Since Loomis reduced all toil and most labor to a basic self-determining technique, whether it was the practice of medicine or the law or banking, he agreed that diplomacy was the craft of lying for one's country against dubious allies or adversaries. Politics, national or international, was nothing but a gull's game. Loomis was no patriot.

His country was a planetary cosmos. After my admiration for and attraction to him had somewhat run its course, I found myself agreeing with Muriel Draper, a far more mature mentor, that Loomis was like a stoppered vial, containing precious elixir, fermented fruit juice, or carbonated spring water. But there was an arrested flow and a disquieting residue of omniscient disdain.

Sometimes discoveries in literature coincide with an early appreciation and hunger for life as adventure. I had devoured the publicized phenomenon of Lawrence of Arabia and written a naively laudatory article about what I could make of his myth; this appeared in *The New Republic* as a review of his first good biography, by Liddell Hart, in April 1934. Hart's book was subtitled "The Man behind the Legend," and was an attempt to scale down to human proportions the icon promulgated by Lowell Thomas in worldwide lecturing. I was, of course, enthralled when "El Lurens" actually responded, on April 12, 1934, from his cottage at Clouds Hill, Moreston, Dorset:

> Dear Kirstein:
>
> Your letter of last December has been troubling me, for you made it hard to answer, and yet I have to answer it. See now, there are, I think, in the world no men very different from ourselves. I walk the streets of an evening, or work in our R.A.F. camps all day, and by

measuring myself against the airmen or passers-by I know I am just an average chap. You write as though there were degrees or distinctions. I see likenesses, instead.

You get your idea from having read *The Seven Pillars* and *The Mint,* apparently. Few people have read *The Mint,* but many *The Seven Pillars.* If they all got this same disproportioned view of myself I would believe that there was some falsity of scale or attitude in what I put down. But these others only find the book natural. I did not mean them to transcend myself, to shout. I hope they do not. Probably they happen upon an unguarded angle of yourself, and so seem to you more significant than is their truth. I have found that in myself. Sometimes a book that is not exceptional to others will mean a great deal to me. From which you should deduce not any superabundance in its writer, but a poverty (in that point) within yourself.

How pompous a paragraph I have written: but you scare me, rather, with your over-impression. Please come and see me, if you get to England again; and then you will see I am your own size—and everybody else's. A very big man will be six feet six; a very small one five feet. Human differences are negligible, except in human eyes.

Pompous again. I am glad you like [Herman] Melville. He is not enough praised by Americans. Nijinski I saw dance once only, across the whole width of a full London theater. It was more than beauty, but not like a man. I suppose if I had seen him off the stage he would have been normal. If we meet let us talk a little upon why some people are greater than their work, and others less. I puzzle myself often over that. And why did you so much like *The Mint,* which is a close photograph of our life in camp?

Now for Gurdjieff. I had read some of his work (in French) a long while ago; not this which you have sent me, but stuff as real. It was closer-knit, too, as prose and argument. I liked it—as I like this *Herald of Coming Good*—but find myself a little to one side, facing perhaps the same question, but from another angle. Perhaps I am English and European, whereas Gurdjieff and yourself are not. Yet Katherine Mansfield . . . but wasn't she a New Zealander? I do not know, but Russia and its books and movements fail to strike me directly. Strange, interesting, moving—but there is no impact, no actuality. I find a common tint or tone or texture in all Russian work, and it all misses me in the end, however I like it for the moment.

"Man of Action" you call me, in the last words of your letter "who has done what he chose to his full extent." Do, for Heaven's sake, travel down to where I am next time you reach England, and put these ideas straight. We are all poor silly things trying to keep our feet in the swirl. Even if we succeed, it is not more than a static performance, nor deserving of applause. So I beg you to see me, and disabuse yourself of an illusion. Or do I take a single letter too seriously? Your somewhat bewildered

T. E. Shaw

It didn't need much prompting for me to warp my accessible Loomis into a sibling of Colonel Lawrence, who was now partially concealing himself in the Royal Air Force, across the broad Atlantic. My idolatry of that shadowy self-styled "Shaw" or "Ross"—and God alone knows what other names adorn his mystery—is further sketched elsewhere in these memories. He was never real to me, but Loomis took on his legend in my imagination, filling it out almost to explosion.

In *Hound & Horn*'s twenty-eighth consecutive number in seven years (July–September 1934), it was announced that publication would cease forthwith. This final issue contained five poems by Stephen Spender, Hart Crane's letters to his patron Otto Kahn concerning "The Bridge," three disconcerting photographs of Havana by Walker Evans, six poems by e. e. cummings, an anonymous translation (Loomis's) of a portion of Andrei Biely's huge novel *St. Petersburg*, and translations of "Twelve Surat of the Holy Quran," signed by Abu-Ali George Khairallah and Payson Walker Loomis. A note prefaced these dozen laconic and careful epitomes:

> Over and above the syntactical difficulties always present in the making of a literal and at the same time intelligible translation from any language into any other, unrelated language, there is also in the case of Arabic and English a peculiar difficulty arising from a difference, as between the Arabic- and English-speaking peoples, in the current usage of the respective inherited vocabularies. In Arabic there is much less of a gap between vernacular and the language of literature. Of the Holy Quran in particular it may be said that it determined the Arabic language as now spoken, and that its language is the language of everyday life, and vice versa. If, then, it be possible to preserve in translation any portion of the force and extreme beauty of the Arabic original, this must be conveyed *insofar as possible* in the language of everyday speech, for the Holy Quran is a popular book, and that is an integral part of its force and beauty.

To me, the Old Testament was merely a pretext for beautiful illustrations by Michelangelo, William Blake, and Gustave Doré. But now, the Quran, through Loomis's ideas, in spite of being an apparently unfocused narrative, nevertheless assumed powerful echoes of vast Arabian Nights.

Later in my days, when I was consumed with admiration for the metaphysic, art, architecture, and poetry of Islam, I came again to these versions, and after memorizing parts of the Quran itself, I feel that Payson (and his friend George Khairallah) had made incomparable renderings, three of which I transcribe. The first is, of course, the mandatory commencement to all abridgment, and I regret most, of the many disappointments I have had over Loomis, that he abandoned a full translation, which might have been undertaken, like Marmaduke Pickthall's familiar version, under exalted patronage.

I

Surat al-Fatihah
(The Opening)

In the name of God, the Merciful, the Compassionate

Praise be to God, the Lord of Creation,
The Merciful, the Compassionate,
King at the day of judgement.
It is Thou we worship
     and it is Thou whose help we ask.
Guide us in the straight path,
The path of the recipients of Thy bounty,
Not of those Thou Art displeased with
     or who have gone astray.

XCIX

Surat al-Zalzala
(Of the Quake)

In the name of God, the Merciful, the Compassionate

When the earth shall quake with its predestined quaking,
When the earth shall cast forth its burden,
And man shall say, What ails it?
Then, on that day, shall it tell its tale:
Yea, the Lord shall have inspired it.
Then, on that day, shall men come forth in throngs

To behold what they have done:
He that does an atom's weight of good shall behold it,
And he that does an atom's weight of evil shall behold it.

Payson introduced me, via the Moghreb, to a peek at Islam. Through his instruction I was in Marrakesh in the summer of 1927, and through local friends had a revelation which amounted almost to conversion. However, a sense of the ridiculous is the most useful demon God gave me, and when I went for an initial lesson of instruction, a wise man, both tolerant and kind, inquired of the romantic ambitions of an Israelite from Rochester, New York. He advised me to return to that faith into which I had been born. But I had no faith, in that or any other dispensation, and I craved solace from fear and anxiety. I felt that the testimony built into the magnificence of the fifteenth-century Governor's Palace was enough to convince me of the majesty of a God who was merciful and compassionate, and who would forgive me, a Jew, for the burden of Jesus.

This was in a small room in a small house off the big souk. The night before I sought his help, I had been taken by my guide, whose name was John Smith (Abd-el-Kad'r) to hear a professional storyteller. A crowd surrounded a fellow who had as aid and abettor a young boy with a silver flute. In a lovely voice, he intoned words in metrical paragraphs the meaning of which was mute to me. But his hearers were in rapt attention. The silver flute-song floated over a mild incense of cinnamon and ginger from market stalls. I was lost in an Arabian night; when I asked my Berber guide (who spoke excellent French), he said the storyteller was recounting the adventures of Sinbad, a mariner.

The mullah, to whom I was sent by an acquaintance of Loomis, gave sage counsel. The religious aspirations of youth are often deceptive; the prestige of myth and substitutes for sex are not equivalents of true hunger. This was true of me. The day before, Abd-el-Kad'r had taken me to a whorehouse where I had performed without talent. It was he whom I desired, not the horrid little twelve-year-old she-kittens who were pushed at me. One of these sank her black, filed teeth into my calf when I pushed her away. The wise man said: "You are a Jew. If there is gold in your purse, spend it. If in the end, you come, without fear, to the essence of Allah, it is well; it is not easy for a Jew, or indeed a Christian, to accept submission to Order, five times a day, on your knees, beside fellows whom your own father would have warned you against. Go in peace. It is likely you'll turn Christian before you take the Haj."

And thus it happened. While I recognize the majesty of Islamic thought as supreme model on this earth—which has created artifacts which, to me, make Michelangelo a midget, which he would have been the first to admit had he known them. My path toward peace was to push, however perilously, to the sacrifice of my Lord, Jesus Christ, in whose birth, death, and resurrection I keep confidence.

When at Mass I repeat the Lord's Prayer, partaking of Body and Blood, I often repeat, in honor of Loomis, this sura:

CXIII

Surat al-Falaq
(Of the Dawn)

In the name of God, the Merciful, the Compassionate

Say: I take refuge in the Lord of Dawn
From the evil of His creatures
And from the evil of utter darkness if it fall
And from the evil of the underminers of the covenants
And from the evil of the envier if he envy.

My school days and college years were gilded by a steady succession of enthusiasms for boys and men whose sweaty brilliance and appetite for hard liquor during Prohibition seemed to liberate them into a princely criminal ambiance. Dynastic breeding, well-nourished muscle resulted in a general arrest of psychic development. They were, for the most part, uninterested in ideas, presupposed cash, and resembled expensive sleep-walkers in a luxurious dream. No hindrance or tragedy touched them, and I was excited by their assurance of command over their immediate situation, even if it led nowhere but to the countinghouses of State and Wall Street or big city law firms. The Harvard Business School had little prestige as yet. The closed code maintaining Gold Coast clubs had its glamor of ancestral association, although I had no contact with any member of the Porcellian. In a sense, this epoch was still redolent of the nineteenth century; men who had rooms in old college dormitories like Hollis and Stoughton could easily have been updated replicas of Henry Adams's compansions, Roony Lee, Wendell Holmes, or Robert Gould Shaw. Some of their direct descendants were my roomates; by their warm invitation I spent gracious weekends in the environs of Boston, north and south, where feudal relics held high state on polo fields, offshore islands, and in big country houses.

To Payson Loomis, all this was not only meaningless, but as oppressive and addictive as a sedative or narcotic. At first, and even later, one might have imagined his antagonism to my bland enjoyments as Marxist rejection. Not at all. Loomis saw Harvard (and Yale) as anachronisms existing from no reality or necessity, as graduating not hedonists, spoilers, or exploiters, but simply somnambulists. Their familial conditioning had reduced them to a company of unreckoning self-condemned sleepers, cursed to repeat a facile habit which corresponded to no need of intense development. At most he found them, in his crisp dismissal "quaint," "amusing," or "lost." Ultimately they gave little to each other, to him, or—as he coolly pointed out—to me. They had names and desires but were papery-thin, lacking any dimension that might count in an extreme situation. Loomis estimated them without contempt; they hardly deserved confirmed judgment, nor would he dignify their mindless idleness by serious castigation.

After I had known him for a couple of years, he had finished Yale, and been hired as an amanuensis for the Grand Duchess Marie of Russia, who was engaged on what would prove to be exceedingly profitable memoirs. Here he was not merely recounting a reconstruction of history. He was experiencing, at but one remove, the courts of Alexander III, Nicholas II, and Rasputin, and events from 1905 through 1917, through a participant eyewitness. The Grand Duchess had her own distinction. She may have been the shrewd operator of a determined survival, but she was effectively charming to me when Payson asked me to tea with her to test my personal attitude toward this employment. She did not speak of her past when I was present and treated Loomis as if he were a secretary or courier, with little curiosity as to his personal history. She had a high style of authority; I was very impressed. In regard to Russia, my inclinations were Bolshevik; near my sister's farm dwelt William Christian Bullitt, who would be ambassador to both France and the Soviet Union. He had married Louise Bryant, the widow of an earlier Harvard graduate, Jack Reed, the flashy journalist of *Ten Days That Shook the World*. My father had been close friends with Lincoln Steffens, the well-known muckraker who was with Reed in Moscow during the days of Lenin's October triumph.

Characteristically, Loomis was heavily anti-Bolshevik. Deeply sympathetic to the Romanov's catastrophe, his interpretation of events caused me such confusion that I seriously considered the possibility that either he was mad, or that he was perpetrating some preposterous joke on me, in which his avowed feelings, perhaps in response to my curiosity, were exactly the reverse of what he actually believed. In his analysis of a situation which I glossed eagerly from the inheritance of American liberal socialism, Rasputin was not a devil from Pokrovskoye, nor was he a *rasputnik,* a libertine, but a powerful Siberian shaman, learned in the crafts of an active religion of Ural-Altaic tribesmen which was also common to North Europe and Asia, and which contained useful methods for the control of disease, nervous or organic—for example, his effect by remote control over the hemophilia of Tsarevitch Alexsei. For Payson, possibly through the revelations of the Grand Duchess, Rasputin was simply a *starets,* a holy pilgrim, a true man of God, who renounced our ordinary world and behaved in a way free of the automatic habits of customary existence. Dostoevski in *The Brothers Karamazov* explains the *starets:* "He seizes your essence, your being into his essence, into his being. Choosing your *starets,* you abdicate from your own will, and offer it to him in absolute fealty and with total self-denial." And why must so drastic a sacrifice be made? Because, declares Dostoevski, "After a life-term of absolute obedience, one may (and this of course quite conditional), gain absolute freedom, liberty from the hampering, the smothering, the devilish: Self."

Langdon Warner was a professor of Oriental art at Harvard. He had kinship by marriage to Franklin Roosevelt, and was able to persuade him to influence his Joint Chiefs of Staff not to firebomb Kyoto and Nara, among the most ancient, holiest sites in Japan. That Nara and Kyoto, with their glorious temples and gardens, were not incinerated depended on the Christian conscience and political shrewdness of this marvelous man. When he died, his ashes were begged by monks of the Horiu-ji monastery, whose founding is attributed to Prince Shotoku, who brought Buddhism and Chinese civilization to the islands. When I went seeking his grave in 1965, it was not marked, but in a space enclosed by granite hedges, there are carved stones which thank an American who, single-mindedly, and almost single-handedly, preserved the patrimony of a nation.

After the Russian Revolution, Langdon Warner was sent to Ekaterinburg to try to determine the exact circumstances of the murder of the Romanovs. His daughter was a college friend of mine; before the Warner's cozy fireplace I heard him tell that when he inspected the walls of the cellar in which the imperial family had been shot, he was puzzled by the fact that the bullet-holes in plaster which laced the whole wall were but three feet from the floor. The tsar, his wife, three daughters, and the sick boy had been shot at prayer. As of today they rank as saints in the company of Orthodoxy. Loomis would have approved.

What indeed were the roots of Loomis's idiosyncratic opinions and recalcitrant attitudes? Was his knowledge revelation, caprice, or the fun of a clever, prepotent conscience? How could he tell me so much of what I needed to know, and yet leave me dangling when I might pop a question which revealed his secret? Why was he so fascinated by the negatives of existence? Why did the purpose of life and death assume such vivid proportions in his lines of thought? Increasingly, I came to judge most action in the terms in which I thought he would have judged. How could a few vacations in Morocco, even adventures among dukes of the High Atlas, or a loose association with exiled Russian aristocrats, add up to a position for which I began to lust?

It was only a bit later that I was to learn that his pressure on me, or rather the presence of his person, declared, proved, or withheld, resulted from instruction by an exterior agency. This was exercise in the manipulation of power or authority, under whose rule he moved and was in service, possibly to others. My attraction to him, psychic or intellectual, rendered me an easy mark, for in those of his realms which I found most fascinating, I had absolutely no instruction. To be sure I was a "brilliant" Harvard sophomore equipped with perfect taste. I took a course in the attribution of quattrocento Italian panel paintings according to the gospel of Bernard Berenson, who, when faced with trying to decide who depicted what pock-marked predella, ingeniously invented the name of an artist to fill the vacuum and declared an anonymous work as surely by the hand of one Amico di Sandro. This was honest enough; he who had painted this partial picture probably had been near the circle of Alessandro di Mariano Dei Filipepi (1444–1510), who from some incident in childhood was nicknamed by an elder brother (a successful broker), "Botticelli," from botticello ("little barrel").

This tasteful data, and more of the same gained by tiresome hours trying to remember names and numbers on slides in the Fogg Museum Library, added little to my skill in navigating deep waters where Loomis fished. But, unknown to myself, he was piloting me. One day in the 1927 Easter vacation, in the Oak Room of the Plaza, always a suitable tapestry against which to gauge one's civilization, Payson handed me a book, found in a style not usual to me at the time, in paper. I assumed it was French, and poetry. He had recently introduced me to Valéry Larbaud, whose *Poésies d' A. O. Barnabooth* I relished and sedulously imitated. Larbaud was the first laureate of contemporary urban luxury, Waldorf Astoria, Savoy, and the Ritz, a devotee of big department stores and historical paintings dusty on the walls of provincial Latin-American city halls. It was his use of the boring immediacy of the close-at-hand which this poet turned into nostalgic golden vapor. From Jean Cocteau's *Le Coq et l'Arlequin* I had been conquered by his theory of modern art as a *ballet des chiffoniers*, a ragpickers' ball, the rehabilitation of the commonplace, the extraordinary ordinary transformed and transcended. Cocteau's brief drama *Orphée* of 1927, upon which the beautiful film of twenty years later would be based, was a vivid recension of an eternal and universal fact, the metaphor of poets and makers who enchant men, birds, and animals, and come to a bloody end. Orpheus would play an important role in my life in theater, in the production of Gluck's *Orfeo ed Euridice* in 1937 at the Metropolitan Opera with Balanchine and Tchelitchev, and with Stravinsky and Balanchine again in their *Orpheus* of 1947, with the gravely elegant scenic investiture of Isamu Noguchi. I particularly cherish the love of Orpheus for animals, how he made big cats tender, horses wise, and dogs intelligent as they listened to the strumming of his lyre, a tortoise shell as sounding board for strings which were, indeed, strung with the twisted guts of cats.

Some hours after I had left Loomis at the Plaza, and seated in a parlor-car back to Boston's Back Bay station, I took a look at the paperback he'd given me. I found, to my astonishment, that it was a pornographic novel entitled *Up and At 'Em*, by one U. P. Standing. It narrated the adventures of an American marine all over the Orient, following the Boxer Rebellion of 1901. Read today, it might seem prim; at the time, over half a century ago, it provided an unsettling shock and jolt which efficient works of its kind are expected to provide, but which the experience of corresponding actuality rapidly defuses. *Up and At 'Em* was swallowed in one gulp. It produced the intended effect, after which I felt empty and calm enough to relax and ponder the meaning of Payson's bounty, if indeed it made any sense.

Before this exchange, Loomis and I had never touched even remotely on the mystery of sex, either as physiology or obscenity. Now his provocation seemed enormous, and I felt raped. What was he trying to tell me? Was he teasing? As for the donation of *Up and At 'Em*, it would be all but naive to say, in terms of today's post-Freudian semiotics, that here was involved a suppressed desire to make love *to* me. In light of what later transpired, it seems likely that Loomis was attempting to "make love" *with* me, but the nature of the operation, the ends in view, and the method used would take me years to clarify. As for sex, Loomis never turned me on; as far as his own carnal predilections went, I know he never knew a man. In a fierce cold style he was a helpless womanizer, and if condemned to a need he could not exhaust, his lack of passion was but concomitant to his omnivorous distrust and distaste for humankind. As for me, I've never been troubled about what is laughingly known as "the body." From my earliest boarding-school days, I've "slept" with whom-ever I liked wherever available, with no aftertaste of guilt, resentment, or fear—elements which have indeed haunted me in relation to money. Naturally, the aura of sexual appetite and personal preference is endlessly apt for gossip, and for me, aged twenty, adult sexual behavior was an un-chartered landscape, paths leading to which always commenced with my father and mother, in their bed, somehow getting me. Since there was a twelve-year gap between my sister and myself, there must have been awkwardness. In any case, my mother, to whom I was closer, once said: "Your father never liked it." His shyness may have come from the mo-ment when, as a young travelling salesman for eyeglasses, he found him-self in St. Louis without money, and temporarily adopted by the kindly madam of a whorehouse from whom he contracted "the clap." The cure, consisting mainly of mercury injections, was so painful that he perhaps abandoned further curiosity as bad luck. His misfortune had no effect on his eldest son. When I was first sent away to Phillips Exeter, he called me for an after-supper conference. These were ominous occasions and usually involved serious criminality, like the theft of cash from my mother's lower drawer, where she kept a stuffed pursed. I needed coin to buy a sur-charged Cape of Good Hope triangular postage stamp for a collection that was entirely built on petty larceny.

As president of the Boston Public Library, Dad nominally controlled miles upon miles of stacks. Obviously he had told some minion to collect a bundle of books about biology for the needs of teenage human bodies. There was an anxious moment when I marked this heap of breviaries: *How Life Begins* (ages 8–12). *What Every Boy Should Know* (ages

12–15). *Your Body and You* (ages 14–17). My father cleared his throat, searched eagerly for the butt of an extinguished cigar (Havana; Romeo y Julieta, with a rose, gilt, and metal-paper band). Somehow I was to get from 506 Commonwealth Avenue to Exeter, New Hampshire, via John O'Brien, chauffeur of our Rolls Royce, and a dedicated researcher into the continuity of the race, methods for which he demonstrated on request. I recognized my father's malaise, and without exactly telling an untruth, relieved him by saying I had already read all the matter pushed at me. He relit his extinguished cigar, pulled out his wallet, gave me two ten-dollar bills, plus a dry kiss on the brow.

At the close of my sophomore year I was with Loomis again in late May; examinations were no problem. These had been surmounted in a mood more of impatience than anxiety. It had been a satisfactory year. The quarterly *Hound & Horn* had been launched with respectable excitement. An editorial in the *New York Herald-Tribune*, written, I think, by Geoffrey Parsons, father of one of my Harvard companions, welcomed a magazine which announced its arrival by a title-page which contained a bar of music marked *allegro con brio*, from Brahms, Op. 40, the theme of his (hunting) horn trio. A quotation from Plato was printed in Greek, without translation; although I could not read it myself, I insisted on an arrogance of erudition. We were supporting traditional values in a young-gentlemanly tone, and were well pleased with our modest boasts. I was eager to show Loomis Volume I, Number One. We had printed a specimen number about half the size of what we hoped later to publish; this was my passport, which would admit me to the cenacle of T. S. Eliot in London and Ezra Pound in Paris. Or so I hoped.

While it didn't exactly turn out that way, it was effort enough to convince Payson of our seriousness; I hoped to enlist his collaboration. Its table of contents was not entirely feeble. Its leading article was by Newton Arvin, professor of English at Harvard and Smith College, who would write excellent studies of Hawthorne and Whitman. There was a poem by my friend Howard Nott Doughty, Jr., whom I had first met at Phillips Exeter, and who had introduced me with enormous excitement both to Algernon Swinburne and (believe it or not) to Wilfred Owen, and this in 1922. Later he would write a fine biography of Francis Parkman. The architectural critics, Henry Russell Hitchcock, Jr., gave us an essay on "The

Decline of Architecture" which acquired a certain fame. Dick Blackmur reviewed Wyndham Lewis's study of Shakespeare under the title *Hubris;* I reviewed a novel by Maurice Baring, then a favorite of my sister and myself. A notice of Eliot's solid magazine *The Criterion* welcomed it as a monthly, graduated from a quarterly. Our salute was a trace *infra dig.* We hoped to hook Eliot, and shortly we did.

Loomis was not enthusiastic. For him *Hound & Horn* was the inevitable result of Harvard's genteel conditioning. Why we should have trouble so much over tasteful printing, good paper, and charming brush and ink vignettes by Rockwell Kent, he didn't know. For whom was this dwarf elegance provided? Who needed it? To what necessity did it correspond? Was there a single piece in our initial number which might not have been published somewhere else? As for my own poem, about term-end at boarding school, although I dared to print it after he had seen it in manuscript, judging it the best of a bunch, nothing was said. He could not wait to shift conversation to summer vacation plans.

His dismissal of my editorial ambition was blunt enough, but I knew enough not to betray disappointment or irritation. His objections were just enough, although I cringed at acknowledgment of blanket inadequacy. There was clinical style in his denigration which read as satisfying pain, iodine on a cut. Loomis's authority, here, his concrete objective disinterest, was something I'd almost been expecting. What he now said did not entirely lack a shock, but instinctively I was prepared for whatever was his final summation. He smiled and, as if to make this more mandatory and impressive, spoke with emphasis. "Now that you're so pleased with yourself, I expect you in Paris by June 15th. Here's my address. Yes, it's Fontainebleau not Paris, but they are close. Wire me your arrival. I'll find you a room. Plan on one free week. Here's where you'll meet Abd-el-Kadr in Marrakesh. Now I've got to go."

The abruptness of his suggestion, which was also by way of challenge or command, left me in a minor nervous tumult. Courage and will were simultaneously twisted and locked. It was as if I was on a rocking chair swung between positive and negative determination. The more I blamed Loomis for his provocation, the more puzzled and irritated I became. Was his presupposed suggestion, invitation, or demand some sort of arcane test like his gift of the randy adventures of the American marine, or was it to challenge my own vague and unstable aims, should I once manage a formulation of what these might be?

There was also "the material question." How was I to get to Paris, or Fontainebleau, or wherever Payson suggested, this side of Morocco? My father gave me a proper allowance as an undergraduate, but this hardly included an expensive couple of months of travel. I explained my need to see Pound and Eliot; he had already paid for the *Hound & Horn* as passport; now I must use it. He was more easily persuaded than I would have thought possible. However, there were serious moral obstacles. The "advance" copy with which we provided ourselves emerged as insubstantial and I was unhappy with the look of the dummy. To make it worse, I had accepted some verse from a man I felt rather sorry for, who had exploited his own self-pity effectively. When I saw his poems in cold print, I was sickened. I couldn't apologize for their dreariness, but the least to be done was elimination from our first public issue. This I did, and gained a life-long paranoid enemy who would pop up in the oddest place and time with murder in his heart. And here I was running off to France, three months before *Hound & Horn* officially appeared, leaving my colleagues to get the damn thing past the press and out to a wholly apathetic audience.

These considerations were overcome by the persistence of Payson's titillation. No one else encountered had taken a more serious interest in my psyche, so I felt a trust and obligation to such attention. I chose to believe that my credence in Loomis was inevitable and inexorable. So, on the predicated day, July 13, 1927, he guided me to a small hotel on the Place de l'Odeon. My room was without bath; it held a big brass bed, a large oak *garderobe,* an ebony washstand with an enormous china pitcher, and a bowl painted with tulips and poppies. The curtains were dusty red velour; there was coarse lace over the double windows, an oval gilt mirror and a framed lithograph of the Odéon theater. I realized this room was the epitome of its period, and easily pictured myself as Rastignac on his arrival from the provinces.

Payson took me for a walk in the Luxembourg Gardens; he spoke of Rémy de Gourmont and Paul Valéry. When I brought up Valéry Larbaud, Loomis announced that he was through with that one; nostalgia, after all, was no subject matter to support a grand scale. Charm, yes. But after all, is it *charm* we are trusting today? I sensed this as disloyal and ungrateful. Larbaud had once meant much to both of us. Payson's coolness chilled me with its tiny treachery. So far, everything had been sunny and fair with us. Suddenly there was a bleak hint of doubt, and not only in the qualitative values of my present opinion (all taken mostly from him): might I, in my turn, be repudiated? Maybe he was not the loyal moral critic I had come to imagine after all. Best be on my guard. We progressed through the gardens, now mottled by big clouds breasting their way toward dusk, in silence. The circus of children playing, their nannies in discreet attendance. People casually populating the trim paths were sufficient to occupy my superficial attention, when Loomis demanded: "Why are you here?"

His tone was not hostile, but his brevity was disarming. I knew it was not enough to counter with "Because you asked me." My arrival, pat upon the date he'd set, called for a modicum of admission. I could use neither Pound in Paris, nor Eliot in London, twin monumental pretexts, as much vindication. They were too slight to weigh against the gravity of possibility which somehow landed me here, bound, as it were, to Loomis. An inexplicable element, undefined, perhaps undefinable, was at play. So I answered with a personal question, fending off his, in a style which I stole from his assumption of mystery. I was after his secret. "What in the world are *you* finding to do here?"

His answer was full, almost as if with relief. He was studying. Ah, of course: languages, since he already had French, Russian, and some Arabic. No, as a matter of fact, not. Then of what was he a student? Dancing. Dancing? Born with some kind of massive predilection for "The Dance," I'd had unappeased curiosity since childhood for "The Ballet." I was surprised that Loomis, whom I'd never suspected had interest in theater, was thus occupying himself. Wasn't he much too old to become a dancer? But, of course; he had no wish to become a professional. He stated that he was more interested in dancing than "The Dance." That's how one might put it; subjects that occupied him were read *without* quotation marks. The essence? Well, yes: an essence.

I had long welcomed his grace of presence. Now, his anonymous and unostentatious elegance was framed in the orderly verdure of the Luxembourg Gardens, a mannered but mannerly background of Gallic "good taste." Flower-beds, hedges, cropped trees, and trimly bordered paths proclaimed civil propriety, an ingrained attention to public habit. The Luxembourg corresponded to one level of luxurious necessity, no equal to which I could recall in America. To be sure there were the Public Gardens in Boston with its tatty swanboats, and Central Park was a genial wilderness. But here gardeners were public servants, and on a level with good cabinetmakers as well. Here one was bathed in winelike richness of air and softness, which led me to breach the customary formal constraint with which I tried to behave when I was with Loomis. I asked him straight out: who was teaching him "dancing"?

No immediate answer; perhaps he had not heard my question. I felt rashness reproved. With him, there were limits not to be passed, yet these applied to my attitude about him, more than to any position he had taken. Now he demanded to know if I had enough money for the next weeks. Money was no problem. I couldn't buy any picture I might fancy, but survival was not in question. Then what *was* my summer plan? I hoped to reach Eliot in London, but that would not be until mid-September. I'd like to wander through Spain; I was planning a dissertation on El Greco for my junior year; I'd just bought Williumsen's big monograph, and I'd been told of a lost "Mary Magdalen" once in the English College at Valladolid; it would be fun to find it. Following his advice and example, I might cross Tangiers and then seek the High Atlas. There was Riffi military action, I knew, but here was another sort of incitement.

Incitement. "Sounds 'exciting,'" Loomis mocked my ingenious proposals, "However first, I think you better come to Fontainebleau." Fontainebleau? "Yes. It's not far." Fontainebleau. "You mean the palace. . . ." Already, I knew the palace fairly well. I had audited Leonard Opdycke's famous survey of French Renaissance architecture; five years before my mother had taken my younger brother and myself on an intensive exploration of Touraine with its châteaux. Fontainebleau is one of the most sumptuous royal residences in all France, consisting of a series of fine courtyards surrounded by rich buildings. These include the famous court of the Cheval Blanc (or des Adieux). Here Napoleon bade farewell to his marshals and the Old Guard, in 1814. There was the Cour Ovale, the Cour Henri IV, a smaller Cour des Princes. The Salle des Fêtes is the grandest sixteenth-century interior in France; under Henri II it was entirely redecorated by Italians, notably Francesco Primaticcio and Niccolo dell' Abbate.

Payson took erudition for granted and curtly cut me short. He said firmly: "Not the palace. The Prieuré." Such was fortuitous introduction to a grand country mansion long known as La Prieuré des Basses Loges. Perhaps Françoise d'Aubigné, Marquise de Maintenon, second wife of Louis XIV, nicknamed his comfortable rural mansion of the "Priory," just as Catherine the Great knew her vast palace as "The Hermitage." The Maintenon was a born teacher, in 1686 she founded the renowned École de St. Cyr, an academy for girls which the "Sun King" endowed with funds from the Royal Abbey of St. Denis. Her time at La Prieuré is forgotten, but historically it prefaced the sage of Gurdjieff's instruction, and before Madame de Maintenon held state, it is thought a religious foundation existed from medieval times. Surely his institute could have enjoyed no more appropriate patronage than from that headmistress of a school for poor but worthy maidens, to whom were first given Racine's splendid dramas, *Esther* and *Athalie,* to perform. Le Nôtre was thought to have laid out the grounds, which were set as formal gardens facing the front of the châteaux, with its more than two hundred acres bordering on the forest of Fontainebleau. Recently, the property was settled on the widow of Maître Labori, who had it from the family of Captain Dreyfus, in payment for Labori's masterful defense in the trials of the great *Affaire.* Currently, it housed "The Institute for the Harmonious Development of Man," directed by a personage recognized as Georges Ivanovich Gurdjieff, who had owned it since October 1922, five years before my visit.

This Gurdjieff, it was, who was teaching Loomis to dance; often when one asked G. who he was, or what he did, he replied: "I am a teacher of dancing." Similarly, when journalists or the ignorant asked what Diaghilev did, he'd answer: "I arrange the lights." When the King of Spain, who was a true friend of the Ballets Russes, asked the impressario his function, the reply was: "Like you, Sire; I am indispensable." Diaghilev, encountering Gurdjieff, with his reputation gathering around his "dances," suggested that these be presented as a "novelty" in one of the seasons. G. refused. In 1915, Diaghilev had tried to persuade Stravinsky to compose a ballet for his stripling choreographer, Léonide Massine, to be entitled *La Liturgie,* exploiting the gravely gorgeous rites of the Orthodox Church. Stravinsky, a communicant, refused. The Eucharist is a sacrament, not a spectacle.

In 1919, Diaghilev, who was the Leonardo da Vinci of theater managers, commissioned Manuel de Falla to write music for *Le Tricorne (The Three-Cornered Hat).* Its scenery and costumes were by Picasso. It was based on *El Sombrero de Tres Picos* by the soldier-poet Pedro Antonio de Alarcón. During a visit to Seville, Diaghilev had found a gypsy youth known as Felix. He realized the boy's value as a source of Andalusian folk-dance, and hired him to teach Massine, who was the same age. Felix conceived a notion that he was to star in the ballet to which he so greatly contributed. But Diaghilev's star *and* choreographer was Massine. The gypsy's fate might have been illustrated by a Capricho of Goya. Betrayed

by Diaghilev after being led to think he would become a world-famous
Spaniard among famous Russians, he went mad, and was found dancing
on the altar steps of a South London church. He was admitted to the Ep-
som asylum. As Madame Lydia Sokolova (Hilda Munnings) wrote in her
Dancing for Diaghilev,

> Felix's reason was the price fate demanded for the creation of a
> masterpiece. With Felix gone, Massine and I had to work hard to
> teach Karsavina not only the dances of the Miller's Wife, but the
> whole Spanish style of dancing. I was then grateful for all the training
> I had under Felix and Massine.

The tragedy of Felix Fernandez echoes that of Vaslav Nijinsky and
contributes to the lurid aura illuminating perils in metaphysical theater.
There is, for those who seek it, a didactic strain in such tales. Gurdjieff's
"dances" were something more than "entertainment." Like the Orthodox
liturgy, they are part of a "service," not of a fixed rite, but of general use.
In time, I was to discover their employment. Such service is multiform, to
many selves, and by observation, to persons magnetized by such motion.

The château of La Prieuré had endured many transformations from
its once princely condition, but still held a grave sense of decent state-
liness and dim grandeur. It had three storeys, built long, broad, and low.
Windows of the two lower floors had black shutters; the room was dor-
mered; two large chimneys with a cluster of multiple flues symmetrically
enclosed slates like massive bookends. The ground floor contained a large
drawing room which, when last completely decorated under the first Empire, maintained the stoic elegance of Percier and Fontaine. Attached was
a cozy salon and library. On the second floor, Mr. Gurdjieff and his con-
sort (or wife?) Madame Ostrowsky, a noble Russian lady, had apartments.
Walls of its corridors were decorated with lightly brushed murals by Alek-
sandr de Salzmann in the manner of the elder Tiepolo. Here also was an
attractive bedroom, known as "The Ritz." The third floor harbored a
range of attic bedrooms; in these ancient servants' quarters slept younger
male students. On my first night as Gurdjieff's guest, I was splendidly
bedded in "The Ritz."

I'd been invited to arrive on a Thursday, after supper. Days were
long; I don't think I came at night. Loomis had taken me into an inn on the
outskirts of neighboring Avon village. He roughly indicated a week's
schedule at the Institute, adding a summary description of its Director,

with something of the nature of the work undertaken there. But not much of either. I was now supine, definitely on the receiving end; it was no longer my place to press for answers. Events transpired with a certain inevitable or even solemn pace. I was happy to place myself under the pressure of Loomis's stewardship. Happenings seemed ominously charged before they came to climax or resolution; meaning would doubtless be unveiled in the fullness of time. Time, oddly enough, became a vivid dimension, and since I wore a wristwatch, I conceived the notion that certain moments, seen for example as 4:56, or 5:43, were actually trying to signify something. Loomis appeared intimately familiar with the local scene, and it became clear that he held some sort of secretarial job, that he was occupied in staff work or translation. Also he appeared free of any formal timetable and he could pass back and forth to Paris as he pleased. Or were such passages fulfilling some plan to which I was not yet privy?

In "The Ritz" I slept well. Payson woke me, waited while I shaved, led me down to breakfast, the classic coffee and croissant, with plenty of fresh butter and clover-honey, milk from the cow and drink from the spring. Other guests were a couple of prim, gray-haired, gray-clad English ladies, past middle age, a fair German girl, matronly and formidable, a very blond American, solid as a draft horse, in his mid-thirties, whose face I was drawn to immediately.

There were a number of other faces and bodies; these made no first impression. Loomis's introductions were formal; there was no apparent curiosity as to my appearance or presence. After breakfast, he piloted me around the gardens. Paths adjoining the château were punctuated by generously heaped big rocks, some of which had holes, three or four feet deep, beside them. Evidently, a renovation of paths, or development of landscaping was in train. Nearby the main house, there were settlements of smaller buildings, in the same style but obviously built later. In a coarse addition to the original mansion there were adequate kitchens, servants' quarters, a large *orangerie* glazed with big panes of glass, and a garden gazebo, or pavilion, known as *Le Paradou*, which appeared smaller than it actually was. Here was housed a considerable band of children supervised by a guardian or housemother whose term was shifted from week to week. Loomis announced, although I had not asked him, that *paradou* was an old French military term for a fortification which stops projectiles launched from the rear. His explanation begged for more, but by now I was pretending to be as secure as he was facing mystery, so I held my peace.

On this initial cursory tour, Loomis guided me to a large building he called The Study House. Its vertebral skeleton was from a surplus World War I airplane hangar, obtained for its haulage from the French Army. Although it covered a considerable tract, there was an unsettling flimsiness about it, as if it were made of cardboard and might collapse in a strong wind. Roof beams were supported by a double wall of rough lath stuffed with dry, dead forest leaves. Laths were plastered with chopped hay. The ceiling was laminated in tarred felt, in some parts quite thick. A glazed clerestory used the glass from old cucumber frames. Beneath was a calligraphic frieze, which may have been Arabic, but to me resembled the false Kufic of Renaissance iconography.

Loomis took discreet pride in explaining that every item of construction had been begged borrowed, or stolen from materials once in use and now at hand. The Study House was a palace of economy; the purpose for which it was raised was manifested by its coherent structure. The floor was trodden earth, stamped hard and dry, covered against dust with a rich layer of oriental rugs, which also draped windows and adorned the walls. In the middle of one side was Mr. Gurdjieff's "Kosshah" or pavilion of honor, a large tentlike enclosure, hung heavily with striped Central Asian textiles. The balcony above, and a whole central area was enclosed by a thin picket fence of white lath. Here the Director might view whatever transpired in the center space. The hall was impressive; my overall impression was more of an oriental circus tent than a ballroom. Elements in it were hideous. Ugly industrial lamps with glaring porcelain reflectors hung at crazy angles from high joists. The structure was at once flagrantly impermanent, yet palatial, with fragments of atavistic precedent. Detailing in carpentry and metalwork was coarse and rough, but there was the harsh fact of completeness, since every inch of wall was crammed with paint or decoration, an insolent patchwork, which irritated me in its contempt for permanence or tidiness. It strained toward theatrical effect, which was in the direction of the blatantly preposterous, far more than any pretence toward the "quasi-religious." It was strange, more exotic than "authentic." Its most effective and undeniable residue was an existential presence; the damn thing was actually, although dubiously, extant, here and now. It was big; it had been whipped up from spare parts by harebrained engineering; for whatever use it intended, the worst weather could be kept out. Its name "The Study Hall" asserted itself without apology. I saw it empty, enigmatic, slightly mocking.

Loomis took me out beyond the garden area. At first, I judged the work at hand as the labor of civilians on vacation, puttering to escape boredom. Parterres were being edged in brick, small bushes were being transplanted, but observation on a longer span revealed that the "students," or whoever they were, seemed to be playing peculiar calisthenic games. Paths abruptly turning to nowhere were being redirected to more dead-ends. Piles of sizeable rocks and damp earth, with big holes beside them, seemed waiting to be filled. We were off on a short walk, past increasingly untidy acreage, toward the ancient forest visible beyond a high, apparently unbreachable brick wall, topped with broken bottles. I asked if he did not have some labor of his own, in which case I could amuse myself. His work (today), he said, was to take me around; it would be inconvenient, even unwise, for me to venture alone. This was no answer; I was stewing with questions. His withholding or arch secrecy maddened me, for I felt a certain disdain or perhaps discipline in the suppressed logic of his mystery-making. Perhaps he thought I didn't deserve to be answered about riddles which I might have figured out for myself.

Yet how could I begin to ask when I had no notion of the basis of such behavior? So I said nothing at all, my curiosity curdling. A few minutes passed in silence. Abruptly, Loomis turned and started back to La Prieuré, almost as if he were leaving me behind. As we went by small gangs of student-gardeners, I had the impression that, while a few seemed to be digging up small stones, more were just throwing the heaps of rocks into holes neatly and deeply dug at their sides. Half a dozen men, of whom one seemed too old for the work, were transferring piles of used brick, which appeared to be rationed to each person, from the edge of one path to another. Although we were walking briskly and the day was bright, there was an unreal atmosphere, as if all the activity encountered was somehow action in reverse, suitably illustrating the adventures of Alice after she had penetrated the looking-glass. Here was a mirror of discrete reality in labor, but its aims were the universe of construction. This instinct for inversion was so strong, that I risked breaking a seemly silence. I asked Loomis, what in the world were these people really *doing*? "In this world," he replied, "They are *really* working."

It was now a few minutes before noon. We had arrived in front of the big house. Loomis said evenly: "Your taxi will be here presently." Taxi? Was I being sent back to Paris, with my overnight bag still left in "The Ritz," all unshriven, because of my graceless stupidity? Not at all. Loomis now had to take dictation for three hours. I would be driven into Fontainebleau, where I could inspect the park and palace. The taxi would return me to The Institute before dark. Then there was The Bath. Bath? Then there was Dancing. Dancing? So I was bundled out of the grounds before murmuring protest or dismay. Sure enough, a taxi was waiting. On the short drive to town, I had a chance to test my undergraduate French. The drive made it easy; he asked me how I liked *le patron. Patron?* "*Monsieur le Patron; le chef, comment dire? Le 'boss.'*" I could only answer "*Je ne sais pas, de tout. . . .*" which was a whole truth. I didn't know what he was talking about. He repeated, as if to himself: "*Le contremaître; oui. Lui. Un trés grand monsieur.*" "*Contremaître?*" The word stuck until, later, I had a proper dictionary: "*Contremaître*, n.m. (*fem: contremaîtresse*). Overseer, foreman, forewoman. (*Naut.*) first mate, boatswain's mate."

He left me at the café. I was about to pay and tip him, but Loomis had arranged everything. Enjoying a delicious lunch at a comfortable table with a view of the palace, I couldn't eat more than half, since I was so aroused by the unexplained and unexpected. I was poised on a brink of grand adventure.

When I was ten years old my parents sent me to a summer camp for boys, directed by A. E. Hamilton ("Chief"), a son-in-law of Dr. Luther Halsey Gulick, an eminent and enlightened educator. He had already founded a camp for girls which was famous for its balanced, thorough regimen. Its name was "Wohelo." When I first heard it, I recognized it as the name of an American Indian princess, probably from "The Song of Hiawatha," which my father liked to read aloud to my brother and myself. Hamilton, then a man of thirty-five, was the first distinguished personality I had ever met, apart from my own family. Some ten years after the foundation of Wohelo, he started a boy's version, on a Maine lake. It was named Timanous. Chief was my first instructor in virtuosity. He had a girlfriend associated with Isadora Duncan's "Isadoreables." It was she who introduced me to theatrical dancing, although she abhorred "the ballet." She gave "movement lessons" to small boys who might have been alarmed by the sissyfied sound of "dancing." These movements, unaccompanied by a piano, occasionally had the benefit of gramophone records (His Master's Voice: that white pup listening). I moved, more or less metrically, to Sinding's "Rustles of Spring," the first movement of Beethoven's "Pastoral," and similar fragments. Following the "method" of Isadora, we were exhorted to fly like a bird, bend like a bough, blossom like a flower. The rapture in moving by measure obliterated any guilt in sissiness. I wished to be a dancer. I *would* be a dancer, that was all there was to it! But organized motor control had other connections which were, for me, far less fun, including not only swimming, which I managed to muster, but diving as well, which I could not.

I was encouraged in my interest in how my body might move by Chief Hamilton, who recognized in unadulterated, energetic, innocent, mindless preadolescence an unformed passion devoid of intellectual prejudice, which was also what I felt for him. While he was experienced enough to keep kids at arm's length, since he was learned in the psychic dislocations of male colts, he would on occasion let me hug him before he punched me in the ribs, to make me let go. All this was nearly seventy years ago, yet I feel again a moment of stupendous euphoria remembering when, one evening after our early supper, when I had been unable even to speak to him for a couple of days, he came up and asked me: "How would you like to go on an *Adventure*?" I was too astonished to believe my ears. He told me to get blanket and mess kit, and meet him at the canoe dock.

Although I could not pull much weight in a canoe, I'd been given my own paddle. Chief set me well in front and pretended I was half the crew. We crossed the lake under darkening clouds, landing in a small inlet in pitch dark. Chief made a fire, laid out our blankets, and said that if I had any questions, having been in camp now a month, he would try to answer them. There was boiling in me such a ferment of violent curiosity, adoration, and excitement, that I could utter no sound. However, I was able to take refuge in the irrelevant, as if to throw the true current of my desire off track and make my ridiculous dwarf self less suspect or vulnerable.

I had been abjectly fascinated by one of Chief's assistant counselors named Karl Nicholson Llewelyn. He was known as Kap, and stationed himself somewhat apart from the rest of the camp's staff. To me, he looked middle-aged, forty at least; but now I know he was under thirty. Lean, almost gaunt, with a small black beard and jet hair crew cut, a scar like a sabre-slice was branded on one cheek. In April 1917 war had been declared against the House of Hohenzollern. There were ugly rumors that circulated after goodnight campfires that Kap was a "Hun," that he had been a U-Boat commander, and lost his job teaching law at Columbia University when his role as an enemy alien had been uncovered.

Hence I asked Chief if Kap was a traitor like Benedict Arnold, why was he not hanged or at least in prison? Chief said shortly, with a firmness which implied he'd heard my question before, that I shouldn't believe everything that was whispered around a campfire. The truth was that Kap was a poet. He had a romantic attitude about Germany; because everyone else was anti-Kaiser, he felt obliged to be pro-Kaiser. Also, he was as much Welsh as German, and Welsh people were poets as a race, and their face was against the world, against the British, or as the thing was today, not exactly anti-American, but anti–American Army. As for Columbia University, big schools for older boys were often more stupid than grammar schools. He reiterated: Kap was a poet. Poetry explained everything.

The scent of the pines, the diminished lapping of still water, glimmering embers of our fire, the small shot of burning liquor that Chief offered me, but which barely filled the bottom of my aluminum cup, settled my fever of curiosity and my need to try to express myself sensibly. There was nothing else to say, thank God. When the fire was black, Chief indicated a hollow in the ground where he had spread our blankets. As I lay in bliss beside him, far too excited to try to sleep, I found I really did have a proper request after all. Tell me the legend of Princess Wohelo. There was no legend. A wise man, his father-in-law Luther Gulick, had invented the name. It was an acronym for Work. Health. Love. Chief said all good things go by number threes. Three is important to remember. One is a start. Two is a difference, but it's three to which you finally come. One is source. Two is what comes from it. Three is the strength or energy that makes it happen. Take Work, Health, and Love. Now Work makes Health, and . . . but by now I dozed off and my lesson in the doctrine of the Blessed Trinity was lost in sleep.

So, ten years later, in Fontainebleau, I recaptured that sense of anxious excitement, a scale of glorious inveterate nervousness which can also be launch for hysteria. I felt like a solo instrument playing in an orchestra of implausible but potent sounds, an initiation adventure that could drag me into landscapes unexpected, even unwanted. I could never recapture the dewdrop glory of infantile innocence and Chief's unblemished splendor. I steeled myself against disillusion which must surely come, within the law of unsteady and unanswerable averages. A clinical neurologist, or what was later to be legitimized as a "psychiatrist," might have diagnosed the initial instance of what would be labelled as manic-depressive psychosis. Such analysis, however magisterial, would have no effect on the sequence of this disturbance or its ultimate effect in the education of a sly fellow.

In Fontainebleau the recollected miracle of my big adventure with Chief Hamilton spurred me into momentary hysteria, triggered by my awed confusion concerning Loomis. Was he a guide, an inquisitor, or a fraud?

I was also troubled by a negative memory of Chief. Young as I was, unfledged and untried, I had once almost come to hate him, or at the least to detest his attitude about art, dancing, poetry, and painting. He was a facile and brisk caricaturist, and sketched in pen and ink in a style which owed much to Frederic Remington and Joseph Pennell, with whom he studied in his youth, when he wished to paint portraits. All boys entering his camp were given blank pine canoe paddles upon which they were told to inscribe personal symbolic figures, expressive of their selves. Most of the kids blotched an animal's head—a fox, a wolf, or a bear, with help from a file of photographs torn from "nature" magazines. My brother was an exception; he conceived abstractly, a straight bar of a line, interrupted by a half-circle, then continuing the straight bar. To him this meant he could overcome obstacles in the straight-and-narrow by circumnavigation. For my symbol, I made a collection or constellation of round shapes, which by a trick of laying in shadows in from their edge, gave a fair enough rendering of plasticity. Color had no correspondence to any tradition; I only wanted to suggest that he who saw or scanned heavens would find a target upon which to keep sanity and come home.

On his paddle, years before, Chief Hamilton had drawn an empty canoe in the middle of a forest lake. Above was a full moon. I had been instructed at The Boston Museum of Fine Arts Schools, and at Harvard by Martin Mower and Pierre la Rose (Peter Ross), that neatness of execution in draftsmanship was three-quarters of the battle. Hamilton had rendered the ripples in the waters of the lake, which filled the bottom curve of his paddle, expertly. Shading was done by pen in india-ink; the paddle was varnished with a clear goo against fading. Chief's forms were rendered by linear design with tight cross-hatching. I knew it was a masterpiece, and I told Chief I thought it and he were *wonderful*. He dashed my enthusiasm by remarking with no heat: "Yes, it's good exercise." Exercise!

Also I had seen his girlfriend dancing alone and unobserved behind our barn dressed in a pale green shift. She flew across the irregular stubble-ground like a butterfly over a bed of flowers. I had never seen anything so magically beautiful. Chief abruptly, from nowhere, came up behind me, and saw the transfiguration effected on her audience of one. The shine in my eyes was instantly darkened when I heard him say: "Yup, it's nice exercise." Exercise, indeed. It was beautiful; what right had he to put it down with such churlish denigration? I bet he couldn't have danced so well. I knew I couldn't, but my inadequacy was diminished by enthusiasm. If this was *exercise*, what could complete accomplishment be?

I was supposed to "qualify" for diving in order to be promoted to a neat superior grade on a document we were to carry home at the end of summer, proving to our parents the fantastic improvement we had made in striving toward physical development. On the last day that count was to be taken I was able to stay on the dock long after everyone else had gone up to change for supper. The young counselor who taught diving was not a cruel man, but he had a conscience. I had not been able to "qualify." Now it seemed that God alone could gain my needed score. If I dived once, I hit the water head-on at least twenty times. I did not realize that anxiety sparked hysterical blockage; my fear and anxiety in poor performing hindered me from any care or effort which might have been productive. If this torture had not been so boring it might have been funny. I knew perfectly well I could never make it, but the instructor was determined, by forcing of *his* will, to make this wretched biped win. He was not indulging himself; doubtless he was doing his best to get out of me what he hoped was the best I had. Perhaps he was also maintaining the prestige of his instruction. After all, I was almost the only boy who had failed him. Finally, after the sun had sunk, my bones were ice and my will was gone, he snapped, mercifully: "O.K.: one more." I almost felt like jumping in, sinking down, and making no try to rise again. But I was hungry, and despite the shame of it all, and the silence in which we walked back to the barn, I knew I would not actually die of failure.

We met Chief Hamilton at the kitchen door. Since the dininghall had been cleared, the tables were wiped clean. The diving-instructor sighed wearily and pointed to an object which resembled a drowned rat which had been eviscerated awaiting a taxidermist. His gesture was replete with battle and defeat. He'd done his best; we both had been defeated. Chief smiled, reassuring my instructor with an ironic but generous pat on his back. I was dug in the ribs, on the bitter verge of tears. He comforted me lightly: "Well, now, that sounds like *quite* an exercise."

Iteration of that word frightened me. I considered how angry his use of it was before, in conjunction with a serious subject—"art." Now, increasingly, a less vague definition in my mind, implemented by immediacy, all but absolved me. An exercise could be repeated twenty times, and still not succeed. End results were not artifact but information. Exercising was about the strain toward extremity. My body had sustained a minute and massive disaster. My psyche, or whatever seeds in it promised possibility, had its rousing tonic. Exercise was now something into which I could sink my teeth, bite, and swallow. A good daemon rewarded me, and thoughtlessly I was grateful. I found I was able to seek the hand of my diving counselor, and while I couldn't formulate the two words "Thank you" aloud I knew he realized what I intended. So did Chief.

Chicago's Bloom
GEORGE LEVINE

The phenomenon of Allan Bloom's *The Closing of the American Mind* is more important than the book. It is an intellectual's book—at least one half of it devoted to a survey and analysis of the history of political philosophy from Plato to Weber—so it is difficult to believe that the more than three hundred thousand people who have reportedly bought it have also actually read it through. Why has it been so successful?

The book's enthusiastic reception by neo-conservatives suggests some obvious political explanations, but these alone are not sufficient. It makes, in addition, a strong emotional appeal. Who, after all, does not share some of Bloom's complaints about the thinness of family and community life in America? I would guess, on the strength of my own experience, that few in the middle class have escaped, in the texture of their lives at home or in what passes for community in cities or suburbia, paying the price of the economic and social organizations of American life. Bloom says what many want to hear about this malaise, and reassuringly does not locate some of the causes in the structure of the American economy and society. He tells the story as though from within, with an authority that seems to certify the argument, and with a rhetoric of considerable persuasiveness.

The rhetoric matters a great deal, suggesting a fearless confrontation with contemporary pieties, and implying emotionally satisfying arguments without actually making them. Bloom consistently pretends to reject positions his rhetoric shows him to be taking. After analyzing the failure of the contemporary family, for instance, he claims that he is not arguing "that the old family arrangements were good or that we should or could go back to them. I am only insisting that we not cloud our vision to such an extent," he says, "that we believe that there are viable substitutes

This article originally appeared as a review essay of *The Closing of the American Mind*, by Allan Bloom (New York: Simon and Schuster, 1987).

for them just because we want or need them." But this, in fact, is what his whole book implies. By rhetorically condemning present social and cultural arrangements and mocking those who try to come to terms with them or improve them, he implies that the only way to go is backwards.

Similarly, he avoids explicitly blaming the failures of contemporary culture entirely on the University and its professoriate. Nonetheless, from the book's title to the final analysis of the inadequacies of the contemporary disciplinary structure of American universities, he implies that a cowardly and ignorant professoriate and the institutions that house them are to blame, and he takes a high moral line against them. The moral indignation that exudes from the rhetoric must be, for many, one of the pleasures of this text, allowing readers to relax into the belief that they can locate the culprits and, by forcing them to behave, make things all better.

One cannot condemn the book for the audience it has attracted nor for the play it has been getting on television, the medium its author unequivocally despises. It is a matter of interest, however, that it could be so quickly assimilated by a culture that Bloom derides. This is a *cri de coeur*, a scholar's letting himself go in a long lamentation about the way the world has turned away from everything he, as scholar, had imagined the University ought to embody. It sounds authentic, and the unacademic texture of the prose, its highly personal nature, makes much of it accessible and credible to a nonacademic audience that values education but feels—fairly enough—that something is the matter with it.

The immediate attractiveness of Bloom's position to neo-conservatives is misguided. His arguments are in fact more conservative than neo-conservatives themselves would like: he wants great books universities, which would exclude technical and practically oriented schools. He wants the University to be a place of pure thought, and of pure thought about fundamental issues of good and evil, life and death, self and other. He sounds like a nineteenth-century liberal in the mode of Matthew Arnold. Like Arnold, he argues that the great intellectual tradition of the West is to understand nature, to see the object as in itself it really is and, again like Arnold, he believes this is possible only by withdrawing from the world. He doesn't use the word, but along with Thomas Arnold, Coleridge, and Matthew Arnold himself, he seeks a "clerisy," disinterested, in touch with their best selves, learning the best that has been thought and said in the West. In this new old vision, the University would be the true church. There is no guarantee that Bloom's clerisy would be capitalists.

It would be unfortunate if, confusing Bloom with the New Right or William Bennett, one were to evade his nineteenth-century excesses by denying that anything is wrong in academia. The book will be invoked as support for all kinds of assaults on the Academy and all kinds of proposals to return to traditional ways of doing things; and it will certainly be used by the back-to-basics movement, although Bloom himself is obviously not interested in "basics." His concern is only with the best students at the best universities. Those who turn to Bloom for quick-answer conservative reforms and for easy condemnations of the universities aren't reading him right. They are building on shaky ground because the immediate strength of the book's rhetoric disguises the intellectual shakiness of its arguments.

Bloom in fact consistently disparages the audience to which his book makes its appeal most directly, and for them the question of the intellectual coherence of his arguments is likely to be secondary. For them, the strength and personal engagement in the analysis of the failings on all sides (except Bloom's) will be sufficient, accompanied as it is by a rhetoric implying that Bloom himself cares deeply both about his students and about the pedagogical goal of "human completeness." This alone is sufficient to establish the book's authority and its appeal for those whose education is as deficient as Bloom says it is. The testimony, on the dust jacket and in reviews, even by educated people I respect, that this book is important, that it will therefore be "savagely attacked," is obviously intended to disarm rejoinders by implying that they will all be motivated by political and partisan prejudice. But quite aside from the rhetorical implications of what Bloom has to say about society, history, and the Academy, none of which I like, the case I would make against the book is that despite Bloom's obvious learning and intelligence, it is intellectually shallow and incoherent. As an argument, his book is difficult to take seriously; it doesn't make sense.

One has a right to expect intellectual coherence of a book that appeals so unabashedly to the universal, the true, the rational, even as it elevates personal disappointment into general cultural analysis. But Bloom totally fails to connect his analysis of the failings of contemporary culture to the failings of the Academy. His argument derives from deeply irrational sources; in its support of "reason," it defies any reasonable standard of what reason might be; and it offers no adequate object of blame or direction for change. His allegations about modern students and his analysis of their "souls" (as one blurb puts it) is entirely anecdotal, Olympian, and condescendingly sentimental. His evidential grounds are outrageously inadequate; and since one of Bloom's major culprits is social science itself, it isn't hard to understand why he refuses to sustain his analysis with the kind of evidence social scientists might find acceptable. Moreover, the essentialist language, the apparently unselfconscious confidence with which Bloom can talk about "nature" and the "good" and the universal aspirations of "human nature" is of a sort that intelligent people have guarded against for decades and that John Stuart Mill was complaining about one hundred and fifty years ago. Bloom must know this, and perhaps he adopted his argumentative strategies and his essentialist language precisely to provoke responses like mine. What's wrong with the world for him is that it is dominated by social science mentalities and antiessentialist thinking.

Bloom's rhetoric, gracefully rejecting the hard abstract language of the disciplines and invoking the highest ideals of Western culture, disguises its own intellectual inconsistencies by implying that it is precisely the loss of his fully humane way of talking and thinking that has caused our present plight. What fuels this book is surely, among other things, Bloom's experience of the sixties, when he felt himself abused, surrounded by cowards and traitors, his beloved dream of the ideal university shattered. There is a venom and bitterness in his anecdotes about those bad old days that makes of this book an act of vengeance. The sixties have been mythologized and trashed since the end of the Vietnam War. Bloom has been nursing his wound since then, and like most commentators who have eased comfortably into the eighties, he has made the years between about 1967 and 1973 the age of the decline of the West, and certainly of the university.

Bloom insists early in the book that he is making no comparisons: "I do not claim that things were wonderful in the past. I am describing our present situation and do not intend any comparison with the past to be used as grounds for congratulating or blaming ourselves." But his title is *The Closing of the American Mind*, with the implication that there was a time when the American Mind was open. Surely, that was before 1968. And he chose, as well, the aggressive subtitle, "How higher education has failed democracy and impoverished the souls of today's students." Apparently, there was also a time when higher education wasn't doing this awful thing, and assuredly too that time was before 1968. For all of his apparently impressive grasp of history, Bloom seems astonishingly insensitive to a long tradition of American lamentation about the country's shallowness and intellectual poverty, its apparently inveterate anti-intellectualism. This didn't start in the sixties, and Bloom knows this. The cowardly professoriate he despises, the treasonable clerks who sold out the idea of education, according to him, for a handful of student approval, were not the caricatures he makes of them. Nor did they sell education down the river. They were part of another phase of continuing struggle within American education, which began at the beginning and continues to this moment, to understand and to define the responsibilities of the University in a democracy.

Bloom's ahistoricism is intrinsic to his argument. Ideas are proof against history, and the issues are to be understood outside of history. Yet with its focus on the culpable sixties, history is nonetheless made to play a role in Bloom's telling of his painful story, and it emerges in his argument through anecdotes about students who provide silly and trivial answers to large moral problems or faculty members and administrators withering under Bloom's sharply intelligent questions. Outside of a few great philosophers, the world of this book is populated by a set of absurdly unintelligent (and hypocritical) intellectuals and painfully shallow and "nice" students. But anecdotes such as Bloom provides were commonplace, if I too may be anecdotal, when I began teaching in the late fifties. The sixties were a mere blip in the course of American history and the history of universities, although for Bloom they were the beginning of the end. The guns have long since disappeared from Cornell; my own experimental college, Livingston, has been absorbed—for better or worse—into the mainstream of Rutgers University. Indeed, all too little of what we learned in the years Bloom finds so terrible has remained part of the academic world.

While it is important to challenge the anecdotal evidence and Bloom's interpretation of the state of our souls and of contemporary culture, the most telling criticism of the book can be directed to its substantive intellectual argument. Let me try to formulate briefly what I take to be Bloom's position, avoiding as far as possible detours into the several thousand interesting but often maddening asides and supplementary arguments, the items that contribute to the book's wide appeal without really substantiating its argument. First of all, Bloom believes—with a passion that I respect but find difficult to comprehend—that ideas, and particularly the great ideas of great thinkers (as defined, of course, by

Bloom) are the primary cause of our behavior, and of our society's. In all of his analysis of the malaise of contemporary culture, there is precisely nothing about economic, industrial, or political forces. Somehow—and Bloom ingeniously shows parallels between the language of the German philosophers and the language of pop psychology and pop culture—there is a direct line from Nietzsche to the man in the street (women get very short shrift in Bloom's world), and the mediator is the University. The man in the street, we are to believe, gets watered-down Nietzsche and guides his life according to Nietzschean principles without knowing it. The determining factors are ideas, not economics, politics, or other subjects of the social sciences.

Cultural relativism, it appears, is the cause of all our woes. This sounds simple, even stupid, but Bloom begins with cultural relativism as the culprit, and he stays there. Cultural relativism is evil, first because every society requires a special faith in itself to insure its coherence and survival; second, because Western culture is superior to all other cultures; third, because all other cultures are entirely closed while ours is open, and they would destroy ours if they could; and fourth, because it means the end of the good, true, and beautiful, of universal verities, of nature itself. (The second point is not overtly stated; Bloom argues that we *can* find some things in other cultures that Western societies might use. But in our rationality and our very capacity to find some good things in other cultures we are clearly superior.) "Cultural relativism," he laments, "succeeds in destroying the West's universal or intellectually imperialistic claims, leaving it to be just another culture." It is a mark of the character of this book that this sentence is apparently intended to register loss, not gain.

Though it is true that sentences like this encourage charges of ethnocentricity, and though I find this book not only ethnocentric, but misogynist, and provincial (and therein lies another part of its grand appeal), I don't want my argument to rest on this kind of accusation. Bloom seems to have heard enough of name calling in the hated sixties, and that got nobody anywhere. More tamely and genially and I fear tediously I want to look at the epistemological implications of his argument.

Bloom believes Western culture is founded on the appeal to reason; cultural relativism denies the priority of reason. Western culture is founded on the understanding of nature; cultural relativism denies the authority if not the reality of nature. Bloom is ready to defend in fairly cogent ways his positions on reason, truth, and nature, and he explicitly argues that these positions are truly antiethnocentric. Nevertheless, as a "cultural relativist" (and part of the problem), I find his language indefensible.

Bloom believes in nature, as opposed to convention, and thus he believes in philosophy as opposed to the social sciences. He argues that "Nature should be the standard by which we judge our own lives and the lives of the people." That sentence left me breathless when I first read it; it still does. The long history of the complexities of the word "nature" seems to have made no impression on Bloom. Whatever he means by it, his "nature" is out there absolutely to be known. It is the standard of both truth and value. Among other things, the sentence suggests a stronger endorsement of sociobiology than Bloom may want to give. But since in his world humanity strives to transcend convention (the subject of the much despised social sciences), in order to get back to *nature*, he must mean, among other things, that humans need to behave in accordance with their biological natures. There is no need to invoke here the various issues revolving around that idea, from sociobiology to behaviorism to the battle of I.Q. testing to feminism.

Bloom argues, moreover, that "what is most characteristic of the West is science, . . . the quest to know nature and the consequent denigration of convention." Science, in this reading, becomes the path to all knowledge and all value, and insofar as it succumbs to cultural relativism and historicism—of the sort philosophers of science like Kuhn and philosophers like Rorty have been practicing—it destroys itself. The whole basis of reality, truth, value of Western society goes down with cultural relativism. While Bloom believes in the possibility of objective, disinterested, and universal truth, the cultural relativist tends to believe in the cultural construction of knowledge.

In Bloom, that belief heralds the death of the West, manifested in such unlikely effects as his students' failure to make love adequately, or the culture's absorption in the dumb animal rhythms of rock music, or the excesses of feminism and ethnic studies. Believing very sensibly that some things are better than others, Bloom strenuously insists on the disasters caused in every aspect of the culture, from top to bottom, by the tendency he finds in his students and their teachers to argue that studying other cultures is the only way to transcend the limits of our own. I'm not sure that very many people really do insist that, and the prominence of

American and Western studies in most curricula—along with the continued manifestations of racial bigotry on ivied campuses—leads me to
think that this particular "threat" is greatly overestimated. Nevertheless,
the point about the intellectual importance of cultural relativism and its
impact on Bloom's kind of faith in absolute and eternal verities is a strong
one. Indeed, it is one that I accept without at all being dismayed by its
effects. Rather, I'm encouraged by it as a provocation to rethink our fundamental assumptions about values and knowledge.

What is most striking to me is that Bloom never once in the entire
book confronts the intellectual substance of the arguments for cultural relativism. His position is, simply, that its *effects* are bad and that most of
the people who espouse it don't know its sources in the great thinkers and
therefore can't understand its full moral and intellectual price. The latter
part of his argument I find persuasive but trivial. That is, it's probably true
that all but the most sophisticated "cultural relativists" haven't read
Nietzsche or Weber, let alone Rousseau and Kant. It also seems that the
consequences of a genuine cultural relativism can be very painful. For
Bloom, cultural relativism is the erasing of value distinctions between cultures (creating the belief that other cultures are not only as good as ours
but perhaps even better). It is also, however, an epistemological notion—
that all perception and thus all knowledge is conditioned if not created by
the cultural assumptions built into our consciousnesses and perceptual
equipment from the time we are born. The confusions, paradoxes, and
creative difficulties issuing from these views are manifest in the dominant
critical theories of our time. Bloom's very reduction of the complex ideas
and states of mind he attacks in the phrase "cultural relativism" suggests
how inadequate his critique of contemporary culture is. Any intellectual
systems that tend to subvert the possibility of absolute objective knowledge, of the essential reality of ideas like "the good" or "nature," are in his
world "cultural relativism."

There are arguments that might begin to contend with the difficulties
of contemporary epistemology, the problems of perspectivalism or what
William James called the egocentric predicament. We get no such arguments from Bloom. Instead, he tells stories about the bad effects of such
thinking. He implicitly urges that we go back to traditions we don't believe in because life was richer and more fulfilling when we did believe in
them. Although he contends that cultural relativism subverts the authority of reason, he doesn't make a single argument to avert the conclu-

sion or to explain why intelligent people might be relativists. Obviously, he doesn't think there are any such people, which accounts for his consistent caricaturing of any figures in his past who disagreed with him. He doesn't talk about the tradition of contemporary hermeneutics that finds all knowledge mediated through personal or cultural biases and distortions; he invokes only to dismiss the deconstructionists and Derrida, Lacan, the Freudians, and the structuralists. And because he doesn't seriously consider the possible contamination of ideas by ideology, contemporary Marxist critics go the way of the deconstructionists.

Everyone from his perspective is intent on denying the importance of the old texts and engaging in a "furious effort" to be up-to-date. The phrase characteristically treats all serious activity of modern thought as faddish and trivial and every effort to deal with the Nietzschean insight into the death of the absolute as derivative and superficial. Bloom's one answer to all these problems is, read his great philosophers. And he justifies his persistence in essentialist language by implying its moral superiority. He talks about nature as if it is not only possible to know exactly what it is but to guide one's behavior in accordance with it. Whose nature? what aspects of it? under what conditions? Is it universal or historical? Can it ever be perceived without the distorting mediation of the perceiver? Does the word refer to some objective nonverbal entity, or does it carry in its very texture the significances, prejudices, ideals of some of the philosophers Bloom constantly invokes?

Yet in insisting on the disastrous consequences of cultural relativism—however foggily undefined along with other of his key words—Bloom is, in fact, putting his finger on a crisis in contemporary thought, the crisis of knowledge and value. Unquestionably, contemporary social dislocations reflected in the dislocations of contemporary epistemology have forced important variations on the questions of how we know, even how we know that we know, and how we affirm, justify, and share values. But Bloom trivializes this important subject by dismissing all who have tried to address it. In effect, he dismisses the crisis itself as the inevitable result of the faddish and cowardly behavior of intellectuals and Americans in general. All of this would have been avoided had we continued to read the great thinkers.

Bloom's language is a desperate retreat to a faith in something in which it is no longer possible to believe. I infer that Bloom doesn't believe in it either. For example, he reprimands Woody Allen in *Zelig* for making fun of the old Jewish dancing men and complains that for Allen "it goes without saying that a return to the old mode of adjustment and apparent health is neither possible nor desirable." But here Bloom is surely practicing the cultural relativism for which he blames his students, since he clearly does not believe in what those old Jewish men believed in, only in the state of "health" that went with the belief. His answer to cultural relativism is to pretend a commitment to older traditions that were healthier. The same kind of answer comes from William Bennett and those of the back-to-basics school who believe that the problems of education can be solved by returning to the very methods and subjects that were so discredited by the late fifties as to inspire the hated sixties to rebel.

The intellectual emptiness of Bloom's high-culture intellectual's attack on what he takes to be the University establishment needs to be recognized. Which is not to say that all is well with the University. His attack would not be so popular if some things weren't very wrong. Obviously, the University is a thoroughly compromised place. It cannot address its curricular and pedagogical problems without contending with finances, entrenched structures, the vagaries of the American economy, immigration policies, professional ambition, self-interest, and innumerable practical exigencies that Bloom does not attend to. And obviously, there are serious curricular problems that follow from social and political changes (and their intellectual counterparts) marking increased democratization and social homogenization—not, I would think, necessarily bad things. The University can address its problems, and lots of faculty are thinking serious non-Bloomian thoughts about how to handle them that make a return to the Great Books University a parochial and even silly response. In many ways, the University is now a more intellectually stimulating and vigorous place than it has been for decades. Many of its most interesting people are dealing uncomfortably but excitingly with the issues that Bloom wants to shove under the table in deference to great ideas by great thinkers. "Cultural relativism" does create profound problems in the establishment and authority of value, and it disrupts the positivist ideal of objective representation of natural truths. It raises the most fundamental of issues—what is knowledge and how is it possible to acquire it? Many people in the University are thinking about these problems, even reading a few great books along the way. The fact that they do not seem to know with dogmatic certainty what nature, "human completeness," or even the ideal curriculum should be is a mark of the integrity not the faddishness of their thought.

Bloom's book is intellectually disreputable because it totally fails to address these issues while pretending that philosophy is the most important of all subjects. Moreover, it absurdly attributes the real crises and weaknesses of contemporary culture entirely to the cowardice and intellectual shabbiness of the Academy and to a professoriate intimidated by the sixties. One of the great ironies of the popularity of his book is that while it looks to be passionately and neo-conservatively pro-American, and shows a charming devotion to knowledge and students, it denigrates *everything* American as shabby, faddish, derivative—except when he waves the flag over America's responsibility to the world. Bloom is, I believe, deeply anti-American in that while he celebrates democracy, the only thing he expressly values in it is what it borrowed from European Enlightenment philosophy when it established democratic government. A look at the index confirms that he makes not a single allusion to important American thinkers, say, Emerson, William James, or Pierce. (Dewey, to be fair, is mentioned three times, for the most part dismissed and belittled, but implicitly praised for boyish optimism.) *All* important ideas in America have been borrowed (and watered down) from Europe, and particularly from Germany. Bloom reveals no feeling for American history, not even American intellectual history, so that while describing the closing of the American mind he talks only about Plato, Aristotle, Locke, Kant, Rousseau, Nietzsche, and Weber. And American universities were at their best when they were suddenly filled, in the 1950s, with European professors.

One last point, which is probably central to any discussion of the subject at state universities. Bloom never connects the failures of the University to larger failures of contemporary society and culture, which he blames implicitly on the University. He oversimplifies intellectual history by ignoring everything that went into producing it, except ideas. I wouldn't for a minute suggest that the American University is an ideal institution, but Bloom's total preoccupation with "great ideas" as the cause of social action and personal behavior leads him to attribute to it and to the people he resented in the sixties the collapse of the whole culture. If we are to do anything about weaknesses in contemporary education it is essential that we dismiss this absurd but forceful part of Bloom's argument. One of the things universities must do is consider the limits of what is genuinely possible for them, within the social, economic, and political constraints of American culture.

Even if Bloom's analysis of the problems of contemporary culture were correct, it wouldn't be of much use to the vast majority of strong institutions of higher education. He is quite explicit at the start about being interested only in the best students at the best universities, and all his anecdotes (which are his evidence) are drawn from experiences at those universities. Not concerned with the state's responsibilities in higher education to the population at large, but only with the best ideas for the best students at the best places, Bloom can't have anything to say about the nature of the curriculum at universities to which financially con-strained parents send their children for training that might help them sur-vive after the B.A. How many parents would be willing to send their children to universities only that they may think great thoughts, struggle to "human completeness," and contemplate or discover the unity of all knowledge—unless, of course, the university's name carried such weight that the diploma would assure employment whatever the actual content of the education. At most universities, questions of curriculum are neces-sarily compromised by economics, state politics, social and ethnic varia-tion. The University has a moral and a legal responsibility to bring along weak and mediocre students as well as to cultivate the outstanding ones, even if it cannot let the shape of its curricula be determined by the weak-est students.

While agreeing with Bloom that cultural relativism has made it very difficult to determine what the best curriculum might be, I welcome that difficulty as a goad to thinking hard and seriously and freshly about the problem. Unlike Bloom, I do not believe that those who argued for radical changes in traditional curricula (which, in any case, wouldn't have satis-fied his objectives) are cowards and charlatans. (Some of these show up everywhere.) And courage seems to me to be the requisite for those will-ing to resist the political and emotional pressures to return to discredited traditions simply because to abandon them caused pain and uncertainty. We should know, though Bloom doesn't, that changing the curriculum isn't in fact going to make much of a difference to the way the family exists in America, or to rock music, or television.

Bloom looks backward and away from the real conditions of American education. Like many in academia, he doesn't like the impurities of history and society as they thrust themselves between great ideas and their embodiment. Grudgingly he modifies at the end his apocalyptic and utopian rhetoric for a melancholy concession that nothing more can be hoped for than to keep the embers of true philosophy alive. I would be happy to fan the flames, but only if "true philosophy" entails coming to terms with the apparently unphilosophical forces that largely determine the shape of our lives, only if it forced Bloom to recognize how much of his American jeremiad is inspired by personal animus, bitterness, and frustration at an early stage of his career, and only if it included a genuine intellectual confrontation with cultural relativism. Otherwise, the best thing to do is to ignore this book and get back to serious business.

Balthus and the Ritualizing of Desire
RONALD PAULSON

*L*A *CHAMBRE*** is a large canvas, ten feet across, painted between 1952 and 1954 by the artist who calls himself Balthus. It shows an adolescent girl, nude except for stockings and pumps, stretched out on a chaise longue in a darkened room, her legs open toward the window. A curtain is being held back from this window by a small gnomish creature so that a strong golden light covers the girl's body, in particular her thighs and torso. There is something under her that looks like a towel, as if she has come from the bath. There are three pieces of furniture in the room, a huge armoire, a solid chest with a bowl and pitcher on it, and a spindly table. On the last lies a book and seated on it, its face turned toward the light, is a cat.

The painting could be a parody of Titian's *Danaë* with the flood of gold pouring into her lap (and in the Prado version her grotesque servant is trying to intercept the downpour in her apron before it impregnates Danaë). Balthus himself painted variations on the subject both before and after *La Chambre*. In *Nu jouant avec un chat* (1949) the girl is semiawake leaning back to touch the now smiling cat; another girl, clothed, has just opened the window. The room has the same furniture but lacks the heavy atmospherics of *La Chambre;* the Derain-like forms and colors, the more uniform distribution of light, imbue the scene with an even greater unease. In a very recent painting, *La Peintre et son modèle* (1980–81) the girl is clothed, engrossed in a book, and it is the painter (his back to us) who pushes the curtain from the window. In one of many other variants (*Les Beaux Jours*, 1944–49) the girl is dressed and there is no window, but her body is in the same relation to the light of a blazing fire being stoked by a boy who is stripped to the waist.

The man who painted these scenes is, as he cabled the cataloguer of the London Tate exhibition of 1968, "a painter of whom nothing is known.

---

*We regret that we were unable to include an illustration of *La Chambre*. It is in a private collection whose owners would not allow it to be reproduced.

Les Beaux Jours, 1944–46—Hirshhorn Museum, photo courtesy of Pierre Matisse Gallery

Now let us look at the pictures." He does, however, make it known that he is called Count Balthazar Klossowski de Rola, though the title is apparently without substance. The two major selections of reproductions of his work, previous to the exhibitions at the Centre Pompidou in Paris and the Metropolitan Museum in New York of a few years ago, were "authorized": one carried out by a close friend, Jean Leymarie, the other by Balthus's son Stanislas. The latter seems to be spokesman for the hauteur of "nothing is known" ("on ne sait rien"). He tells us nothing in his preface to *Balthus* (Harper & Row, 1983), but he urges admirers, instead of seeking biography, to "contemplate" the paintings.

> By "contemplation" I mean the elevation from mere perusal and observation to vision, from the empirical to the ideal—a state wherein the act of seeing, the seen and the seer become one. . . . Any other way is doomed to failure, for Balthus' art pertains to a mysterious tradition whose secret and sacred tenets he is constantly in the process of rediscovering.

However fatuous it may sound, this statement from the son of Balthus carries some authority. He tells us that "the fabled theme of the young adolescent girl" as expressed in *La Chambre*

> has nothing whatsoever to do with sexual obsession except perhaps in
> the eye of the beholder. These girls are in fact emblematic archetypes
> belonging to another, higher realm. Their very youth is the symbol of
> an ageless body of glory, as adolescence (from the Latin *adolescere:* to
> grow toward) aptly symbolizes that heavenward state of growth which
> Plato refers to in the *Timaeus*. Eroticism is nowadays confused with
> libidinousness, thus obscuring the true intelligence of esoteric works
> ultimately pertaining to the divine cosmic mystery of love and desire.

These words may to some extent be the result either of a paternal leg-pull or a filial misunderstanding, but they do reflect in however dim a way one aspect of Balthus's paintings. His figures, including those suggestive adolescent girls, are not only behaving very strangely; they are represented in an extremely hieratic, even hieroglyphic stylization. Their bodies are often mannequinlike; the diagonal line favored by Balthus influences the shape of their shoulders seen from the back, the brittle inclination of their heads, and often their whole bodies; the girl he sometimes paints leaning over a table to read a book seems to have been cut from a pattern book.

Balthus is important to contemporary artists because he is one of the exemplary figurative painters of our time. It is possible that a figurative painter, struggling in the wake of the great modern traditions of abstraction, has to adopt a "mystery" or a myth; indeed, if his work is genuinely *figurative* (as in figurative speech) it is metaphorical rather than literal in its depiction of the objective world. The two great continuing art movements of this century, both contending for place in Balthus's work, are cubism and surrealism. His figures often assume cubist forms, and in some of his later work his whole canvas dissolves into cubist patterns, often resembling the still-lifes and fabrics of analytic cubism. What is known of Balthus the painter, however, is that he emerged in the wake of the surrealist movement in 1930s Paris (bearing some traces of Derain's "classical" phase), and the signs of the movement can be detected in the incongruity of the grotesque attendant and the cat as well as the cavernous *chambre*.

Balthus's largest compositions, like *La Chambre*, may be in the tradition of Degas's baigneuses but on a scale and with an imagery to recall history paintings such as Titian's *Venus of Urbino* or *Danaë*. In the same way, he painted panoramic landscapes carrying a pedigree from Poussin (the *Seasons*) to Courbet and Corot; still-lifes from Chardin to Cézanne; card-players from the Le Nain brothers to Courbet and Cézanne; views through the windows onto landscapes from the frescoes of the Villa d'Este to the scenes of Friedrich, Bonnard, and Matisse; and cityscapes that recall the frescoes of Lorenzetti and Piero della Francesca. The viewer is aware of all these masters as he looks at a Balthus in much the same way we are aware that he calls himself Count Balthazar Klossowski de Rola, but also in the positive sense of an academic tradition carried into the present—and with the growing awareness of odd discrepancies and surrealist dislocations.

We can date the advent of surrealism about 1932, when Balthus dated the second version of *La Rue*. The first version is still in the postimpressionist style of *Le Pont Neuf* and the other cityscapes of the 1920s. But the later version, expanded to the huge size he was to affect for his major works, has abandoned impressionism for the smooth texture and odd juxtapositions of surrealism. Balthus has added the molestation of the little girl, the strange roundish child bouncing her ball, and the boy leaning diagonally in his mother's arms. These additions turn the central figure, the one odd element in the earlier version, into something more bizarre, resembling Lewis Carroll's Tweedledum or Tweedledee.

In the cityscape *Le Passage du Commerce Saint André* (1952–54), Balthus paints a Paris street with (characteristically) its exit closed off by a cross street. The colors, texture, space, and composition are of a Piero fresco, but there are two strange figures painted in a grotesque convention, and these draw our attention to the irrationalities in the architecture—the sidewalks that disappear where they should close, the formal but implausible variations of the window spaces, including blocked windows—as if we were looking at a capriccio, one of those cityscapes the Romans and Venetians loved in which St. Peter's was represented standing next to the Leaning Tower of Pisa.

This is the surrealist method of René Magritte, but Balthus's canvases are interesting at precisely the point where Magritte's stop, with the flat, absolutely unexpressive paint that produces the effect of mechanical reproduction and focuses undivided attention on the content of his images (often illustrative of a verbal paradox). Balthus also painted bland surfaces in the early 1930s, but in his characteristic pictures these passages are en-

Toilette de Cathy, *1933—Musée national d'art moderne, Centre Georges Pompidou, photo courtesy of The Metropolitan Museum of Art*

livened by charged areas of paint that involve the viewer emotionally in a way quite foreign to Magritte. One's attention is drawn to some passage of rich, buttery paint, usually a highlight; or to some unfinished detail or emendation, or a face or body that is drawn in a different convention of representation or style, such as the grotesque hairdresser with Cathy in *Toilette de Cathy* (1933) who appeared earlier in *Pont Neuf* and later in *Passage du Commerce* and many other pictures as well. All of these break the solid Magritte surface by acknowledgment of the painter's presence and introduce into the very paint texture chance and the unconscious. It is at this point that Balthus also evokes André Masson, Max Ernst, and the surrealists who draw attention to the act of metamorphosis both within the image and in the gestural performance of the painter.

Balthus's paintings are influential among younger painters today partly because of the rich working of the paint surface: sun *and* the bold play of the paint brilliantly illuminate the crucial parts of the female body. Magritte's painting of a room filled with one gigantic apple could never be mistaken for a Balthus. Magritte's rooms and apples, before being composited, are taken from posters and magazine illustrations, not from old-master paintings. He paints not a nude but a truncated sculpture of a nude, a headless torso on a coat hanger, or a pair of amputated feet. Balthus simply paints a nude, but the genre of Nude is juxtaposed with the very particularized face of a little girl's portrait and with the clearly focal intersection of the relaxed legs (sometimes, in the manner of brothel photographs, wearing only stockings) that designates the genre of erotic art; and all of this is juxtaposed also with the elegant form and paint surface. It is this divided focus, this odd juxtaposition, that creates the Balthusian incongruity.

In his *Nu allongé* of 1950 Balthus represents a girl stretched out on a bed; he has painted the white of the bedding subsequent to painting the girl's body, so that the white of his pigment penetrates noticeably between her legs to the very intersection, impinging physically upon her body. In an earlier version, *La Victime* of 1938, the knife lying near the outstretched nude assigns the aggression to an outsider rather than to the artist, but the aggression in both is sexual. (In the same way, it is only when we notice that the apricot in a Balthus still life is cut and placed to resemble a vagina or turned to show its stem-end that we realize we are still within the metamorphic realm of Magritte's famous *Le Viol*, in which a woman's face becomes a nude female torso and vice versa.)

Magritte's truncated objects are evocations of male anxiety; Balthus's girls hold the attention because the aesthetic experience—the paint and the almost cubist formality of his pattern—is so erotically charged, not without some menace. His rooms are distant cousins of Magritte's anxiety-ridden rooms. From the composition and the style we expect Titian's *Venus of Urbino*, but we are confronted instead with an adolescent girl. The shock value Balthus seeks is clarified when we recognize that, though he begins with a Titian Venus, he pivots on Manet's *Olympia*, the true graphic prototype of all his girls. He has picked up the Olympia's particularity, her antithetical attendant (black to her white), her youth and her unselfconscious indifference in the presence of the viewer, the brilliant clarity with which the body is painted, the emphasis on the bedding, and above all the sense of the outrageous, of the break with tradition in a picture so strongly affirming the tradition, that has been associated with the *Olympia* ever since its first showing. Balthus makes the nude a girl just on the edge of womanhood, embodying a metamorphosis that seems to be represented by both the sunlight flooding in from the window and the artist's own play of pigment.

The surrealist-related writers of the 1930s one immediately connects with Balthus are Antonin Artaud, the theorist of the "theater of cruelty," and Georges Bataille, the center of a group much concerned with eroticism and death that included Balthus's brother Pierre Klossowski.

Balthus designed the sets for Artaud's play *The Cenci* in 1935 and drew his portrait; Artaud had already reviewed Balthus's first exhibition in 1934, commenting: "If he uses 'reality,' it is the better to crucify it." Crucifixion was a central theatrical formula in Artaud's *Le Théâtre et son double* (1938), one of the more influential books on theater published in this century. Painting is one of Artaud's two master similes for theater, the other being plague: "like the plague, the theater has been created to drain abscesses collectively"; it is "a crisis which is resolved by death or cure." Like the painter's *tableau* (the French word means both picture and dramatic scene), Artaud calls for a theater that replaces the spoken word with the visual gesture, the text with a foregrounding of the mise-en-scène. The "concrete physical language" Artaud advocates, which "is truly theatrical only to the degree that the thoughts it expresses are beyond the reach of the spoken word," could be used to describe a Balthus scene. By "cruelty" Artaud means an "extreme action" or situation like the plague— "everything that is in crime, love, war, or madness," but which comes down to a ritual of pain and exorcism.

The painting Artaud refers to is Lucas van Leyden's mannerist extravaganza *Daughters of Lot* in the Louvre, which happens to deal with the taboo theme of incest, and he also adduces the "extreme" tableaux painted by Bosch and Grünewald of temptation, damnation, and crucifixion. From the dramatic repertoire he invokes Jacobean tragedy, built "around famous personages, atrocious crimes, superhuman devotions," and in particular John Ford's *'Tis Pity She's a Whore,* in which a brother and sister flamboyantly commit incest. Artaud is most interested in the young heroine Annabella: "If we desire an example of absolute freedom in revolt, Ford's Annabella provides this poetic example bound up with the image of absolute danger." The theatrical elements here are youth, vigor, obsession, the narcissistic mirror image of brother and sister as lovers, and the suicidal sacrifice of Annabella to her obsession.

Jacobean tragedies may not at first seem relevant to Balthus's quiet domestic interiors. But almost everyone who has written on Balthus notices the threat exuded by his extraordinarily theatrical (in Artaud's sense) interiors. And youth is, of course, the locus of Balthus's world. His figures are either children or adults who have the bodily proportions of children. The pseudonym *Balthus* itself is derived from Baltusz, the Polish diminutive of Balthazar (as Sasha is of Alexander), latinized. Balthus's official commentators (his friends and son) connect his juvenile world with the golden age; but less purity than the free play of instinct is to be seen in Balthus's images. His children only make sense in the context of Artaud's "theater of cruelty," and also in the context of Balthus's own set of illustrations for Emily Brontë's *Wuthering Heights*, fourteen pen and ink drawings made in 1933 on which a number of his later paintings were based. In this series, which is in fact the nucleus of his later work, Balthus makes Heathcliff a self-portrait.

Cathy and Heathcliff are a disguised version of the brother and sister in *'Tis Pity She's a Whore:* their love is not specifically incestuous, but it is forbidden. (Heathcliff, however, was given by the Earnshaws the name of Cathy's dead brother and slept in the same bed with her as a child.) Spiritual siblings, they are children passionately driven to pursue each other despite the world of adult taboos. The large heads and small bodies that distinguish Balthus's work first appear in these illustrations. The younger generation stifled by the elder (a state of nature compromised by society) is summed up in the illustration that shows Cathy being dressed up into respectability while Heathcliff sits nearby expostulating with her: "Why have you put that silk frock on then?" When Balthus made a painting based on this scene (*Toilette de Cathy*, 1933), he reversed the roles: Balthus/Heathcliff is fully, formally dressed and Cathy is outrageously undressed, her head thrown back and her nipples pointing in different directions; but despite the developed breasts her pubic area is that of a child. The boy has donned the veneer of adulthood that so annoyed Heathcliff. The girl, as in all of Balthus's later work, remains a girl, that is a free and—as suggested by her unfastened robe—accessible spirit.

Georges Bataille wrote an essay on *Wuthering Heights* in a book called *Littérature et le mal* (1957), which sets out to prove "that literature is a return to childhood" and therefore to a natural evil. "The fundamental theme of *Wuthering Heights*," he writes, is "childhood when the love between Catherine and Heathcliff originated," and his image of the "two children [who] spent their time racing wildly on the heath," who "abandoned themselves, untrammelled by any restraint or convention," sounds rather like Artaud's description of the brother and sister of *'Tis Pity*. "There is no character in romantic literature who comes across more convincingly or more simply than Heathcliff," Bataille writes, "although he represents a very basic state—that of the child in revolt against the world of Good, against the adult world, and committed, in his revolt, to the side of Evil." Although Heathcliff appears only infrequently in Balthus's scenes (perhaps as the boy stoking the fire in *Les Beaux Jours*) Cathy, either a pre-Linton Cathy or a Cathy who retains the wild Heathcliff in her, is the subject of a great many paintings. The grotesque old woman who was dressing her hair also recurs, recalling one of those old crones in Hans Baldung Grien's paintings who mock the beautiful young girl as Death mocks Life; or possibly one of Goya's duennas or bawds.

Bataille continues the theme in the other essays in *Littérature et le mal*—on Blake, Baudelaire, and de Sade. Thus Baudelaire "deliberately refused to behave like a real man, that is to say, like a prosaic man"— rather he "chose to be wrong, like a child." This is clearly the ethos Balthus chose with his name and his personal iconography, but embodied in the girl Cathy (Annabella). Although it is hard, without more biographical information, to establish precedence between the interpretations of *Wuthering Heights* by Balthus and Bataille (a third, related interpretation appeared in Buñuel's *Abísmos de Pasión* of 1954), Bataille's ideas were already set out in his notorious pornographic novel of 1928, *Histoire de l'oeil*. It opens, for example, with a chapter called "The Cat's Eye" which seems to herald the ubiquitous Balthusian cat. A boy and girl, both sixteen years old, are involved in some sexual play with a cat's saucer of milk. It is no secret what *that* cat means, and therefore what in demotic French the feline signifies positioned near the girl's legs in Balthus pictures. The cat may also, as some critics have suggested, be a self-reference to Balthus (in a painting of 1935 he refers to himself as "king of the cats," a deeply ambiguous phase). But in the series of prints called *Mitsou* (1920), Balthus's earliest surviving work (he was twelve), the cat is found, cherished, and lost by a little boy modelled, I suppose, on Balthus. This is not a *louche* cat à la Bataille, but it is worth noticing that if the little boy in this

Jeune Fille au chat, *1937—Mr. and Mrs. E. A. Bergman Collection, photo courtesy of The Metropolitan Museum of Art*

series parallels Heathcliff in the later one, the cat, ultimately lost, parallels Cathy. Certainly in the paintings of girls in the 1930s the cat is primarily a sexual index to the concealed (or not concealed) center of the painting, the flash of underpants or flesh. In *Thérèse revant* (1938), to take another case, the cat is in fact drinking milk from a saucer just below the girl's exposed crotch. In *Jeune Fille au chat* of 1937, the cat is in the same position, alertly couchant. The saucer in *Histoire de l'oeil*, and the girl's anatomical part that rests in it, activate a series of round shapes that include eyes, eggs, testicles, and above all, the sun.

The sun, so important a presence in Balthus's paintings, embodies Bataille's central doctrine of *dépense*—a generous, wasteful expenditure, like the child's "sin" of squandering time, which increases the intensity of life by drifting carelessly toward death. "Eroticism," in Bataille's famous definition, "is assenting to life to (virtually beyond) the very point of death" ("L'érotisme est l'approbation de la vie jusque dans la mort"). At its most elemental natural level the effect of the Balthus girl is heliotropic: she is stretching and opening like a flower in the warmth of the sun. But the ambiguous pose (heads inclining as if on broken necks, bodies bending like discarded puppets), and the presence of the old crone, keep this otherwise positive and banal moment in check.

Bataille associates *dépense* and the sun with self-immolation, not only with Semele but with the Aztec deity to which human sacrifices were offered. Indeed, the Bataille philosophy of *dépense* (formulated in *La Part maudite* [1949], and *L'Érotisme* [1957], but in circulation earlier) may be that secret/sacred mystery to which Stanislas Klossowski alludes. Bataille writes that for eroticism to be erotic it has to be a sin, a transgression of a taboo (it "has been hard put to survive in a world of freedom whence sin has vanished"). First then, there must be the taboo subject, for example a prepubescent girl; and second a threat or danger of death. (Bataille quotes de Sade, "There is no better way to know death than to link it with some licentious image," and adds: "The sight or thought of murder can give rise to a desire for sexual enjoyment.")

From both Artaud and Bataille, then, comes the centrality of theater and art of ritual human sacrifice, the voluntary offering of the innocent, as also the evocation of the Black Mass—a taboo version of Christ's Passion—laid out on a prone female body. In Balthus's *La Victime* (1938) the nude is stretched out on a crumpled bed sheet, prepared for love-making or—we see a knife on the floor—murder or sacrifice. As Camus wrote of Balthus, "Ce n'est pas la crime qui l'interesse, mais la pureté." In *L'Érotisme* Bataille remarks on how sacrifice like the act of love involves an unclothing to "reveal the flesh," and (in the manner of Artaud) he compares these actions to "a rudimentary form of stage drama reduced to the final episode where the human or animal victim acts it out alone until his death."

Bataille sees the ceremony of his scene as an iconographical alternative to the crucifixion, but it is obviously also a suggestive ritual that draws on older myths, of Greek origin in Danaë or Semele (young women who are "given" or give themselves to a lustful god), or of pre-Columbian origin in the sacrifice to the sun god. Behind Bataille and his group, of course, was a general interest in latter-day Gnostic ideas and Rosicrucian doctrines, all centered on the opposition of light to dark, good to evil, or in Bataille's terms *dépense* to in-turned adult prudence: the young girl to the old hag. But the girl herself, with the particularized, inscrutable, and perhaps somnolent face, denotes a turning inward, a kind of frigidity at odds with the open body. There is a withholding that is in tension with the acceptance of the body to the sunlight pouring over it which returns us to the conflicting centers of interest in individualized face and exposed underpants, to which we can now add closed, self-contained face and open body; and the two aspects of time externalized in a watchful *dépense*-ful cat and an old crone. This attendant can open or close curtains to introduce or exclude the sun; can emblematize adult prudence or some subrational desire, whether Old Age/Death or the Goya duenna/bawd.

I would like to conclude with a brief confirmatory survey of Balthus's paintings in chronology. After beginning to paint in various modes in the 1920s, from Rousseau-primitive groups of figures in park settings to copies of Piero della Francesca frescoes and Bonnard-like landscapes, in 1932 Balthus painted *Jeune Fille assise*, a portrait of a clothed girl throwing back her arms and reclining into a position of relaxed openness. By the next year he had transformed this figure into the absolutely characteristic girl of the notorious *Leçon de guitare*, a composition which combines in one image the acts of guitar playing, sexual arousal, and sacrificial display, carried out on a prone body, its lower parts exposed with emphasis on the prepubescently bald genitals. The composition takes off from (and alludes to) Max Ernst's equally notorious *The Blessed Virgin Chastises the Infant Jesus* (1926); Balthus has transformed the Christ Child's backside (distinctly feminine as Ernst paints it), being spanked by the Virgin, into the girl's frontside being played upon by the older woman as if she were the guitar that lies abandoned on the floor. Both Balthus and Ernst are mockingly alluding to pietàs. The woman's face bears a disquieting resemblance to Heathcliff's (and so to Balthus's) in *Toilette de Cathy* of 1933, just as her exposed and upturned breast is precisely Cathy's.

The nudes in sacrificial positions take two forms. One is the recumbent figure, most blatant in *La Victime* of 1938 and its later version, *Nu allongé* of 1950, where the knife is absent and the artist himself has taken the role of the officiant. In the pictures of the later 1930s, where the paint texture begins to appear in all its richness, the light also makes itself felt in a more powerful and direct way. In *Nu adossé* (1939) the girl's thighs and belly are picked out by a ray of light, the rest remaining in shadow. There are many other pictures of this general sort, the girl sometimes clothed, more often unclothed, including the girls in *Le Salon* (1940–43) and the wonderfully painted *Jeune Fille endormie* of 1943. There are, of course, gaps during which Balthus painted in other modes, and when we look at the whole series of paintings of the war years we see other preoccupations. But in 1944–46, with the large *Les Beaux Jours*, he made the first of a series of summations of the subject, with the mythological overtones emphasized. Here the girl is open not to sunlight but to firelight; the fire, being stoked by a boy, is borrowed from an engraving of Vulcan stoking his furnace while Venus lies stretched out behind him.

While painting the second version of *La Victime* and other languid girls stretched out on beds, Balthus also painted a clothed girl lying on a hillside (but skirt hitched up to retain her receptivity to the sexual dimension of nature) in a landscape that echoes the curves of her body (1942–45). She recalls Claude's Echo and, ultimately, Giorgione's sleeping Venus. This and *Le Cérisier* (1940) are two of the three landscapes that directly connect the female figure with nature. The third is the monumental *La Montagne* (1937) which combined the horizontal, recumbent, sleeping, or dead girl with the vertical, upstretched girl, later developed in *Le Cérisier*. They reflect respectively the horizontal and vertical aspects of the natural setting, the hillside and the mountain. Balthus's other landscapes, while omitting the human presence, are extended panoramas analogous to the close-ups of the female torso he painted in *Nu addossé* and *Jeune Fille endormie*. In the later landscapes where girls appear, they are within a room looking out through a window at the landscape.

As the summation of the recumbent nudes, and a response to the fire of *Les Beaux Jours*, Balthus painted a series of nudes stretching backward in a flood of sunlight and playing with a cat (1948–54), which led up to the huge *La Chambre*, with which we began this essay. There the sacrificial element is emphasized by having the gnomish creature, acting as officiant, introduce the sun. The girl in *La Chambre*, as we have noticed, lies on a towel. The idea of a bath, once introduced, leads to the standing girls of the 1950s who had just risen from a bath.

This second series of standing nudes began, however, much earlier with the surrealist *La Fenêtre* of 1933. Here the girl, an upright version of the girl in *La Leçon de guitare* or *La Victime*, perches on the sill of an open window overlooking a townscape of rooftops. She appears threat-

La Fenêtre, *1933—Indiana University, Bloomington, photo courtesy of Pierre Matisse Gallery*

ened: she holds one hand up as if to ward off an intruder, one breast is exposed, and with the other hand she braces herself against the sill, apprehension in her eyes. This figure, however, is related to the two standing nudes of the same years, Cathy of *Toilette de Cathy* and the large figure, straight out of Otto Dix's work of the 1920s, called *Alice* with its raised, exposing leg that was to become a signature of Balthus's female "portraits." Both of these are cases of proud self-presentation, hardly involving victimization. The exposed breast of *La Fenêtre,* also present in the instructress of the guitar, may indicate the collapsing distinction between the victim and the attacker.

This upright figure has to be seen also in the context of the strange frontal portrait groups, primarily one parent and his or her offspring posed in a cross between a formal photograph for a family album and a Holy Family. One parent is always missing. The physical resemblance between parent and child is emphasized to an odd extreme. In the best-known of these, *Joan Miró et sa fille Dolorès* (1933–38), there is a marked tension between the father and daughter, whose images are nearly the same size: he seems to be both holding her back and displaying her; she seems to be clinging to him with one hand while her left arm and leg thrust her out toward the spectator, her eyes combining anticipation and apprehension. The association with a Madonna and Child is fruitful, for it is the girl who fits the position of the sacrificial component; moreover, to complete the Balthusian irony, her father is an artist. In this context, another portrait of an artist, André Derain, shows the subject dominating the foreground, left hand pressed against his torso, presenting himself in the way the nudes later present themselves. In the background sits his young model, fitting into the pattern of a father and daughter, or even in some perverse way (given his prominence in the foreground), a mother and child, as in *la Leçon de guitare*.

The offshoot of the Derain figure, and the alternative to the threatened girl of *La Fenêtre*, is the self-contained *Jeune Fille en vert et rouge* (1939) who (her right hand to her torso) seems to be a dressed, indeed costumed, version of Cathy, apparently an officiant of some vaguely eucharistic ritual involving altar, bread, knife, ewer, and candle—and yet still with the possibility that she may herself be the sacrifice. Finally, in 1948–49, as the series of recumbent nudes in sunlit rooms was approaching its fulfillment in *La Chambre*, Balthus painted a number of frontal nudes emerging from the bath. They are in a pose that combines the Christ of an Ecce Homo with the Baptism and a Salvator Mundi (as well as, in its later forms, the heavy female figure of Rembrandt's *Juno*). These figures, who in later versions become pure baigneuses drying themselves or disturbingly violent figures leaping from the tub (a Christus Victor or a pagan Athena?), nevertheless continue to be accompanied by the old crone who goes all the way back to *Toilette de Cathy*.

Balthus also undertook a series of nudes in profile in the 1950s. These lead in one way to the Lehman *Nu devant la cheminée* (1955), the nude whose back is turned to the light, engrossed, looking at her own reflection in the mirror above the fireplace, and in another way to the *Nu de profil*

Jeune Fille en vert et rouge, *1939—Museum of Modern Art, New York, photo
courtesy of Pierre Matisse Gallery*

(1973–77), in which she does face the light, standing before a window in a
room with only a table and a washbasin. Suggesting a pose both offertory
and receptive, she recalls more strongly than any of the previous paintings in this series one of Vermeer's naturalized Annunciations, a Dutch
matron (sometimes reading a letter, sometimes pregnant) facing the window in a sun-drenched interior. But then one also wonders whether Balthus had seen Edward Hopper's *Woman in the Sun* of 1961.

In the majority of the pictures, however, the bather is turned away
from the light. In *Katia lisant* (1968–76), though her thighs are still open
to it, she is holding a book up to her face, between herself and the light.
In *Le Peintre et son modèle* (1980–81) the girl is engrossed in a book obliv-
ious to the painter who (replacing the dwarf of *La Chambre*) himself
opens the blind to let in the light. Another girl holds the mirror between
herself and the light, looking into it rather than at the light; or she holds
the mirror between herself and the figure of a cat, who has now become

an admonitory emblem. In one picture the girl plays with a toy bird which is eyed by the cat, who is borrowed from Hogarth's *Graham Children,* where he is hungrily watching a caged bird, supposedly showing the children to be on the brink of experience in the adult world. The nudes engrossed in mirrors recall the pose of the lady in Vanitas emblems.

In 1955, pictures of one girl combing another's hair, and then one awake and the other sleeping, are mythologized into an Annunciation or a Cupid and Psyche. Balthus replaces the sun by an intruder bearing flowers or fruit or a light to the recumbent girl. The flower connects with the Annuciation, the blazing, sunlike lemon (or orange) with the story of Psyche approaching through curiosity her sleeping lover, to see his face by the illumination of a candle. Because he is revealed in his proper person (and burnt by the wax) Cupid disappears and leaves her literally loveless and lightless. The story, used by mystics from the Middle Ages onward as an allegory of the progress of the soul, is also a final echo of Balthus's story of Mitsou, the lost cat. The girl, the Cupid figure, is not only asleep; her face is turned away and her body shrouded in clothes. The ambivalent receptiveness of the earlier girls is denied; only closure and voyeurism remain in these darkening interiors. Even the oriental girls Balthus paints, though nude, are crawling belly-downward across a floor and engrossed in a mirror.

What one notices in these recent paintings is how the women are subsumed to decorative pattern. Compared with the heavy Junoesque figures of the frontal baigneuses, they are becoming younger and thinner, almost Giacometti-like in their attentuation. Their faces have lost the particularity of the early girls, whose piquancy to some extent derived from the blunt, tomboyish, altogether unconcerned features above the smooth body and open legs. These are now the sweet faces of angels by Piero or Leonardo. They are painted in chalky, gravelly, rather monotonous pigments, frescolike. The tension between *dépense* and self-absorption, embodied in the contrast of face and body, is now externalized and emblematized in the mirror and the story of Cupid and Psyche. We can follow Balthus from the 1930s to the present as he supports his strange portraits with an increasingly heavy mythological freight, progressing from a disguised Danaë to a not-so-disguised Annunciation and an overt Cupid and Psyche. Myth, pattern, style, and sentiment: all become more emphatic until the paintings sometimes resemble blown-up Hallmark greeting cards.

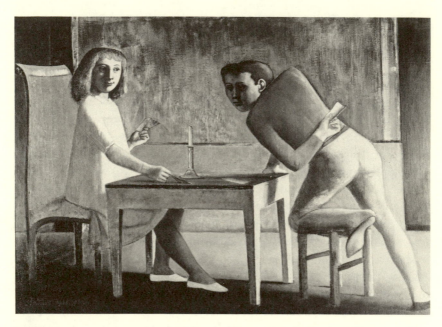

La Partie de cartes, 1948–50—Thyssen-Bornemisza Collection, Lugano, photo courtesy of The Metropolitan Museum of Art

The recent mythological paintings most easily confirm Stanislas's esoteric mysteries about the ascent of the soul through love. The interest of the earlier paintings survives in other genres Balthus has continued to explore: his very suggestive still lifes and the landscapes seen through a window, observed from the inside by a girl whose back is to us. His paintings of card games, undertaken in the late 1940s, began as two girls and then, in their most finished form, as boy and girl (1948–50 and 1966–73), and from time to time as single girls playing solitaire. The image, a modern amalgam of Pope's *Rape of the Lock* (in the intense expressions of the players) and Cézanne's *Card-Players*, makes plain the restrained tensions of a game not unlike the one implied in the outstretchings and withdrawings of the sun-drenched girls. The card game sums up the ritualizing of desire that is Balthus's central concern. The Balthus doctrine, which may have begun as surrealist incongruity, can be seen as the situating of erotic energy (*dépense*) within various sedate orders which restrain or withhold desire: the prepubescent female, for example; or the tradition of old-master painting; or the portrait genre (or the convention of an angel's face); or, above all, the elaborate formal pattern of the composition (some paintings can be said to be as much about the Golden Section as about the girl). At an extreme, in *Nu devant la cheminée*, precise geometrical lines are incised into the paint surface but blurred by the freedom of brush-work, the incongruence of lines and paint contours, and the use of rough charcoal smudges where precise lines of the fireplace are called for. The withholding or restraining of desire, the sense of representing the moment just before or *at* violence ("jusque dans la mort")—this Balthus embodies in these tensions of classical form, autonomous paint, and pro-vocative image.

Venerable Complications: Why Literature Is a Little Hard to Read

RICHARD POIRIER

T HIS IS TO BE a parable about Literature and Technology, their problematic relations to each other and to a third party named People. I begin with an observation which though quite obvious is generally ignored by pietistic devotees of Literature: for nearly all of human history practically no People could read. Literature included them as subjects, compliant to the comic and idealizing tendencies of Literature, but People seldom knew that they were being "used" unless they happened in on a masque or a play or the oral transmission of, say, the *Iliad*. Except for an extremely small number, People did not count as an *audience* for Literature, and even when some rare lower-class person did acquire a reading capacity—like the sixteenth-century miller named Menocchio described in Carlo Ginzburg's *The Cheese and the Worm*, a study of the Inquisition—the books he was provided with were reduced and aphoristic versions that bore little resemblance to the versions read by his betters. The author did not have to think of People as readers. Literature was a minority enterprise, read and supported by the economically and politically privileged classes. But even though it was written by them, for them, and under their patronage, it was and still is the best exhibition of a kind of human power working within language which is not exclusive to writers, readers, or the literate, a power to shape and trope language in obedience to human desire that is everyone's inheritance regardless of how he invests it.

Meanwhile, the relative historical positions of Literature and People have undergone an extraordinary change. Literature in recent times has found itself worried about and worried by People. There are, for one thing, so many of us. Sanitation, agricultural methods, transportation, medicine, and manufacturing—all these forms of Technology have allowed a fantastic growth in the production of People and in the prolongation of lives. There are now five billion People, and the current increase among illiterates and semiliterates is approximately twice what it is among the largely literate ones. But in respect to Literature, People are different from what they were not simply because they are more numerous. They are different because nearly all of them, at least in England, the United States, and Western Europe, can now read. This is a wholly unprecedented development, and it follows that People are at last able, if they choose, to assert a new authority over a Literature which heretofore was not obliged even to speak to them.

People have acquired enormous cultural power. But they do not exercise it by reading; they choose instead, as they could never have done before, not to read, at least not to read Literature. Indifference to Literature is consistent with the aims of mass education as it began to get formulated only about a hundred years ago. It was created and motivated by a desire less to make Literature more available, except in token doses, than to make goods and services more abundant, and as an instrument for civic regulation. The same Technology that produced billions of People also created an economy that required a mass of skilled and relatively docile labor. The literacy given them had and has little to do with Literature, nor should it. Literature is scarcely for everyone now, any more than it ever was; I mean, of course, Literature in the sense in which I will try to describe it. But in being exclusive (and ultimately partisan) about Literature, I am not being condescending to People. In fact I would hope to see People rid of the idea that unless they have a productive relationship to Literature they are necessarily denied the moral or ethical benefits reputedly accruing to those who do. Literature is a particularly disciplined form of language and, therefore, of life. But there are other forms of life whose disciplines and vocabularies can be equally beneficial to human beings, like sports or gardening, like the achievements of domestic intimacy, like any kind of creative work. As Emerson tells us in "Self-Reliance," there can be "prayer in all action. The prayer of the farmer kneeling in the field to weed it, the prayer of the rower kneeling with the stroke of the oar." Would anyone argue for long that those who read and write Literature, especially as a profession, are therefore in any way morally or ethically superior to those who cannot read or write at all? It seems sometimes as if the reverse were true. In my view Literature is preeminently an activity, an example of what I have called elsewhere, with respect to poetry, "the work of knowing."

Such "work" can go on in many places, and one such place is in Literature. It is most successful when it creates still more work, when it leads, that is, not only from density into clarification but out of clarification into still other densities. That there are ways of knowing that have nothing to do with the writing or reading of Literature is clear from Literature itself. That is why it is forever finding analogues to its own compositional acts. It proposes metaphors for literary composition in the act of love (Herbert or Donne), in farming (Thoreau), in apple picking (Frost), in sports (Hemingway), in exploration, scholarship, or the cultivation of roses (Parkman), in money-making (Dreiser), in social manipulation (Henry James), and in raids upon nature for images and tropes (Wordsworth). "Is it only poets and men of leisure and cultivation, who live with nature?" Emerson asks in "The Poet." No; but also hunters, farmers, grooms, and butchers, though they express their affection in their choice of life, and not in their choice of words." Literature allows these analogies between itself and other activities, however, only on condition: the lover, the explorer, the athlete must be committed to his or her task with a dedication, a genius, a discipline worthy of a great writer. It is not to be supposed that Literature is more available than Thoreau's harvest of beans. "I was determined," he tells us, "to know beans."

Literature is necessarily a less available harvest, since we cannot ever merely watch it grow or reap it. The performance of Literature is complete neither in the writing nor in the reading. Reading is writing in that it produces language; writing is reading in that it interprets the possibilities in what has already been written for what subsequently can be written. The "work" required by Literature is in that sense never finished and cannot be. I would therefore define Literature, for the time being, as any written text whose points of clarification, whether these occur by local or by larger design, bring you only to densities different from but flexibly related to those from which you have previously emerged. Literature is that writing whose clarities bring on precipitations of density.

This can be said, I think, of the Literature of any period. But for the last hundred years or so Literature has become, to an unprecedented degree, self-conscious and defensive about its own complications. It has developed a sort of bunker mentality and begun to insist not only on its necessary density but on its necessary difficulty. *Moby-Dick* is an obvious instance of difficulty, *Bleak House*, in the peculiarity of its narrative organization, only a somewhat less obvious one, and by the beginning of the century Henry James directly attributes the causes of difficulty to what he calls "monstrous masses." Literature, he says, cannot catch the life of the modern city or touch its inhabitants, a deduction expressed both in *The*

American Scene, with respect to New York, and, with respect to London, in the Prefaces, especially the Preface to *The Altar of the Dead.* "The general black truth," he remarks, is "that London was a terrible place to die in":

> It takes space to feel, it takes time to know, and great organisms as well as small have to pause, more or less, to possess themselves and to be made aware. Monstrous masses are, by this truth, so impervious to vibration that the sharpest forces of feeling, locally applied, no more penetrate than a pin or a paper-cutter penetrates an elephant's hide. Thus the very tradition of sensibility would perish if left to their care. It has here and there to be rescued, to be saved by independent, intelligent zeal; which type of effort, however, to avail, has to fly in the face of the conditions.

What is imagined here is not a mere standoff between "monstrous masses" and "the tradition of sensibility." James proposes a more drastic alienation. If the "tradition" is to be saved by "independent" effort, then both the effort and the independence call for the abdication by Literature of a kind of public power it once enjoyed. Instead of applying its forces "locally," instead, that is, of creating "vibrations" within a civilization known to be susceptible, Literature must now "fly in the face of the conditions," and these are nothing less than the civilization's "imperviousness." James's image, with its suggestion of movement prompted by an encounter with something hostile, well enough describes how he and other late Edwardian writers, specifically including the line from Pater to Joyce, were to confront the common reader. If the "tradition of sensibility" is to be rescued, it is implied, then it will be by embedding it within stylistic fortifications made intentionally and necessarily intricate. James perceived this well before World War I and its aftermaths. Let it be remembered that Literature by its very nature would already have excluded even a solicitous semiliterate People. But even a literate People are in James's account grown elephantine in size and thickness, and his own later novels are an instance of the stylistic release from any determining obligation to them.

All this suggests some reasons why in England, from about 1900 to 1914, modernist characteristics began to manifest themselves in some central examples of Literature. This had happened earlier in America during the decade before the Civil War, with Poe, Hawthorne, and Melville. In each country these were times when demographic and educational developments helped to produce James's "monstrous masses," in America first for a number of reasons, including extraordinary growth in the economy, in compulsory education, and, later on, in land grant universities. There emerged great numbers of People who could read and write and make unprecedented demands on cultural production. But the "tradition of sensibility," assumed to be the preserve of Literature, was not necessarily a tradition for them.

Literature was forced, as it were, to extemporize an audience *out of itself*. The consequences are measurable not only with respect to modernist difficulty, but in the efforts of literary criticism, as led by T. S. Eliot, F. R. Leavis, and the Southern "new critics," to locate a tradition of sensibility in earlier English literature, especially of the seventeenth century. Here, too, the cult of difficulty expressed itself. It was suggested that because of the degenerative effects of life in the twentieth century, its barbarisms, discontinuities, and vulgarizations of taste, even the works of the past had become inaccessible to all but a few trained readers. In England, the critical enterprise of Leavis's *Scrutiny* (following in 1932 on the earlier *Calendar of Modern Letters*, 1925–27) and in America the bimonthly called *The Fugitive* (published at Nashville, Tennessee, from 1922 to 1925, with writings by John Crowe Ransom, Allen Tate, and Robert Penn Warren) was in large part meant to show that only by a quite strenuous sort of reading was it possible to recover from the past those values that presumably were disappearing everywhere else. The Southern regionalism of the Fugitive group had its corollary in *Scrutiny*'s celebration of Bunyan's and Lawrence's England. It was proposed that Literature offered an experience not of ideas but of sounds and movements in the English language that carried with them traces of a rich and fulfilling community of assumptions. The experience could be had only by those who could enter most fully into Literature's vital and dramatic and exploratory uses of language. Tradition, Eliot warned, "cannot be inherited, and if you want it you must obtain it by great labor." It was to be largely a labor of close reading.

I have previously argued in *The Performing Self* ("What Is English Studies? And If You Know What That Is, What Is English Literature?") that there are ways in which these notions might be quite sentimental, wrong-headed, even pernicious, and I am trying here only to describe the consequences of believing in them, consequences that have had much to do with the place assigned to Literature within the discourses of modern culture. Working your way into a text by "close reading" was supposed to be a way to get close also to a "tradition of sensibility" otherwise fading from daily life, along with the institutions which had supported it. Reading was in that sense implicitly a critique and rejection of the new civilization of People which Technology had helped create. Thus the reader of the Literature of the past, no less than the modernist writer of Literature, was to find a community only in remnants, redoubts, pockets of resistance within a larger civilization that was indifferent even to their existence, like a whale to some mollusk encysted on its flank.

Lawrence was an especially important and complicating figure in this imagination of the estrangement of Literature from twentieth-century life. For Leavis and others he suggested that there still might be tenuous connections between contemporary life, if conducted in a certain way, and surviving shreds of a redeeming past. Leavis's gradual disenchantment with Eliot is best understood, I think, as part of his larger conviction that by nationality, religious feeling, and sexual fastidiousness Eliot was rendered incapable of understanding what the barely existing English culture of the mining villages could still have meant to Lawrence. No American like Eliot, so it was suggested, no Irishman like Joyce, for that matter, could really know, as instinctively as did Lawrence (and Leavis himself), the vital resources alive in the English language. But there is no need here to rehearse or enter into these arguments except to note that they are a rather touching symptom of how desperate were the efforts to imagine some possible resuscitation of a tradition of sensibility. Not only Literature but the proper way to read it were fraught with difficulty because, it would seem, the only way the tradition could affirm itself was by being at once radical and reactionary.

Distortions of form, dislocations in language, exclusivity and effortfulness in criticism—these were meant to restore certain kinds of life presumably displaced by the emergence and empowerment of People. That not all Literature or criticism subscribed to these notions is evident enough from the careers of, say, Hardy in the novel, Frost in poetry, and, in criticism, both a figure like Edmund Wilson and a brilliant antagonist of modernist fashions like Edward Thomas, whose reviews of Pound, suitably wary from the first, are among the most subtle diagnoses of literary modernism ever written. The death of Thomas in the First World War probably made an immense difference, as David Bromwich suggests, to the direction of criticism thereafter, as it moved, subserviently in most cases, into the service of modernist apologetics. The point was made and it held: Literature was not even to pretend that it was meant for People. Instead it was to be, as was criticism, an extraordinarily demanding and self-conscious inquiry into its own resources and procedures. Literature was deemed to be necessarily unpopular; it was to be ignored by People; it was to be read and understood by an elite. And yet it wanted at the same time to claim for itself a degree of historical and cultural significance which it had never before so explicitly and under such compulsion been required to claim. Literature assumed an enormous historical mission—to record the demise of the cultural traditions that sustained it—precisely in the act of abdicating its traditional centrality, its place in the community. At the moment of its exile, Literature said to People, "I banish *you*," and then set about, as Coriolanus never could, to build another empire.

Literature feels, if anything, even more embattled now. It found itself after World War II confronted with People still more indifferent, as if Literature were not there at all. Starting with radio early in the century, then with recording mechanisms, tape machines, television, and the miniaturization of these, Technology, which created vast numbers of People to begin with, then provided the equipment which allowed People, to a degree they could never before have expected, to become both visible and articulate *to themselves*. Visibility and articulateness had, till recently, been for the most part exclusively in the selective giving of the literary minority, who chose to represent the illiterate classes only sporadically and to suit its own esthetic and political sense of things. It was not intended that People should be given a history. For the first time People who in earlier centuries had no way to register their existence at all, except in church records, no way to tell anyone what it was like to be as they were day by day, could now record, could re-present themselves, could tell their story—or so it seemed—and hope that it would be heard by those who before had suppressed it.

But in what if any sense is this really the case? And who is to say that the relative obscurity of People was not for them a preference and a blessing? It is only literate clerks, after all, who are given to the lamentation that "Full many a flower is born to blush unseen, / And waste its sweetness on the desert air." If, nonetheless, writers, readers, and critics need to be reminded that much of the world is excluded from Literature, it does not then follow that more of the world or of its People will in any important sense be accounted for by Literature's rival, the electronic media. Should the development by which these media now promise to give visibility and voice to People prove a hoax, as I suspect it already has done, then that will in itself prove immensely instructive. It will further demonstrate that there is perhaps no way in which expression is ever free from the economic, political, and cultural structures that are implicated in the very nature of any and all media. Third World and displaced minorities are now encouraged to insist, for example, upon a history for themselves which is not simply a subplot in the Western story of man, but there is little evidence so far of success in the West, partly for reasons which I explore in "Watching the Evening News" (*Raritan*, Fall 1982).

Literature, and those who want to care for it, ought to acknowledge, as the other media dare not do, that it does not and cannot reveal much of the history even of those it favors with attention. It is in this regard, too, that the literary modernist claim that the twentieth is the worst of centuries might be questioned. Worst for whom? One presumption of Anglo-American-Europeans is that their experience, or what it is said to be by certain writers, defines the nature of contemporary life. So that the recorded ravages of the twentieth century, while indeed horrible by any standard, are given unquestioned predominance over what can nonetheless be known about the mute, sporadically recorded, unnarrativized miseries of vast numbers of people in centuries past, as in the greatest genocide in history during the hundred years after Columbus landed in the New World, an episode examined in Tzvetan Todorov's *The Conquest of America: The Question of the Other.* Those who say in common-room banter that really they belong in the eighteenth century imagine that if transported there they would still be in the common room, though differently dressed, when in all likelihood they would be sweeping chimneys, assuming they had survived long enough even to do that.

But who, it must nonetheless be asked, can inquire most effectively into this question of narrativity, of a place for People in the plot of history, if it be not those—like Todorov or Edward Said in *Orientalism*—who have been prepared to do so in large part by their educated knowledge of analogues in the necessarily repressive plottings of Literature? It may be encouraging to suppose that Technology has, for the new mass of People, removed literacy as a prerequisite for securing a place of sustained significance in historical narrative, and in a nicer world that might be the case. In fact, however, the allowance for such a place is now within the giving of corporate institutions far less disposed than is Literature to surrender any of its power to the powerless. Technology, in this parable, seems to grant to the hitherto "invisible man" an opportunity for self-articulation, and this might persuade him that Literature is even less essential now than it was in the past. Such technological benefits are utterly illusory however. And it is not surprising that when it calls attention to this illusion, Literature also likes to exult in itself. Literature as a custodian of language and as a representation of life is now in a position to show the consequences for People of a Technological power which only pretends to rescue them from obscurity. It can show what it is like for People to live under the aegis of media other than Literature. What Henry Adams half suspected in *The Education* Thomas Pynchon projects as a saturnalia in *Gravity's Rainbow*.

If at this point in the story one is tempted to commiserate with Literature, give thought, however, to a few historical contradictions and peculiarities. Before Technology struck back, it had for centuries been victimized by Literature. There is a haunting instance in Book II of Spenser's *The Faerie Queene*. Book II was given to the printer in 1589, but Spenser describes it as an "antique" mirror of a faery land. The past for which it is an image has always been an imaginary past. Near the end of that book Sir Guyon descends from the open fields and virgin lands of chivalric England into the Cave of Mammon. The Cave has ascribed to it the detailed horrors of what would later be called an industrial-factory system, along with many of the blandishments of finance capitalism. For one thing, it is filled with currency that reproduces its own value without in the process contributing to the growth of anything other than money, filthy lucre. The Cave is a perversion of nature in the interests of financial and industrial progress. Guyon is so appalled—or tempted—that he faints when he reaches the surface. Milton, whose father was a moneylender, finds Guyon's heroism validated by the fact that in order to confront Mammon he had to digress from his main business, which is to discover and bring to governance those extremes of eroticism which can weaken the zeal for public service to the Queen. But the encapsulation of the Mammon episode within this larger purpose is also, I think, a symptom of the difficulty, given Spenser's historical situation in an England determined on economic development, of dealing with financial enterprise and its technological counterparts. Apparently the misuse of the body for private pleasure could be more critically and dialectically treated than could the misappropriations of the body by economic institutions. Perhaps that is why the standards and ideals evoked in the episode seem already for the sixteenth century to be rather wistful.

What I am suggesting is that Literature, from some of its earliest and now classic instances seems *always* to have been nostalgic for something that has been lost. What can be the origin of a loss that was always there? It was to meet such a logistical and logical gap that Literature introduced Technology as a villain. It is obvious, again, that I am using the term Technology to describe manifestations whose early forms are quite unlike later, more familiar ones. Literature did not wait for Mark Twain or Lawrence or Pynchon before it ascribed demonic and destructive powers to what can be called Technology. Nearly from the beginnings of English literature, images of exploitative control over environment are, embryonically, images also of Technology. Usury is an aspect of this, of money that begets only money so that, as in the opening of *Volpone*, accumulated wealth rivals the sun, the source of natural energy and generative power. In writing about this, R. H. Tawney helps bring me to the point I want to make—that Literature, paradoxically, depends on and partakes of Technology: "Behind the genii of beauty and wisdom who were its architects"—he is speaking of the emergence of the modern from the feudal world—

> there moved a murky, but indispensable figure. It was the demon whom Dante had met muttering gibberish in the fourth circle of the Inferno, and whom Sir Guyon was to encounter three centuries later, tanned with smoke and seared with fire, in a cave adjoining the mouth of hell. His uncouth labors quarried the stones which Michael Angelo was to raise, and sank deep in the Roman clay the foundations of the walls to be adorned by Raphael.

To read Tawney is to be reminded that electronic media are, for Literature, only the most recent version of what was anciently imagined as a Technological threat to cultural health and continuity. With precedents for which there are forever other precedents, Literature has always asked us to be nostalgic for some aspect of the human and the natural whose essential purity resides in the fact that it begins to perish under Technology's pressure. So much so that it seems as if the ideal forms of the human and the natural do not in fact or in reality ever actually exist; as if when they appear, even in represented life, they can be no more than fleeting and pitiable remnants, like Sir Guyon, or shepherds, like Melville's Starbuck or Wordsworth's Michael, like Lawrence's Mellors or Joyce's Bloom. One might call it the Cordelia syndrome—these creations of a nostalgia for human goodness uncontaminated, a nostalgia so strong that its embodiments emerge from the doom that awaits them.

Again, why has Literature persuaded itself and us that this should be so? When a villain is hard to find, there is always, after all, original sin. But original sin is one likely source of Literature itself. Original sin was probably invented to explain and relieve some feeling in each of us that something was lost, abandoned, betrayed in the process of our becoming human. We love our cats and dogs with a certain pathos, a sense that we left them behind, along with other creatures, in an inarticulateness that once was also ours. The Fall of Man according to Emerson "is the discovery we have made that we exist." This is the fall from the womb into some terrible consciousness of unitary existence. Literature, one of the great human creations, is in this view a compensation for the Fall. It offers consoling evidence of a community of loss but also (implicit in the shaping of language itself), a promise of corporate creation. Without the Fall there could be, as Milton tells us, no *Paradise Lost*. What then has compelled Literature to invent yet another instrument of loss and call it Technology?

Even to ask this question reveals why Literature has so frequently expressed a suspiciousness of its own enterprise. And why should it not? Because if it locates a cause for human alienation in Technology, what prevents the indictment from reaching back, beyond the Fall to the prelapsarian human attribute of Reason itself and thence to the mental technologies, including Literature, to which Reason gave birth? Not only science but the very act of interpretation, of which Literature is a species? For Literature to deny its collusion with Technology would require it to claim not merely that it re-presents life but that it actually created it. Indeed, Literature does frequently indulge in such exorbitant and heroic self-assertions even while asking to be pardoned for them. This is the beautiful pathos of Joyce/Stephen in *A Portrait*, of Shakespeare in the Sonnets, of Marlowe in the punishments meted out to his overreachers, of Milton's Satan, and of Coleridge, who worried about his "genius" as something that might cut him off from the supposedly natural bonds between man and nature.

Literature acknowledges in these instances that its own operations are akin to exercises of the technological power which it writes against. Like Technology, Literature appropriates, exploits, recomposes, arranges—within inherited but constantly "modernized" mechanisms of literary form—materials that all the while are also said by Literature to belong to something called "life." This concern for the power of technique in Literature is especially pronounced in the English Romantics, as in such poems of Wordsworth's as "Nutting" and Book I of *The Prelude* where, as David Ferry and others have shown, human intrusions, acquisitive destructiveness, or theft, all of them visited upon an otherwise silent, awe-ful, and serene nature, are a metaphoric equivalent for the poet's own seizure of objects for use in poetry. Wordsworth includes in his poetry the criticism later made of him by Lawrence, that he was "impertinent."

The dialectic concern for form as against fluidity, for figuration as against fracture, for a protean self—these are not, however, original to the Romantic or modernist concern about the usurpatory-creative nature of writing. They are everywhere in Literature expressions of concern for order that is always and also an anxiety about its possibly brutal and deforming rigidities. More recent literature is especially useful for illustration only because it tends to treat earlier writing as if in itself it were a kind of Technology, as if it had created forms and predictable movements that have become reified and potentially deadening.

Literature's distaste for Technology reveals, at last, a squeamishness about its own operations. This is perhaps most evident in the degree to which it idealizes an emphatically nonliterary contingent of People. I refer to characters who are themselves almost never interested in Literature. In some central instances—and there are of course many exceptions to this—the most admired and commendable human figures in works of genius, especially since 1800 or so, are either unliterary or positively suspicious of Literature. The worthy rustics of Wordsworth's poetry, no less than Faulkner's enduring Dilsey, could hardly be expected to *read* about themselves. Indeed you might say that the reason they are exemplary is that they do not engage in the exploitative enterprise of reading and writing. Leopold Bloom can, of course, read, but would anyone expect him to read *Ulysses?* Literature seldom includes among its implied readers the kind of people it most admires, and when it includes literary people they are often a shady or tortured lot. If Literature is something "we" need, why is it apparently not needed at all by some of the finest types Literature has imagined? This was the case long before such "ordinary" people were presumably corrupted or lost to Literature by the television screen. A little of such literary demography might dampen the bravado of those who take it for granted that since Literature makes such redeeming use of ordinary people, it follows that ordinary people can make redeeming use of Literature.

To put it another way, it is quite generally assumed that because ordinary people are available to Literature as a resource, they are also available to it as an audience, had they not been otherwise seduced. How else explain the voluble and confused disparagement visited, in the name of print culture, on television? But if critical competence in the reading of Literature requires some sort of productive engagement with difficulties made inevitable by the nature of language itself, then it requires some measure of critical incompetence to complain that Literature should or could be in competition with TV for the attention of a general public. Many avid readers of Literature spend, as I do, a great deal of time watching television, but it does not follow that the reverse might also be true—that inveterate watchers could care about Literature and language in ways they can most rewardingly be cared about. Leaving aside the masses in the world who cannot read at all, it is evident that reading citizens, wherever they are, would not necessarily read more or read better if they watched television less. And much of what they do read in newspapers, magazines, and what passes for good fiction is often lacking in the nuances that can be heard not only in movies but on videotape. Arguments that the emergence of video is largely responsible for the decline of reading or literacy are no more tenable than long-faced suggestions that the so-called art of conversation (never a conspicuous feature in the TV-less childhoods of people my age) disappeared from the family circle because of the intrusion of the tube. To judge from the endless conversational murmur in movie houses, which used to be much quieter, people may have been convinced by TV that they can and should become more, not less, voluble before any available screen.

A habit of phrasing epitomizes the confusions I am trying to sort out: the tendency to refer to all instruments of expression *except* Literature as "the media," often with the omission of such qualifiers as "electronic" or "mass." The implications are especially glaring in linked phrases like "print and media culture." What is being suggested is that video is one of "the media" and that print is not; that print, and especially Literature, are exonerated from the contaminations associated with media.

The implication, not dispelled by any amount of critical theory however ancient, is that language and Literature are "natural" while all other media, like TV or the movies are not. This is at the heart of the confusions of those who assume that life would somehow be better if Literature could prevail over video for a general audience. What seems to be forgotten is that language is in itself a mediation—another point that cannot be emphasized enough, no matter how embarrassingly obvious. Every word is a form of re-presentation. And Literature, by virtue of its formal conventions and the conscious struggle by which it appropriates language to poetry or the novel, is yet another and still more formidable example of media and re-presentation. Language and Literature are the most indispensable and resilient cultural resources which human beings have invented for themselves. And yet, no matter how "natural" language is judged to be, it is obviously an artifact in large part created and fashioned by all kinds of social, religious, economic, and political pressures.

Language itself is a particular form of Technology. Perhaps the tendency to think otherwise, to think that language partakes of nature— instead of knowing that nature partakes of language—is a result of the quite understandable desire to believe that language and Literature should be identical with the *kinds* of nature and humanity which they idealize and preserve. It is a very costly mistake, however, an unnecessary concession to vulgarians, mediacratic or literary. It implies that culture, in its literary or high-artistic manifestations, can be absorbed pretty much the way TV is absorbed, that somehow, in its competition with popular culture, high culture has gotten not less but more readily available than it has ever been in history.

Language, however, is not virgin "nature" available as fully to video or to radio or to movies as it is to Literature. It is a resource which Literature, more effectively than any other media, can productively mine and develop. The detrimental effect of video on the general public has been exaggerated to the extent that the positive effects of Literature on the general public have been idealized. Régis Debray's remark that "the darkest spot in modern society is a small luminous screen" is a sample of the kind of silliness that can pass for thinking on this subject. What has happened—and for a variety of reasons that include but are not exhausted by Technology—is that there have been in the last hundred years or so some accelerated changes in ideas of the natural, the traditional, and, especially, of the human. These ideas, which are in part the invention of

Literature, are essential to its prosperity and to the prospect of its being able to maintain some degree of its ancient cultural-social power. But this is not to say, in the mood of the culturally conservative, that Literature ought to preserve any particular image of nature, the human, or the past. Precisely the reverse. Literature exists to challenge the inherited forms of language. It exists in and by the act with which it questions what at the same time it proposes; it challenges in one period—in one phrase—the images predominant in another, and it exposes as a figuration, a shadow, any term, like "human" or "natural," which the culture at large may want to idealize for its own political or historical convenience. So that what is truly threatened by Technology in the form of electronic media is exactly that play of dialectical complication in language that is inseparable from the act of literary creation.

What I have been implying can now be said more directly. A feature of Literature essential to its value is quite simply its refusal to offer, in the parlance of TV, a clear image. The obvious implication of electronic media is that Literature's kind of opacity is inessential, evasive, and obscurantist. This is also, to expose the full and tortuous ironies of our cultural situation, the charge customarily levelled against Literature itself by those middle-, would-be high-brow, elements of the literary-critical establishment (as featured in such politically and culturally conservative journals as *Commentary, The American Scholar,* and *New Criterion*) whenever the canon is disrupted by the appearance of experimental or theoretical work. "Inessential," "evasive," "obscurantist"—this has at some point been said of nearly every innovative writer, specifically including what have proved to be the most important critics, in recent history. Those who want Literature to be widely available, on the assumption that it is socially and morally enhancing, generally oppose TV on the grounds that it is socially and morally injurious, but their criteria are as simplistic in the one case as in the other.

We are left with the task of finding a way to describe how Literature, unlike TV, manages to put itself out of focus no matter how hard we try to bring it into focus. I have already said that Literature is a kind of writing whose clarities bring on precipitations of density and have used the word "difficulty" to characterize a particularly self-conscious or modernist aspect of this. I want briefly to discuss these terms and their utility in the larger argument I am making. By *density* I mean to describe a kind of writing which gives, or so it likes to pretend, a fairly direct access to pleasure but which becomes, on longer acquaintance, rather strange and imponderable. Shakespeare is a good example, so is Herbert or Marvell or Emerson's essays or *Middlemarch* or Frost. Another kind of writing may, on first encounter, seem quite bristly, resistant, "difficult." If somehow, maybe with the help of notes and annotations, you master the "difficulty"—you cannot in the same sense master density—you may then find that there is little or no density behind it. Stephen Dedalus's tortured prose in the "Proteus" section of *Ulysses* is for me a case in point, as are such episodes as "Oxen of the Sun" and "Ithaca," where formal mechanisms, more than the information carried by them, rather statically communicate the significance. To put it very crudely, the Joyce of "The Dead" is more dense than is the Joyce of *Ulysses*, where he is being both difficult and dense; *Ulysses*, relatively speaking, is difficult, while *Nostromo* and *Women in Love* are dense; Pound is difficult; Stevens is dense, as are Dickinson and Whitman who are deceptively easy.

Twentieth-century criticism and theory have tended to prefer difficulty to density. Difficulty gives the critic a chance to strut his stuff, to treat Literature as if it really were a communication of knowledge rather than a communication of being. Difficulty also carries with it a lineage of theoretical, historical, and cultural justification. George Chapman, in "The Shadow of Night" (1594) had religious theories about the virtues of obscurity in poetry, but in this century, as I have elsewhere remarked, difficulty has been made to seem the inescapable social and political responsibility of the artist. You were already on notice that when something is hard to read there are Big Reasons for its being so, and that you, reader, had better shape up. Density is another matter. No guidebook will help you. It does not announce itself in Literature, any more than it does in some of our most intimate conversations, and it can go unnoticed in either case by those who do not care to encounter it. Density is very often something that strikes the ear rather than the eye; it is often something you hear happening to voices as they modify words and phrases which, at another point, seemed quite clear or casual. Density is usually accompanied not by the extruding allusiveness of modernism but by the covert allusiveness of troping.

Troping, the turning of a word, gives evidences of the human involvement in the shaping of language and it prevents language from imposing itself upon us with the force and indifference of a Technology. It frees us from predetermined meanings. Troping is the turning of a word in directions or detours it seemed destined otherwise to avoid. Thus Emerson, admitting that "this charming landscape which I saw this morning is indubitably made up of some twenty or thirty farms," owned by people he then proceeds to name, goes on to say that "none of them owns the landscape. There is a property in the horizon which no man has but he whose eye can integrate all the parts, that is, the poet." This is a nice example, because even while Emerson is troping on the idea of possession, he is at the same time claiming that the power to trope is greater than any more obviously economic power. Frost is being notably Emersonian, for example, when he remarks in a letter to Untermeyer that "Marx had the strength not to be overawed by the metaphor in vogue . . . great is he who imposes the metaphor." In that sense, to be a great poet, and Marx would surely count as one, is also to be a great scholar.

Anyone who uses language is, even without knowing it, accepting an entitlement and, along with it, an obligation that is honored more by resentment than by gratitude. Words have a way of suggesting that they have already had an earlier, very likely a better, life than any we purpose to offer. And in reaction everyone likes, as it were, to "turn a phrase." By the turning, the troping of it, language can be made into a sign not of human subservience but of human power, though that power might also consist at some point in deciding not to trope any further, to leave the world to its own changes, free of human intrusion, as I argue in "Writing Off the Self" (*Raritan*, Summer 1981). At least some of the time, especially in playful conversation, everyone is a kind of poet—without intending thereby to be a modernist one who feels there is something unique in recent times which compels him, in Eliot's phrase, self-consciously "to force, to dislocate, if necessary, language into his meaning." Nothing can be more gratifying than those conversational witticisms that come by chance, unintended jokes that are like a gift of the words we utter. So that while language makes limiting claims on any effort to express life, it seems at the same time to lend itself to human inventiveness, to incite or even initiate it by hints of its promiscuity, as in the mere slip of the tongue.

Literature goes the crucial step beyond this. It is the Olympics of talk and of writing, an Olympics which requires that the spectator actively compete in the games. Literature records itself, shows how its records might be broken, and how the assumptions of a given discourse or culture might thereby be challenged. Shakespeare is, again, the great example. He is amazingly dense but almost never turgid, except for special or comic purposes as in, say, *Troilus and Cressida,* and for the reason that his dialogue proceeds in a manner completely natural to each of his characters while it manages simultaneously to be full of echoes and reverberations that create possibilities of meaning of which these characters are mostly innocent. Those telling repetitions that anyone can hear in the casual talk of a friend—grist for the psychoanalytic mills—is transformed by Shakespeare into the exploratory shapings of his plays. In act 5 of *Julius Caesar,* for example, Antony berates Brutus and Cassius by saying that "your vile daggers / Hacked one another in the sides of Caesar"—a gruesome bit of talk, and nastier than Antony realizes because what he cannot know is that *hacked* had been given unusual prominence earlier in the play by Brutus himself when, in the conspirators' scene in act 2, he voiced opposition to Cassius's recommendation that Antony should also be assassinated. "Our course will seem too bloody, Caius Cassius," he argued, "To cut the head off and then hack the limbs." And he goes on to say that they should proceed like "sacrificers, but not butchers," that they should "carve him as a dish fit for the gods, / Not hew him as a carcass fit for hounds." Because of Brutus's earlier discriminations among "carving," "hewing," "hacking," "hunting," "cutting," and the like, the later accusation that his own dagger "hacked" with Cassius's inside the body of Caesar will strike the reader with a force beyond anything that Antony, in the fullness of his contempt, could have wished for. The troping of terms creates significances that have far less to do with expressions of character than with the larger expressive intentions of the whole work. At such junctures Shakespeare himself is to be discovered within the deployments of his language. The troping of terms having to do with killing and bloodletting points to a central problem in nearly all of his tragedies and histories: how is it possible to kill, how bleed or cause others to bleed, so that instead of making the time more gory and slaughterous it may instead be redeemed, as by the bleeding and killing of Christ? Can a butcher become a sacrificer? Can an assassination become a ceremony? How is it ever possible effectively to trope murder?

Literature makes the strongest claims on my attention because more than any other form of art or expression it demonstrates what can be made, what can be done with something shared by everyone, used by everyone in the daily conduct of life, and something besides which carries most subtly and yet measurably within itself, its vocabulary and syntax, the governing assumptions of a society's social, political, and economic arrangements. Works of music, dance, painting, filmmaking—any of these may be more enjoyable or affecting than a given work of Literature and may also, of course, exhibit comparable operations of genius. But none depends for its principle or essential resource on materials that it must share in an utterly gregarious way with the society at large and with its history. None can teach us so much about what words do to us and how, in turn, we might try to do something to them which will perhaps modify the order of things on which they depend for their meaning. To Literature is left the distinction that it invites the reader to a dialectical relationship to words with an intensity allowable nowhere else, which Technology, especially in the form of video, cannot offer in any sustained way, and which many kinds of writing (including most of the poetry and novels now being written) are quite anxious to abridge. Despite its own affiliations with Technology, and perhaps because it feels guilty about them, Literature tells us not that we are in what is often glibly called "the prison house of language" but that we are on parole.

Travelling Theory

EDWARD W. SAID

LIKE PEOPLE and schools of criticism, ideas and theories travel—
from person to person, from situation to situation, from one period to
another. Cultural and intellectual life are usually nourished and often sustained by this circulation of ideas, and whether it takes the form of acknowledged or unconscious influence, creative borrowing, or wholesale
appropriation, the movement of ideas and theories from one place to another is both a fact of life and a usefully enabling condition of intellectual
activity. Having said that, however, one ought to go on to specify the
kinds of movement that are possible, in order to ask whether by virtue of
having moved from one place and time to another an idea or a theory
gains or loses in strength, and whether a theory in one historical period
and national culture becomes altogether different for another period or
situation. There are particularly interesting cases of ideas and theories
that move from one culture to another—as when so-called Eastern ideas
about transcendence are imported into Europe during the early nineteenth century, or when certain European ideas about society are translated into traditional Eastern societies during the mid- to late-nineteenth
centuries. Such movement into a new environment is never unimpeded.
It necessarily involves processes of representation and institutionalization
different from those at the point of origin. This complicates any account of
the transplantation, transference, circulation, and commerce of theories
and ideas.

There is, however, a discernable and recurrent pattern to the movement itself, three or four stages common to the way any theory or idea
travels. First, there is a point of origin, or what seems like one, a set of
initial circumstances in which the idea came to birth or entered discourse;
second, there is a distance traversed, a passage through the pressure of
various contexts as the idea moves from an earlier point to another time
and place where it will come into a new prominence; third, there is a set
of conditions—call them conditions of acceptance or, as an inevitable part
of acceptance, resistances—which then confronts the transplanted theory

or idea, making possible its introduction or toleration, however alien it might appear to be; fourth, the now fully (or partly) accommodated (or incorporated) idea is to some extent transformed by its new uses, its new position in a new time and place.

It is perfectly obvious that any satisfactorily full account of these stages would be an enormous, if not impossible task. But while I have neither the intention nor the capacity to undertake it, it seemed worthwhile to describe the problem in a sketchy and general way so that I might at length and in detail address a particularly topical, highly limited aspect of it. Of course the discrepancy between the general problem and any particular analysis is itself deserving of comment. To prefer a local, detailed analysis of how one theory travels from one situation to another is also to betray some fundamental uncertainty about specifying or delimiting the field to which any one theory or idea might belong. Notice, for example, that when professional students of literature now use words like "theory" and "criticism" it is not assumed that they must or should confine their interests to *literary* theory or *literary* criticism. The distinction between one discipline and another has been blurred precisely because fields like literature and literary study are no longer considered to be as all-encompassing or as synoptic as, until recently, they once were. While some polemical scholars of literature can still, nonetheless, attack others for not being literary enough, or for not understanding (as who should not?) that literature, unlike other forms of writing, is essentially mimetic, essentially moral, essentially humanistic, the resultant controversies are themselves, I would think, an evidence of the fact that no consensus exists on how the outer limits of the word "literature" or, for that matter, the word "criticism" are to be determined. Several decades ago, literary history and systematic theory of the kind pioneered by Northrop Frye promised an orderly, inhabitable, and hospitable structure in which, for instance, it might be demonstrated that the mythos of summer could be transformed definably into the mythos of autumn. "The primal human act in Frye's system," writes Frank Lentricchia in *After the New Criticism*, quoting Frye's *The Educated Imagination*, "and a model for all human acts, is an 'informative,' creative act which transforms a world that is merely objective, set over against us, in which we 'feel lonely and frightened and unwanted' into a home." But most literary scholars find themselves now, once again, out in the cold. Similarly, the history of ideas and comparative literature, two disciplines closely associated with the study of literature and literary criticism, do not routinely authorize in their practitioners, as they once did, quite the same Goethean sense of a concert of all literatures and ideas.

In all these instances the specific situation or locality of a particular intellectual task seems uneasily distant from, and only rhetorically assisted by, the legendary wholeness, coherence, and integrity of the general field to which professionally it belongs. There seem to be too many interruptions, too many distractions, too many irregularities interfering with the homogeneous space supposedly holding scholars together. The division of intellectual labor, which has meant increasing specialization, further erodes any direct apprehension one might have of a whole field of literature and literary study; conversely, the invasion of literary discourse by the *outré* jargons of semiotics, poststructuralism, and Lacanian psychoanalysis has distended the literary critical universe almost beyond recognition. In short there seems nothing inherently "literary" about the study of what have traditionally been considered "literary texts," no *literariness* that might *prevent* a contemporary literary critic from having recourse to psychoanalysis, sociology, or linguistics. Convention, historical custom, appeals to the protocols of humanism and traditional scholarship are of course regularly introduced as evidence of the field's enduring integrity, but more and more these seem to be rhetorical strategies in a debate about what literature and literary criticism ought to be rather than convincing definitions of what in fact they are.

Geoffrey Hartman has nicely dramatized the predicament by analyzing the tensions and vacillations governing contemporary critical activity. New criticism, he says, is radically revisionist. "Freed from a neoclassical decorum that, over the space of three centuries, created an enlightened but also over-accommodated prose," criticism is undergoing what he calls "an *extraordinary language* movement." At times this language movement is so eccentric as to approach, even challenge, literature itself; at others it obsesses the critics who were borne along its currents toward the ideal of a completely "pure" language. At still others, the critic discovers that "writing is a labyrinth, a topological puzzle and textual crossword; the reader, for his part, must lose himself for a while in a hermeneutic 'infinitizing' that makes all rules of closure appear arbitrary." Whether these alternatives for critical discourse are called "terrorist" or "a new type of sublimity or an emerging transcendentalism," there remains the need for the humanist critic both to define more clearly "the special province of the humanities" and "to materialize" (rather than spiritualize) the culture in which "we" live. Nevertheless, Hartman concludes, "we are in transition," which is perhaps another way of saying, as he does in his title *Criticism in the Wilderness*, that criticism today is alone, on the loose, unlucky, pathetic, and playful because *its* realm defies closure and certainty.

Hartman's exuberance—for his attitude is at bottom exuberant—ought to be qualified by Richard Ohmann's devastating observation in *English in America* that English departments represent "a moderately successful effort by professors to obtain some benefits of capitalism while avoiding its risks and, yet, a reluctance to acknowledge any link between how we do our work and the way the larger society is run." This is not to say that literary academics present a united ideological front, even though Ohmann is right *grosso modo*. The divisions within cannot be reduced simply to a conflict between old and new critics, nor to a monolithically dominant antimimetic ideology, as Gerald Graff very misleadingly argues. Consider that if we restrict the number of debated issues to four, many of those in the vanguard on one issue are very conservative on another:

1) Criticism as scholarship, humanism, a "servant" to the text, mimetic in its bias versus criticism as revisionism and as itself a form of literature.

2) The role of critic as teacher and good reader: safe-guarding the canon versus subverting it, or creating a new one. (Most Yale critics are revisionist with respect to #1, conservative with respect to #2.)

3) Criticism as detached from the political/social world versus criticism as a form of philosophical metaphysics, psychoanalysis, linguistics; or, either of these versus criticism as actually having to do with such "contaminated" fields as history, the media, economic systems. (Here the distributional spread is much wider than in (1) or (2) above.)

4) Criticism as a criticism of language (as negative theology, as private dogma, as ahistorical metaphysics) versus criticism as an analysis of the language of institutions; or, either of these versus criticism as a study of relationships between language and nonlinguistic things.

In the absence of an enclosing domain called literature with very clear outer boundaries, there is no longer an authorized or official position for the literary critic. But neither is there some new sovereign method, some new critical technology compelling allegiance and intellectual loyalty. Instead there is a babel of arguments for the limitlessness of all interpretation; for ideologies that proclaim the eternal, yet determinate value of literature or "the humanities"; for all systems that in asserting their capacity to perform essentially self-confirming tasks allow for no counterfactual evidence. You can call such a situation pluralistic if you like or, if you have a taste for the melodramatic, you can call it desperate. For my part, I prefer to see it as an opportunity for remaining skeptical and critical, succumbing neither to dogmatism nor to sulky gloom.

Hence the specific problem of what happens to a theory when it moves from one place to another proposes itself as an interesting topic of investigation. For, if, as I have tried to suggest, fields like literature or the history of ideas have no intrinsically enclosing limits, and if, conversely, no one methodology is imposable upon what is an essentially heterogeneous and practically open area of activity—the writing and interpretation of texts—it is wise to raise the questions of theory and of criticism in ways suitable to the situation in which we find ourselves. At the outset, this means a historical approach. Assume therefore that, as a result of specific historical circumstances, a theory or idea pertaining to those circumstances arises. What happens to it when, in different circumstances and for new, perhaps no less convincing reasons, it is used again and, in still more different circumstances, again? What can this tell us about theory itself—its limits, its possibilities, its inherent problems—and what can it suggest to us about the relationship between theory and criticism on the one hand, and society and culture on the other? The pertinence of these questions will be apparent at a time when theoretical activity seems both intense and eclectic, when the relationship between social reality and a dominant yet hermetic critical discourse seems hard to determine, and when, for all of these reasons and some of the ones I have just referred to, it is futile to prescribe theoretical programs for contemporary criticism.

Lukács's *History and Class-Consciousness* (1923) is justly famous for its analysis of the phenomenon of reification, a universal fate afflicting all aspects of life in an era dominated by commodity fetishism. Since, as Lukács argues, capitalism is the most articulated and quantitatively detailed of all economic systems, what it imposes upon human life and labor under its rule has the consequence of radically transforming everything human, flowing, processual, organic, and connected, into disconnected and "alienated" objects, items, lifeless atoms. In such a situation then,

> time sheds its qualitative, variable, flowing nature; it freezes into an
> exactly delimited, quantifiable continuum filled with quantifiable

'things' (the reified, mechanically objectified 'performance' of the worker, wholly separated from his total human personality): in short, it becomes space. In this environment where time is transformed into abstract, exactly measurable, physical space, an environment at once the cause and effect of the scientifically and mechanically fragmented and specialised production of the object of labour, the subjects of labour must likewise be rationally fragmented. On the one hand, the objectification of their labour-power into something opposed to their total personality (a process already accomplished with the sale of that labour-power as a commodity) is now made into the permanent ineluctable reality of their daily life. Here, too, the personality can do no more than look on helplessly while its own existence is reduced to an isolated particle and fed into an alien system. On the other hand, the mechanical disintegration of the process of production into its components also destroys those bonds that had bound individuals to a community in the days when production was still 'organic'. In this respect, too, mechanisation makes of them isolated abstract atoms whose work no longer brings them together directly and organically; it becomes mediated to an increasing extent exclusively by the abstract laws of the mechanism which imprisons them.

If this picture of the public world is bleak, it is matched by Lukács's description of what happens to intellect, "the subject" as he calls it. After an astonishingly brilliant account of the antinomies of classical philosophy from Descartes to Kant to Fichte, Hegel, and Marx, in which he shows the increasing retreat of the subject into passive, privatized contemplation, gradually more and more divorced from the overwhelmingly fragmented realities of modern industrial life, Lukács then depicts modern bourgeois thought as being at an impasse, transfixed and paralyzed into terminal passivity. The science that it produces is based on mere fact-gathering; the rational forms of understanding therefore cannot cope with the irrationality of physical *données*, and when efforts are made to compel "the facts" to submit to "system," their fragmentation and endlessly atomized *thereness* either destroy the system or turn the mind into a passive register of discrete objects.

There is, however, one form of experience that concretely represents the very essence of reification as well as its limitations: crisis. If capitalism is the embodiment in economic terms of reification, then everything, including human beings, ought to be quantified and given a market value:

this of course is what Lukács means when he speaks of articulation under capitalism, which he sometimes characterizes as if it were a gigantic itemized list. In principle, then, nothing—no object, person, place, or time—is left out, since everything can be calculated. But there are moments when "the qualitative existence of the 'things' that lead their lives beyond the purview of economics as misunderstood and neglected things-in-themselves, as use values [Lukács here refers to such "irrational" things as sentiment, passion, chance] suddenly becomes the decisive factor (suddenly, that is, for reified, rational thought). Or rather: these 'laws' fail to function and the reified mind is unable to perceive a pattern in this 'chaos.'" At such a moment, then, mind, or "subject" has its one opportunity to escape reification: by thinking through what it is that causes reality to appear to be only a collection of objects and economic *données*. And the very act of looking for process behind what appears to be eternally given and objectified, makes it possible for the mind to know itself as subject and not as a lifeless object, then to go beyond empirical reality into a putative realm of possibility. When instead of an inexplicable shortage of bread you can imagine the human work and, subsequently, the human beings who produced the bread but are no longer doing so because there is a bakers' strike, you are well on your way to knowing that crisis is comprehensible because process is comprehensible; and if process is comprehensible so too is some sense of the social whole created by human labor. Crisis, in short, is converted into criticism of the status quo: the bakers are on strike for a reason; the crisis can be explained, the system does not work infallibly, the subject has just demonstrated its victory over ossified objective forms.

Lukács puts all of this in terms of the subject-object relationship, and proper justice to his argument requires that it be followed to the point where he shows that reconciliation between subject and object will be possible. Yet even he admits that such an eventuality is very far in the future. Nevertheless, he is certain that no such future is attainable without the transformation of passive, contemplative consciousness into active, critical consciousness. In positing a world of human agency outside the reach of reification, the critical consciousness (that is, the consciousness that is given rise to by crisis) becomes genuinely aware of its power "unceasingly to overthrow the objective forms that shape the life of man." Consciousness goes beyond empirical givens, and comprehends, without actually experiencing, history, totality, and society as a whole—precisely those unities that reification had both concealed and denied. At bottom, then, class consciousness is thought thinking its way through fragmentation to unity; it is also thought aware of its own subjectivity as something active, energetic, and, in a profound sense, poetic. (Here we should remark that several years before *History and Class-Consciousness* Lukács had argued that only in the realm of the aesthetic could the limitations of pure theory and of pure ethics be overcome; by the former Lukács meant a scientific theory whose very objectivity symbolized its own reification, its thralldom to objects, by the latter a Kantian subjectivity out of touch with everything except its own selfhood. Only the Aesthetic rendered the meaning of experience as lived experience—*der Sinn des Erlebnisses*—in an autonomous form: subject and object are thereby made one ("Die Subjekt-Objekt-Beziehung in der Ästhetik," *Logos*, 1917–18, republished in *Heidelberger Ästhetik*, Luchterland, 1975).

Now because it rises above objects, consciousness enters a realm of potentiality, that is, of theoretical possibility. The special urgency of Lukács's account of this is that he is describing something rather far from a mere escape into fantasy. Consciousness attaining self-consciousness is no Emma Bovary pretending to be a lady in Yonville. The direct pressures of capitalist quantification, that relentless cataloguing of everything on earth, continue to be felt, according to Lukács; the only thing that changes is that the mind recognizes itself as a mind, which means that it also recognizes a class of beings like itself who have the power to think generally, to take in facts but to organize them in groups, to recognize processes and tendencies where reification only allows evidence of lifeless atoms. Class consciousness therefore begins in critical consciousness. Classes are not real the way trees and houses are real; they are imputable by consciousness, using its powers to posit ideal types in which, with other beings, it finds itself. Classes are the result of an insurrectionary act by which consciousness refuses to be confined to the world of objects, which is where it had been confined in the capitalist scheme of things.

Consciousness has moved from the world of objects into the world of theory. Although Lukács describes it as only a young German philosopher could describe it—in language bristling with more metaphysics and abstractions than even I have been using—we must not forget that he is performing an act of political insurgency. To attain theory is to threaten reification, as well as the entire bourgeois system on which reification depends, with destruction. But, he assures his readers, this destruction "is no single unrepeatable tearing of the veil that masks the process [of reification] but the unbroken alternation of ossification, contradiction and movement." Theory, in fine, is won as the result of the process which begins when consciousness first experiences its own terrible ossification in the general reification of all things under capitalism; then when consciousness generalizes (or classes) itself as something opposed to other objects, and feels itself as a contradiction to (or crisis within) objectification, there emerges a consciousness of change in the status quo; finally, moving toward freedom and fulfillment consciousness looks ahead to complete self-realization, which is of course the revolutionary process stretching forwards in time, perceivable now only as theory or projection.

This is very heady stuff indeed. I have summarized it in order to set down some small indication of how powerfully responsive Lukács's ideas about theory were to the political order he described with such formidable gravity and dread. Theory for him was what consciousness produced not as an avoidance of reality, but as a revolutionary will completely committed to worldliness and to change. According to Lukács, the proletariat's consciousness represented the theoretical antithesis to capitalism; as Merleau-Ponty and others have said, Lukács's proletariat cannot by any means be identified with a ragged collection of grimy-faced Hungarian laborers. The proletariat was his figure for consciousness defying reification, mind asserting its powers over mere matter, consciousness claiming its theoretical right to posit a better world outside the world of simple objects. And since class consciousness derives from workers working and being aware of themselves that way, theory must never lose touch with its origins in politics, society, economics.

This then is Lukács describing his ideas about theory—and of course his theory of socio-historical change—in the early twenties. Consider now Lukács's disciple and student Lucien Goldmann, whose Le Dieu caché (1955) was one of the first, and certainly among the most impressive, attempts to put Lukács's theories to practical scholarly use. In Goldmann's study of Pascal and Racine, class consciousness has been changed to "vision du monde," that is, something which "is not an immediate, empirical fact" but a collective consciousness expressed in the work of certain highly gifted writers. But this is not all. Goldmann says that these writers derive their world vision from determinate political and economic circumstances common to members of their group, yet the world vision itself is premised not so much on empirical detail as on a human faith that "a reality" exists "which goes beyond them as individuals and finds its expression in their work." Writing as a politically committed scholar (and not like Lukács as a directly involved militant), Goldmann then argues that because Pascal and Racine were "highly privileged writers," their work can be constituted into a "significant whole" by a process of dialectical theorizing, in which part is related to assumed whole, assumed whole verified empirically by empirical evidence. Thus individual texts are seen to "express a world vision"; secondly, the world vision is "analysed as constituting a whole made up of the intellectual and social life of the group" (the Port-Royal Jansenists); thirdly, "the thoughts and feelings of the group . . . [can] be seen as an expression of their economic and social life." In all this—and Goldmann argues with exemplary brilliance and subtlety—the theoretical enterprise, an interpretive circle, is a demonstration of coherence: between part and whole, between world vision and texts in their smallest detail, between a determinate social reality and the writings of particularly gifted members of a group. In other words, theory is the *researcher's* domain, the place in which disparate, apparently disconnected things are brought together in perfect correspondence: economics, political process, the individual writer, a series of texts.

Goldmann's indebtedness to Lukács is clear, although it has not been noted that what in Lukács is an ironic discrepancy between theoretical consciousness and reified reality is transformed and localized by Goldmann into a tragic correspondence between world vision and the unfortunate class situation of the *noblesse de robe* in late seventeenth-century France. Whereas Lukács's class consciousness defies, indeed is an insurgent against, the capitalist order, Goldmann's tragic vision is perfectly, absolutely *expressed* by the works of Pascal and Racine. True, the tragic vision is not directly expressed by those writers, and true also that it requires an extraordinarily complex dialectical style of research for the modern researcher to draw forth the correspondence between world vision and empirical detail; the fact nevertheless is that Goldmann's adaptation of Lukács removes from theory its insurrectionary role. The sheer existence of class, or theoretical, consciousness for Lukács is enough to suggest to him the projected overthrow of objective forms; for Goldmann an awareness of class or group consciousness is first of all a scholarly imperative, and then—in the works of highly privileged writers—the expression of a tragically limited social situation. Lukács's *zugerechnetes*

Bewusstsein (imputed consciousness) is an unverifiable, yet absolutely prior theoretical necessity if one is to effect a change in social reality; in Goldmann's version of it, admittedly limited to an acutely circumscribed situation, theory and consciousness are expressed in the Pascalian wager upon an unseen and silent god, the *deus absconditus;* they are also expressed for Goldmann the scientific researcher, as he calls himself, in the theoretical correspondence between text and political reality. Or to put the matter in another way, for Lukács theory originates as a kind of irreducible dissonance between mind and object, whereas for Goldmann theory is the homological relationship that can be seen to exist between individual part and coherent whole.

The difference between the two versions of Lukács's theory of theory is evident enough: Lukács writes as a participant in a struggle (the Hungarian Soviet Republic of 1919), Goldmann as an expatriate historian at the Sorbonne. From one point of view we can say that Goldmann's adaptation of Lukács *degrades* theory, lowers it in importance, domesticates it somewhat to the exigencies of a doctoral dissertation in Paris. I do not think, however, that degradation here has a moral implication, but rather (as one of its secondary meanings suggests) that degradation conveys the lowering of color, the greater degree of distance, the loss of immediate force that occurs when Goldmann's notions of consciousness and theory are compared with the meaning and role intended by Lukács for theory. Nor do I want to suggest that there is something inherently wrong about Goldmann's conversion of insurrectionary, radically adversarial consciousness into an accommodating consciousness of correspondence and homology. It is just that the situation has changed sufficiently for the degradation to have occurred, although there is no doubt that Goldmann's reading of Lukács mutes the latter's almost apocalyptic version of consciousness.

We have become so accustomed to hearing that all borrowings, all readings and interpretations are misreadings and misinterpretations that we are likely to consider the Lukács-Goldmann episode as just another bit of relatively conclusive evidence that everyone, even Marxists, misreads and misinterprets. I find such a conclusion completely unsatisfying. It implies, first of all, that the only possible alternative to slavish copying is "creative" misreading, and that no intermediate possibility exists. Secondly, when it is elevated to a general principle the idea that all reading is misreading is fundamentally an abrogation of the critic's responsibility. In my opinion, it is never enough for a critic taking the idea of criticism seriously simply to say that interpretation is misinterpretation, that borrowings inevitably involve misreadings, etc. Quite the contrary: it seems to me to be perfectly possible to *judge* misreadings (as they occur) as part of a historical transfer of ideas and theories from one setting to another. Lukács wrote *for* as well as *in* a situation that produced ideas about consciousness and theory that are very different from the ideas produced by Goldmann in his situation. To call Goldmann's work a misreading of Lukács's, and then to go on immediately to relate that misreading to a general theory of interpretation as misinterpretation is to pay absolutely no critical attention to history and to situation, both of which play an important determining role in changing Lukács's ideas into Goldmann's. The Hungary of 1919 and post–World War II Paris are two quite different environments. To the degree that Lukács and Goldmann are read carefully, then to that precise degree we can understand the critical change—in time and in place—that occurs between one writer and another, both of whom depend on theory to accomplish a particular job of intellectual work. I see no need here to resort to the theory of limitless intertextuality as an Archimedean point outside the two situations; the particular voyage from Hungary to Paris, with all that that entails, seems to me to be compelling enough, adequate enough for critical scrutiny unless, as I shall be showing later, we want to give up critical consciousness for critical hermeticism.

In measuring Lukács and Goldmann against each other, then, we are also recognizing the extent to which theory—even when it is borrowed—is a response to a specific social and historical situation, of which an intellectual occasion is of course a part. Thus what is insurrectionary consciousness in one instance becomes tragic vision in another for reasons that are elucidated when the situations in Budapest and Paris are seriously compared. I do not at all wish to suggest that Budapest and Paris *determined* the kinds of theories produced by Lukács and Goldmann respectively. I do mean that "Budapest" and "Paris" are irreducibly first conditions, and they provide limits and apply pressures, to which each writer, given his own gifts, predilections, and interests, responds.

Let us now take Lukács, or rather Lukács as used by Goldmann, a step further: the use made of Goldmann by Raymond Williams. Brought up in the tradition of Cambridge English studies, trained in the techniques of Leavis and Richards, Williams was formed as a literary scholar who had no use whatever for theory. He speaks rather poignantly of how intellectuals educated as he was could use "a separate and self-defining language" which made a fetish of minute, concrete particulars; this meant that the intellectuals could approach power but speak antiseptically only of "microcosm," profess not to understand reification and to speak instead of the "objective correlative," not to know mediation "although they knew catharsis." Williams tells us that Goldmann came to Cambridge in 1970 and gave two lectures there. This visit, according to Williams in the moving commemorative essay that he wrote about Goldmann after his death, was a major event. It introduced Cambridge to theory, Williams claims, understood and employed as it had been by thinkers trained in the "major continental tradition." Goldmann induced in Williams an appreciation of Lukács's contribution to our understanding of how, in an era of "the dominance of economic activity over all other forms of human activity," reification was both "a false objectivity" so far as knowledge was concerned, and a "deformation" more "thoroughly penetrating . . . life and consciousness" than any other form. Williams continues:

> The idea of totality was then a critical weapon against this precise deformation; indeed, against capitalism itself. And yet this was not idealism—an assertion of the primacy of other values. On the contrary, just as the deformation could be understood, at its roots, only by historical analysis of a particular kind of economy, so the attempt to overcome and surpass it lay not in isolated witness or in separated activity but in practical work to find, assert and to establish more human social ends, in more human and political and economic means.

Once again Lukács's thought—in this instance the avowedly revolutionary idea of "totality"—has been tamed somewhat. Without wishing in any way to belittle the importance of what Lukács's ideas (via Goldmann) did for the moribund state of English studies in late twentieth-century Cambridge, I think it needs to be said that those ideas were originally formulated in order to do more than shake up a few professors of literature. This is an obvious, not to say easy, point. What is more interesting, however, is that *because* Cambridge is not revolutionary Budapest, because Williams is not the militant Lukács, because Williams is a reflective *critic*—this is very crucial—rather than a committed revolutionary, he *can* see the limits of a theory that begins as a liberating idea but can become a trap of its own.

At the most practical level [Williams continues] it was easy for me to agree [with Lukács's theory of totality as a response to reification]. But then the whole point of thinking in terms of a totality is the realization that we are part of it; that our own consciousness, our work, our methods, are then critically at stake. And in the particular field of literary analysis there was this obvious difficulty: that most of the work we had to look at was the product of just this work of reified consciousness, so that *what looked like the methodological breakthrough might become, quite quickly, the methodological trap.* I cannot yet say this finally about Lukács, since I still don't have access to all his work; but in some of it, at least, *the major insights* of History *and Class-Consciousness,* which he has now partly disavowed, *do not get translated into critical practice* [Williams refers here to Lukács's later, much cruder work on European realism] and certain cruder operations—essentially still those of base and superstructure—keeping reappearing. *I still read Goldmann collaboratively and critically asking the same question,* for I am sure the practice of totality is still for any of us, at any time, profoundly and even obviously difficult. (*Problems in Materialism and Culture;* emphasis mine)

This is an admirable passage. Even though Williams says nothing about the lamentable repetitiveness of Goldmann's later work, it is important that as a critic who has learned from soneone else's theory he should be able to see the theory's limitations, especially—and this is why I am so impressed with Williams's insight—the fact that a breakthrough can become a trap if it is used uncritically, repetitively, limitlessly. What he means, I think, is that once an idea gains currency because it is clearly effective and powerful, there is every likelihood that during its peregrinations it will be reduced, codified, institutionalized. Lukács's remarkably complex exposition of the phenomenon of reification can, and indeed did, turn into a simple reflection theory; to a degree of course, and Williams is too decently elegiac to say it about a recently dead old friend, it did become this sort of idea in Goldmann's hands. Homology is, after all, a refined version of the old Second International base-and-superstructure model.

Beyond the specific reminder of what could happen to a vanguard theory, Williams's ruminations enable us to make another observation about theory as it develops out of a situation, begins to be used, travels, and gains wide acceptance. For if reification-and-totality (to turn Lukács's theory now into a shorthand phrase for easy reference) can become a reductionist implement, there is no reason why, given the nature of this particular theory, it could not become too inclusive, too ceaselessly active and expanding a habit of mind. That is, if a theory can move *down*, so to speak, become a dogmatic reduction of its original version, it can also move *up* into a sort of bad infinity, which—in the case of reification-and-totality—is the direction intended by Lukács himself. To speak of the unceasing overthrow of objective forms, and to speak, as he does in the essay on "Class-Consciousness," of how the logical end of overcoming reification is the self-annihilation of the revolutionary class itself, means that Lukács had pushed his theory too far forward and upwards unacceptably (in my opinion). The contradiction inherent in this theory—and perhaps in most theories that develop as responses to the need for movement and change—is that it risks becoming a theoretical overstatement, a theoretical parody of the situation it was formulated originally to remedy or overcome. To prescribe "an *unbroken* alternation of ossification, contradiction and movement" toward totality as a theoretical remedy for reification is in a sense to substitute one unchanging formula for another. To say of theory and theoretical consciousness, as Lukács does, that they intervene in reification and introduce process is not to calculate carefully enough, and allow for, the *details* and the *resistances* offered by an intransigent, reified reality to theoretical consciousness. For all the brilliance of his account of reification, for all the care he takes with it, Lukács is unable to see how even under capitalism reification itself cannot be *totally* dominant—unless, of course, he is prepared to allow something that theoretical totality (his insurrectional instrument for overcoming reification) says is impossible, namely, that totality in the form of totally dominant reification is *theoretically* possible under capitalism. For if reification is totally dominant, how then can Lukács explain his own work as an alternative form of thought under the sway of reification?

Perhaps all this is too fussy and hermetic. Nevertheless, it seems to me that however far away in time and place Williams may be from the fiery rebelliousness of the early Lukács, there is an extraordinary virtue to the distance, even the coldness of his critical reflections on Lukács and Goldmann, to both of whom he is otherwise so intellectually cordial. He takes from both men a sophisticated theoretical awareness of the issues involved in connecting literature to society—as he puts it in his best single theoretical essay. The terminology provided by Marxist aesthetic theory for mapping the peculiarly uneven and complicated field lying between base and superstructure is generally inadequate, and then he goes on to do work that embodies *his* critical version of the original theory ("Base and Superstructure in Marxist Cultural Theory"). He puts this version very well, I think, in *Politics and Letters:* "however dominant a social system may be, the very meaning of its domination involves a limitation or selection of the activities it covers, so that by definition it cannot exhaust all social experience, which therefore always potentially contains space for alternative acts and alternative intentions which are not yet articulated as a social institution or even project." *The Country and the City* records both the limits and the reactive alternatives to dominance, as in the case of John Clare, whose work "marks the end of pastoral poetry [as a systematic convention for describing the English countryside] in the very shock of its collision with actual country experience." Clare's very existence as a poet was threatened by the removal "of an acceptable social order" from the customary landscape idealized by Jonson and Thomson; hence Clare's turning—as an alternative not yet fully realized, and not yet completely subdued by the inhuman relationships that obtained under the system of market exploitation—to "the green language of the new Nature," that is, the Nature to be celebrated in a new way by the great romantics.

There is no minimizing the fact that Williams is an important critic because of his gifts and his insights. But I am convinced it would be wrong to underestimate the role in his mature writings played by what I have been alluding to as borrowed, or travelling, theory. For borrow we most certainly must if we are to elude the constraints of our immediate intellectual environment. Theory we most certainly need, for all sorts of reasons that would be too tedious to rehearse here. What we also need over and above theory, however, is the critical recognition that there is no theory capable of covering, closing off, predicting all the situations in which it might be useful; this is another way of saying, as Williams does, that no social or intellectual system can be so dominant as to be unlimited in its strength. Williams therefore has the critical recognition, and uses it consciously to qualify, shape, and refine his borrowings from Lukács and Goldmann, although we should hasten to add that it does not make him infallible or any less liable to exaggeration and error for having it. But unless theory is answerable, either through its successes or its failures, to the essential untidiness, the essential unmasterable presence that constitutes a large part of historical and social situations (and this applies equally to theory that derives from somewhere else, or theory that is "original"), then theory becomes an ideological trap. It transfixes both its users and what it is used on. Criticism would no longer be possible.

Theory, in short, can never be complete, just as one's interest in everyday life is never exhausted by simulacra, models, or theoretical abstracts of it. Of course one derives pleasure from actually making evidence fit or work in a theoretical scheme, and of course it is ridiculously foolish to argue that "the facts" or "the great texts" do not require any theoretical framework or methodology to be appreciated or read properly: no reading is neutral or innocent, and by the same token every text and every reader is to some extent the product of a theoretical standpoint, however implicit or unconscious such a standpoint may be. I am arguing, however, that we distinguish theory from critical consciousness by saying that the latter is a sort of spatial sense, a sort of measuring faculty for locating or situating theory, and this means that theory has to be grasped in the place and (of course) the time out of which it emerges as a part of that time, working in and for it, responding to it; then, consequently, that first place can be measured against subsequent places where the theory turns up for use. The critical consciousness is awareness of the differences between situations, awareness too of the fact that no system or theory exhausts (or covers or dominates) the situation out of which it emerges or to which it is transported. And above all, critical consciousness is awareness of the resistances to theory, reactions to it elicited by those concrete experiences or interpretations with which it is in conflict. Indeed, I would go as far as saying that it is the critic's job to *provide* resistances to theory, to open it up toward historical reality, toward society, toward human needs and interests, to point up those concrete instances drawn from everyday reality that lie outside or just beyond the interpretive area necessarily designated in advance and therefore circumscribed by every theory.

Much of this is illustrated, I think, if we compare Lukács and Williams on the one hand with Goldmann on the other. I have already said that Williams is conscious of what he calls a "methodological trap"; Lukács, for his part, shows in his career as a theorist (if not in the fully-fledged theory itself) a profound awareness of the necessity to move from hermetic aestheticism (*Die Seele und die Formen, Die Theorie des Romans*) toward the actual world of power and institutions. By contrast, Goldmann is enmeshed in the homological finality that his writing, very brilliantly and persuasively in the case of *Le Dieu caché*, demonstrates. Theoretical closure, like social convention or cultural dogma, is anathema to critical consciousness, which loses its profession when it loses its active sense of the open world in which its faculties must be exercised. One of the best lessons of that is to be found in Frank Lentricchia's powerful recent book, *After the New Criticism*, a wholly persuasive account of what he calls "the currently paralyzed debates" of contemporary literary theory. In instance after instance he demonstrates the impoverishment and the rarification that overtake any theory relatively untested by and unexposed to the complex enfolding of the social world, which is never a merely complaisant context to be used for the enactment of theoretical situations. (As an antidote to the barrenness afflicting the American situation, there is in Fredric Jameson's *The Political Unconscious* an extremely useful account of three "semantic horizons" to be figured in dialectically by the interpreter as parts of the decoding process, which he also calls "the cultural mode of production.")

Yet we must be aware that the social reality I have been alluding to is no less susceptible to theoretical overtotalization, even when, as I shall be showing in the case of Michel Foucault, extremely powerful historical scholarship moves itself out from the archive toward the world of power and institutions, toward precisely those resistances to theory ignored and elided by most formalistic theory—deconstruction, semiotics, Lacanian psychoanalysis, the Althusserian Marxism attacked by E. P. Thompson. Foucault's work is most challenging because he is rightly considered to be an exemplary opponent of ahistorical, asocial formalism. But he too, I believe, falls victim to the systematic degradation of theory in ways that his newest disciples—with few exceptions—consider to be evidence that he has not succumbed to hermeticism.

Foucault is a paradox. His career presents his contemporary audience with an extraordinarily compelling trajectory whose culmination, most recently, has been the announcement made by him, and on his behalf by his disciples, that his real theme is the relationship between knowledge and power. Thanks to the brilliance of his theoretical and practical performances, *pouvoir* and *savoir* have provided his readers (it would be churlish not to mention myself; but see also Jacques Donzelot's *La Police des familles*) with a conceptual apparatus for the analysis of instrumental discourses that stands in stark contrast to the fairly arid metaphysics produced habitually by the students of his major philosophical competitors. Yet it is not often noticed that Foucault's earliest work was, in many ways, remarkably unconscious of its own theoretical force. Reread *Histoire de la folie* after *Surveiller et punir*, and you will be struck with how uncannily prescient the early work is of the later; and yet you will also be struck that even when Foucault deals with *renfermement* (confinement), which has always been his obsessive theme, in discussing asylums and hospitals, power is never referred to explicitly. Neither, for that matter, is *volonté*, "will." *Les Mots et les choses* might be excused for the same neglect of power on the grounds that the subject of Foucault's inquiry was intellectual, not institutional history. In *The Archaeology of Knowledge* there are intimations here and there that Foucault is beginning to approach *power* through a number of abstractions, surrogates for it: thus he refers to such things as acceptability, accumulation, preservation, and formation that are ascribed to the making and the functioning of statements (*enoncés*), discourses, and archives, yet he does so without spending any time on what might be the common source of their strength within institutions, or fields of knowledge, or society itself.

Although it is only referred to once, and rather briefly at that, in *The Archaeology of Knowledge*, the *episteme* stood in Foucault's way in these first three or four books. It rather mysteriously gave coherence to historical epochs; it seemed at the same time to be able to hold in, as well as to constitute thought; because it underwent silent metamorphoses, the *episteme* also somehow managed the transition from one kind of thinking to another. But whatever else the *episteme* did for Foucault's archaeologies until *Surveiller et punir*, its shadowy dominance obscured the workings of power within society.

Not that Foucault employed the *episteme* as either socially determining or determined by social forces. He has always had numerous possible versions of strict dialectical materialism available to him, but he has preferred not to use them to get at power. Perhaps this is because in his first works Foucault had learned Althusserian Marxism too well, confining his awareness of praxis to a scrupulous regard for wholly textual problematics. So between his strangely insistent use of the *episteme* and his avoidance of Marxist categories, Foucault developed a peculiar attitude toward powerful individuals who, in more traditional historical analyses than Foucault's, might have been supposed to play important roles in the process of historical change. The Marquis de Sade, Nietzsche, and Mallarmé, for example, are pivotal figures in *Les Mots et les choses:* they indicate, if they do not adequately symbolize or cause, the transformation of one epistemological era into another. In several respects they also exceed the limits of their age, in others they embody them. Their status vacillates between being bearers of a symbolic adversarial power and victims of a sovereign *Zeitgeist*. In the end, of course, they are casualties of "the death of man," which Foucault commemorates repeatedly after *Les Mots et les choses* in various essays and in *The Archaeology*. Thereafter, man's place, along with the places formerly occupied by kings, authors, great men, heroes, and victims, is dissolved, to be replaced by the relatively anonymous archives, discourses, and statements of *The Archaeology*, which in turn is superseded by the "microphysics of power" put forward in *Discipline and Punish* and "la volonté de savoir" in the first volume of his *History of Sexuality*.

Foucault's theory of power—to which I shall restrict myself here—derives from his attempt to analyze working systems of confinement from the inside, systems whose functioning depends equally on the continuity of institutions as on the proliferation of justifying *technical* ideologies for the institutions. These ideologies are what Foucault calls "discourses" and "disciplines." In his concrete presentation of local situations in which such power and such knowledge are deployed, Foucault has no peer, and what he has done is remarkably interesting by almost any standard. As he says in *Surveiller et punir*, for power to work it must be able to manage, control, even create *detail:* the more detail, the more real power, management breeding manageable units, which in turn breed a more detailed, a more finely controlling knowledge. Prisons, he says in a memorable passage, are factories for producing delinquency, and delinquency is the raw material for disciplinary discourses.

With descriptions and particularized observations of this sort I have no trouble. It is when Foucault's own language becomes general (that is, when he moves his analyses of power from the detail to society as a whole) that the methodological breakthrough becomes the theoretical trap. Interestingly, this is slightly more evident when Foucault's theory is transported from France and planted in the work of his overseas disciples. Recently, for example, he has been celebrated by Ian Hacking in *The New York Review of Books* as a kind of hardheaded alternative to the too-backward and forward-looking "Romantic" (*sic*) Marxists (which Marxists? all Marxists?), and as a ruthlessly anarchistic opponent of Noam Chomsky, who is described quite inappropriately as "a marvelously sane liberal reformer." Other writers, who quite rightly see Foucault's discussions of power as a refreshing window opened on to the real world of politics and society, uncritically misread his pronouncements as the latest thing about social reality. (There is much evidence of this in an issue of *Humanities in Society*, 3, Winter 1980, entirely devoted to Foucault.) There is no doubt that Foucault's work is indeed an important alternative to the ahistorical formalism with which he has been conducting an implicit debate, and there is great merit to his view that as a specialized intellectual (as opposed to a universal intellectual—the distinction is made by Foucault in *Radical Philosophy*, 17, Summer 1977) he, and others like him, can wage small-scale guerilla warfare against some repressive institutions, and against "silence" and "secrecy."

But all that is quite another thing from accepting Foucault's view in *History of Sexuality* that "power is everywhere" along with all that such a vastly simplified view entails. For one, as I have written elsewhere, Foucault's eagerness not to fall into Marxist economism causes him to obliterate the role of classes, the role of economics, the role of insurgency and rebellion in the societies he discusses. Let us suppose that prisons, schools, armies, and factories were, as he says, disciplinary factories in nineteenth-century France (since he talks almost exclusively about France), and that panoptic rule dominated them all. What resistances were there to the disciplinary order, and why, as Nicos Poulantzas has so trenchantly argued in *State, Power, Socialism*, does Foucault never discuss the resistances which by implication always end up incorporated and dominated by the system he describes? The facts are more complicated, of course, as any good historian of the rise of the modern state can demonstrate. Moreover, Poulantzas continues, even if we accept the view that power is essentially relational, that it is not held by anyone but is strategic, dispositional, effective, that, as *Discipline and Punish* claims, it invests all areas of society, is it correct to conclude, as Foucault does, that power is exhausted *in its use?* Is it not simply wrong, Poulantzas asks, to say that power is not *based* anywhere, and that struggles and exploitation—both terms left out of Foucault's analyses—do not occur? The problem is that Foucault's use of the term "power" moves around too much, swallowing up every obstacle in its path (resistances to it, the class and economic bases which refresh and fuel it, the reserves it builds up), obliterating change and mystifying its micro-physical sovereignty. A symptom of how overblown Foucault's conception of power can become when it travels too far is Hacking's statement that "nobody knows this knowledge;

no one yields this power": surely this is going to extremes in order to prove that Foucault is not a simple-minded follower of Marx.

In fact, I think, Foucault's theory of power is a Spinozist conception, which has captivated not only Foucault himself but many of his readers who wish to go beyond left optimism and right pessimism so as to justify political quietism with sophisticated intellectualism, at the same time that they wish to appear to be realistic, in touch with the world of power and reality, as well as historical and antiformalistic in their bias. The trouble is that Foucault's theory has drawn a circle around itself, constituting a unique territory in which Foucault has imprisoned himself and others with him. It is certainly wrong to say, with Hacking, that hope, optimism, and pessimism are shown by Foucault to be mere satellites "of the idea of a transcendental or enduring subject," since empirically we experience and act according to those things daily without reference to any such ridiculously irrelevant "subject." There is, after all, a sensible difference between Hope and hope, just as there is between the Logos and words: we must not let Foucault get away with confusing them with each other, nor with letting us forget that history does not get made without work, intention, resistance, effort, or conflict, and that none of these things is silently absorbable into micro-networks of power.

There is a more important criticism to be made of Foucault's theory of power, and it has been made most tellingly by Chomsky. Hacking, alas, misrepresents the disagreement between them, and unfortunately most of Foucault's new readers in the United States seem not to know of the exchange that took place between them several years ago on a Dutch television program (a transcript of which may be found in *Reflexive Water*, edited by Fons Elders, London, Souvenir Press, Ltd., 1974), nor of Chomsky's succinct critique of Foucault contained in *Language and Responsibility*. Both men agreed on the necessity of opposing repression, a position Foucault has since found it more difficult to take unequivocally. Yet for Chomsky the socio-political battle had to be waged with two tasks in mind: one, "to imagine a future society that conforms to the exigencies of human nature [the need for justice, self-development, creative work] as best we understand them; the other, to analyze the nature of power and oppression in our present societies." Foucault assented to the second without in any way accepting the first. According to him, any future societies that we might imagine now "are only the inventions of our civilization and result from our class system." Not only would imagining a future society ruled according to justice be limited by false consciousness, it would also be too utopian a project for anyone like Foucault, who believes that "the idea of justice in itself is an idea which in effect has been invented and put to work in different societies as an instrument of a certain political and economic power or as a weapon against that power." This is a perfect instance of Foucault's unwilllingness to take seriously his own ideas about "resistances" to power. If power oppresses and controls and manipulates, then everything that resists it is not morally equal to power, is not neutrally and simply "a weapon against that power." Resistance cannot equally be an adversarial alternative to power, and also a dependent function of it, except in some metaphysical, ultimately trivial sense. Even if the distinction is hard to draw, there is a distinction to be made—as, for example, Chomsky does, when he says that he would give his support to an oppressed proletariat if as a class it made an ideal of justice the goal of its struggle.

The disturbing circularity of Foucault's theory of power is a form of theoretical overtotalization superficially more difficult to resist because, unlike many others, it is formulated, reformulated, and borrowed for use in what seem to be historically documented situations. But note that Foucault's history is ultimately textual, or rather textualized; its mode is one for which Borges would have an affinity. Gramsci, on the other hand, would find it uncongenial: he would certainly appreciate the fineness of Foucault's archeologies, but would find it odd that they make not even a nominal allowance for emergent movements, and none for revolutions, counter-hegemony, or historical blocks. For in human history there is always something beyond the reach of dominating systems, no matter how deeply they saturate society, and this is obviously what makes change possible, limits power in Foucault's sense, and hobbles the theory of that power. One could not imagine Foucault undertaking a sustained analysis of powerfully contested political issues nor, like Chomsky himself and writers like John Berger, would Foucault commit himself to descriptions of power and oppression with some (perhaps misguided) intention of alleviating human suffering, pain, or betrayed hope.

It may seem an abrupt conclusion to reach, but the kinds of theory I have been discussing can quite easily become cultural dogma. Appropriated to schools or institutions, they quickly acquire the status of authority within the cultural group, guild, or affiliative family. While of course they are to be distinguished from grosser forms of cultural dogma like racism

and nationalism, they are insidious in that their original provenance—
their history of adversarial, oppositional derivation—dulls the critical
consciousness, convincing it that a once insurgent theory is still insurgent, lively, responsive to history. Left to its own specialists and acolytes,
so to speak, theory tends to have walls erected around itself, but this neither means that critics should ignore theory, nor look despairingly around
for a newer variety. To measure the distance between theory then and
now, there and here; to record the encounter of theory with resistances to
it; to move skeptically yet investigatively in the broader political world
where such things as "the humanities" or "the great classics" ought to be
seen as small provinces of the human venture; to map the entire territory
covered by all the techniques of dissemination, communication, and interpretation; to preserve some modest (perhaps shrinking) belief in non-
coercive human community: if these are not imperatives, they do at least
seem to be very attractive alternatives. And what is critical consciousness
at bottom if not an unstoppable predilection for alternatives?

Homophobia, Misogyny, and Capital:
The Example of Our Mutual Friend

EVE KOSOFSKY SEDGWICK

In the efflorescence of theory and scholarship on gender that has accompanied the feminist and gay movements of the last fifteen years, one strand of argument that has begun to seem important within the discourse of several disciplines has nevertheless remained mostly unarticulated and theoretically inchoate. That is the relation of same-sex bonds (and more specifically, the bonds of men with men) to the apportionment of power between the sexes. A literature and the beginnings of a theory and history of both lesbian and less sexualized female bonds are being composed and discovered; and the range of possible relations (subversive, directly oppositional, or even enforcing) between those bonds and the shape of the gender system as a whole is now a subject of active investigation. But the importance for women and for the gender system of the spectrum of relations between men themselves has received no correspondingly sustained attention, whether from feminist, gay male, or more traditional scholarship. Nevertheless, all those discourses are by now bristling with intimations that this complicated question is likely to prove quite important. For instance, Heidi Hartmann, one of the most influential of the contemporary feminist theorists, frames patriarchal power over women firmly in terms of bonds between men. She defines patriarchy itself as *"relations between men,* which have a material base, and which, though hierarchical, establish or create interdependence and solidarity among men that enable them to dominate women" (emphasis mine).

Perhaps the most powerful recent argument made through (and against) a traditional discipline that bears on these issues has occurred with anthropology. Based on readings and critiques of Lévi-Strauss and Engels, in addition to Freud and Lacan, Gayle Rubin has argued in an important essay ("The Traffic in Women: Notes Toward a Political Economy of Sex") that patriarchal heterosexuality can best be discussed in terms of one or another form of the traffic in women: it is the use of women as exchangeable, perhaps symbolic, property for the primary purpose of cementing the bonds of men with men. For example, Lévi-Strauss writes, "The total relationship of exchange which constitutes marriage is not established between a man and a woman, but between two groups of men, and the woman figures only as one of the objects in the exchange, not as one of the partners." Thus, Lévi-Strauss's normative heterosexual man uses a woman as a "conduit of a relationship" in which the true partner is a man. Rejecting Lévi-Strauss's celebratory treatment of this relegation of women, Rubin offers instead an array of tools for specifying and analyzing it. One of the consequences of her analysis which she does not examine is to suggest that male hetero- and homosexuality are potentially closer in structure than the common sense of our age perceives. Rubin seems to view patriarchal culture as necessarily homophobic, but the example of ancient Greece, for instance, suggests that in fact a seamless continuity among male bonds of genital homosexuality, mentorship, comradeship, the transmission of culture and power, *and* the traffic in women is possible under certain historical conditions. Even though modern Western culture has erected an almost insuperable barrier of homophobia between male genital bonds and the other, power-enforcing forms of "male bonding," it can be structurally illuminating to view the entire spectrum of male-to-male bonds as a potential whole. We seem to find it easier to view women's bonds in that way: the continuity of lesbianism with the other relationships by which women nurture, support, or protect the interests of women seems more immediately intelligible.

In this essay I will refer to the entire spectrum of same-sex bonds as "homosocial," reserving "homosexual" for those parts of the homosocial spectrum that seem most marked by genital sexuality. Using these terms, we can go beyond Rubin's account to hypothesize that in any male-dominated society, there is a special relationship between male homosocial (*including* homosexual) bonds and the institutions for maintaining and transmitting patriarchal power over women: a relationship founded on an inherent and potentially active structural congruence. For historical reasons, this special relationship may take the form of ideological homophobia, ideological homosexuality, or some highly conflicted but intensively structured combination of the two. I should make explicit that in positing this "special relationship" of structural congruence between patriarchy and male homosexuality, I am not arguing either that patriarchy is primarily or necessarily homosexual, or that male homosexual desire has a primary or necessary relationship to misogyny. Either of those arguments would be homophobic and, I believe, inexact. (Lesbianism also must always be in a special relation to patriarchy, but on different—sometimes opposite—grounds and working through different mechanisms.) There are several aspects of homosexual activity that vary across cultures and have changed radically within Western culture itself over the centuries. These aspects include frequency of occurrence, exclusivity, class associations, relation to the dominant culture, ethical status, and the degree to which homosexuality is seen as defining nongenital aspects of the lives of those who practice it. But perhaps the most radical historical change can be seen in homosexuality's association with what is considered femininity or masculinity in societies in which gender is a profound determinant of power. The "masculinity" of the homosexual orientation of male desire seemed as self-evident to the ancient Greeks, and perhaps to Whitman, for instance, as its effeminacy seems in contemporary popular culture. The importance of women (not merely of "the feminine" but of actual women as well) in the etiology and the continuing experience of male homosexuality is just as vexed a question as the importance of other men in male heterosexuality.

Some of Freud's writing on this subject begins to do justice to the complicated intertwining of gender identity and sexual choice, especially when refracted through late-twentieth-century lenses that de-emphasize his (often implicitly prescriptive) emphasis on development and fixation. An essay by Richard Klein offers an elegant summary of Freud's argument:

> In the normal development of the little boy's progress towards heterosexuality, he must pass, as Freud says with increasing insistence in late essays like "Terminable and Interminable Analysis," through the stage of the "positive" Oedipus, a homoerotic identification with his father, a position of effeminized subordination to the father, as a condition of finding a model for his own heterosexual role. Conversely, in this theory, the development of the male homosexual requires the postulation of the father's absence or distance and an abnormally strong identification by the child with the mother, in which the child takes the place of the father. There results from this scheme a surprising neutralization of polarities: heterosexuality in the male . . . presupposes a homosexual phase as the condition of its normal possibility: homosexuality, obversely, requires that the child experience a powerful heterosexual identification.

Thus Freud's "heterosexual," like the normative man in Rubin's reading of Lévi-Strauss, uses a woman as a conduit to a relationship with a man. At the same time, in Rubin's terms, the prudent man who is unwilling or unable to entrust his all-important link with patriarchal power to a powerless symbol, a woman, and who therefore makes the direct object-choice of a man, risks acting out the same powerless status in his own relations with patriarchy; he is feminized by his unmediated approach to male patriarchal power.

Freud's account of the effeminizing potential of desire for a woman and the masculinizing potential of subordination to a man is argumentatively powerful because its symmetry allows it to bring femininity and masculinity into a schematic relation. Its very symmetry introduces a potential for ahistorical blindness, however. Another powerfully symmetrical formulation, closely tied to Freud, offers an even clearer example of the dangers of abstracting desire from history. It is also—perhaps for the same reasons—one of the formulations that has been most productive in making Freud accessible to readers of novels.

René Girard's early book *Deceit, Desire, and the Novel* was both a reading of Freud and a schematization of the folk wisdom of erotic triangles. Through readings of major European fictions, Girard traced a calculus of power that was structured by the relation of rivalry between the two active members of an erotic triangle. What is most interesting for our purposes in his study is its insistence that, in any erotic rivalry, the bond that links the two rivals is as intense and potent as the bond that links either of the rivals to the beloved: that the bonds of "rivalry" and "love," differently as they are experienced, are equally powerful and in many senses equivalent. For instance, Girard finds many literary examples in which the choice of the beloved is determined in the first place, not by the qualities of the beloved, but by the beloved's already being the choice of the person who has been chosen as a rival. In fact, Girard seems to see the bond between rivals in an erotic triangle as being even stronger, a more important determinant of actions and choices, than anything in the bond between the lover and the beloved. And within the male-centered novelistic tradition of European high culture, the triangles Girard traces are most often those in which two males are rivals for a female; it is the bond between males that he most assiduously uncovers. Girard's argument suggests that rivalry is indeed one of the most important homosocial institutions for the male traffic in women. Girard's model has an additional, elegantly heuristic quality: to hypothesize that in all erotic triangles the homosexual pairing is as strongly charged as the two heterosexual ones sharpens our perception of an obvious symmetry—one woman involved with two men—by suggesting a hidden symmetry: one man involved with a woman and a man.

The index to Girard's book gives only two citations for "homosexuality" per se, and it is one of the strengths of his formulation not to depend on how homosexuality as an entity was perceived or experienced—indeed, on what was or was not considered *sexual*—at any given historical moment. As a matter of fact, the symmetry of his formulation always depends on suppressing the subjective, historically determined account of which feelings are or are not part of the body of "sexuality." The transhistorical clarity gained by this organizing device naturally has a cost, however. Gender and sexuality become known or recognized as such only within a larger productive process in which all human actions are to be codified and named. Recent gender theory and scholarship—the tradition from which our "homosocial spectrum" is drawn—all suggest, however, that the place of drawing the boundary between the sexual and the nonsexual, like the place of drawing the boundary between the realms of the two genders, is variable, but is not arbitrary. That is, the placement of the boundaries in a particular society affects not merely the definitions of those terms themselves—sexual/nonsexual, masculine/feminine—but also the apportionment of forms of power that are not obviously sexual. These include control over the means of production and reproduction of goods, persons, and meanings. So that Girard's account, which thinks it is describing a structural imperative of power abstracted from either the male/female or the sexual/nonsexual dichotomies, is leaving out of consideration categories that in fact preside over the distribution of power in every known society. And because the distribution of power according to these dichotomies is not and possibly cannot be symmetrical, the hidden symmetries that Girard's triangle helps us discover will always in turn discover hidden obliquities.

In principle, then, any male-centered literary text is likely to be about homosocial/homosexual as well as heterosexual object choices, and in this way about relations to patriarchal power. Dickens's *Our Mutual Friend* in particular emboldens one to make such a statement because it is thick almost to redundancy with themes associated with male homosexuality. It is by now a critical commonplace that *Our Mutual Friend* is the English novel that everyone knows is about anality—though to say so is, as we shall see, a kind of dodge. The inheritance at the center of the plot is immensely valuable real estate that contains a cluster of what Dickens calls "dust heaps." Layers of scholarly controversy have been devoted to the contents of Victorian dust heaps, and, led by Humphry House's *The Dickens World,* many critics have agreed that human excrement was an important (and financially valuable) component of the mounds. Such critics as Earle Davis, Monroe Engel, J. Hillis Miller, and Sylvia Bank Manning have given this thematic element a good deal of play, often, as F. S. Schwartzbach says, "with the intention of establishing whether Dickens did or did not understand Freud's later formulation of the psychic relation between human waste and money." But although many of those who write about Dickens's conjunction of excrement and money refer to Freud, sometimes by way of Norman O. Brown, most of the substance of Freud's (and Brown's) argument is missing from their accounts. Their point is most often far simpler and essentially moralistic: namely that money and excrement are alike because (more or less) they are worthless or bad. Thus Earle Davis writes:

> Economically speaking, [Dickens's] world could see no difference between unearned increment and diffused excrement. . . . [I]n every part of London he saw mankind straining and struggling over a dung heap. . . . His pen became an excretory organ sprouting out a sizzling cover for all the organic corruption which lay festering in the values that money set, the awful offal of Victorian standards.

Davis concludes his "post-Freudian" reading with the old favorite text of Chaucer's Pardoner: "At the bottom of all is money, the love of money at the cost of everything else. It is the overweening desire for money which lands most people in the filth of Hell." Perhaps it would be more precise, then, to say that *Our Mutual Friend* is the only English novel that everyone *says* is about excrement in order that they may *forget* that it is about anality. For the Freudian insights, elided in the critics' moralistic yoking of filth and lucre, are erotic ones. They are insights into the pleasures, desires, bonds, and forms of eros that have to do with the anus. And it is precisely the repression of these pleasures and desires that, in Freud, turns feces into filth and filth into gold. A novel about the whole issue of anal eroticism, and not merely a sanitized invective against money or "filthy lucre"—or what critics have come to call "the dust-money equation"—would have to concern itself with other elements in the chain Freud describes: love between man and man, for instance; the sphincter, its control, and the relation of these to sadism; the relations among bodily images, material accumulation, and economic status. It would also offer some intimations, at least, of adult genital desire and repression in relation to the anus. Furthermore it follows from what I have said so far that a novel that treated these issues would necessarily cast them in the mold of a particular, historical vision of society, class, power, money, and gender.

Is *Our Mutual Friend* such a novel? Yes, and richly so, although you would never know it from the critical tradition I have been summarizing. I do not mean that it is prophetic or merely prefigurative of Freud; the novel has its own labyrinths and explores its own narrative of the body. Indeed, although post-Freudian readers may find its genital allegory clearer in some respects (but factitiously so?) than Dickens's contemporaries did, we also lose something by reading it through the medium of the twentieth century and Freud. Dickens's economic and class awareness was of course more acute than Freud's—or than our own for that matter—and his argument about desire is more signally political than Freud's or, certainly, than that of most contemporary theorists of "desire." In another obvious way, we simply lose a certain perspective by our temporal distance and by the fact that our twentieth-century categories for certain acts (notably sexual ones) are often foreign to the way Dickens's readers might have categorized the same acts. Still, the novel itself tries to educate us in the terms by which to interpret it.

One curious thematic marker in the novel that has gone critically unnoticed, and that the novel itself tends to muffle, is a name. An important character in the novel chooses to call herself Jenny Wren, but we are told—just once—that that is not the name she was born with. Her real name is Fanny Cleaver. Unlike the later, funny, almost childishly deflationary name, Fanny Assingham, in *The Golden Bowl*, Fanny Cleaver is a name that hints at aggression—specifically at homosexual rape. The pun would seem a trivial accident, except that in Dickens names are not trivial accidents. In fact, the name is a small pointer to something much more striking: that there are two scenes in *Our Mutual Friend* whose language does indeed strongly suggest homosexual rape. These are Bradley Headstone's attack on Rogue Riderhood, discussed below, and the attack on John Harmon in chapter thirteen. Yet another "clue" functions at a different level to solicit the twentieth-century reader's attention to homosexual components in the book: one of the male protagonists lives in domestic happiness with another man, and at moments of particular intensity he says things like, "I love you, Mortimer."

In some sense, therefore, this must be a novel that delineates something close to the whole extent of the male homosocial spectrum, including elements of homosexual genitality. Just what version of male homosexuality most concerns it, however? The sweet avowal, "I love you, Mortimer," almost promises the impossible in the nineteenth-century English novel: homosexual love rendered in the absence of homophobia. At the same time, to give a woman a name like Fanny Cleaver suggests the opposite, and equally impossible: homophobia in the absence of homosexuality. And those golden dust heaps are the emblem of a wholly abstracted anality; they do not refer us to the anus of any particular person or persona. To understand the very excess, the supervisibility of homosexual thematics in this novel, requires us to see that for Dickens the dust heaps are inextricable from another preoccupation—that the erotic fate of every female or male is also cast in the terms and propelled by the forces of class and economic accumulation.

Let me begin by tracing a chain of Girardian triangles within one of the novel's plots, a chain reaching from the lowest class up to the professional class. It begins with the three members of the Hexam family: Gaffer Hexam, the father, an illiterate scavenger who makes his living by fishing corpses from the Thames and robbing them; Lizzie Hexam, his beautiful, good, and loyal daughter; and Charley Hexam, his son, whom Lizzie protects from their father's violent resentment until Charley is old enough to run away and go to school. These three comprise the first triangle.

Charley is determined and industrious enough to go from a Ragged School to a National School, where he becomes a pupil-teacher under the sponsorship of a young schoolmaster, Bradley Headstone. Bradley, like Charley, began as a pauper, and Dickens says, "regarding that origin of his, he was proud, moody, and sullen, desiring it to be forgotten." Yet an intense bond soon develops between the schoolmaster and young Charley. After the father's death, Bradley advises Charley to have no more to do with his impoverished, illiterate sister. Charley begs Bradley to come meet Lizzie first, however, and Bradley finds himself, as if by compulsion, violently in love with her.

The triangles of the Hexam family and of Charley, Lizzie, and Bradley are complicated by another triangle. Eugene Wrayburn, a young barrister

and one of the heroes of the novel, also falls in love with Lizzie. He, like
Bradley, has an intense encounter with Charley before meeting Lizzie,
although in this case the intensity takes the form of instant, almost allergic
dislike on both sides. And Eugene has another, apparently nontriangular,
love relationship—it is he who says, "I love you, Mortimer." Mortimer
Lightwood is an old friend and protégé of Eugene's from public school,
and the two, while making languid efforts to succeed in the law, make a
household together.

Already contrasts of class are appearing under the guise of contrasts
of personality and sexuality. One great evidence of class and control divides this little world in two as absolutely as gender does, though less permanently—that is the division of the literate from the illiterate. And after
Gaffer's early death, only one of these people—Lizzie, the desired
woman—remains illiterate. The quarrel between the schoolmaster and
Eugene is over who will teach her to read. But even within the masculine
world of literacy, the gradations of class are unforgiving. Charley's and
Bradley's relation to knowledge is always marked by the anxious, compulsive circumstances of its acquisition. Dickens says of the schoolmaster,

> From his early childhood up, his mind had been a place of mechanical
> stowage. . . . There was a kind of settled trouble in the face. It was
> the face belonging to a normally slow or inattentive intellect that had
> toiled hard to get what it had won, and that had to hold it now that it
> was gotten.

Bradley seems always to be in pain, "like . . . one who was being physically hurt, and was unwilling to cry out"; his infliction of pain on others
seems to come from even greater spasms of it within himself; talking to
Lizzie about his desire to teach her to read, for example, he seems to be
hemorrhaging internally: "He looked at Lizzie again, and held the look.
And his face turned from burning red to white, and from white back to
burning red, and so for the time to lasting deadly white." In fact, to borrow an image from a patient of Freud's, the schoolmaster behaves socially
like a man with a hungry rat in his bowels. And for him, the rat represents
not money but more specifically his small private capital of knowledge. Or
rather, it represents the alienation from himself of the profit of this knowledge. For the knowledge never makes *him* wiser; it is quite worthless outside the schoolroom, and it merely places him, more decisively even than
illiteracy would, in a particular, low position in the line of production of

labor for a capitalism whose needs now included a literate, rather than merely a massive, workforce. Bradley's one effort to invest his nest egg for his own profit—to teach Lizzie to read, as part of that triangular transaction with Charley—is imperiously overruled by Eugene, who wants to pay his own person to do the teaching. "Are you her schoolmaster as well as her brother's?" asks Eugene scornfully, and instead of using his name, will only call him "Schoolmaster." Bradley, as usual, loses control of his composure and complexion—for he is merely "used to the little audience of a school, and unused to the larger ways of men."

Eugene, on the other hand, though not wealthy, is a gentleman and a public-school boy. His relation to his own store of knowledge is the confident one of inconspicuous consumption. He can afford to be funny and silly. He likes to say things like "But then I mean so much that I—that I don't mean." Or:

> You know that when I became enough of a man to find myself an embodied conundrum, I bored myself to the last degree by trying to find out what I meant. You know that at length I gave it up, and declined to guess any more.

Mortimer sees him affectionately as "this utterly careless Eugene." He has no consciousness of knowledge, or even of power, as something to be struggled for, although his unconscious wielding of them makes him not only more lovable and relaxed than Bradley but also much more destructive. The moral ugliness of Eugene's taunts against the schoolmaster is always less striking, in the novel's presentation, than the unloveliness of the schoolmaster's anxiety and frustration. Bradley the pauper, thinking to make himself independent by his learning, finds that he has struggled himself into a powerless, alienating position in an impervious hierarchical economy. Eugene Wrayburn, imagining himself as marginal, passive, and unempowered in his relation to the economy, nevertheless speaks with the full-throated authority of a man near its very center.

Bradley's relationship with Charley and Eugene's with Mortimer differ on the basis of class, and the position of Lizzie in each relationship is accordingly different. Charley's offer of Lizzie to his schoolmaster represents the purest form of the male traffic in women. Charley explains it to Lizzie this way:

> "Then *I* come in. Mr. Headstone has always got me on, and he has a good deal in his power, and of course if he was my brother-in-law he

wouldn't get me on less, but would get me on more. Mr. Headstone
comes and confides in me, in a very delicate way, and says, 'I hope
my marrying your sister would be agreeable to you, Hexam, and
useful to you?' I say, 'There's nothing in the world, Mr. Headstone,
that I could be better pleased with.' Mr. Headstone says 'Then I may
rely upon your intimate knowledge of me for your good word with your
sister, Hexam?' And I say, 'Certainly, Mr. Headstone, and naturally I
have a good deal of influence with her.' So I have; haven't I, Liz?"

"Yes, Charley."

"Well said! Now you see, we begin to get on, the moment we begin
to be really talking it over, like brother and sister."

To Bradley, his triangle with Charley and Lizzie represents not access to power within the patriarchy but a dire sliding away from it; and
this is true whether one takes his desire for Lizzie or for Charley to represent the main erotic bond. No wonder he says to Lizzie, in an example of
his resentful style of courtship:

"You are the ruin—the ruin—the ruin—of me. . . . I have never
been quit of you since I first saw you. Oh, that was a wretched day for
me! That was a wretched, miserable day!"

No; the closest relation to patriarchal power for Bradley in this tangle
comes in the link of rivalry between himself and Eugene Wrayburn. And
it soon emerges that this is, indeed, for him, the focus of the whole affair.
In the painful scene with Lizzie I have been quoting, Bradley makes a
threat against Eugene, and when she responds indignantly, "He is nothing
to you, I think," he insists, "Oh yes he is. There you mistake. He is much
to me." What? she asks.

"He can be a rival to me *among other things.* . . . I knew all this
about Mr. Eugene Wrayburn, all the while you were drawing me to
you. . . . With Mr. Eugene Wrayburn in my mind, I went on. With
Mr. Eugene Wrayburn in my mind, I spoke to you just now. With
Mr. Eugene Wrayburn in my mind, I have been set aside and I have
been cast out." (emphasis mine)

After Lizzie has refused Bradley and left London, the desiring relationship between Bradley and Eugene, far from dissipating, becomes hotter
and more reciprocal. The schoolmaster decides—wrongly—that he can
find Lizzie by following Eugene everywhere he goes, and, Eugene says,

"I goad the schoolmaster to madness. . . . I tempt him on, all over London. . . . Sometimes, I walk; sometimes, I proceed in cabs, draining the pocket of the schoolmaster, who then follows in cabs. I study and get up abstruse No Thoroughfares in the course of the day [while Bradley is teaching]. With Venetian mystery I seek those No Thoroughfares at night, glide into them by means of dark courts, tempt the schoolmaster to follow, turn suddenly, and catch him before he can retreat. Then we face one another, and I pass him as unaware of his existence, and he undergoes grinding torments. . . . Thus I enjoy the pleasures of the chase. . . . just now I am a little excited by the glorious fact that a southerly wind and a cloudy sky proclaim a hunting evening."

In Surtees's *Handley Cross,* Mr. Jorrocks declaims that "'Unting" is "the image of war without its guilt, and only five-and-twenty per cent. of its danger," but it is less lucky than that for the men who are caught up in this chase. One day on a towpath Bradley attacks Eugene from behind; the two men struggle in an embrace, and Eugene, both arms broken, nearly drowns. Soon after that, another man, a lockkeeper with the sinister and important name Rogue Riderhood, who has been dogging and blackmailing Bradley Headstone, finds himself, too, attacked from behind. This is one of the scenes whose language is that of homosexual rape:

> Bradley had caught him round the body. He seemed to be girdled with an iron ring. . . . Bradley got him round, with his back to the Lock, and still worked him backward. . . . "I'll hold you living, and I'll hold you dead! Come down!"
>
> Riderhood went over into the smooth pit, backward, and Bradley Headstone upon him. When the two were found, lying under the ooze and scum behind one of the rotting gates, Riderhood's hold had relaxed, probably in falling, and his eyes were staring upward. But, he was girdled still with Bradley's iron ring, and the rivets of the iron ring held tight.

Sphincter domination is Bradley Headstone's only mode of grappling for the power that is continually flowing away from him. Unfortunately for him, sphincter control can't give him any leverage at all with women, certainly not with Lizzie, who simply never engages with him, who eludes him from the start. It only succeeds in grappling more closely to him men who have already been drawn into a fascinated mirroring relation to him—Eugene, with whom he has been engaged in that reversible hunt, and Rogue Riderhood, in whose clothing he had disguised himself for the assault on Eugene. His initial hating terror of Lizzie was a terror of, as he kept putting it, being "drawn" from himself, having his accumulated value sucked from him down into the great void of her illiteracy and powerlessness. But, classically, he is the man who, fearing to entrust his relations with patriarchy to a powerless counter, a woman, can himself only be used as a woman, and valued as a woman, by the men with whom he comes into narcissistic relation.

In the novel's social mapping of the body, Bradley, like some other figures at the lower end of the respectable classes, powerfully represents the repressive divorce of the private thematics of the anus from the social forces of desire and pleasure. Dickens does precede Freud, Norman O. Brown, and Deleuze/Guattari, among others, in seeing digestion and the control of the anus as the crucial images for the illusion of economic individualism: "The first organ to be privatised, to be excluded from the social field," Deleuze/Guattari remark in *Anti-Oedipus*, "was the anus. It gave privatisation its model." One thematic portrayal of this exclusion is a splitting of the body between twin images of a distended gut and a distended disembodied head. Bradley Headstone (and note his name), the most wrackingly anal of the characters, also appears repeatedly as a floating "haggard head in the air"; Mr. Venus, a taxidermist and articulator of skeletons, with his shop full of hydrocephalic babies in jars, is himself given to "floating his powerful mind in tea"; illiterate "Noddy" Boffin dandles the head of his walking stick at his ear like the head of a floating "familiar spirit" or baby, and himself seems to turn into a great heavy-headed puppet at the end of the novel; and so on. The unanxious version of *homo digestivus* is the "hideous solidity" that the firmly bourgeois Podsnaps and their circle share with their "corpulent straddling" tableware:

> Everything said boastfully, "Here you have as much of me in my ugliness as if I were only lead; but I am so many ounces of precious metal worth so much an ounce; wouldn't you like to melt me down?". . . . All the big silver spoons and forks widened the mouths of the company expressly for the purpose of thrusting the sentiment down their throats with every morsel they ate. The majority of the guests were like the plate.

This strain of imagery, of course, culminates in the monstrous dust-heaps themselves. In short, one thing that goes on when the human body is taken as a capitalist emblem is that the relation of parts to wholes becomes problematic; there is no intelligible form of circulation; the parts swell up with accumulated value, they take on an autonomous life of their own, and eventually power comes to be expressed as power over reified doubles fashioned in one's own image from the waste of one's own body. Power is held over dolls, puppets, and articulated skeletons, over the narcissistic, singular, nondesiring phantoms of individuality.

For Bradley Headstone, anxiety, toil, dissociation, and a crippling somatic self-consciousness mark the transition into respectability, and make heavy and humiliating work of his heterosexual involvement. How differently they manage these things in the upper classes. While Bradley's intentions toward Lizzie, however uneasy, had been strictly honorable, Eugene Wrayburn has no intentions toward her at all. Mortimer asks him,

> "Eugene, do you design to capture and desert this girl?"
> "My dear fellow, no."
> "Do you design to marry her?"
> "My dear fellow, no."
> "Do you design to pursue her?"
> "My dear fellow, I don't design anything. I have no design what-soever. I am incapable of designs. If I conceived a design, I should speedily abandon it, exhausted by the operation."

This is the opposite of Bradley's compulsive, grasping relation to power. Eugene sees himself as a little leaf borne upon a stream, and an image that is often associated with him is the pretty river that supplies power to the papermill where Lizzie finally finds work. But Eugene's lack of will is enormously more potent than Bradley's clenched, entrapping will, simply because the powerful, "natural" trajectory of this stream is eternally to-ward swelling the exploitive power of ruling-class men over working-class women. Resolute and independent as Lizzie is, weak and passive as he is, Eugene barely has to make a decision, much less form a design, in order to ruin her.

> The rippling of the river seemed to cause a correspondent stir in his uneasy reflections. He would have laid them asleep if he could, but they were in movement, like the stream, and all tending one way with a strong current. . . . "Out of the question to marry her," said Eugene, "and out of the question to leave her."

It is traditional, in criticism of *Our Mutual Friend*, to distinguish two groups of thematic imagery, that surrounding the river and that surrounding the dust-heaps. If, as I have suggested, the dust-heaps can be said to represent an anthropomorphization of capital that is most closely responsive to the anxieties of the petite bourgeoisie, then the river, in a sense, offers a critique of that in terms of a more collectively-scaled capitalism, organized around alienation and the flow of currency. Its gender implications are pointed and odd: all the men in this waterside novel are strikingly incompetent about the water; there are seven drownings or near-drownings, all of them males; men are always dragging each other into the river; and only one person, Lizzie, has the skill to navigate a rescue. At the same time, women are in control only in correctly understanding the current of power as always flowing away from themselves. Gazing into the river, both Lizzie and Eugene read in it the image of Lizzie's inability to resist ruin.

Just as Eugene's higher status enables his heterosexual relationship to be at once more exploitive and less guilty than Bradley's, so his desiring relationship with a man can be at once more open and much less embroiled in repressive conflict than any of Bradley's. Interestingly, though it is more open, it also seems much less tinged with the sexual. Imagery of the sphincter, the girdle, the embrace, the "iron ring" of the male grasp, was salient in those murderous attacks on men by Bradley Headstone. By contrast it is utterly absent from the tenderer love between Eugene and Mortimer. They live together like Bert and Ernie on "Sesame Street"—and who ever wonders what Muppets do in bed? This thematic reticence—if it is reticence—in contrast to the hypersaturation with homosexual thematics of Bradley's part of the story, can perhaps best be accounted for not by some vague invocation of "Victorian prudery," but by thinking about how the libidinal careers of Victorian gentlemen were distinguished, in fiction and in ideology at any rate, from those of males of higher and lower class.

The obstacles to mapping this territory have been suggested earlier in this essay. The historical research on primary sources that would add texture and specificity to generalizations is only beginning to be done, or at any rate published. At the same time, the paradigms available for understanding the history of sexuality are in rapid (and productive) flux. The best that I can attempt here is perhaps to lay out in a usefully codified form what the "common sense" or "common knowledge" of the (essentially middle-class) Victorian reader of novels might likely have been, buttressed by some evidence from biographies. I wish to make clear how tentative and how thoroughly filtered through the ideological lens of middle-class literature these generalizations are, but still to make them available for revision by other scholars.

With respect to homosocial/homosexual style, it seems to be possible to divide Victorian men among three rough categories according to class. The first includes aristocratic men and small groups of their friends and dependents, including bohemians and prostitutes; for these people, in 1865, a distinct homosexual role and culture seem already to have been in existence in England for several centuries. This milieu, at once courtly and in touch with the criminal, seems to have constituted a genuine subculture, facilitated in the face of an ideologically hostile dominant culture by money, privilege, internationalism, and, for the most part, the ability to command secrecy. Pope's lines on Sporus in the *Epistle to Dr. Arbuthnot* do, however, presuppose his audience's knowledge that such a role and culture exist, as does Wollstonecraft's condemnation of it in her *Vindication of the Rights of Woman*. This role is closely related to—is in fact, through Oscar Wilde, the antecedent of—the particular stereotype that at least until recently has characterized American middle-class gay homosexuality; its strongest associations are with effeminacy, transvestism, promiscuity, prostitution, continental European culture, and the arts.

For classes below the nobility, however, there seems in the nineteenth century not to have been an association of a particular personal style with the genital activities now thought of as "homosexual." The class of men about which we know most—the educated middle class, the men who produced the novels and journalism and who are the subjects of the biographies—operated sexually in what seems to have been a cognitive vacuum. A gentleman (I will use the word "gentleman" to distinguish the educated bourgeois from the aristocrat as well as from the working-class man—a usage that accords, not with Victorian ideology, but with Victorian practice) had a good deal of objective sexual freedom, especially if he were single, having managed to evade the great cult of the family and, with it, much of the enforcing machinery of his class and time. At the same time, he seems not to have had easy access to the alternative subculture, the stylized discourse, or the sense of immunity of the aristocratic/bohemian sexual minority. So perhaps it is not surprising that the sexual histories of English gentlemen, unlike those of men above and below them socially, are so marked by a resourceful, makeshift, *sui generis* quality, in their denials, their rationalizations, their fears and guilts, their sublimations, and their quite various genital outlets alike.

Biographies of English gentlemen of the nineteenth and early twentieth centuries are full of oddities, surprises, and apparent false starts. They seem to have no predetermined sexual trajectory. Good examples include Lewis Carroll, Charles Kingsley, John Ruskin, and, a little later, T. E. Lawrence, James M. Barrie, T. H. White, and J. R. Ackerley (who describes in an autobiography how he moved from a furtive, promiscuous homosexuality to a fifteen-year-long affair of the heart with a female dog). The sexuality of a single gentleman was silent, tentative, protean, and divorced from expectations of genre, though not of gender. In fiction, a thematically tamer but structurally interesting and (very often) emotionally turbid and preoccupying relationship was common between single middle-class men: Pendennis and Warrington, Clive Newcome and J. J. Ridley, the two Armadales of Collins's *Armadale*, the gentlemen of the Pickwick Club, all resemble Eugene and Mortimer in the lack of remark surrounding their union and in the shadowy presence of a mysterious imperative (physical debility, hereditary curse, secret unhappy prior marriage, or simply extreme disinclination) that bars at least one of the partners in each union forever from marriage.

Of the sexuality of English people below the middle class, reliable accounts are difficult to assemble. Both aristocratic and (in the early twentieth century) middle-class English male homosexuality seem to have been organized to a striking degree around the objectification of proletarian men, as we read in accounts by or of Forster, Isherwood, Ackerley, Edward Carpenter, Tom Driberg, and others. At the same time, there is no evidence from these middle-class-oriented accounts of a homosexual role or subculture indigenous to men of the working class, apart from their sexual value to more privileged men. It is possible that for the great balance of the non–public-school-educated classes, overt homosexual acts may have been recognized mainly as instances of violence: English law before the Labouchère amendment of 1885 did not codify or criminalize most of the spectrum of the male bodily contacts, so that homosexual acts would more often have become legally visible for the violence that may have accompanied them than for their distinctively sexual content. In middle-class accounts of the working class, at any rate, and possibly within the working class itself, there seems to have been an association between male homosexual genitality and violence, as in Dickens's treatment of Bradley Headstone's anal eroticism in terms exclusively of murder and mutilation.

Since most Victorians neither named nor recognized a syndrome of male homosexuality as our society thinks of it, the various classes probably grouped this range of sexual activities under various moral and psychological headings. I have suggested that the working class may have grouped it with violence. In aristocrats—or, again, in aristocrats as perceived by the middle class—it came under the heading of dissolution, at the very time when dissolution was itself becoming the (wishful?) bourgeois-ideological name for aristocracy itself. In Victorian novels almost all profligate young lords share the traits of the Sporus-like aristocratic homosexual "type," and it is impossible to predict from their feckless, "effeminate" behavior whether their final ruin will be the work of male favorites, female favorites, the racecourse, or the bottle; waste and wastage is the presiding category of scandal.

Fictional examples of this ambiguous style include Lord Frederick Verisopht (with his more "masculine," less aristocratic sidekick, Sir Mulberry Hawk) in *Nicholas Nickleby;* Count Fosco, (with his more "masculine," less aristocratic sidekick, Sir Percival Glyde) in *The Woman in White;* Lord Porlock, in *The Small House at Allington* and *Doctor Thorne;* in a more admiring version, Patrick, Earl of Desmond (with his more "masculine," less aristocratic sidekick, Owen Fitzgerald) in Trollope's *Castle Richmond;* and Lord Nidderdale (with Dolly Longstaffe) in *The Way We Live Now.* In each case there is explicit mention of only female erotic objects, if any, but in each case the allegedly vicious or dissolute drive seems more visibly directed at a man in more immediate proximity. Perhaps the most overtly sympathetic—at any rate the least grotesque, the closest to "normal"-seeming—of the men in this category is also one who is without a title, although within the context of the novel he represents the vitiated line of a rural aristocracy. That is Harold Transome, in *Felix Holt.* To his sexual history we receive three clues, each tantalizing in its own way: we hear—mentioned once, without elaboration—that the woman he had married in his Eastern travels was one whom he had bought as a slave; we hear—mentioned once, without elaboration—that he has brought a (different) woman back with him from the East. But the person of whom we hear incessantly in connection with Harold is his plangent, ubiquitous manservant-companion:

"I don't know whether he's most of a Jew, a Greek, an Italian, or a Spaniard. He speaks five or six languages, one as well as another. He's cook, valet, major-domo, and secretary all in one; and what's more, he's an affectionate fellow. . . . That's a sort of human specimen that doesn't grow here in England, I fancy. I should have been badly off if I could not have brought Dominic."

Throughout a plot elaboration that depends heavily on the tergiversations of a slippery group of servants-who-are-not-quite-servants, who have unexplained bonds from the past with Dominic, one waits for the omniscient, serviceable, ingratiating character of Dominic to emerge into its full sinisterness or glamor or sexual insistence—in vain, since the exploitive "oriental" luxuries of his master can be perceived only in a sexually irresolute blur of "decadence." Perhaps similarly, the lurid dissipations of the characters in *The Picture of Dorian Gray* are presented in heterosexual terms when detailed at all, even though (biographical hindsight aside) the triangular relationship of Basil, Dorian, and Lord Henry makes sense only in homosexual terms.

Between the extremes of upper-class male homosocial desire, grouped with dissipation, and working-class male homosocial desire, grouped apparently with violence, the view of the gentleman, the public-school product, was different again. School itself was, of course, a crucial link in ruling-class male homosocial formation. Disraeli (who was not himself an Etonian) offers the flattering ideological version of Eton friendships in *Coningsby*:

At school, friendship is a passion. It entrances the being; it tears the soul. All loves of after life can never bring its rapture, or its wretchedness; no bliss so absorbing, no pangs of jealousy or despair so crushing and so keen! What tenderness and what devotion; what illimitable confidence; what infinite revelations of inmost thoughts; what ecstatic present and romantic future; what bitter estrangements and what melting reconciliations; what scenes of wild recrimination, agitating explanations, passionate correspondence; what insane sensitiveness, and what frantic sensibility; what earthquakes of the heart, and whirlwinds of the soul, are confined in that simple phrase—a school-boy's friendship!

Candid accounts seem to agree that in most of the public schools the whirlwinds of the soul were regularly acted out in the flesh. Like the young aristocrat, the young gentleman at those same public schools would have seen or engaged in a variety of sexual activities among males. But unlike the aristocrat, the gentleman found neither a community nor a shared, distinctive sexual identity ready for adults who wanted more of the same. A twentieth-century writer, Michael Nelson, reports asking a school friend, "Have you ever had any homosexual inclinations since leaving Eton?" "I say, steady on," his friend replies. "It's all right for fellows to mess one another about a bit at school. But when we grow up we put aside childish things, don't we?"

David Copperfield, among other books, makes the same point. David's infatuation with his friend Steerforth, who calls him "Daisy" and treats him like a girl, is simply part of David's education—though another, later part is the painful learning of how to triangulate from Steerforth onto women, and finally, although incompletely, to hate Steerforth and grow at the expense of his death. In short, a gentleman will associate the erotic end of the homosocial spectrum, not with dissipation, not with viciousness or violence, but with childishness, as an infantile need, a mark of powerlessness which, while it may be viewed with shame or scorn or denial, is unlikely to provoke the virulent, accusatory projection that characterizes twentieth-century homophobia.

This slow, distinctive, two-stage progression from schoolboy desire to adult homophobia seems to take its structure from the distinctive anxieties that came with being educated for the relatively new class of middle-class "gentlemen." Unlike title, wealth, or land, the terms that defined the gentleman were not clearly and simply hereditary but had somehow to be earned by being a particular kind of person who spent time and money in particular ways. But the early prerequisites for membership in this powerful but nebulous class—to speak with a certain accent, to spend years translating Latin and Greek, to leave family and the society of women—all made one unfit for any other form of work, long before they entitled one to chance one's fortune actively in the ruling class.

The action of *Our Mutual Friend* brings to a close that long abeyance in Eugene's life between, so to speak, being *called* and being *chosen* for the professional work of empire. (For instance, he has been called to the Bar, but no one has yet chosen to employ him.) His position is awash with patriarchal authority, the authority of the law itself, but none of it belongs to him yet. In just the same way, having been removed from the family as a child, he will soon be required to return—and in the enforcing position of paterfamilias, a position that will lend a retroactive meaning and heterosexual trajectory to his apparently aimless courtship of Lizzie. In the violence at the end of the novel, we see the implacability with which this heterosexual, homophobic meaning is impressed on Eugene's narrative: Bradley, his rival, nearly kills him by drowning; Lizzie saves him; while he seems to be dying, Mortimer interprets his last wishes as being that he might marry Lizzie; and when he comes back to life, he is already a married man. "But would you believe," Lizzie asks afterwards, "that on our wedding day he told me he almost thought the best thing he could do, was to die?"

There is one character to whom this homophobic reinscription of the bourgeois family is even more crippling than it is to Eugene, who already, by the end of the novel, looks almost "as though he had never been mutilated." That person is, of course, Lizzie. The formal, ideological requirements for a fairytale "happy ending" for her are satisfied by the fact that she is not "ruined" by Eugene, not cast into the urban underclass of prostitution, but raised up into whatever class the wife of a Victorian barrister belongs to. Eugene is determined to fight for his right to have her regarded as a lady. But with all that good news, Dickens makes no attempt to disguise the terrible diminution in her personal stature as she moves from being the resentful, veiled, muscular, illiterate figure rowing a scavenger boat on the Thames, to being a factory worker in love, to being Mrs. Eugene Wrayburn *tout court*. Admittedly, Lizzie has been a reactionary all along. But she has been a blazing, courageous reactionary: she has defended and defied her violent father; she has sacrificed everything for her beastly brother; she gave up a chance to form an alliance with an older woman, a tavern-keeper, just because the woman would not accept her father; she took off for the countryside to save her honor from the man she loved; and she unhesitatingly risked her life to save his life. But all her reactionary courage meets with a stiflingly reactionary reward. Lizzie stops being Lizzie once she is Mrs. Eugene Wrayburn.

As we see how unrelentingly Lizzie is diminished by her increasingly distinct gender assignment, it becomes clearer why "childishness," rather than "femininity," should at that moment have been the ideological way the ruling class categorized its own male homosexuality. As Jean Baker Miller points out in *Toward a New Psychology of Women*, an attribution of gender difference marks a structure of permanent inequality, while the relation between adult and child is the prototype of the temporary inequality that in principle—or in ideology—exists only in order to be overcome: children are supposed to grow up into parents, but wives are not supposed to grow up into husbands. Now the newly significant class of "gentlemen," the flagship class of high capitalism, was to include a very wide range of status and economic position, from plutocrats down to impoverished functionaries. In order to maintain the illusion of equality, or at any rate of meritocratic pseudoequality, *within* the class of gentlemen, and at the same time justify the magnification of distinctions within the class, it clearly made sense to envision a long, complicated period of individual psychic testing and preparation, full of fallings-away, redefinitions, and crossings and recrossings of lines of identification. This protracted, baffling narrative of the self, the direct forerunner of the twentieth-century Oedipal narrative, enabled the process of social and vocational sorting to occur under the less invidious shape of different rates of individual maturation.

Not until this psychologistic, "developmental" way of thinking had been firmly established was the aristocratic link between male homosexuality and "femininity" allowed to become an article of wide public consumption—a change that was crystallized in the Wilde affair and that coincided (in the 1890s) with the beginnings of a dissemination across classes of language about male homosexuality (e.g., the word "homosexual"), and with the medicalization of homosexuality through an array of scientific "third sex" and "intersex" theories.

But during all this time, for women, the immutability of gender inequality was being inscribed more and more firmly, moralistically, and descriptively in the structure of every bourgeois institution. As the contrasting bodily images in *Our Mutual Friend* suggest, woman's deepening understanding, as she sees the current flowing away under her own image, comes for the most part at the cost of renouncing individual ownership and accumulation. The division of cognitive labor that emerges with the bourgeois family is not a means of power for women, but another part of the edifice of master-slave subordination to men. Woman perceives the triangular path that enforces patriarchal power as being routed through her, but never ending in her; while capitalist man, with his prehensile, precapitalist image of the body, is always deluded about what it is that he pursues, and in whose service. His delusion is, however, often indistinguishable from real empowerment; and indeed it is blindest, and closest to this empowerment, in his triangular transactions through women with other men.

Plate Glass

RICHARD SENNETT

THE SKYSCRAPER should be fatally attractive to suicides; the tall buildings thrust up into nothingness, their very height creating an abyss below. Plate glass, however, is the great modern protection against suicide and lesser acts of spontaneity. Smashing a window of plate glass is hard work; unscrewing the glass from its metal frame requires patience and steady hands. A person who suddenly feels he has had enough might press his face yearningly against the glass, yet he is protected by a material which lets him see everything inaccessible to desire.

This is the centenary of the birth of Ludwig Mies van der Rohe, the architect who did more than anyone else to make plate glass the material through which our century defines the relation between inner and outer— the outside entirely visible from within, yet hermetically sealed off. It was Mies who in 1921 conceived an office building for the Friedrichstrasse in Berlin entirely sheathed in glass, Mies who a year later built a model of a glass tower whose walls were not straight sides but billowing curves and folds, thus converting the metaphor of a "curtain wall" into a literal if ideal vision of curtains of glass rising forty stories into the air. It was Mies who, exiled to Chicago in 1939, began to build these ideal visions of glass in that city where Sullivan's skyscrapers, with their inner glass atriums, had already suggested that the transparency of a window might be extended to the transparency of an entire wall, from which it was only a logical next step to an entire tower that might become transparent. And of course it is Mies, the archon of modernism, who is now accused of fathering a soulless environment of glass towers in which men and women are as cut off from one another as from the outside, an architecture if not of suicide, at least of despair.

Manufactured glass is at least four thousand years old, but not until the Christian era did men learn how to make it transparent; they discovered transparency through experiments in heating and cooling the mixture of soda and lime which is simple glass. Not until 1676 was it known how to alter the properties of glass by changing the very materials of which it could be made. In that year the British chemist George Ravenscroft replaced the soda lime mixture by a lead alkali one. This glass, which we use still for fine crystal objects, had far greater transparency and strength than soda lime glass, but it was much too expensive for windows. The older glass cost little to make but broke easily when cast in large panes. Until quite recently, then, the visual experience of joining inside and outside was a matter either of direct exposure, through an open window, or of looking through an often ripply material cut into small pieces and framed in wood or metal. Fully apprehending the outside from within, yet feeling neither cold nor wind nor moisture, is a modern sensation.

Toward the end of the eighteenth century, the technology was perfected for reliably producing sheet glass, thanks to the use of cast-iron rollers for smoothing. Windows in all kinds of structures could now be made larger, but in the nineteenth century truly radical glass architecture appeared in two special building forms—the greenhouse and the arcade.

Greenhouses like those Joseph Paxton built for the Duke of Devonshire at Chatsworth, which we know only from drawings and photographs, or Kew Gardens, or the Jardin des Plantes, are extraordinary buildings. The dappling play of light and shadow in these enormous glass halls, as clouds pass, as time passes, make space into action. The rooms constantly change their form, just as a stage is transformed through lighting, but here there is no sense of artifice; the sunlight alone does the work. Or rather, there is an artifice which does not register on our senses as a stage set because all the actors here are plants: the nineteenth-century greenhouse abolished the distinction between inside and outside, in terms of light, while radically controlling this barrier in terms of heat, the penetration of smoke, or whatever, permitting an experience of walking outside and inside simultaneously, which remains as magical to us as it was to the Victorians.

Moreover, glass created a more obvious drama, a drama of scale. A building sheathed in iron-framed glass radically reduced the cost of building big and also cut the time necessary for construction. Kew Gardens outside London and the Jardin des Plantes in Paris rose in a fraction of the time required to build St. Paul's or the Madeleine. Thus architects accomplished a division of the senses in buildings whose scale had before only been seen in cathedrals or the palaces of kings.

Glass was the material which overcame men's sense of great space as difficult to enclose. The material was used more tentatively, however, in dwellings for human beings. This ambivalence appeared in the arcades. With the prominent exception of the Galerie d'Orleans in the Palais-Royal, most of the nineteenth-century arcades are ordinary stone or brick buildings shoved close together, the space between them roofed over by glass. The great exhibition structures, like the Crystal Palace in London, or the Palais de l'Exposition in Paris, were, however, designed as temporary structures. To *live*, exposed to the outside, seemed akin to walking around naked, not an appealing condition to our Victorian forebears. This is why they used glass less freely than their technology permitted, even in factories or offices. And indeed there is an inherent Victorian logic to their deferral in constructing glass houses until the elevator, the steel skeleton, and the other technological advances of the late nineteenth century ensured that exposure would take place far above the ground, up in the sky, where no one could see it. Indeed, neither Mies in his Berlin days nor Corbusier dreaming at the same time of his Ville Radieuse imagined the towers, manufactured by machine entirely of man-made materials, would so thicken and reproduce themselves mechanically in cities, crowding close together. Instead Mies usually drew his earlier towers as single structures alone on the horizon, places where "up" meant "alone"; up and alone, visibility entailed no risk.

Can one blame Mies for not understanding the rules of industrial multiplication? Is he accountable for all these illegitimate offspring? Perhaps, but imitation is a form of homage hard to forbid. A better question is whether Mies understood the cultural implications of the tool he wielded so much more gracefully than others. The answer, I think, is that he did not.

The architecture of Mies van der Rohe is an architecture of decree. Its grace and harmony depend on finely calculated balances, on the exact placement of furniture (his own, naturally), the presence or absence of paintings, the textures and colors of rugs. His work is unlike that of Frank Lloyd Wright, who also designed his own furniture as an integral part of his architecture. If you can get away with it, try moving the furniture around in a Wright room; you find you can do so without affecting the sense of volume or the play of wall planes; in a Mies room, the least change of the position of a chair alters how big the room feels, or the proportions of wall to floor.

Mies's architecture makes the esthetics of the whole depend on one man's absolute control of the parts. Delicate and graceful a dictator as Mies is, his esthetic blinded him intellectually to the consequences of glass. He decreed that large sheets of glass would dissolve the distinction between inner and outer in his buildings. Transparent equals visually nonexistent. Yet we know that the suicide's dilemma, when one day on the fortieth floor his family and his failed novel seem too much for him, is but an extreme version of the problem others have with sealed glass walls. We see the division of people from their environment. There is the man who sees from his office window a tree blowing in the wind but cannot hear the wind blowing. Or observe people working in Detroit's Renaissance Center (a very bad pastiche of the wavy glass tower Mies conceived in 1922): during the course of a day they labor steadily, unruffled because insulated from the sound of police sirens continually wailing in the streets below. Or again, think of the barrier of transparency embodied in plate glass shop windows ensuring that an object for sale cannot be touched. This division of the physical senses that began in the Victorian greenhouse has become absolute, sight now insulated in its operations from sound, smell, and touch. In the case of Mies's own architecture, this division of the senses is carried a step further: his space is immobilized in time, since in it nothing can be moved once it is designed. Here Mies's work contrasts with the Victorian greenhouse, where light created motion; but it's hardly a change for the better. Mies decreed the unity of space; like all the members of the Bauhaus, "unity" and "wholeness" were for him compelling ideals, but he fell victim to his own purity.

Why? A philosophic friend might have whispered to Mies that to join any two conditions, you must also make their differences significant: to exclaim how wonderfully unobstructed a view is, you must first establish visible boundaries between inside and outside. But Mies would not have listened to such a philosophic friend; he was as indifferent to philosophy as he was to politics, an isolated man quite content to make an architecture of isolation. Mies believed that visual thinking involved laws unto itself; speculation of the sort Breuer or Gropius dabbled in seemed to him a distraction from drawing.

Whatever the importance of these personal limits, there are larger reasons why Mies failed. These have to do with a failure of historical imagination. They apply not just to a single genius but to inferior architects who are creating for us an environment of isolation without any redeeming elegance.

The architects of Mies's generation proclaimed an abyss between their own work and that of the past, thanks in part to their ability to use materials like plate glass as they had never been used before. This conviction of an abyss between modernism and the past was false—an observation about modern art in general which has become something of a cliché. But architecture is a special case. Having failed to learn their own place in history, the Miesian modernists were condemned to repeat history. The plate glass canyons on Park Avenue in New York or on the Ginza in Tokyo embody one of the great Romantic dramas of social thought: that of making sense of the incommensurate relationship between the human spirit—the soul—and the world around it. The acerbic, determinedly modern and tough-minded Mies would have smiled at the very mention of the word *soul*. Yet the Romantic philosophers were preoccupied with why and how spiritual life had become divorced from the physical environment. Mies's work shows what this divorce looks like, even though he imagined he was in marital bliss.

In the writing of Hegel, for instance, we find the philosopher worrying about the kind of space Mies would later build. Hegel believed that a soul divorced from the world would yet clearly see the shapes and movements of things and other men; the spirit would observe physical reality without participating in it. This, Hegel says, is the most primitive social condition we can imagine, the most animal reality. In it there are no illusions, no myths; human animals scan each other as they scan the horizon for danger, trying to see everything but feeling no desire to reach out to the other animals. A man in this condition would look about him without wonder or confusion; his hunter's sight would be unclouded—unclouded, say, by the sense of a destiny to be shared with the other animals. The illusion of a common destiny must await a later stage of spiritual evolution, when the discovery of one's own loneliness has clouded the watchful eye.

Throughout the *Phenomenology of the Spirit* Hegel sought for visual images to express the state of primitive spiritual life and its evolution. Plate glass was not yet available to him for this imagery, but another celebrated philosophic material was. This was, of course, the wall of Plato's cave. The denizens of the cave are undeveloped spiritually; they lack knowledge, and so they mistake the character of the visible world, imagining shadows thrown by firelight on the cave's wall to possess reality, an entire world before them of flickering phantoms which they think are solid. These drudges are literally afflicted by mysterious darkness. In the parable of the cave, Plato argued that the more knowledge men have, the clearer are the operations of their senses; visibility, clarity, and truth are inseparable. Hegel set himself against this eminently logical and organic view of the relations between mind and body. Relations between the physical and the spiritual seemed to him more perverse. The eyes of the primitive see everything; his are scanning eyes, measuring eyes, but he has no desire to share, to speak, and so he cannot collaborate with others to change the world he sees. Visibility and passivity conjoin: this is what Hegel feared in the divorce of spirit from world. There will be no mystery, and no experience, for one who coolly takes the measure of everything.

Sometimes Hegel called the creature in this condition a scientist; more often a slave; never, to my knowledge, an architect. But then, though Hegel wrote interestingly on some aspects of classical architecture, he died before modern architecture was announced. Perhaps these few remarks make clear why that announcement seems to me so suspicious. Far from breaking with the nineteenth century, our architecture embodies in glass and concrete and steel the fear which many philosophers influenced by Hegel had of spiritual emptiness. This fear wasn't frivolous or empty; following Hegel, they defined spiritual emptiness as a life in which sense data cannot be transmuted into social communication, a condition we can see in walking around the center of any modern city. Or more generously, we might say Mies converted into the most exquisite visual form the Romantic philosopher's fear of slavery, the slavery of being pent-up inside yet knowing the outer world, a prison without bars or even walls.

It's easy to reduce this connection between modernism and Romantic social thought to clichés like the "new Brutalism." What if we took the connection more seriously? In other words, what does it matter that, far from being as advertised, the architecture inspired by plate glass draws us into the spiritual problems of an earlier age? Once we connect these buildings with their cultural past, the enormous body of Romantic writing on solitude seems less a matter for smiles and indulgence. The practical problem of urban design now is how men and women can cope with the solitude imposed upon them by modernism. The Romantics knew more about it than we do; solitude had not yet been reduced to a badge of honor for the alienated or a wound to be treated by collective compulsion.

The glass world imposes solitude upon its habitants: if I put the matter thus, I write just another crude cliché. For glass has to be used in a certain way to arouse a sense of lonely space. Think of the glass houses built by Phillip Johnson and the glass house built in America by Mies. There is an immense difference between the domestic structures of the two architects, though the form—the glass box—seems virtually identical. The glass boxes of Phillip Johnson (his own in Connecticut, or an earlier glass house in Cambridge, Massachusetts) sit directly on the ground, the floor plane and the ground virtually continuous. The Cambridge house forms one side of a rectangular courtyard, the other three sides enclosed by a high fence, the court paved, its edges planted; the inside of the house achieves a real unity with this protected exterior space. In the Connecticut house, the trees and shrubs seem as much a part of the decor as the lamps and paintings. In these glass boxes there is no feeling of isolation.

Yet in the Farnsworth House of Mies, there is such a feeling. Here, intimate space is governed by the same esthetic as the generic skyscraper. It is perhaps culturally the most important structure in Mies's work, for it is an exact lesson in how, even on a domestic scale, the use of plate glass can create an architecture of spiritual solitude.

Mies built the Farnsworth House in Plano, Illinois, just after the Second World War. It is a rectangle of glass walls sheathed in white-painted steel; the box floats on eight steel stilts four feet above the ground; a rectangular terrace, also on stilts, lies along one side of it and slightly lower. There is a functional reason for the stilts, for the land is the floodplain of the Fox River, nearby; but form has not "followed function" here. As the irate owner was later to complain, there were far more efficient ways to design a flood-proof house. A house on stilts, however, proclaims that this is a threatened dwelling; when you look at the Farnsworth House, especially up from the ground as you approach by foot, you sense it. I'm told the ground is usually soft and squishy on this floodplain as it was the day I visited—beautiful land but uncomfortable. Among other things, there are snakes. The Farnsworth House, with its base at chest level, its terrace at waist level, seems to hover, floating like a spaceship, and you hurry forward to hoist yourself up to this refuge.

The house, however, does not feel like a refuge. The threat of nature which urged you toward it is reinforced once you reach the terrace; there is no refuge here for you, or for any other living thing. The use of glass for every exterior vertical surface means you have not got inside safe at all. The sight of people within is not reassuring; they look as if they don't belong there, as if no one belongs inside. Mies achieves this effect in part by the unusual height of the glass walls, in part by the heaviness of the wood pedestal, containing the kitchen and bathrooms, which sits in the center of the glass box. The pedestal is a perfectly balanced weight against the wall planes, the furniture precisely and elegantly defined within the interplay of central mass and outer boundaries. But the intrusion of someone dozing in a chair (though it's hard to nap in a Barcelona chair), someone else reading a magazine while munching potato chips—all these normal signs of domesticity become obscene. This building is meant for emptiness.

I've described in some detail the sensations Farnsworth House arouses because they would be familiar to Romantic writers, sensations about which those writers had something unexpected to say. Here is a work of art set in hostile nature, a work in its very perfection inhospitable to human beings. To both Schiller, in his *Letters on the Aesthetic Education of Man,* and Senancour, in his novel of ideas, *Obermann,* the conjunction is a logical one. When a person shuns society, gives him- or herself over to solitude, he or she does not find the natural world to be a friendly shelter; *this* Senancour declared, with the childish sentimentality of Rousseau and the eighteenth-century naturalists. Solitude in nature reveals the utter indifference of the physical world to the projects of human beings, especially artistic projects. Nature so experienced no longer can serve, Senancour believed, as a friendly inspiration for art.

Many writers and painters in the Romantic era did, of course, continue to draw that friendly inspiration. There was in the domain of letters, however, a sensibility parallel to Gericault's image of nature's cruelty in the *Raft of the Medusa,* or Delacroix's drawings of storms and of the desert. These writers tried to understand the meaning of epithets like "inhuman," "lifeless," "cold," the vocabulary used so easily today to describe modern architecture. They tried to understand these words as naming complex processes occurring within the human psyche, "coldness" in art or life being not simply a sign of failure, but perhaps something more complex, more disturbing than simple judgments of success and failure suggest. Why, for instance, did Mies build the Farnsworth House as a testament to solitude? Schiller might have been answering for the architect as he defended his own poetry. Only when the artist creates a space of

solitude for himself, only then can he realize in pure, still form a contrast
to the viciousness of the outer world. The coldness testifies to the artist's
will, his refusal to be either an animal in nature or a servant of others in
society. In Schiller's *Letters*, as in the poems of the young Baudelaire, the
writer *wills* himself to withdraw; Hegel might accuse these writers, as he
did Rousseau, of therefore losing their humanity, to which Schiller's reply
was that he had at least gained the power to practice his art. This might
serve Mies as well; the Farnsworth House is a good illustration of an art
practiced in a hostile natural setting which is in turn hostile to human intervention and mess. The Phillip Johnson houses are by contrast friendlier to plants, animals, and man, and less powerful visually, less dramatic.

From this reasonable position, the writers I have referred to made an
imaginative leap. Its boldness is today buried in a cliché; recovering its
boldness might help us take stock not just of a great and severe artist of
our time, but of the medium of severity on which his art is based. If I try
to imagine how Senancour might explain why Mies has greater force than
Phillip Johnson, I think of him making that imaginative leap in *Obermann*, when the protagonist, depressed by the people around him, joyless in his attempts to escape and find comfort in the Alps, withdraws
within himself, and feeling absolutely empty suddenly experiences a wave
of terror and awe, as though he were in a church. It is a moment Baudelaire understood, as did, above all, Kierkegaard—the moment when a
person realizes that the sacred consists of experiences of the absent, of the
Other. I am thus certain they could name the architectural power of
Mies's buildings: here too absence acquires a sacred character. Its very
inhumanity makes it so.

The Romantic's understanding of that phrase, "the religion of art,"
has thus a very different sense once we begin to ask what it might now
mean. For it bears on a problem that vexes us both theoretically and practically—our conviction that works of art are inviolable, the very word
inviolable suggesting that these human products have a magic which subsequently renders them untouchable by men. The recent arguments over
Richard Serra's sculpture in New York, the artist defending his cold and
inhuman metal scrap by appealing to ideas of the inviolability of his labor—the defense of this particular art would have made perfect sense to
Senancour or Kierkegaard. In the same way, we try to defend buildings
like Breuer's Whitney Museum or Wright's Guggenheim Museum against
changes, we do so; whereas the public in Renaissance Rome had no fear

that the churches might be profaned if additions or alterations were made to them. This change of consciousness is what the Romantics sought to plumb, by understanding the conditions in which a man-made thing acquires, as it were, rights against them. Most broadly, this problem appears in an architecture whose elements, like steel-framed glass, are not subject to easy adaptation or modulation through use in time. These elements aspire to create an object with, as we say, "its own integrity," with "an internal logic," and so on. They express a withdrawal of objects from the world of human beings, an authentic solitude in which, through their very coldness and estrangement, the objects are invested with their own mana. And in spaces where this coldness works, like the public areas of Mies's Seagram Building or the entrance to Breuer's Whitney Museum, we do feel awed, awed by space alien to us, space drawn into itself. The ways in which people talk about, and experience, architecture betray evidences, I believe, that the esthetics of modern architecture are really those of religion as the Romantics understood religious experience, religion in which there is a divorce between the inner spiritual and outer physical or social world, a transmutation of inner solitude into work which, in its very estrangement, will resist the depredations of nature or other people. Such an art aspires to formal perfection, the awesomeness and untouchable qualities of a sacred object.

Art reveals to us, in this perspective, something quite unexpected, I think, about the material environment in which we live. Far from being neutral, the space created by the architecture of glass is highly charged. It is space which, in its hostility to livability, in its very hostility to nature, seeks to consecrate itself, to become sacred, inviolable. Mies succeeded in this Romantic quest: spaces, whether small, like the Farnsworth House, or large, like the public areas of the Seagram Building, are spaces we experience as untouchable, ones through which we move, but which do not belong to us. The quest of Mies's followers is the same. Their architecture, in its very inhospitability, claims a privileged position for itself, the highest, most arrogant privilege, Schiller said, a human being could claim—that his or her works had become so perfect in themselves that it would be sacrilege to touch them. The Romantics tried to ask what would become of man's need for the sacred, for the inviolate, once formal religion waned. Lacking faith in God, he could invest it in things, but these works would become hostile to himself.

Since I am interested in glass, let me say something about its place in this larger scheme. The glass panel can, and should be, the most flexible of all building media. This was the lesson of Paxton's Crystal Palace and the other exhibition halls of its type. Some modern architects have learned this lesson well, even for glass buildings on a small scale. For instance, the Cambridge Maximum Space House, built by students at Cambridge University in the summer of 1969, is a structure which allows great and continuing design flexibility on the part of its users. But the bias in the use of glass elements is against this kind of flexibility; it is a prejudice, or rather, an unthinking practice, which uses glass for the sake of the kind of cultural ends I've described, rather than for creating malleable human space.

Think, for instance, of Buckminster Fuller's geodesic domes. Nothing in form could seem farther from Mies, especially as the domes were articulated by François Dallegret to cover both a building and the area just around it, so that inner and outer space become absolutely one. Dallegret's was a reasonable version of Fuller's own dream to cover all of Manhattan with a dome. In fact, the hemispherical shape creates serious practical problems of air stratification and heating, as one of its critics, John Hix, has noted; it is also hard to accommodate the workings of windows and doors to a curved integument. Most seriously, and revealingly, the sites for the domes are usually in the woods, yet domes don't combine easily with structures which aren't domes. This, supposedly the most radical of modern glass structures, betrays the same Romantic logic as do the glass towers of Mies. Again there is total visibility, and again the visible is cut off from the other senses, the very geometry of the geodesic elements making adaptation difficult. Fuller recognized that glass might be a truly modern material, in the sense of truly flexible material, much more flexible in deployment than brick or stone. But in practice he used it Romantically. If Fuller can no more be held accountable for the excesses of his followers than Mies, the esthetic provoking the excess is for both men the same—an esthetic which invests karma, charisma, mana in a building by virtue of its very aloofness and indifference.

I hope I have suggested one way of understanding what it means to call modern architecture *cold*. It means that this architecture isn't modern, or exclusively so: cold was a temperature in art which the Romantics felt and sought to explain. They did so by asking what happens when inner and outer life become incommensurate and the artist becomes a spiritual solitary; what happens, as Erich Heller once put it, on a "journey to the interior"? The second meaning of cold when applied to solitary art is that this art acquired, in the history of culture, rights of inviolability, aroused sentiments of veneration that formerly had been attached to religious artifacts and rites. All the writers of the early nineteenth century I have cited were ambivalent about this transformation, this displacement from religion to art, this privilege accorded the interior over the exterior—refuge and prison becoming inseparable. Hegel spoke for Kierkegaard and for Baudelaire in declaring that freedom requires people to reach beyond the boundaries of their own spiritual life; he wrote in the *Philosophy of Right*, "If the free will is not to remain abstract, it must in the first place give itself an embodiment, and the material primarily available to sensation for such an embodiment is things, i.e., objects outside us." Modern architecture as exemplified in the elegant glass objects of Mies has yet to afford us this sense of freedom in space.

I suppose there are practical consequences to knowing more precisely and more historically what we mean when we say an architecture is cold. These consequences flow from disputing the integrity of the architectural object, challenging the protection of form per se. This is why one could make a principled objection to the work of landmark preservation commissions and the like, or, conversely, why planning commissions should be able to require that plans submitted to them make provision for change and modification of the original structures. We have a right to demand that buildings used by the public be capable of being altered over the course of time as we need them and use them in different ways—and few modern buildings can be gracefully violated.

What interests me more, however, is the very recovery of a sense of materiality, of the sensual, of the physical in the built environment. The term "material necessity" was not invented by Marx. Long before him artists thought about it, indeed, in the most direct way: is there a necessary character to materials? Does a melody in D minor have a different character from the same melody in G minor? Does blue arouse inherently different responses than white? In the Romantic era these questions became important in a new way: how could an artist, of all people, escape from material necessities, from thingness, from responsive sensation? The voyage of the solitary might deaden the artist—dull gray, Senancour declared, was the color of solitude.

Postmodern taste at the moment replaces plate glass, whenever feasible, with older, friendlier materials like brick or wood. As with most postmodern tastes, these efforts often mistake decoration for art. Moreover, it avoids the question of how a man-made material, mass produced, might somehow contain within itself the possibility for a different esthetic, an esthetic use which might redress the imbalance which produces cold architecture.

Recently I went to a cocktail party in Chicago, at one of the apartment towers Mies built at 830 Lake Shore Drive. The rooms seemed at first like all his other elegant cubicles in the sky. The furniture was his; even the paintings, my host told me, had been chosen and hung by the architect. When the party began, with just a few people, it felt as parties usually do at first: no one seemed to belong there. Then, as is the way of cocktail parties, the living room filled up with people spilling drinks, flipping cigarette ashes on the exquisite rug, shouting at the top of their voices, their very numbers freeing them from the mournful hush that tends to fall over two or three people in a Miesian chamber. I found myself at the edge of this yacking mass, near the windows/walls of unobstructed plate glass. Beyond them was only the emptiness of Lake Michigan. Now the glass seemed, if I can put it this way, like a mediation: if any more exuberant Chicagoans pushed into this hot party, I might be pushed out into the lake. Visually there seemed no way to avoid this danger. But the glass also reflected as a mirror the surging mass of drinking and carousing people within, so that I knew I wouldn't fall out. It reflected the humanity within to which I belonged.

At that moment I thought of a line somewhere in Baudelaire's letters: only when people feel vulnerable do they feel alive. And violation aroused in me the sense of being vulnerable. It seemed indeed that the space Mies made had come alive by violation, the glass as window and as mirror reporting and responding. For the first time in a building by Mies, I felt comfortable leaning back against the glass. I don't want to make too much of this moment, only that it gave me an intimation, through the material, of what the phrase *modern* might truly and positively imply. It was just a sense of the inherent ambiguity of glass; more than a metaphor, it was a field on which the exchange between inner and outer occurs, a field reflecting the violation of space but also enclosing and protecting. And I suppose this is why plate glass is so interesting: now a window on nothing, a mirror of solitude, its possibilities have yet to be explored in the practice of an ambiguous, permeable, violating, warm, and thus truly modern art.

Critical Crossing-Dressing: Male Feminists and The Woman of the Year
ELAINE SHOWALTER

"It's better to be a woman in our day. With us is all the joy of
advance, the glory of conquering. . . . Thank heaven we are
women!" —from George Gissing, *The Odd Women* (1893)

A NUMBER of prominent English and American male theorists have
recently begun to recognize the intellectual claims of feminist criticism,
and to connect it with their own critical positions. Wayne Booth led the
way by linking feminism and interpretation at the conference on "The
Politics of Interpretaion" at Chicago, when he declared his conversion to a
feminist criticism that had finally persuaded him that "our various canons
have been established by men, reading books written mostly by men for
men, with women as eavesdroppers," and that "now is the time for men to
join women in working at the vast project of reeducating our imaginations." Robert Scholes allied feminism and semiotics in a racy chapter on
the literary suppression of the clitoris in his *Semiotics and Interpretation*.
Jonathan Culler used feminist theories of reading to bring deconstruction
down to earth, political earth, that is, in his *On Deconstruction*. And
Terry Eagleton, in his sustained advocacy of Marxist and feminist criticism in several recent books and TV appearances, seems to be even more
interested in leading women than in joining them in their educational
project.

To women who have been writing feminist criticism this phenomenon must be both gratifying and unsettling. To begin with, we can hardly

---

This article originally appeared as a review essay of *On Deconstruction: Theory and Criticism after Structuralism*, by Jonathan Culler (Ithaca, N.Y.: Cornell University Press, 1982);
The Rape of Clarissa, by Terry Eagleton (Minneapolis: University of Minnesota Press,
1983); *Literary Theory: An Introduction*, by Terry Eagleton (Oxford: Basil Blackwell, 1983);
Woman and the Demon, by Nina Auerbach (Cambridge, Mass.: Harvard University Press,
1982); *Clarissa's Ciphers*, by Terry Castle (Ithaca, N.Y.: Cornell University Press, 1982); and
Making Tootsie, by Susan Dworkin (New York: Newmarket Press, 1983).

fail to welcome male feminist criticism when we have so long lamented the blindness, deafness, and indifference of the male critical establishment toward our work. "As every feminist critic knows," Sandra Gilbert has protested, "many—indeed, most—of our male colleagues don't come to our talks, don't read our essays and books, don't in fact concede that we exist as thinkers, teachers, and writers who are part of a significant intellectual movement." The exclusion of feminist criticism from the institutions of critical discourse, the omission of feminist criticism from histories of modern criticism (such as those by Gerald Graff, Grant Webster, and Frank Lentricchia), shows how, in Jane Marcus's words, "male bonding" is a more cohesive force among American cities than the theoretical enmities that divide them intellectually.

The move to feminist criticism on the part of other male theorists, in fact, seems motivated in many cases by the recognition that it offers the mixture of theoretical sophistication with the sort of effective political engagement they have been calling for in their own critical spheres. In *Walter Benjamin; or Towards a Revolutionary Criticism* (1981), for example, Terry Eagleton imagines the ideal shape of a revolutionary criticism: It would

> dismantle the ruling concepts of "literature," reinserting "literary" texts into the whole field of cultural practices. It would strive to relate such "cultural" practices to other forms of social activity, and to transform the cultural apparatuses themselves. It would articulate its "cultural" analyses with a consistent political intervention. It would deconstruct the received hierarchies of "literature" and transvaluate received judgments and assumptions; engage with the language and "unconscious" of literary texts, to reveal their role in the ideological construction of the subject; and mobilize such texts, if necessary by hermeneutic "violence," in a struggle to transform those subjects within a wider political context. If one wanted a paradigm for such criticism, already established within the present, there is a name for it: feminist criticism.

After this announcement, one might have predicted that it would not be long before Eagleton would try to incorporate the revolutionary paradigm of feminist criticism within his own problematic stance as an English Marxist aesthetician, a political position whose historical impotence he has often remarked.

Jonathan Culler has also taken note of the success of feminist criticism in opening the literary canon, changing the curriculum, and challenging entrenched theoretical positions. In an interview with Fredric Jameson in *Diacritics* (Fall 1982), he asked whether other modes of criticism that seek political impact might have lessons to learn from feminist criticism, which he calls "the most politically effective movement in literary criticism." Jameson (whose political unconscious, like his political conscious, has been unabashedly phallocentric) conceded that feminism had been a force whose power he attributed to its "collective dimension, its status as the culture . . . of a genuine social group," and asked rather plaintively in return, "with what organic social group the straight white male intellectual has any particular affinities?"

The organic social group with which this lonely soul found a bond used to be called the Old Boys' Network; and if, at last, it no longer provides a secure status and a collective identity, then the women's movement has been more successful than it often thinks it has. Indeed, feminist criticism is currently so appealing to male theorists that some feminists are beginning to regard the development with suspicion. In the 1890s, Gissing's "odd women" congratulated themselves on their fortunate position in history, and pitied men who had no movement to serve. As one of his fin-de-siècle feminists remarks, "A woman with brains and will may hope to distinguish herself in the greatest movement of our time—that of emancipating her sex. But what can a man do, unless he has genius?" Gissing's heroes acquired a vicarious sense of history through their contact with these ambitious feminists. Gayatri Spivak, however, is sharply skeptical of the motives of "straight white male intellectuals" who have turned to feminism: "Why is it that male critics in search of a cause find in feminist criticism their best hope?" she asks in *Critical Inquiry*.

> Perhaps because, unlike the race and class situations, where academic people are not likely to get much of a hearing, the women's struggle is one they can support "from the inside." Feminism in its academic inceptions is accessible and subject to correction by authoritative men; whereas . . . for the bourgeois intellectual to look to join other politico-economic struggles is to toe the line between hubris and bathos.

Feminist critics disagree, moreover, about the potentialities of male feminist reading. Annette Kolodny sees feminist reading competence as a skill that men can learn through patience, practice, and effort. Reading, she maintains, is a "learned activity . . . inevitably sex-coded and gender-inflected." Although most men are poor readers of women's writing because they are ignorant of women's values and inexperienced in interpreting female codes, they "will be better readers . . . of women's books when they have read more of them." But others would find this functional view of feminist reading as an acquired expertise superficial and politically suspect. Ten years ago Carolyn Heilbrun and Catherine Stimpson warned that feminist techniques could be copied and lifted out of their personal and political contexts: "Like French or Esperanto, they will comprise a language that a person may practice or learn, learn or practice, without having it affect his or her actions outside of the study or the classroom." Kolodny's argument is limited to the reading of women's texts, but other feminist critics would also question the reduction of feminist reading to a cognitive skill easily transferrable to male texts or critical theories. Gayatri Spivak is one who insists on the "political or historical and indeed ideological differential that irreducibly separates the male from the female critic of phallocentrism."

In general, I think Spivak is right to question the contexts in which male feminist criticism is produced, to point out the different stake that men and women have in a critique of phallocentrism, and to remind us that the habits of academic training make women critics peculiarly susceptible and vulnerable to the judgments of male authority figures. Feminist criticism has worried too much already, in my opinion, about communicating with the white fathers, even at the price of translating its findings into the warp of their obscure critical languages. If some of them are now learning *our* language, all the better; but there is more than a hint in some recent critical writing that it's time for men to step in and show the girls how to do it, a swaggering tone that reminds me of a recent quip in the *Yale Alumni Magazine* about a member of the class of 1955, Renée Richards: "When better women are made, Yale men will make them."

Nevertheless we must not prejudice male feminist criticism, refuse to give it a hearing, or go after it with a hatchet *pour encourager les autres*. It strikes me, in fact, that this first wave comes from friends rather than rivals, that it is genuinely exciting, serious, and provocative, and that it has large and important cultural implications. Booth, Scholes, Culler, and Eagleton have taken some chances of their own in supporting a feminist politics. Culler, for example, has already been attacked by Robert Alter in *The New Republic*, ostensibly for making feminism his latest "true revolution" and for trying to "harness Deconstruction to a political program," but more likely for having betrayed the patriarchy by finding feminist criticism intellectually challenging. It's no accident that these initial recognitions should have come from strong and secure writers of criticism who have little to gain by aligning themselves with a constituency or a cause.

Still, there are questions raised by the phenomenon of male feminist writing which are both pragmatic and theoretical. Why does this criticism make its appearance now? What does male feminist criticism tell us about the current impasse in literary theory? Most important, what are its uses and its dangers for women, and for feminist criticism in general? Is male feminism a form of critical cross-dressing, a fashion risk of the 1980s that is both radical chic and power play? Or is it the result of a genuine shift in critical, cultural, and sexual paradigms, a break out of the labyrinth of literary theory? In pursuing these questions, I want to begin with a parallel phenomenon in popular culture: the rise of the male heroine. What is the sudden cultural appeal of serious female impersonation?

Acting as a Woman: Dustin Hoffman and Making Tootsie

"One of the things about being a man in this society is giving away as little as possible," Mr. Hoffman notes. "Part of manhood is not to be taken advantage of. Poker is a masculine sport, where the whole thing is bluff and knowing where someone's vulnerability is so you can attack and try to take something away from them."

—"*Tootsie* Taught Dustin Hoffman About the Sexes," *New York Times*, December 1982

The 1980s fascination with cross-dressing, manifested in such recent and popular plays and films as *La Cage aux folles*, *Torch Song Trilogy*, *The World According to Garp*, *Victor/Victoria*, *Cloud 9*, and especially *Tootsie*, is symptomatic of a fin-de-siècle ambiance in which sex roles are under attack, and gender anxieties take a variety of cultural forms. The parallels with the nineteenth century are striking. In the 1880s and 1890s, New Women, homosexuals, and sexual radicals symbolized the apocalypse to Victorian patriarchs, and warnings of epidemic syphilitic infection convinced frightened conservatives that racial degeneration or extinction was at hand. Yet the androgyne became a compelling figure in theater and art; themes of cross-dressing began to appear in popular fiction and feminist fantasies; and some advanced novelists of the period (including Gissing, Hardy, and Wells) imagined a better social order beyond what Gissing called "sexual anarchy." In the 1980s, as Reaganism tries to demolish every legislative and social advance of the women's movement, and as epidemics of herpes and AIDS convince the Moral Majority that God is punishing the perverted, the promiscuous, and the depraved, we are seeing ludicrous, panicked reactions to the erosion of gender distinctions. In "La Différence," for example, a last-ditch op-ed polemic in the *New York Times* against the admission of women to the Century Club in Manhattan, Lewis Lapham insisted that only Nature's "dynamic symmetries" of masculine and feminine keep us from chaos: "The clarity of gender makes possible the human dialectic. Let the lines of balanced tension go slack and the structure dissolves into the ooze of androgyny and narcissism." This could be straight from the 1890s, an echo of its urbane diatribes against feminist "erotics, neurotics, and Tommy-rotics."

Yet the immense popularity of *Tootsie*, and the reverently received Hollywood hype about gender meanings that accompanied it, indicates the contemporary mass appeal of the androgynous ooze, and also of the narcissism of sexual introspection. American audiences took very seriously the questions that *Tootsie*'s several makers raised in interviews about the film: "What does it mean to be a man? What does it mean to be a woman? What would a given individual be like if he or she were to change gender?"

Dustin Hoffman's motivations received especially close media attention and praise, often from feminist film critics. According to Susan Dworkin, in her book *Making Tootsie*, Hoffman and his producer Sydney Pollack located the film in the "sexually political atmosphere" of the 1980s, and described its origins as "the ferment of feminist awakening." Even before Pollack signed on as director-producer, Hoffman had been earnestly researching feminist theory; in July 1981 I saw him several times in London sitting attentively in the audience at avant-garde feminist plays (two were on George Eliot and Virginia Woolf), presented in the dark attics or dank basements of small lunchtime theaters. Hoffman's motivations, according to Dworkin, were more personal than political. In playing Dorothy Michaels, he was "not looking for the truth about women. He was looking for the woman in himself."

American film critics seem to have accepted this; Molly Haskell, for instance, calls Dorothy "the first genuinely mainstream feminist heroine of our era." I should make clear, however, that, to my mind, *Tootsie* is not a feminist film. In England, where the drag act is one of the last preserves of a virulent misogyny, the minstrel show of sexist culture, film critics were skeptical of *Tootsie*, seeing the buxom Dorothy as a familiar caricature, and the film's pretensions to raised consciousness as insulting to women. Insofar as *Tootsie* is a commentary on the women's movement, teaching women how to stand up for their rights, it borrows what little politics it has from *Nine to Five*, even using the same actor, Dabney Coleman, to play the male chauvinist boss. It says more, I think, about Dustin Hoffman's sense of the actor's career—its passivity, vulnerability, and physical exposure—as feminine. The woman in Hoffman is the rejected actor; as Dworkin notes, "the insecurity of the actor, who knows what it's like to wait by the phone for twenty years, parallels the insecurity of the woman who is less than pretty, who has waited by a few silent phones herself."

At the same time, to act as a woman means access to a kind of biological stardom or supremacy. "There's a lot about being a woman I've always felt robbed about," Hoffman told a reporter. "I can't carry children; I can't bear children. I can't breastfeed. When it comes to all that, I've always felt like a stagehand." In *Kramer vs. Kramer,* Hoffman took centerstage as the parent, getting Meryl Streep offscreen to demonstrate that he could be a better mother than a woman could. In one of the original takes for the courtroom scene in this film, Hoffman improvised his own dialogue about the child: "I'm his *mother!* He didn't come out of my vagina, but I'm his mother!" (Molly Haskell has called the films in which women are cast out or killed in order to make room for Daddy in his new role as male mother, "male weepies.") For Hoffman, maternity seems to be the essential attribute of feminine completion; the most positive (real) woman in *Tootsie*, Jessica Lange's Julie, has a baby, and Hoffman has joked in interviews that in a sequel to *Tootsie* he too will give birth.

The actor's need to be the star is also at variance with some of Hoffman's views of the character Dorothy Michaels. For him, she is not only childless, but a homely sexual loser. "This character makes me cry," he told Gene Siskel of the *Chicago Tribune*. "She doesn't have a man. She never got married. She never had kids. And it hurts me 'cause she's not pretty." The pain of identifying with this feminine marginality and frustration, according to the press releases about the film, humanized both Michael Dorsey and Dustin Hoffman, and taught them both how to be better men. The crudeness of Hoffman's criteria of feminine success is amply revealed in his remarks; but oddly enough, the film never *shows* Dorothy Michaels as a lonely and unattractive woman who is rejected by men. The two men in her age group both pursue her hotly; she has more sexual invitations than she can accept. Whereas in nineteenth-century feminist literature, cross-dressing is redressing of an emotional debt owed to women, and dressing like a woman is the hero's penitential and instructive immersion in humility, impotence, and subordination, Michael Dorsey is a male failure who becomes a female success. Playing Dorothy is an ego trip.

This success comes primarily, the film suggests, from the masculine power disguised and veiled by the feminine costume. Physical gestures of masculinity provide *Tootsie's* comic motif of female impersonation. Dorothy Michaels drops her voice to call a taxi, lifts heavy suitcases, and shoves a hefty competitor out of the way. Dorothy's "feminist" speeches too are less a response to the oppression of women than an instinctive situational male reaction to being treated like a woman. The implication is that women must be taught by men how to win their rights.

In this respect, *Tootsie's* cross-dressing is a way of promoting the notion of masculine power while masking it. In psychoanalytic theory, the male transvestite is not a powerless man; according to the psychiatrist Robert Stoller, in *Sex and Gender,* he is a "phallic woman," who can tell himself that "he is, or with practice will become, a better woman than a biological female if he chooses to do so." When it is safe or necessary, the transvestite "gets great pleasure in revealing that he is a male-woman. . . . The pleasure in tricking the unsuspecting into thinking he is a woman, and then revealing his maleness (e.g., by suddenly dropping his voice) is not so much erotic as it is a proof that there is such a thing as a woman with a penis." Dorothy's effectiveness is the literal equivalent of speaking softly and carrying a big stick.

Acting as a woman, therefore, is not necessarily a tribute to the feminine. If, however, the female impersonation of *Tootsie* often seems to be part of the masculine sport of knowing where people are vulnerable so you can then try to take something away from them, the film winningly and finally mocks and deflates this characteristic in itself. As Hoffman/Dorsey, drunk with success, fantasizes playing Medea, Blanche DuBois, and Eleanor Roosevelt, his agent reminds him that he has nothing to say to women. *Tootsie* does, in fact, have a message for women, although not the one the filmmakers intended. It says that feminist ideas are much less threatening when they come from a man.

Reading as a Woman: Jonathan Culler and
the Deconstruction of Feminist Criticism

It's a quantum leap from the flamboyant self-promotion of *Tootsie* to Jonathan Culler's account of the theoretical issues of women's reading in *On Deconstruction*. If the seriousness of a book is in inverse relation to the figuration of its cover, the white jacket of *On Deonstruction*, adorned only with the title, the author's name, and three small lines, is the peak of minimalist prestige. Scrupulous, lucid, and tough-minded, *On Deconstruction* not only clarifies debates within feminist criticism, but moves the arguments a step ahead. Culler takes feminism seriously as a political ideology and a critical practice, describing it as "one of the most powerful forms of renovation in contemporary criticism." He takes to task "self-styled historians of criticism and critical theory" who have left feminist criticism out of history; and he is one of the few critics under discussion here who gives detailed and knowledgeable references to feminist texts, instead of vague well-meaning gestures in the direction of *Signs*.

The alliance of feminism and deconstruction is not new; male theorists such as Derrida and Lacan have for some time used woman as the wild card, the joker in the pack who upsets the logocentric and phallocentric stack of appellations, and a number of brilliant young feminist critics, including Jane Gallup, Nancy Miller, Peggy Kamuf, Gayatri Spivak, and Margaret Homans, have made common cause with deconstructionist theory. But Culler's analysis cuts two ways. First he uses deconstructive techniques to demonstrate some difficulties in the feminist appeal to the woman reader's experience, an experience and an identity which is always constructed rather than given. Second, he uses feminist criticism to give deconstruction a body, to link its philosophical abstractions to specific literary and political choices. Feminist critics confront, on immediately practical terms, many of the issues deconstruction defines. Where Derrida insists that hierarchical oppositions (such as man/woman) must be deconstructed through reversal rather than denial, feminist critics must put this principle into action, must choose whether to ally themselves with the reformist position of sexual equality, which denies difference, or with the radical position which asserts the difference, the power, and the superiority of the feminine. Their position on the specificity of women's writing, their critical style and voice, will be determined by this choice. Culler recognizes that both positions are valid, although as a Derridean he prefers the rhetorical reversal. Most feminist critics, in fact, play both ends against the middle—advocating social, academic, institutional equality, but textual difference. These positions are not oppositional, but responsive to women's different roles as citizens or as writers.

Feminist criticism also poses in dramatic and concrete terms the poststructuralist concern with the reader's experience as constitutive of the text. While reader-response criticism in general proposes a reading self or an informed reader who produces textual meaning, it prefers not to discuss the nature of the reader in specifically human terms. But as Culler observes, feminist criticism "has a considerable stake in the question of the relation of the reading self and the experience of the reader to other moments of the self and other aspects of experience." The question of the *woman* reader brings this relation forward, and "issues often swept under the carpet by male stories of reading are brought into the open in the debates and divisions of feminist criticism."

In tracing out feminist approaches to "reading as a woman," Culler sees three modes or stages. In the first, the critic appeals to female experience as a source of authority on female characters, on values, and on phallocentric assumptions. Yet, he points out, the "nature" of woman is a social construct, so "to ask a woman to read as a woman is in fact a double or divided request. It appeals to the condition of being a woman as if it were a given and simultaneously urges that this condition be created or achieved." In its second phase, feminist criticism confronts the reasons why women often read as men do, given their indoctrination by male literary and critical values. While identification with male experience may, as Dorothy Dinnerstein has argued in *The Mermaid and the Minotaur,* be the widespread result of nurturing arrangements which lead both sexes to reject and resent the female mother on whom they are initially dependent, it is reinforced and intensified in the case of academic women by their professional training and their prolonged immersion in patriarchal institutions. Reading as a woman thus becomes a willed project of unlearning, a resistance to what Judith Fetterley has called "immasculation." In this mode, the hypothesis of a woman reader, rather than a call upon female experience, serves to expose the misreadings, distortions, and omissions, of phallic criticism.

Culler sees the third mode of feminist criticism as the investigation of the "way our notions of the rational are tied to or are in complicity with interests of the male." This investigation includes the French feminist attack on phallogocentrism and the interrogation of current critical assumptions. Its task is to "develop critical modes in which the concepts that are products of male authority are inscribed within a larger textual system." More theoretical than the other two, this third phase is nevertheless still linked to female experience, Culler argues, through its stress on maternal thematics and marginality. He concludes that "reading as a woman" is always a paradoxical act, in that the identity as "woman" must always be deferred: "For a woman to read as a woman is not to repeat an identity or an experience that is given but to play a role she constructs with reference to her identity as a woman, which is also a construct, so that the series can continue: a woman reading as a woman reading as a woman."

But can a *man* read as a woman? Culler does not ask what might happen when a man attempts to produce a feminist reading, a situation in which the construction of the reader's gender identity is foregrounded. He does not present himself as a feminist critic, but rather as an analyst of feminist critical work. For the most part, Culler places himself outside of, although sympathetic to, feminist reading. Yet in two instances, he does offer his own feminist readings of texts, and these raise interesting questions as to whether a male feminist is in fact a man reading as a woman reading as a woman.

Near the beginning of the section on feminist criticism, Culler comments on Geoffrey Hartman's observation in *The Fate of Reading* that "much reading is indeed like girl-watching, a simple expense of spirit," explaining that "the experience of reading seems to be that of a man (a heart-man?) for whom girl-watching is the model of an expense of spirit in a waste of shame. When we posit a woman reader, the result is an analogous appeal to experience; not to the experience of girl-watching, but to the experience of being watched, seen as a 'girl,' restricted, marginalized." Here Culler invokes the woman reader as a preamble to his inversion of Hartman's text.

But by the end of his excursus on "Reading as a Woman," Culler has abandoned the hypothesis of a woman reader and produces his own rhetorically unmediated reading of Freud's *Moses and Monotheism*. Freud, he points out, links the development of speech, the Mosaic prohibition of material images of God, and the turn from a matriarchal to a patriarchal social order, and treats the result as an advance to a more symbolic and thus higher stage of intellectuality. In doing this, says Culler, Freud is really promoting the elevation of the paternal principle which values the invisibility and the symbolic nature of its own relation with the child. Culler proceeds from this argument to speculate on the relation between the "promotion of the paternal" and the likely concerns of literary criticism in a patriarchal culture: (1) the conception of the author's role as paternal and the assimilation of any valued maternal function to paternity; (2) the investment in paternal authors; (3) the obsession with the legitimacy of meaning and with the prevention of illegitimate interpretations.

I would argue that what Culler has done here is to read consciously from his own gender experience, with an ironic sense of its ideological bounds. That is to say that he has read not as a *woman*, but as a man and a feminist. Indeed, Culler's deconstructionist priorities lead him to overstate the essentialist dilemma of defining the *woman* reader, when in most cases what is implied and intended is a *feminist* reader. Reading as a feminist, I hasten to add, is not unproblematic; but it has the important aspect of offering male readers a way to produce feminist criticism that avoids female impersonation. The way into feminist criticism, for the male theorist, must involve a confrontation with what might be implied by reading as a man, and with a questioning or surrender of paternal privileges.

Writing as a Woman: Terry Eagleton and the Rape of Feminist Criticism

But when male theorists borrow the language of feminist criticism without a willingness to explore the masculinist bias of their own reading system, we get a phallic "feminist" criticism that competes with women instead of breaking out of patriarchal bounds. Terry Eagleton's *The Rape of Clarissa: Writing, Sexuality, and Class Struggle in Samuel Richardson* (1982) brings together three "revolutionary" reading strategies: feminist criticism, historical materialism, and poststructuralist textualism. Although Eagleton refuses to give priority to any of these methods (indeed the copyright page of the American edition states that "The University of Minnesota is an equal-opportunity educator and employer," as if to guarantee the constitutional equality of ideas as well), the aggressive title and the erotic cover of *The Rape of Clarissa* (Fragonard's *Le Verrou*) certainly foreground the sexual issues. Eagleton also acknowledges the centrality of the feminist revolution in his text when he declares that "if Richardson may once again become readable, it will be in large measure because of the women's movement."

Eagleton presents the book as a bold incursion into several alien territories, and it is meant to have the dash and daring of a highwayman's attack. First, it is a foray into psychoanalysis, a "terrain," he notes, "which the English have always found a little unnerving." Second, it is an invasion of the eighteenth century, "long the preserve of literary conservatism, rarely penetrated by Marxist criticism." And finally, it is a raid of feminist criticism, in order to claim overdue recognition for *Clarissa* as "the major feminist text of the language." Richardson, according to Eagleton, was the most "gifted and popular ideologue" of the eighteenth-century exaltation of the "feminine," and *Clarissa* is "the true history of women's oppression at the hands of eighteenth-century patriarchy." Like his "eighteenth century," Eagleton's "feminist criticism" is another well-barricaded preserve to be penetrated by the daring Marxist Macheath. Obviously more is at stake than the recuperation of Richardson.

Clues to precisely what *is* at stake may be deciphered in the textual strategies Eagleton employs, the "hermeneutic violence" he deploys in the name of revolutionary criticism. He is very good at exposing the sexism of those critics who have been of Lovelace's party: Dorothy Van Ghent, V. S. Pritchett, and especially William Beatty Warner, who reads the rape as Lovelace's clever way of deconstructing Clarissa. But Eagleton's own reading sees Clarissa, in her apparently infinite accessibility to interpretation, as the Lacanian "transcendental signifier"—the phallus itself. It is her phallic power that the anxiety-ridden Lovelace really craves: "Lovelace must possess Clarissa so that he may reunite himself with the lost phallus, and unmask her as reassuringly 'castrated.'"

What then, we ask, is Lovelace so anxious about? In part, Eagleton suggests, he is anxious about writing, about the appropriation of a womanly, or at any rate, an unmanly act. "What is worrying about Lovelace," according to Eagleton, "is that for a man he spends too much time writing." If the letter, in the eighteenth-century context, is associated with the feminine entrance into literature, and, more generally, with the expression of those concerns for the individual and for the emotional that Eagleton also describes as part of the bourgeois "feminization of discourse," then the scribbling Lovelace may be less than virile. And on a different level, the written word in fiction seems to share the metaphoric properties of the feminine. As Eagleton asserts, "The problem of writing is in this sense the problem of the woman: how is she to be at once decorous and spontaneous, translucently candid yet subdued to social pressure? Writing, like woman, marks a frontier between public and private, at once agonized outpouring and prudent strategem."

The allegory here of "Writing as a woman" seems forced, especially when we recognize that what is being described is neither female anxiety of authorship, such as Sandra Gilbert and Susan Gubar analyze in *The Madwoman in the Attic,* nor the dilemma of Clarissa herself as correspondent and narrator. Instead it is the male gender anxiety of the character, the novelist, and ultimately the Marxist critic, who fears that his writing (rather than revolutionary action) is effeminate. By possessing feminist criticism, so to speak, Eagleton effectively recuperates for himself its "phallic" signifying power. In his synthesis of feminism, Marxism, and poststructuralism, Eagleton also intermingles (or ignores) critics, so that there is no sense of a background of feminist readings of *Clarissa* against which his reading defines itself. This may be the inadvertent result of haste, or an aspect of English critical style, but it also suggests a disconcerting insensitivity to the politics of acknowledgment.

What happens if we contrast Terry Eagleton's reading of *Clarissa* to another feminist reading by a woman? Like Eagleton, Terry Castle, in *Clarissa's Ciphers,* locates her reading at the intersection of feminism, deconstruction, and politics. Like him too she deplores the Lovelacean bias of Warner and Van Ghent, and sees Lovelace as infantile and banal. But unlike Eagleton, Castle sees Clarissa as the *victim* of "hermeneutic violence" practiced against women. Interrupted, "shut up," censored, silenced, violated, Clarissa's powers of expression, her access to language and to literary modes of production are severely constrained, while her oppressors' rights to language go unquestioned. Despite her eloquence, Clarissa's rhetoric is powerless because it is not grounded in the political authority and force that backs up the patriarchal discourse of Lovelace and the Harlowes. In the "black transaction" of the rape, *Clarissa* as novel inevitably tends to polarize its male and female readers, encouraging us to "examine the ways in which the gender of the reader (along with resulting differences in socialization and *power*) may condition the meanings he or she finds in the text." In particular, Castle argues, the female/feminist reader responds to the silences in *Clarissa* and these correspond to the

silences in the cultural history of women. The rape is the ultimate silenc-
ing, and a form of "hermeneutic intimidation" for Clarissa's efforts to define her own nature.

Terry Eagleton describes *Sir Charles Grandison* as Richardson's
effort to appreciate the "tide of feminization" for patriarchy, to produce a
new kind of hero who would combine Clarissa's feminine virtues—tenderness, feeling, goodness, chastity—with masculine power and effectiveness. The effort failed, however, because without the reality of female
dependency and powerlessness behind it, goodness seemed priggish,
chastity pointless, and tenderness merely effeminate. Thus Grandison's
unreality indicates "a genuine ideological dilemma." If Eagleton had gone
one step further, to consider his own ideological dilemma, *The Rape of
Clarissa* would have been a more important book for feminist critics. Energetic, entertaining, and inventive though it be, Eagleton's phallic feminism seems like another raid on the resources of the feminine in order to
modernize male dominance. We are led back to the politics of *Tootsie*—
the appropriation of the tide of feminist feeling in the interests of patriarchy, the production of a new kind of (critical) hero. Whereas Terry
Castle, breaking hermeneutic silence by reading and writing as a woman,
testifies to the increased power of women to define their own nature, and
builds her case on the work of such feminist critics of *Clarissa* as Nancy
Miller, Janet Todd, Rachel Brownstein, Judith Wilt, and Margaret
Doody, the effect of Eagleton's text is to silence or marginalize feminist
criticism by speaking for it, and to use feminist language to reinforce the
continued dominance of a male literary canon.

As Eagleton points out with reference to Sir Charles Grandison, the
"genuinely progressive drive to generalize the discourse of femininity to
men, exposes, in the very thinness of the text, an insurmountable sexual
difference." In critical terms, as Larry Lipking disarmingly concedes in
his essay "Aristotle's Sisters," sexual difference begins with "a fact that few
male theorists have ever had to confront: the possibility of never having
been empowered to speak." As women understand it, the problem of
writing as a woman is initially one of overcoming fear. Eagleton notices
that the people around Clarissa would prefer her *not* to write, that Mrs.
Harlowe, for example, would prefer her daughter to read—that is, "to
conform herself to another's text rather than to produce her own meanings." Like other kinds of criticism, of course, feminist criticism is both
reading and writing, both the interpretation of a text and the independent

production of meaning. It is through the autonomous act of writing, and the confrontation with the anxiety that it generates, that feminist critics have developed theories of women's writing, theories proved on our own pulses. What I chiefly miss in *The Rape of Clarissa* is any sign from Eagleton that there is something equivocal and personal in his own polemic, some anxiety of authorship that is related to his own cultural position.

It has to be added, nevertheless, that in his latest book, *Literary Theory: An Introduction*, where he is no longer scolding feminist criticism for its separatist tendencies and lack of theoretical rigor (as he does in his book on Benjamin), or speaking for it (as in *The Rape of Clarissa*) for his own interpretative ends, Eagleton is persuasive, pungent, and self-aware. At his best—and *Literary Theory* is his best—Eagleton is a persuasive analyst of literary culture, and his clearheaded account of the mutual goals—yet mutual independence—of socialist and feminist criticism makes this book immensely valuable. If in *The Rape of Clarissa* Eagleton's use of feminist criticism is self-interested, here he accords it a full measure of autonomy and respect. One senses in this book that feminist ideas have penetrated Eagleton's reading system everywhere, that, along with Marxist aesthetics, they inform his entire account of the development of contemporary critical discourse.

Looking for the Woman: Demons, Diacritics, and The Woman of the Year

> Mercedes Kellogg, at table with Raquel Welch, who wore a bow tie, wing collar and tuxedo: "What does it mean when 'The Woman of the Year' dresses like a man?"
>
> —John Duka, *New York Times*, December 1982

To a considerable degree, recent debates within feminist criticism about the importance of gender in the production of the feminist text have made a space for male theorists like Eagleton, Culler, Booth, and Scholes to enter the field. Nina Auerbach's *Woman and the Demon: The Life of a Victorian Myth* challenges the feminist critical commonplace that literary stereotypes of women (such as the angel in the house, the victim, the queen, the witch, the old maid, and the fallen woman) are male mystifications, reducing and dehumanizing women. Properly understood, she argues, these figures are paradigms, or better, myths, of ascendant womanhood. George MacDonald's malevolent Lilith, Rossetti's monumental "stunners," Dickens's expiring angels, all testify to female grandeur and to the woman-worship of an age losing its religious faith. In textual terms, then, male writers and artists inscribed "subversive paradigms of a divine and demonic female power at the cultural center of Victorian patriarchy and chivalry." Auerbach's analysis turns conventional interpretation on its head: although she does not exactly claim that Rossetti, Dickens, Thackeray, are feminist writers, she explains that their work is part of a Victorian "feminism" so "pervasive"—in the broad power of this many-faceted myth of a mobile presiding woman—that the word had lost its meaning." Certainly, for Auerbach's purposes, there is no point in distinguishing between male and female purveyors of the myth.

Within French/deconstructionist feminist criticism, these issues take a different and even more enabling form for male critics. First of all, after the decentering of the human subject, and the alleged disappearance or death of the author, "the question of whether a 'man' or a 'woman' wrote a text," as Alice Jardine explains, "becomes nonsensical." Second, for French theorists, *"l'écriture féminine,"* or women's writing, stands for a style, not a signature. Writing is feminine when it is open-ended, playful, avant-garde, audacious, nonlinear; *l'écriture féminine* can as well be signed by a man as by a woman.

In recent years, in fact, it has been necessary for American feminist critics to argue in behalf of our special commitment to women's writing as a historical and social category. The material conditions and contexts of women's writing have to be repeatedly stressed, because the patriarchal literary canon has a centripetal force and a social power that pulls discussion toward its center; women's writing gets left out unless feminist criticism insists that historically speaking, the question of whether a man or a woman wrote a text is of primary importance. Reviewing the first wave of male feminist criticism, one notes that it nearly all "happens" to be about texts signed by men: Rabelais, Richardson, Hemingway, Lawrence. As Culler predicts, patriarchal criticism tends to disclose whatever it values in the maternal by assimilating it to the paternal function. Unless male feminist critics become more aware of the ways they too have been constituted as readers and writers by gender systems, their books may continue to be written for men and in behalf of male literary traditions.

Without closing the door on male feminists, I think that Franco-American theory has gone much too far in discounting the importance of signature and gender in authorship. The male author occupies a different literary place; the author of an *écriture féministe* needs to consider his or her own cultural circumstance. The movement away from the historical specificity of gender is hinted in the cover of the *Diacritics* special issue of summer 1982, titled "Cherchez la Femme: Feminist Critique/Feminine Text." On a white background is a figure in a black tuxedo and high heels, resting one knee on a bentwood chair à la Marlene Dietrich. The figure has no hands or head. On the back cover, a dress, hat, gloves, and shoes arrange themselves in a graceful bodiless tableau in space. No "vulgar" feminist, the chic Diacritical covergirl hints at the ephemera of gender identities, of gender signatures.

There is an interview with Derrida in this issue of *Diacritics*, but all the other contributors are women, as are the editors. Yet I am haunted by the ambiguity of that cover. Sometimes I have a dream of the feminist literary conference of the future. The demonic woman rises to speak, but she mutates before our eyes into a mermaid, a vampire, a column of fire. The diacritical woman rises to speak, but she has no head. Holding out the empty sleeves of her fashionable jacket, she beckons to the third panelist. He rises swiftly and commands the podium. He is forceful; he is articulate; he is talking about Heidegger or Derrida or Lévi-Strauss or Brecht. He is wearing a dress.

The Play of Sexes in Bruegel's Children's Games

EDWARD SNOW

IT MIGHT seem unlikely that Peter Bruegel the Elder, of all artists, would be much interested in the difference between the sexes. The horizons of his paintings are too vast and their concerns too far-reaching. They confront us with both our common lot as a species and our isolation as solitary units of existence, and in either case whether we are men or women would seem a relatively trivial distinction. Nevertheless, in Bruegel's *Children's Games* (fig. 1) there is a marked tendency to distinguish between male and female versions of the evolving self and its imaginative grasp on reality, and in terms more complex than conventional notions of the sexual hierarchy (our own as well as those of Bruegel's age) might lead us to expect.

Consider, to begin with, the boy perched high on stilts and the open-armed girl paired with him at the right corner of the building near the painting's center (fig. 2). Everywhere one looks one finds some variation on one or the other of these figures (climbing and balancing on the one hand, outstretched arms on the other): they constitute something like a key to the painting's anthropology. The human animal rises precariously on two feet (whose black, cumbersome boots provide immunity from the earth as well as anchored contact with it), and as a result winds up having to devise for itself the world of functions and purposes which in nature seems merely given. One result is a paradox that the boy on stilts neatly illustrates: the means he invents for acquiring a sense of balance and a feel for the laws of the physical universe nurtures in him both a fantasy of transcendence and a preoccupation with downfall and ruin. (It is hard to say which motive is host and which parasite in this complex symbiosis.) And having planted itself on two feet (the girl and the painting's many variations on her gesture are emblematic here), this same creature suddenly finds itself with two arms which—deprived, as it were, of their natural function—can reach, cling, grasp, contend, exult, assist, despair, express isolation and connection, register fullness of being and emptiness of self. They generate, in short, the entire *human* world of care unknown to those rooted trees in the upper left whose calm uprightness moves us so.

Primarily, then, the pairing at the corner of the building implies a dialectic that is constitutive of human beings in general. But it also provides an emblem for the difference between male and female horizons. The boy enjoys a privilege in the realm of transcendence that the girl is denied; but his position there entails a constant sensation of instability and forces him to gaze anxiously at the ground immediately beneath his feet. The girl, on the other hand, apparently deprived of the means to rise or strive beyond herself, paradoxically stands firm, and opens her empty arms (which conjure up no lifting presence) to the whole of what encompasses her. Her gesture is one of the most elusive, and at the same time evocative, in the entire painting. It is closely related to the family of reaching and groping arms which weave into the scene both a need for connection and a lack of fulfillment (cf. the blindfolded woman, the boy running up the cellar door, the children on the sandpile, and the figures circling in the shadow of the central building). Bruegel tempts us to read it as a distraught address to the boy above her (there is even a subliminal allusion to crucifixion and lamentation imagery), but then projects it forward toward something unspecified and limitless, and stretches her arms open—past the limits of abjectness, as it were—until they become a wide embrace. Even if we perceive her gesture as a response to the boy, it reads less persuasively as a desire for what he has than as an expression of the vicarious elation of his adventurousness evokes in her. It is ironic, in fact, that a sense of expanding horizons and an experience of the surrounding whole register in her open arms, not in his risk-taking. She, rather than he, looks like the ontologically adventurous one.

The two barrels in the foreground are the focus of a similar difference (fig. 3). One sits upright, a stable, maternal-seeming object into which a single girl simultaneously peers and shouts. The other has been tipped over on its side and transformed into a precarious surface with which two boys awkwardly contend. There is something archetypal about the material presence of these barrels: they are like surrogates for the world's body, that "first" object of the incessant human dialectic of attachment and separation. The uses to which they are being put represent antithetical modes of appropriating the given and experiencing the self in relation to it. And once again the difference is expressed in male and female terms.

The two boys are indifferent to the self-sufficient, strangely answering presence of this given object; it interests them only insofar as they can surmount and master it. (They are apparently working together to rock the barrel back and forth, pushing first off one foot and then the other. But

Fig. 1. Children's Games, 1560—Kunsthistorisches Museum, Vienna, photo courtesy of museum

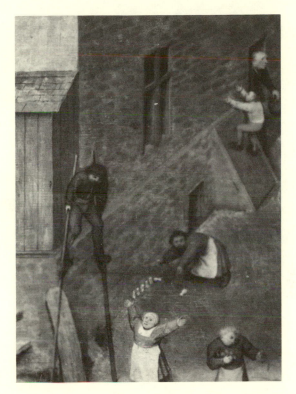

Fig. 2. Children's Games *(detail)*

Bruegel characteristically stresses the difference in the way they go about the task: the boy nearest us exerts himself violently against the barrel—and, it appears, against his counterpart—while the one farthest from us holds on for dear life.) To do this they must convert it into something they can struggle with, something in opposition to which they can establish a more precarious equilibrium of their own making. The hole in the barrel's side, which for the girl opens into a resonating inner realm, becomes for them a means of taking hold of and dominating the barrel. Their game, then, like that of the fence riders on the left, manages to transform a container into a conveyance—in this it asserts a precious human capacity—but only by treating the object's original equilibrium and sufficiency of being with disdain. Although they are perched atop something whose most obvious properties are depth, inwardness, and circumference, they have appropriated it as an external surface, and use it as a neutral ground

Fig. 3. Children's Games *(detail)*

upon which to play out a version of the human connection that, even in collaborative projects, generates feelings of opposition and competitiveness.

The girl's curiosity appears diametrically opposed to the aggressively appropriative instincts of the boys. The barrel is for her a mystery to be sounded, without, however, invading or disturbing it. Her activity may be less inventive than the boys', and may lack the social instinct theirs is an expression of, but it also involves her in what looks like a more nourishing relation. She appears, like the tree climber at the edge of the stream, to be still in touch with the world's largely obliterated maternal aspect, and to draw nourishment from it. Though she doesn't seek to transform her object, she does fill it with her voice, which the barrel amplifies and returns to her. If this is an image of narcissism, it is a primary narcissism that responds instinctively to the object-world's mysterious appeal. The image has to do, like so many in the painting, with the filling of vacant, unrealized spaces (the hobbyhorse rider and the boy in the window peering through the oversized mask are more problematic variations on the theme). It evokes an imaginative desire to grow bigger that seems incidental to the actual maturing process, and that in fact the passage into the adult world seems to stifle: witness the diminution that takes place in the receding street, and the hollow silence that seems to reign there.

It only takes a brief scan of the painting's layout to become convinced that the contrast between these two modes of experience is one of its primary interests, and that their embodiment in boys and girls respectively is not fortuitous. Indeed, the many intricate variations on this difference are compelling signs of the painting's intelligence. The sandpile just in front of the stream at the far left, for instance, is the site of a contrast that closely parallels the one located by the two barrels (fig. 4). On it two boys are playing a version of "king of the mountain"—a game that involves competitiveness, violence, a sense of opposition, and a will to dominate. At the same time a girl kneels at its base (her posture is clearly evocative of the girl at the barrel), immersed in building sand castles. Here, especially, the nuances of the configuration seem to valorize the difference it depicts. Bruegel has portrayed the boys not locked in struggle but failing to connect, as if they had migrated from the shadowy area of the street at the upper right. The girl, however, is quiet and self-absorbed, and her arms are as happily occupied as those of the boys are empty-looking and distraught. She appears as connected and contentedly in place as the boys seem lost and blindly driven.

There is in turn a precise, though more neutral, variation on this set

Fig. 4. Children's Games *(detail)*

of images in the lower right-hand corner of the painting. There two boys playing mumblety-peg are juxtaposed with a single girl below them grinding red powder with a brick (fig. 5). The boys, whose gestures and expressions seem calculated to resemble those of the boys on the sandpile, relate across a vacancy that their game again turns into a charged space of contention, and the knife which the player on the left holds between his teeth injects into it an element of violence. (He recalls "armed to the teeth" from Bruegel's *Netherlandish Proverbs* [fig. 6].) The girl, however, is another instance of solitary, quietly absorbed inventiveness.

One would search in vain for a sixteenth-century context which might account for the subtle distinctions these paired images delineate.

Fig. 5. Children's Games *(detail)*

Fig. 6. *Netherlandish Proverbs, 1559 (detail)—Staatliche Museen, Berlin, photo courtesy of museum*

To be sure, the difference between the sexes was a much theorized-about topic in Bruegel's age, and the question of superiority became the focus of an increasingly heated philosophical quarrel. (Ian Maclean, *The Renaissance Notion of Woman*, and M. A. Screech, *The Rabelaisian Marriage*, provide useful historical accounts.) But the nuances of Bruegel's images so extravagantly exceed the text-bound limits of the contemporary debate as to remain for all practical purposes innocent of it. It is not even that they encode ideas ahead of their time; rather they establish contact with the realm of vital impulse upon which culture rests and which cultural perception is in many ways an attempt to adapt and control. In this respect they are as likely to call into question *our* culture's accounts of gender difference as they are those of Bruegel's own. I am thinking specifically of Erik Erikson's classic study of children's play, which purports to show that the imaginations of boys and girls are structured according to different spatial modes—one dominated by "height and downfall and by strong motion and its channeling and arrest," the other by "static interiors which [are] open or simply enclosed, and peaceful or intruded on"—and that these modes correspond to differences in the way the sexes experience "the ground plan of the human body." The pairings in *Children's Games* clearly depict differences related to the one proposed in such passages, and Erikson would probably take Bruegel's images as straightforward support for his observations.

Yet if this artist and this psychoanalyst observe similar phenomena— and with a similar interest in ontological implications—they see with very different eyes. Bruegel's images, in fact, provide touchstones for a critique of Erikson. For one thing, they can make us see the maleness of Erikson's gaze, and the extent to which it is as Other that he observes—and in the process domesticates—his female subjects. The girls in *Children's Games* may engage in activities that are vulnerable to Erikson's terms, but their bodies are clearly animated by active selves, not hollowed out by vacant "interiors" that can be imagined as "static," "passive," or "expectant"; and the motives that issue from them (as we shall see in greater detail later) have to do with creation, exploration, and self-expression, and only in a secondary sense with bearing, caretaking, and containment. Erikson concludes that "the girls emphasized *inner* and the boys *outer* space." Bruegel's images, on the other hand, make it clear that all the games involve both "inner" and "outer" space, and suggest that a difference lies in the way the two sexes experience the interchange between those realms.

The main result of this contrast is not, it seems to me, to make us feel the presence of historical difference (much less just two dissimilar ways of looking at things): on the contrary, Bruegel's sixteenth-century images restore complexities that Erikson's modern observations elide. The painter's images feel less culture-bound, less occluded by sexual stereotypes, than the psychoanalyst's observations—not least of all because of their urge to inhabit the behavior they depict—to imagine human experience, as it were, from the inside out. Erikson's account of the sexual differences underlying children's play does little more than betray the fantasies that structure his empirical observations:

> Here sexual difference in the organization of a play space seems to parallel the morphology of sexual differentiation itself: in the male, an external organ, erectile and intrusive in character, serving the channelization of mobile sperm cells; in the female, internal organs, with vestibular access, leading to statically expectant ova.

What appears most irreducibly real in Bruegel's games, however, is the transaction between self and world in which both self and world take shape. Sexuality seems a metaphorical dimension of this transaction, not what it unconsciously symbolizes. We can at least say that Bruegel shows us a "prior" realm where sexuality is subsumed in ontological imaginings. The child who is inflating a bladder while gripping it as if it were his or her own belly (fig. 7), for instance, may be indulging, consciously or uncon-

Fig. 7. Children's Games (*detail*)

sciously, in a fantasy of pregnancy (Bruegel deliberately obscures signs of gender, as if to emphasize that either sex can *play* at this), but the primary dimensions of the game have to do, again, with filling empty spaces and "growing bigger"—it provides a portable, body-centered version of the experience which the girl shouting into the barrel devises.

Even in the games which are more concerned with the energy that animates the body than with its ontological horizons, Bruegel's focus is on the process which channels that energy into an expressive relation with the world. The painting treats this transaction as something common to both sexes, but also as something that differentiates them. A good example is the juxtaposition of the hobby-horse rider in the foreground with the two girls playing in his path (fig. 8). There is something almost demonically introverted and compulsive-looking about the figure of the boy. As

Fig. 8. Children's Games *(detail)*

he goads his imaginary horse by striking his whip against his own bare thigh, he experiences himself as both the driven animal and the rider who dominates it. He exacerbates in himself a violence that thrusts him compulsively into the outer world, but in a way that appears to lead him only further inside fantasies of dominance and control. The two girls in front of him are equally absorbed in what they are doing, but their activity issues spontaneously from them—unlike the boy's, which he whips up and channels into a kind of phallic will. One plays a pipe and tabor, while the other pokes a stick into a pile of mud or dung, and perhaps (as if under the primitive influence of a creative urge) stirs circles into it. The curiosity of the one and the musical expressiveness of the other are like two aspects of an extrovertive principle whose opposite is the driven solipsism of the hobbyhorse rider. The girls are portrayed, in fact, as if they were different aspects of a single figure, and may be meant to suggest complementary poles of the creative process—one its upright, flowering aspect, the other its less reputable generative origins. (The girl at the barrel combines these aspects: peering into the barrel matches the exploratory curiosity of the girl with the stick; making it reverberate with her voice parallels blowing on a flute while beating on a drum.) Certainly they are two of Bruegel's happiest images of bodily experience and the human motives that issue from it.

The girl who leans over the pile of dung is also linked visually to a boy in the upper center of the painting who similarly crouches over an upsidedown pot and either bangs or sharpens a knife against it (figs. 9 and 10). The visual echo again juxtaposes contrasting feelings of what it is like to

Figs. 9 (left) and 10. Children's Games *(details)*

inhabit a body and to be inhabited by its energies. The girl is all round-
ness and circles. The ball she holds in her free hand, the outline of her
white kerchief, and even the concentric rings of the dung pile underscore
the centered, spherical feel of the physical space she operates from. Not
that Bruegel consigns her, in the manner of Erikson's observations, to this
immanence: a kind of egoless curiosity about the nature of things issues
instinctively from it. But as she reaches out ever so discreetly with an exploratory gesture, she remains planted in her own separate physical
space, and the gentle curve of her reaching arm is what, more than anything else, creates the effect of self-containment. All this tends to make
her an ideal of well-being reminiscent of the rounded, self-absorbed
shapes that contribute to the peaceful atmosphere of Bruegel's *Fall of Icarus*, where all movement outward and away ultimately curves back toward its beginning. She especially resembles the fisherman in the lower
right-hand corner of that painting, who reaches out into the destructive
element from the security his own ponderous body provides (fig. 11).

The boy, on the other hand, is all discordant angles and vectors (his
legs resemble those of Icarus as he plunges awkwardly into the sea), and
his presence has a fugitive, menacing quality about it. The effect is a
matter not just of the knife and masklike face but of the body itself. Forces
seem to be pulling it in opposite directions, twisting it into a posture that
resembles the torque of the peripheral figures in Bruegel's *Procession to
Calvary* who respond almost in spite of themselves to the impersonal momentum sweeping things toward the site of the Crucifixion (fig. 12). The
result is a tense, coiled energy, produced, unlike the girl's curiosity, as
much by forces acting from without as from within, and more likely

Fig. 11. Landscape with the Fall of Icarus, *c. 1555–58 (detail)—Musées Royaux des Beaux-Arts, Brussels, photo courtesy of museum*

Fig. 12. The Procession to Calvary, *1564 (detail)—Kunsthistorisches Museum, Vienna, photo courtesy of museum*

to explode in violence than find its way into the rhythms of creative experience.

This difference is explored in more complex terms in a contrast between the boys spinning tops in the loggia of the central building and the girls twirling skirts nearby in a grassy area bordering the stream (fig. 13). The tops the boys spin are a kind of metaphoric displacement of the inner gyroscope that so many of the games are ways of discovering and developing. (The left-to-right progress of the fence riders depicts stages in its mastery.) The activity of the boys externalizes the gyroscopic principle, where it is experienced as something subject to the will (rather than as an inner, sustaining origin), something that must be animated by external violence and continually exacerbated. Their figures convey the excitement and sense of power in being able to concentrate all the body's energy at a single, willed point outside the self (in pointed contrast to the girl who sits hunched against the wall behind them, the image of a bodily self with only itself and its natural functions as its object); yet at the same time they suggest an immobilizing, trancelike compulsiveness. Although they par-

Fig. 13. Children's Games *(detail)*

Fig. 14. Children's Games *(detail)*

ticipate as a group, they all seem locked inside their near-identical gestures, alone together, as it were, hypnotically preoccupied with making
the objects of their separate wills perform at their bidding.

The two girls with red skirts are by contrast one of Bruegel's most
felicitous images of companionship (fig. 14). Although they don't act out
the human bond (or its tensions) with the direct visceral intensity of the
barrel riders or the boys playing tug-of-war, they mirror each other in a
more fundamental and reassuring way. Amid all the games of opposition
and conflict, they evoke the happiness of an identity based in sameness.
The pleasure each takes in her own red skirt is inseparable from its agree-
ment with the other's, and the same appears true of their bodies and the
selves that inhabit them. Like the boy who embraces the material reality
of the tree behind them, they are emblems of an assurance the skeptic
despairs of—in their case, that there is a sharing of experience, that the
other can be present to the self not as an opponent or an enigma or a
threat but as its complement, the source of its experience of itself as something outward and manifest. In this respect they are the antithesis not
only of the top spinners but also of the diminutive couple playing "odd or
even," who are in the process of discovering both their own and the
other's capacity for withholding and concealment (fig. 15).

The game the girls play involves spinning in place (apparently in opposite directions), and then plopping down on the grass so that their skirts
spread full around them. It thus opposes the activity of the top spinners

Fig. 15. Children's Games *(detail)*

not only with a different sense of what it is like to be (inside) a body, but with a different teleology as well. The girls are portrayed in this final state, sitting at the edge of the stream like two red flowers blossoming there. The metaphor may be fanciful, but the impression of compatibility with the natural setting and its simple manifestness of feeling is not; Bruegel has even emphasized it by coloring in the apron of the girl on the left with the same rich blue the stream deepens to at its intensest point.

Both the skirt twirlers and the top spinners are arranged so that a single figure is detached from the shared activity of the rest. But unlike the isolated top spinner, the girl who stands alone still twirling her skirt seems continuous with the red-skirted pair, even though she is active and alone while they are at rest and together. And she is similarly "opposite" the top spinners. Instead of projecting outward toward an object, her game generates a sensation of the whole body and makes her experience herself as the center of an encompassing environment—an exterior that becomes her surroundings as a function of her own centrifugal energy. Whereas the boy's game objectifies the gyroscopic principle as something dominated by the will, the girl experiences it as an axis around which she revolves. The purpose of her game, ontologically speaking, is to fill the body with the self's energy rather than to inflict that energy on an object. Unlike the isolated top spinner, who (as we shall see) makes us think of the hidden and repressed, she is an image of the self as whole and free, centered yet open and radiating outward.

The disjunction Bruegel creates within the top spinners is more complex, and opens on questions of inner motive and instinctual violence that the theme of gender difference can only partially contain. The four boys who cluster together under the right arch of the loggia are separated by a column from another boy who stands alone under the arch on the left, dressed in what looks like a monk's habit and holding his lash poised high above him (fig. 16). Crossing over the threshold marked by this central column is like passing from one world into another. Physical presence, psychic charge, and mode of representation all change radically in these two adjoining spaces. It is as if Bruegel's purpose were to bring a certain difference into focus in order to examine the nearly imperceptible transformation of one sort of animating energy into something almost its opposite.

The top spinners on the right are portrayed realistically, and they elicit from the viewer an immediate visceral response. They are possessed

Fig. 16. Children's Games *(detail)*

by what looks like pure instinctual energy—the violence that issues from them seems to satisfy a bodily need as basic as that of the girl who sits against the wall in the background relieving herself. Yet in spite of the violence with which the boys assert their will-to-power over the objects of their attention, it would seem willfully misanthropic to deduce from such behavior a "sadistic instinct." The energy that possesses them seems more innocent, more spontaneously extrovertive. They experience the exhilaration of being able to concentrate the will and to focus it on an external object: the top is less an object of aggression than a natural symbol for the feeling of centered power into which the game converts the energy that drives the boys to play it. Though it is difficult to see how the object-relation the game embodies could translate at the social level into anything very creative or altruistic, the relation itself is not what motivates the boys; rather, their energy of self spills over into it. And though this energy may seem too violent and compulsive to supply the impetus for anything like purposive behavior, its ontological grounds do appear neutral, not destructive.

But all this changes when we pass to the single top spinner on the other side of the central column. A mental element intrudes into the boy's activity and our perception of it, and at both levels the result is something like a loss of innocence. The stiff, hieratic pose into which the boy is frozen robs his body of any sense of animation, and turns it into a container of controlled psychic energy. Suddenly there is a question about what is hidden inside the self, and what motivates its need for an object. The top spinners on the right are caught at the peak of their gestures by the instant of representation; but the hand of the boy on the left appears to pause of its own accord. He seems to eye his top from a greater distance—and a qualitatively different one—than the strictly pragmatic arm's length that separates the boys on the right from theirs. The net effect is a space of measured reflection in which the boy "administers" the lashing of the top and at the same time stands back and observes the effect of his blows. We can read his attitude as either brutality or detached curiosity—it is in fact the affectless combination of the two that makes the image so peculiarly disturbing.

These accidents of the boy's posture combine with his monk-like habit and the framing arch to make the spontaneous motorvisual empathy we experience with the top spinners on the right virtually impossible in his case. It is difficult *not* to "see through" the boy's activity to the iconography of the flagellation, or to the current practices of the Inquisition, or to the legal punishments whose administration Bruegel had catalogued less than a year earlier in his depiction of *Justicia* (fig. 17). Indeed, the boy's gesture seems a direct evocation of the raised arms of that print's executioner and flagellator. The posture of the girl hunched against the wall is similarly reminiscent of the heads bowed beneath the two raised swords in *Justicia*. Her presence as well succumbs to the emblematic mode of perception triggered by the figure beneath her. Realistically perceived, she is an instance of uninhibited curiosity about the sexuality and the body's natural functions; but at the same time we tend to "read" her as a figure of abject passivity. The arch couples her with the boy in such a reading, and installs her in the "mental" space above him. There she can function not only as a fantasized object but also as a subjective complement, an image of the inner state where his sadistic impulse originates. (The top spinner, with his raised whip and monkish garb, condenses into a single figure the executioner and priest who bracket the peasant about to be beheaded in *Justicia* [fig. 18]—an operation which internalizes both the criminal-victim and the distance which civilized Christianity main-

Fig. 17. *After Bruegel,* Justicia, *1559–60—photo courtesy of the National Gallery, Washington, D.C.*

tains from the institutional violence it sanctions. This gap is the most sardonically observed interval in all of Bruegel: note how the mindless gaze of the armed soldier falls into it, and how the work of the flagellator presides over it.) There is a similar linking of impersonal, measured cruelty and abject submissiveness in the relationship between executioner or torturer and victim in *Justicia.* But in *Children's Games* the coupling reveals even darker energies: besides acquiring an internal, purely subjective aspect, it is polarized in terms of male and female and given sexual connotations by the boy's monkishness and girl's wide-open legs.

The image thus frames a "male" impulse and at the same time poses a question about human nature. The isolated top spinner is the one image of childhood in the painting that evokes a potential for something we might be tempted to call "evil." But instead of attributing this potential to

Fig. 18. Justicia *(detail)*

carnal instinct, Bruegel's imagery frames a complex question about its derivation. The body's urges remain innocent, or at least neutral. It is only when the physical impulse embodied in the boys on the right is clothed and framed in the emblems of religion, and brought under what looks like mental control, that it assumes a menacing aspect. The boy's monklike appearance generates an especially vicious circle: it makes the attitude in which he is frozen suggest both repression and channeling of the repressed energy into the agency that administers its repression. Yet the spontaneity of the group of boys on the right is too demonic, and the isolated figure's connection with them too strong, to allow us to be satisfied with any notion of childhood as an innocence destined to be corrupted by the forms of adulthood. Clearly it is something *in* those boys on the right that is transformed in the top spinner on the left. One can imagine Bruegel, having just catalogued the institutionalized forms of violence with which society enforces order in the name of justice, turning to the spontaneous disorder of children's games with a sense of relief, only to discover the capacity for violence there from the beginning, animating the body and organizing the whole of things into a kind of Heraclitean strife.

Yet to encounter it in this form is itself the discovery of a kind of innocence, albeit an innocence which the moral sense and its need for order
are bound to find unsettling. It clarifies what the vision of Bruegel's *Justicia* implies—that evil springs not from an innate, anarchic violence, but
from the human capacity to detach oneself from it and administer it in the
service of order.

I have been especially aware in these last comparisons of having to restrict an unmanageable plurality of images in order to stabilize an object
of analysis. It is not that the comparisons are not in some sense marked
by the painting (my claim has been that they are), but that they are subsumed in a play of differences which ultimately exceeds whatever idea
one can construct to contain them. The skirt twirlers, for instance, contrast as obviously with the tree climber as with the top spinners, and the
doublet they form with him is a variation on the pairing between the boy
on stilts and the girl with widespread arms. Or to take another example:
the girl balancing the broom complements the skirt twirler, projecting out
from herself the still-point which the latter locates deep within. The equilibrium which is affirmed for the one in the vertiginous dependency of the
self and its surroundings is experienced by the other as a delicate balancing act performed at the end of one finger. This connects the girl with
the broom to the boys spinning tops—like them she projects outward,
and concentrates her will and attention at an external balance point—in
a way, to be sure, that locates another difference, but a *different* difference from that between the top spinners and the skirt twirlers. The girls'
broom also inverts the stilt walker's enterprise, and both echoes and contrasts with the many similarly raised sticks held in the boys' hands and
connected with destruction, random violence, or the will-to-power.
(Though even here there are exceptions: the raised lashes of the fence
riders, for instance, are expressions of pure exuberance, just like the spinning girl's outstretched arms.) The skirt twirler and the piggyback rider
are similarly alike in the way they fill the body to its furthest extent (the
one in an open relation to her surroundings, the other in a struggle against
an opponent), while the girl who pokes her stick into the dung pile's
circles connects (especially if she is stirring them) with the boys who lash
their spinning tops. And finally: though the single skirt twirler is the

image of a "centered" self, her game—this surely must be the fun of it—induces instability and vertigo, and serves to dislodge the world. Like the boy on stilts, she is playing with downfall, and from this point of view the difference is in the way her two companions blossom in their fallen state. As such gender-marked disjunctions and connections proliferate through the painting, they are continually being absorbed and reformulated by a play of differences that is always on the move, and can neither be reduced to gender differences nor considered apart from them.

Given the intricacy of this play, one might expect the overall structure of *Children's Games* to involve a marriage or at least some form of dialectical intermingling of the two ontological modes Bruegel tends to locate in images of male and female activity. But this isn't really how the painting works. Instead, when one steps back and attempts to take in the painting as a whole, the "female" images virtually disappear. Both the linear patterns that thrust across the painting in what appear to be all directions at once, and the general mood of restless, driven activity suggest a world attuned almost exclusively to the energy that manifests itself in the boys' games. In this respect female difference is present in the painting much as it is present in the society whose formations the painting explores. But reflected at the level of spontaneous play rather than socially regulated activities, this marginal invisibility seems less a matter of forced exclusion than voluntary indifference. There is something virtually asocial about the contentedness of the skirt twirlers, the girls at the barrel and the sandpile, the pair with the musical instruments and the "mudpie," and the girl at the lower right with her improvised brick grinder. All seem too happily immersed in primary activities and relations to be concerned with coagulating into larger patterns and power centers. But Bruegel appears to celebrate rather than be threatened by this asociality: these images are among his most affectionately rendered, and the ones with which as an artist he seems most closely to identify. Their apartness underscores, on the contrary, what is problematic about the social order. For the painting makes the violence that undermines social stability appear intrinsic to the social impulse, not alien and opposed to it. The overall impression is of human order emerging from a matrix of unrest, and driven by the energy it supplies. For the most part this insight is conveyed neutrally, even exuberantly. And to the degree that the painting does look askance at the generative instability it depicts, the values that control its critical perspective do not appear in images of the well-ordered society (the bleakness of the receding street suggests what Bruegel thinks of that ideal), but in the peacefulness of the pastoral landscape at the upper left and in the scattered pockets of solitary female activity—the very areas of experience that tend to become inaccessible to society in its walled-in, smoothly functioning form.

Excellent Things in Women

SARA SULERI

LEAVING Pakistan was, of course, tantamount to giving up the company of women. I can only tell this to someone like Anita, knowing that she will understand, as we go perambulating through the grimness of New Haven and feeding on the pleasures of our conversational way. Sue, who lives in Boston, would also understand. She will one day write a book about the stern and secretive life of breast-feeding, and is partial to fantasies that culminate in an abundance of wealth. And Fawzi, with a grimace of recognition, knows because she knows the impulse to forget.

To a stranger or an acquaintance, however, some vestigial remoteness obliges me to explain that my reference is to a place where the concept of woman was not really part of an available vocabulary: we were too busy for that concept, just living, and conducting precise negotiations with what it meant to be a sister or a child or a wife or a mother or a servant. By this point of course I am damned by my own discourse, and doubly damned when I add that yes, once in a while we naturally thought of ourselves as women, but only in some perfunctory biological way that we happened on, perchance. Or else it was a hugely practical joke, we thought, hidden somewhere among our clothes. But formulating that sentence is about as hopeless as attempting to locate the luminous qualities of an Islamic landscape, which can on occasion generate such esthetically pleasing moments of life. My audience is lost, and angry to be lost, and both of us must find some token of exchange for this failed conversation. I try to put the subject down and change its clothes, but before I know it, it has sprinted off evilly in the direction of ocular evidence. It goads me into saying, with the defiance of a plea, you did not deal with Dadi.

Dadi, my father's mother, was born in Meerut toward the end of the last century. She was married at sixteen and widowed in her thirties, and in her later years could never exactly recall how many children she had borne. When India was partitioned in August 1947, she moved her thin, pure Urdu into the Punjab of Pakistan and waited for the return of her eldest son, my father. He had gone careening off to a place called Inglestan, or England, fired by one of the several enthusiasms made available by the proliferating talk of independence. Dadi was peeved. She had long since dispensed with any loyalties larger than the pitiless give-and-take of people who are forced to live in the same place, and she resented independence for the distances it made. She was not among those who, on the fourteenth of August, unfurled flags and festivities against the backdrop of people fleeing and cities burning. About that era she would only say, looking up sour and cryptic over the edge of her Koran, and I was also burned. She was, but that was years later.

By the time I knew her, Dadi, with her flair for drama, had allowed life to sit so heavily upon her back that her spine wilted and froze into a perfect curve, and so it was in a posture of a shrimp that she went scuttling through the day. She either scuttled, or did not: it all depended on the nature of her fight with the devil. There were days when she so hated him that all she could do was lie out straight and tiny on her bed, uttering the most awful imprecations. Sometimes, to my mother's great distress, she could only berate Satan in full eloquence after she had clambered on top of the dining room table and lain there like a little moldering centerpiece. Satan was to blame: he had, after all, made her older son linger long enough in Inglestan to give up his rightful wife, a relative, and take up instead with a white-legged woman. He'd taken her only daughter Ayesha when Ayesha lay in childbirth. And he'd sent her youngest son to Swaziland, or Switzerland: her thin hand waved away such sophistries of name.

God she loved, understanding him better than anyone. Her favorite days were those when she could circumvent both the gardener and my father, all in the solemn service of her God. She'd steal a knife and weedle her way to the nearest sapling in the garden, some sprightly poplar, or a eucalyptus newly planted. She'd squat, she'd hack it down, and then she would peel its bark away until she had a walking stick, all white and virgin and her own. It drove my father into tears of rage. He must have bought her a dozen walking sticks, one for each of our trips to the mountains, but it was like assembling a row of briar pipes for one who will not smoke. For Dadi had different aims. Armed with implements of her own creation, she would creep down the driveway unperceived to stop cars and people on the street, to give them all the gossip that she had on God.

Food, too, could move her to intensities. Her eyesight always took a sharp turn for the worse over meals, so that she could point hazily at a perfectly ordinary potato and murmur with an Adamic reverence, what *is* it, what *is* it called. With some shortness of manner, one of us would describe and catalog the items on the table. *Alu ka bhartha*, Dadi repeated with wonderment and joy. Yes, Saira begum, you can put some here. Not too much, she'd add pleadingly. For ritual had it that the more she demurred, the more she expected her plate to be piled with an amplitude that her own politeness would never allow. The ritual happened three times a day.

We pondered on it but never quite determined whether food or God constituted her most profound delight. Obvious problems, however, occurred on occasions which brought the two together. One was the Muslim festival called Eid, not the one that ends the month of fasting, but the second Eid, which celebrates the seductions of the Abraham story in a remarkably literal way. In Pakistan, at least, people buy sheep or goats and fatten them up for weeks with all sorts of delectables. Then, on the appointed day they're chopped, in place of sons, and neighbors graciously exchange silver trays heaped with raw and quivering meat. After Eid prayers the men come home, the animal is cooked, and shortly thereafter, they rush out of the kitchen steaming plates of grilled lung and liver, of a freshness quite superlative.

It was a freshness to which my Welsh mother did not immediately take. She observed the custom but located in it a conundrum that allowed for no ready solution. For, liberal to an extravagant degree on thoughts abstract, she found herself to be remarkably slow and squeamish on particular things. Chopping up animals for God was one. She could not quite locate the metaphor, and was therefore a little uneasy. My father, the writer, quite agreed, for he was so civilized in those days.

Dadi didn't agree. She pined for choppable things. Once she made the mistake of buying a baby goat and bringing him home months in advance of Eid. She wanted to guarantee the texture of his festive flesh by a daily feeding of tender peas and ghee, or clarified butter. Ifat and Shahid and I greeted a goat into the family with boisterous rapture, and soon after, he ravished us completely when we found him nonchalantly at the clothesline, eating up Shahid's pajamas. Of course there was no fight: the little goat was our delight, and even Dadi knew there was no killing him. He became my brother's and my sister's and my first pet, and he grew huge, a big and grinning thing.

Years after, Dadi had her will. We were all old enough, she must have thought, to make the house sprawl out, abstracted, into a multitude of secrets. That was true, but still we all noticed one another's secretive ways. So my sisters and I just shook our heads when the day before Eid our Dadi disappeared. We hid the fact from my father, who at this time of life had begun to equate petulance with extreme vociferation. So we went about our jobs and were Islamic for a day. We waited to sight moons on the wrong occasions and we watched the food come into lavishment. Dried dates change shape when they are soaked in milk, and carrots rich and strange can turn magically sweet when deftly covered with green nutty shavings and smatterings of silver.

Dusk was sweet as we sat out, the day's work done, in an evening garden. Lahore spread like peace around us. My father spoke, and when Papa talked it was of Pakistan. But we were glad, then, at being audience to that familiar conversation, till his voice looked up, and failed. There was Dadi making her return, and she was prodigal. Like a question mark interested only in its own conclusions, her body crawled through the gates. Our guests were spellbound; then they looked away. For Dadi, moving in her eerie crab formations, chose to ignore the hangman's rope she firmly held. And behind her in the gloaming minced, hugely affable, a goat.

That goat was still smiling the following day, when Dadi's victory meant that the butcher came and went just as he should, on Eid. Goat was killed and cooked: a scrawny beast that required much cooking and never melted into tenderness, he muscularly winked and glistened on our plates as we sat eating him on Eid. Dadi ate, that is: Papa had taken his motification to some distant corner of the house; Ifat refused to chew on hemp; Tillat and Irfan still gulped their baby sobs over such a slaughter. Honestly, said Mamma, honestly. For Dadi had successfully cut through tissues of festivity just as the butcher slit the goat, but there was something else that she was eating with that meat. I saw it in her concentration. I know that she was making God talk to her as to Abraham, and see what she could do—for him—to sons. God didn't dare, and she ate on, alone.

Of those middle years it is hard to say whether Dadi was literally left alone or whether a quality of being apart and absorbed was always emanated by her bodily presence. In the winter, I see her alone, painstakingly dragging her straw mat out to the courtyard at the back of the house, and following the rich course of the afternoon sun. With her would go her

Koran, a metal basin in which she could wash her hands, and her ridiculously heavy-spouted watering pot that was made of brass. None of us, according to Dadi, was quite pure enough to transport these particular items: the rest of the paraphernalia we could carry out. These were baskets of her writing and sewing materials and her bottle of most pungent and Dadi-like bitter oils, which she'd coat on the papery skin that held her brittle bones. And in the summer, when the night created an illusion of possible coolness, and all held their breath while waiting for a thin and intermittent breeze, Dadi would be on the roof, alone. Her summer bed was a wooden frame latticed with a sweetly smelling rope, much aerated at the foot of the bed. She'd lie there all night, until the wild monsoons would wake the lightest and the soundest sleeper into a rapturous welcome of rain.

In Pakistan, of course, there is no spring but just a rapid elision from winter into summer, which is somewhat analogous to the absence of a recognizable loneliness from the behavior of that climate. In a similar fashion it is quite hard to distinguish between Dadi with people and Dadi alone. She was just impossibly unable to remain unnoticed. In the winter, when she was not writing or reading, she would sew for her delight tiny and magical reticules out of old silks and fragments that she had saved, palm-sized cloth bags that would unravel into the precision of secret and more secret pockets. But none of them did she ever need to hide, for something of Dadi always remained intact, however much we sought to open her. Her discourse, for example, was too impervious to allow for penetration, so that when one or two of us remonstrated with her in a single hour she never bothered to distinguish her replies. Instead, generic and prophetic, she would pronounce, the world takes on a single face. Must you, Dadi, I'd begin, to be halted then by her great complaint: "the world takes on a single face."

It did. And often it was a countenance of some delight, for Dadi also loved the accidental jostle with things belligerent. As she went perambulating through the house, suddenly she'd hear Shahid, her first grandson, telling me or one of my sisters that we were vile, we were disgusting women. And Dadi, who never addressed anyone of us without first conferring the title of lady, so we were Tillat begum, Nuzhat begum, Ifat begum, Saira begum, would halt in reprimand and tell her grandson never to call her granddaughters women. What else shall I call them, men? Shahid yelled. Men, said Dadi, men. There is more goodness in a woman's little finger than in the benighted mind of man. Hear, hear, Dadi, *hanh hanh*, Dadi, my sisters cried. For men, said Dadi, shaking the name off her fingertips like some unwanted water, live as though they were un-suckled things. And heaven, she grimly added, is the thing Mohammed says (peace be upon him) lies beneath the feet of women! But he was a man, Shahid still would rage, if he weren't laughing, as all of us were laughing, while Dadi sat among us like a belle or a May queen.

Toward the end of her middle years my father stopped speaking to his mother, and the atmosphere at home appreciably improved. They se-cretly hit upon novel histrionics that took the place of their daily battle. Instead they chose the curious way of silent things: twice a day, Dadi would leave her room and walk her long length of the corridor to my fa-ther's room. There she just peered round the door, as though to check if he were real. Each time she peered, my father would interrupt whatever adult thing he may have been doing in order to enact a silent paroxysm, an elaborate facial pantomime of revulsion and affront. At teatime in par-ticular, when Papa would want the world to congregate in his room for tea, Dadi came to peer at her ghostly peer. Shortly thereafter conversa-tion was bound to fracture, for we could not drown the fact that Dadi, invigorated by an outcast's strength, was sitting in the dining room and chanting an appeal: God give me tea, God give me tea.

At about this time Dadi stopped smelling old and smelled instead of something equivalent to death. It would have been easy to notice if she had been dying, but instead she managed the change as a certain grada-tion into subtlety, just as her annoying little stove could shift its hanging odors away from smoke and into ash. During the middle years there had been something more defined about her being, which sat in the world as solely its own context. But Pakistan was increasingly complicating the question of context, as though history, like a pestilence, was insisting that nothing could have definition outside relations to its own fevered sleep. So it was simple for my father to ignore the letters that Dadi had begun to write to him every other day, in her fine wavering script, letters of advice about the house or the children or the servants. Or she transcribed her complaint: Oh my son, Zia. Do you think your son, Shahid, upon whom God bestowed a thousand blessings, should be permitted to lift up his grandmother's chair and carry it into the courtyard, when his grand-mother is seated in it? She had cackled in a combination of delight and virgin joy when Shahid had so transported her, but that little crackling sound she omitted from her letter. She ended it, and all her notes, with her single endearment. It was a phrase to halt and arrest when Dadi actually uttered it: her solitary piece of tenderness was an injunction, really, to her world. Keep on living, she would say.

Between that phrase and the great Dadi conflagration comes the era of the trying times. They began in the winter war of 1971, when East Pakistan became Bangladesh and Indira Gandhi hailed the demise of the two-nation theory. Ifat's husband was off fighting, and we spent the war together with her father-in-law, the brigadier, in the pink house on the hill. It was an ideal location for anti-aircraft guns, so there was a bevy of soldiers and weaponry installed upon our roof. During each air raid the brigadier would stride purposefully into the garden and bark commands at them, as though the success of the war rested upon his stiff upper lip. Then Dacca fell, and General Yahya came on television to resign the presidency and accede defeat. Drunk, by God, barked the brigadier as we sat watching, drunk.

The following morning General Yahya's mistress came to mourn with us over breakfast, lumbering in with swathes of overscented silk. The brigadier lit an English cigarette—he was frequently known to avow that Pakistani cigarettes gave him a cuff—and bit on his moustache. Yes, he barked, these are trying times. Oh yes, Gul, Yahya's mistress wailed, these are such trying times. She gulped on her own eloquence, her breakfast bosom quaked, and then resumed authority over that dangling sentence. It is so trying, she continued, I find it so trying, it is trying to us all, to live in these trying, trying times. Ifat's eyes met mine in complete accord: mistress transmogrified to muse; Bhutto returned from the U.N. to put Yahya under house arrest and become the first elected president of Pakistan; Ifat's husband went to India as a war prisoner for two years; my father lost his newspaper. We had entered the era of the trying times.

Dadi didn't notice the war, just as she didn't really notice the proliferation of her great-grandchildren, for Ifat and Nuzzi conceived at the drop of a hat and kept popping babies out for our delight. Tillat and I felt favored at this vicarious taste of motherhood: we learned to become that enviable personage, a khala, mother's sister, and when our married sisters came to visit with their entourage, we reveled in the exercise of khala-love. I once asked Dadi how many sisters she had had. She looked up with the oceanic gray of her cataracted eyes and answered, I forget.

The children helped, because we needed distraction, there being then in Pakistan a slightly musty taste of defeat to all our activities. The children gave us something, but they also took away: they initiated a slight displacement of my mother, for her grandchildren would not speak any English, and she could not read them stories as of old. Urdu always remained a shyness on her tongue, and as the babies came and went she let something of her influence imperceptibly recede, as though she occupied an increasingly private air space. Her eldest son was now in England, so Mamma found herself living in the classic posture of an Indian woman, who sends away her sons and runs the risk of seeing them then succumb to the great alternatives represented by the West. It was a position that preoccupied her, and without my really noticing what was happening, she quietly handed over many of her wifely duties to her two remaining daughters, to Tillat and to me. In the summer, once the ferocity of the afternoon sun had died down, it was her pleasure to go out into the garden on her own. There she would stand, absorbed and abstracted, watering the driveway and breathing in the heady smell of water on hot dust. I'd watch her often, from my room upstairs. She looked like a girl.

We were aware of something, of a reconfiguration in the air, but could not exactly phrase where it would lead us. Dadi now spoke mainly to herself, and even the audience provided by the deity had dropped away. Somehow there was not a proper balance between the way things came and the way they went, as Halima the cleaning woman knew full well when she looked at me intently, asking a question that had no question in it: Do I grieve, or do I celebrate? Halima had given birth to her latest son the night her older child had died in screams of meningitis; once heard, never to be forgotten. She came back to work a week later, and we were talking as we put away the family's winter clothes into vast metal trunks. For in England, they would call it spring.

We felt a quickening urgency of change drown our sense of regular direction, as though something was bound to happen soon, but not knowing what it was that was making history nervous. And so we were not really that surprised when we found ourselves living through the summer of the trials by fire. That summer's climax came when Dadi went up in a little ball of flames. But somehow sequentially related were my mother's trip to England, to tend to her dying mother, the night I beat up Tillat, and the evening I nearly castrated my little brother, runt of the litter, serious-eyed Irfan.

It was an accident on both our parts. I was in the kitchen, so it must have been a Sunday when Allah Ditta, the cook, took the evening off. He was a mean-spirited man with an incongruously delicate touch when it came to making food. On Sunday at midday he would bluster one of us into the kitchen and show us what he had prepared for the evening meal, leaving strict and belligerent instructions about what would happen if we overheated this or dared brown that. So I was in the kitchen heating up some food, when Farni came back from playing hockey with that ominous asthmatic rattle in his throat. He, the youngest, had been my parents' gravest infant: in adolescence he remained a gentle invalid. Of course he pretended otherwise, and was loud and raucous, but it never worked.

Tillat and I immediately turned on him with the bullying litany that actually is quite soothing, the invariable female reproach to the returning male. He was to do what he hated, and stave off his disease by sitting over a bowl of camphor and boiling water, inhaling its acrid fumes. I insisted that he sit on the cook's little stool in the kitchen, holding the bowl of water on his lap, so that I could cook and Farni could not cheat and I could time each minute he should sit there thus confined. We seated him and flounced a towel on his reluctant head. The kitchen jointly reeked of cumin and camphor, and he sat skinny and penitent and swathed for half a minute before begging to be done. I slammed down the carving knife and screamed *Irfan* with such ferocity that he jumped literally and figuratively quite out of his skin. The bowl of water emptied onto him, and with a gurgling cry he leapt up, tearing at his steaming clothes. He clutched at his groin, and everywhere he touched the skin slid off, so that between his fingers his penis easily unsheathed, a blanched and fiery grape. What's happening, screamed Papa from his room; what's happening, echoed Dadi's wail from the opposite end of the house. What was happening was that I was holding Farni's shoulders, trying to stop him jumping up and down, but I was jumping too, while Tillat just stood there frozen, frowning at his poor ravaged grapes.

This was June, and the white heat of summer. We spent the next few days laying ice on Farni's wounds: half the time I was allowed to stay with him, until the doctors suddenly remembered I was a woman and hurried me out when his body made crazy spastic reactions to its burns. Once things grew calmer and we were alone, Irfan looked away and said, I hope I didn't shock you, Sara. And I was so taken by tenderness for his bony convalescent body that it took me years to realize that yes, something female in me had been deeply shocked.

Mamma knew nothing of this, of course. We kept it from her so that she could concentrate on what took her back to the rocky coastline of Wales, and to places she had not really revisited since she was a girl. She sat waiting with her mother, who was blind now and of a fine translucency, and both of them knew that they were waiting for her death. It was a peculiar posture for Mamma to maintain, but her quiet letters spoke mainly of the sharp astringent light that made the sea wind feel so brisk in Wales, and so many worlds away from the daily omnipresent weight of a summer in Lahore. And there, one afternoon, walking childless among the brambles and the furze, Mamma realized that her childhood was distinctly lost. It was not that I wanted to feel more familiar, she later told me, or that I was more used to feeling unfamiliar in Lahore. It's just that familiarity isn't important, really, she murmured absently, it really doesn't matter at all.

When Mamma was ready to return she wired us her plans, and my father read the cable, kissed it, then put it in his pocket. I watched him and felt startled, as we all did on the occasions when our parents' lives seemed to drop away before our eyes, leaving them youthfully engrossed in the illusion of knowledge conferred by love. We were so used to conceiving of them as parents moving in and out of hectic days that it always amused us, and touched us secretly, when they made quaint and punctilious returns to the amorous bond that had initiated the unlikely lives through which we knew them.

That summer, while my mother was away, Tillat and I experienced a new bond of powerlessness, which is the white and shaking rage of sexual jealousy in parenthood. I had always behaved toward her as a belligerent surrogate parent, but she was growing beyond that scope, and in her girlhood asking me for a formal acknowledgment of equality that I was loath to give. My reluctance was rooted in a helpless fear of what the world could do to her, for I was young and ignorant enough not to see that what I could do was worse. She went out one evening, when my father was off on one of his many trips. The house was gaping emptily, and Tillat was very late. Allah Ditta had gone home, and Dadi and Irfan were sleeping; I read, and thought, and walked up and down the garden, and Tillat was very very late. When she came back she wore that strange sheath of complacency and guilt which pleasure puts on faces very young. It smote an outrage in my heart until despite all resolutions to the contrary I heard my hiss: and where were you? Her returning look was both fearful and preening at the same time, so that the next thing to be smitten was her face. Don't, Sara, Tillat said in her superior way, physical violence is so degrading. To you, maybe, I answered, and hit her once again.

It made a sorrowful bond between us, for we both felt complicit in the shamefulness that had made me seem righteous, when I had felt simply jealous, which we tacitly agreed was a more legitimate thing to be. But we had lost something, a certain protective aura, some unspoken myth asserting that love between sisters at least was sexually innocent. Now we had to fold that vain belief away and stand in slightly more naked relation to our affection. Till then we had associated such violence with all that was outside us, as though, somehow, the more historical process fractured, the more whole we would be. But now we were losing a sense of the differentiated identities of history and ourselves, and were guiltily aware that we had known it all along, our part in the construction of unreality.

By this time, Dadi's burns were slowly learning how to heal. It was she who had given the summer its strange pace by nearly burning herself alive at its inception. On an early April night Dadi awoke, seized by a desperate need for tea. It was three in the morning and the household was asleep, so she could do the great forbidden thing of creeping into Allah Ditta's kitchen and taking charge, like pixies in the night. As all of us were so bored with predicting, one of her many cotton garments took to fire that truant night. But Dadi deserves credit for her resourceful voice, which wavered out for witness to her burning death. By the time Tillat awoke and found her, she was a little flaming ball: *Dadi*, said Tillat in the reproach of sleep, and beat her quiet with a blanket. In the morning we discovered Dadi's torso had been quite consumed and nothing recognizable remained, from collarbone to groin. The doctors bade us to some decent mourning.

But Dadi had different plans. She lived through her sojourn at the hospital; she weathered her return. And then after six weeks at home she angrily refused to be lugged daily to the doctor's to get her dressings changed, as though she were a chunk of meat: Saira begum will do it, she announced. And thus developed my great intimacy with the fluid properties of human flesh. By the time Mamma left for England, Dadi's left breast was still coagulate and raw. When Farni got his burns she was growing pink and livid tightropes, strung from hip to hip in a flaming advertisement of life. And in the days when Tillat and I were wrestling,

Dadi's vanished nipples started to congeal and turn their cavities into triumphant little loveknots.

I learned about the specialization of beauty from that body. There were times like love when I felt only disappointment to carefully ease the dressings off and find again a piece of flesh that would not knit, happier in the texture of a stubborn glue. But then, on some more exhilarating day, I'd peel like an onion all her bandages away and suddenly discover I was looking down at some literal tenacity, and was bemused at all the freshly withered shapes she could create. Each new striation was a triumph to itself, and when Dadi's hairless groin solidified again, and sent firm signals that abdomen must do the same, I could have wept with glee.

During her immolation, Dadi's diet underwent some curious changes. At first her consciousness teetered too much for her to pray, but then as she grew stronger it took us a while to notice what was missing: she had forgotten prayer. It left her life as firmly as tobacco can leave the lives of only the most passionate smokers, and I don't know if she ever prayed again. At about this time, however, with the heavy-handed inevitability that characterized his relation to his mother, my father took to prayer. I came home one afternoon and looked for him in all the usual places, but he wasn't to be found. Finally I came across Tillat and asked her where Papa was. Praying, she said. *Praying?* I said. Praying, she said, and I felt most embarrassed. For us it was rather as though we had come upon the children playing some forbidden, titillating game, and decided it was wisest to ignore it calmly. In an unspoken way, though, I think we dimly knew we were about to witness Islam's departure from the land of Pakistan. The men would take it to the streets and make it vociferate, but the great romance between religion and the populace, the embrace that engendered Pakistan, was done. So Papa prayed, with the desperate ardor of a lover trying to converse life back into a finished love.

And that was a change, when Dadi sewed herself together again and forgot to put back prayer into its proper pocket, for God could now leave the home and soon would join the government. Papa prayed and fasted and went on pilgrimage and read the Koran aloud with the most peculiar locutions. Occasionally we also caught him in nocturnal altercations that made him sound suspiciously like Dadi: we looked askance, but did not say a thing. And my mother was quite admirable. She behaved as though she always knew she'd wed a swaying, chanting thing, or that to register surprise would be an impoliteness to existence. Her expression reminded me somewhat of the time when Ifat was eight, and Mamma was urging her recalcitrance into some goodly task. Ifat postponed, and Mamma, always nifty with appropriate fables, quoted meaningfully: "I'll do it myself, said the little red hen." Ifat looked up with bright affection. Good little red hen, she murmured. Then a glance crossed my mother's face, a look between a slight smile and a quick rejection of eloquent response, something like a woman looking down, and then away.

She looked like that at my father's sudden hungering for God, which was added to the growing number of subjects about which we, my mother and her daughters, silently decided we had no conversation. We knew that there was something other than trying times ahead and would far rather hold our breath than speculate about what other surprises the era held up its capacious sleeve. Tillat and I decided to quash our dread of waiting around for change by changing for ourselves, before destiny took the time to come our way. I moved to America and Tillat to Kuwait and marriage. To both intentions my mother said, I see, and helped us in our preparations: she knew by now her son would not return and was not unprepared to extend the courtesy of waiting to her daughters, too. We left, and Islam predictably took to the streets, threatening and shaking Bhutto's empire. Mamma and Dadi remained the only women in the house, the one untalking, the other unpraying.

Dadi behaved abysmally at my mother's funeral, they told me, and made them all annoyed. She set up loud and unnecessary lamentations in the dining room, somewhat like an heir apparent, as though this death had reinstated her as mother of the house. While Ifat and Nuzzi and Tillat wandered frozen-eyed, dealing with the roses and the ice, Dadi demanded an irritating amount of attention, stretching out supine and crying out, your mother has betrayed your father; she has left him; she has gone. Food from respectful mourners poured in, cauldron after cauldron, and Dadi rediscovered a voracious appetite.

Years later, I was somewhat sorry that I heard this tale because it made me take affront. When I went back to Pakistan, I was too peeved with Dadi to find out how she was. Instead I heard Ifat tell me about standing there in the hospital, watching the doctors suddenly pump upon my mother's heart—I'd seen it on television, she gravely said, I knew it was the end. Mamma's students from the university had found the rickshaw driver who had knocked her down, pummeled him nearly to death, and then camped out in our garden, sobbing wildly, all in hordes.

By this time Bhutto was in prison and awaiting trial, and General Zulu was presiding over the Islamization of Pakistan. But we had no time to notice. My mother was buried at the nerve center of Lahore, a wild and dusty place, and my father immediately made arrangements to buy the plot of land next to her grave: we are ready when you are, Shahid sang. Her tombstone bore some pretty Urdu poetry and a completely fictitious place of birth, because there were some details my father tended to forget. Honestly, it would have moved his wife to say.

So I was angry with Dadi at that time, and I didn't stop to see her. I saw my mother's grave and then came back to America, and hardly reacted when, six months from then, my father called from London and mentioned that Dadi was now dead. It happened in the same week that Bhutto finally was hanged, and our imaginations were consumed by that public and historical dying. Pakistan made rapid provisions not to talk about the thing that had been done, and somehow accidentally Dadi must have been mislaid into that larger decision, because she too ceased to be a mentioned thing. My father tried to get back in time for the funeral, but he was so busy talking Bhutto-talk in England that he missed his flight. Luckily, Irfani was at home and saw Dadi to her grave.

Bhutto's hanging had the effect of making Pakistan feel quite unreliable, particularly to itself. There was a new secretiveness its landscape learned, quite unusual for a formerly loquacious place. It accounts for the fact that I have never seen my grandmother's grave, and neither have my sisters. I think we would have tried, had we been together, despite the free-floating anarchy in the air that—like the heroin trade—made the world suspicious and afraid. Now there was no longer any need to wait for change because change was all there was, and we had quite forgotten the flavor of an era that stayed in place long enough to gain a name. One morning I awoke to see that, during the course of the night, my mind had completely ejected the names of all the streets in Pakistan, as though to assure that I could not return, or that if I did, it would be returning to a loss. Overnight the country had grown absentminded, and patches of amnesia hung over the hollows of the land like fog.

But I think we would have mourned Dadi in our belated way, except that the coming year saw Ifat killed in the consuming rush of change and disbanded the company of women for all times. It was a curious day in March, two years after my mother died, when the weight of that anniversary made us all disconsolate for her quietude. I'll speak to Ifat, though, I thought to myself in America. But in Pakistan someone had different ideas for that sister of mine and thwarted all my plans. When she went walking out that warm March night a car came by and trampeled her into the ground, and then it vanished strangely. By the time I reached Lahore, a tall and slender mound had usurped the grave space where my father hoped to lie, next to the more moderate shape that was his wife. Children take over everything.

So, worn by repetition, we stood by Ifat's grave and took note of the narcissi, still alive, that she must have put upon my mother's on the day that she had died. It made us impatient, in a way, as though we had to decide there was never anything quite as farcical as grief, and that it had to be eliminated from our diets for good. It cut away, of course, our intimacy with Pakistan, where history is synonymous with grief and always most at home in the attitudes of grieving. Our congregation in Lahore was brief, and then we swiftly returned to a more geographic reality. We are lost, Sara, Shahid said to me on the phone from England. Yes, Shahid, I firmly said, we're lost.

Today, I'd be less emphatic. Ifat and Mamma must have honeycombed and crumbled now, in the comfortable way that overtakes bedfellows. And somehow it seems apt and heartening that Dadi, being what she was, was never given the pomposities that enter the most well meaning of farewells, but seeped instead into the nooks and crannies of our forgetfulness. She fell between two stools of grief, which is quite appropriate, since she was greatest when her life was at its most unreal. Anyway, she was always outside our ken, an anecdotal thing, neither more nor less. And so some sweet reassurance of reality accompanies my discourse when I claim that when Dadi died, we all forgot to grieve.

For to be lost is just a minute's respite, after all, like a train that cannot help but stop at way stations, in order to stage a pretend version of the journey's end. Dying, we saw, was simply change taken to points of mocking extremity; it wasn't a thing to lose us but to find us out, and catch us where we least wanted to be caught. In Pakistan, Bhutto became rapidly obsolete after a few successions of bumper harvests, and none of us can fight the ways that the names Mamma and Ifat have become archaisms and quaintnesses on our lips.

Now I live in New Haven and feel quite happy with my life. I miss of course the absence of "woman," and grow increasingly nostalgic for a world where the modulations of age are as recognized and welcomed as the shift from season into season. But that's a hazard that has to come along, since I have made myself an inhabitant of a population which democratically insists that everyone from twenty-nine to fifty-six roughly occupies the same space of age. When I teach topics in third world literature, much time is lost in trying to explain that such a place is not locatable, except as a discourse of convenience. It is like pretending that history or home is real and not located precisely where you're sitting, I hear my voice quite idiotically say. And then it happens. A face, puzzled and attentive and belonging to my gender, raises its intelligence to ask why, since I am teaching third world writing, I haven't given equal space to women writers on my syllabus. I look up, the horse's mouth, a foolish thing to be. Unequal images battle in my mind for precedence—there's imperial Ifat, there's Mamma in the garden and Halima the cleaning woman is there too, there's uncanny Dadi with her goat. Against all my own odds I know what I must say. Because, I'll answer slowly, there are no women in the third world.

Notes on the Contributors

LEO BERSANI is Professor of French at the University of California, Berkeley. His latest book, *The Culture of Redemption*, will be published by Harvard University Press.

HAROLD BLOOM is Sterling Professor at Yale and Berg Professor at New York University. His most recent books are *The Poetics of Influence* and *Ruin the Sacred Truths*, essays which were the Charles Eliot Norton lectures at Harvard in 1987–88.

DAVID BROMWICH is Professor of English at Yale. He is the author of *Hazlitt: The Mind of a Critic* and *A Choice of Inheritance: Self and Community from Edmund Burke to Robert Frost*.

STANLEY CAVELL is Professor of Philosophy at Harvard. His latest books are *In Quest of the Ordinary* and *This New Yet Unapproachable America*, published in 1989 by the University of Chicago Press, which next year will bring out his Carus lectures, entitled *Conditions Handsome and Unhandsome*, on Emersonian perfectionism.

THOMAS R. EDWARDS teaches at Rutgers and is the executive editor of *Raritan*. He is the author of *This Dark Estate: A Reading of Pope* and *Imagination and Power*.

ROBERT GARIS has written widely on literature, the ballet, music, and film. He teaches English at Wellesley.

CLIFFORD GEERTZ is Harold F. Linder Professor of Social Science at The Institute for Advanced Study, Princeton. His most recent book is *Works and Lives: The Anthropologist as Author*.

REGINALD GIBBONS is the author of three books of poems and other works and is the editor of *TriQuarterly* and Professor of English at Northwestern.

MIRIAM HANSEN, Associate Professor of English at Rutgers, is a co-editor of *New German Critique*. Her book, *Babel and Babylon: Spectatorship in American Silent Film*, is forthcoming from Harvard University Press. She is working on a study of the film theory of the Frankfurt School.

VICKI HEARNE is a poet and dog and horse trainer. She is currently working on *Bandit: Dossier of a Dangerous Dog*, a book of essays that deals with how a particular court case raised general questions about animal and human rights.

JOHN HOLLANDER teaches at Yale. His latest book of poetry is *Harp Lake*, published by Knopf, and his latest book of criticism is *Melodious Guile*, published by Yale University Press.

GEORGE KATEB teaches political theory at Princeton and is the author of *Hannah Arendt: Politics Conscience, Evil*.

LINCOLN KIRSTEIN is the president of the School of American Ballet.

GEORGE LEVINE is Kenneth Burke Professor of English at Rutgers. Director of the Rutgers Center for the Critical Analysis of Contemporary Culture, he is coauthor of the ACLS pamphlet, *Speaking for the Humanities*. His most recent book is *Darwin and the Novelists*, published by Harvard University Press.

RONALD PAULSON, the Mayer Professor of Humanities at Johns Hopkins, is the author of, among others, *Hogarth's Graphic Works*, *Representations of Revolution*, and the forthcoming *Breaking and Remaking: Aesthetic Practice in England, 1700–1820*.

RICHARD POIRIER, the founding editor of *Raritan*, is Marius Bewley Professor of English at Rutgers and chairman of the board of The Library of America. His several books include *A World Elsewhere, The Performing Self, Robert Frost: The Work of Knowing*, and, most recently, *The Renewal of Literature*.

EDWARD W. SAID is Parr Professor of English and Comparative Literature at Columbia. His most recent book is *After the Last Sky: Palestinian Lives*. He also co-edited *Literature and Society* and contributed an essay to *After Foucault* (Rutgers University Press).

EVE KOSOFSKY SEDGWICK teaches at Duke. She is the author of *Between Men: English Literature and Male Homosocial Desire* and the forthcoming *Epistemology of the Closet*.

RICHARD SENNETT is a writer living in New York City. He teaches at N.Y.U.

EDWARD SNOW teaches English at Rice and is the author of *A Study of Vermeer*. His translations of Rilke's *New Poems* and *New Poems: The Other Part* have recently been published by North Point Press. He is completing books on Bruegel and Shakespeare.

ELAINE SHOWALTER is Avalon Professor of the Humanities at Princeton University. She is author of *A Literature of Their Own* and *The Female Malady: Women, Madness, and Culture*. Most recently, she has published *Border Lines: Gender and Culture in the "Fin de Siècle"* and *The Tenth Muse: Traditions and Contradictions in American Women's Writing*. She is also co-editor of Rutgers' American Women Writers Series.

SARA SULERI teaches at Yale. She is the author of *Meatless Days* and is working on a project entitled "The Rhetoric of English India."